LETITIA ELIZABETH LANDON

SELECTED WRITINGS

11 - 31
✓37 - 42
3/15 ✓ 46 - 42
51 - 50
83 - 82

87 - 101
102 - 27
143 - 46
3/17 160 - 46
169 - 68
173 - 72
173 - 86

3/22 209 - 262

3/24 352 - 84
Reviews 1, 2, 4, 5 & 11
+ Poems of
tribute

LETITIA ELIZABETH LANDON:

SELECTED WRITINGS

edited by Jerome McGann and Daniel Riess

broadview literary texts

Canadian Cataloguing in Publication Data

L.E.L. (Letitia Elizabeth Landon),
1802–1838
        Letitia Elizabeth Landon: selected writings

(Broadview literary texts)
Includes bibliographical references.
ISBN 1-55111-135-7

I. McGann, Jerome J.   II. Riess, Daniel.   III. Title.
IV. Series.

PR4865.L5A6 1997   821'.7   C97-930850-X

Broadview Press
Post Office Box 1243, Peterborough, Ontario, Canada K9J 7H5

in the United States of America:
3576 California Road, Orchard Park, NY 14127

in the United Kingdom:
B.R.A.D. Book Representation & Distribution Ltd.,
244A, London Road, Hadleigh, Essex SS7 2DE

Broadview Press is grateful to Professor Eugene Benson for advice on editorial matters for the Broadview Literary Texts series.

Broadview Press gratefully acknowledges the support of the Canada Council, the Ontario Arts Council, and the Ministry of Canadian Heritage.

Book design and typesetting by George Kirkpatrick

PRINTED IN CANADA

Acknowledgements

First of all we would like to give our special thanks to Cynthia Lawford, who worked tirelessly on the bibliography at a very late date. Thanks go as well to Lawford and to Glenn Dibert-Himes, for granting permission to publish their Landon bibliography and providing access to their research materials; to Michael Landon, for supplying valuable biographical information; and to Anne Mellor, Jeanne Moskal, Jim Nohrenberg, Charles Robinson, and Gene Ruoff who helped in various ways from their stores of learning. Thanks go as well to the staffs of the Alderman Library, U. of Virginia, and the Harry Ransom Research Centre, U. of Texas. Finally we were fortunate to work with Barbara Conolly, our editor at Broadview, who worked so hard to make this book successful.

Portrait of Landon by Henry William Pickersgill (1782–1875), exhibited at the Royal Academy in the summer of 1825. Reproduced by permission of Michael and Carole Landon.

Contents

Editorial Preface

Unless otherwise indicated, the texts used are the first published versions of each work (purged of printer's errors). Normalization of accidentals has been avoided, including spelling, punctuation, italicization, and capitalization.

Most annuals were published the Christmas before the year included in the title; e.g., *The Keepsake for 1829* was published in December 1828. Publication dates in the table of contents use the date given in the title of the annual.

Many of the poems Landon published in *Fisher's Drawing Room Scrap Book* were republished posthumously with different titles in *The Zenana and Minor Poems* (1839). Because no available evidence suggests that Landon authorized the title changes, this edition uses the original titles.

Introduction

LIKE Burns and Byron, Letitia Elizabeth Landon names a legendary figure of nineteenth-century British culture. No English writer of the 1820s and 1830s was more well known or more popular than "L.E.L." When she took those initials as her literary signature, she began to fashion an arresting cultural presence – the very emblem of the conflicted Victorian sentimentalist, at once critical of and enslaved by the worldliness and hypocrisies of her age. She herself would see in her condition the dialectic of "Romance and Reality." Dying young (she was only thirty-six), in an exotic land, and under dark circumstances, Landon consummated the myth that had been gathering about her life for over fifteen years. We need to know the myth in order to understand her writings, and we need to know the life in order to appreciate the myth.

She was born on 14 August 1802 in Chelsea, the eldest of three children including a brother, Whittington Henry (1804-1873), and a sister Elizabeth Jane (1806-1819). Landon's ancestors had been Herefordshire landed gentry, but her great-grandfather lost most of the family money through bad speculation. Her father, a partner in the army agency of Adair & Co. in Pall Mall, earned a respectable income during the wars with France, but Napoleon's defeat brought a serious decline in his business prospects.

Letitia – or "Letty" as she was nicknamed – had received instruction for several months at a school run by Frances Rowden, a poet who had also taught Mary Russell Mitford and Caroline Lamb. Her education was subsequently taken up by her cousin, Elizabeth Landon, who found her a quick pupil and an avid reader. Her childhood reading included the works of Walter Scott, *Robinson Crusoe*, Plutarch's *Lives*, the *Thousand and One Nights*, Cook's *Voyages*, and Elizabeth Smith's *Fragments in Prose and Verse* (1811). Later she became a voracious reader of contemporary writers of all kinds, including John Keats, Leigh Hunt, William Godwin, Maria Edgeworth, Thomas Moore, and Germaine de Staël. She was deeply read in Byron.

Landon wrote verse from an early age, and her poems were soon submitted to William Jerdan, the Landons' neighbour in Brompton.

In 1817 Jerdan had advanced to the editorship of *The Literary Gazette*, which was rapidly becoming one of the most widely-read literary reviews in the nation. Impressed by Landon's efforts, he began publishing her verse in the *Gazette* in 1820. She first signed herself "L.," but soon changed to "L.E.L."

Landon specialized in writing "poetical sketches" for the *Gazette* – that is, poems on the subject of paintings and mass-produced engravings of contemporary artists. These sentimental commodity-poems made ambiguous capital of a popular spectacle of beauty. They also proved a useful apprenticeship for the Gift Books and Annuals, which would soon begin to dominate the literary and cultural scene. Weekly publication of the *Gazette* ensured the frequent production of her poems, whose anonymity stimulated the curiosity of the reading public. Poems addressed to "L.E.L." began to be submitted to the *Gazette* and *The Literary Magnet* after Jerdan revealed that his poet was a young woman "yet in her teens!" (In reality, Landon was twenty at the time of the notice.)

Determined to make her way as a writer, Landon extended her burgeoning periodical success by publishing a book of poems in July 1824, *The Improvisatrice and Other Poems*.[1] It was a tremendous success, going through six editions in a year. Landon soon repeated her success with another book of verse, *The Troubadour, Catalogue of Pictures and Historical Sketches* in July 1825, which went through four editions. Landon earned an estimated 900 pounds from the sale of her two books and was rapidly becoming a celebrated figure in London society.

The unexpected death of her father in 1824 left Landon the sole support of her mother and younger brother, who aspired to a clerical life. With Jerdan's support she assumed greater responsibilities for the *Gazette,* becoming its head literary reviewer and contributing to its "Original Poetry" section until her death. These obligations brought a much increased work-load and may have contributed to her troubled relationship with her mother. Whatever the case, she left her mother's house and moved in with her grandmother. The latter died in 1826, at which point Landon removed to an upper apartment in the boarding-school she had attended briefly as a child.

It was about this time that the first of a series of slanderous attacks on her character appeared anonymously in the press, where it was suggested that she had been involved in a romantic liaison with Jerdan.[2] In a letter to Katherine Thomson dated June 1826, Landon attributed the slander to her lack of social standing:

> It is only because I am poor, unprotected, and dependent on popularity, that I am a mark for all the gratuitous insolence and malice of idleness and ill-nature. And I cannot but feel deeply that had I been possessed of rank and opulence, either these remarks had never been made, or if they had how trivial would their consequence have been to me. (Blanchard, 1:50)

Her biographer Laman Blanchard adds that the slander may have resulted from envy of Landon's considerable success or from the wounded pride of a writer she had reviewed negatively. It is also possible that her social behaviour, which was said to lack discretion, encouraged the malice of her anonymous enemy. Certainly her sex did not protect her, and may well have been a further provocation.

Landon's next two volumes of poetry, *The Golden Violet, with Its Tales of Romance and Chivalry, and Other Poems,* published in December 1826, and *The Venetian Bracelet, The Lost Pleiad, A History of the Lyre, and Other Poems,* published in October 1829, show a real advance over her earlier work, and a more self-conscious engagement with contemporary social issues, as a poem such as "Lines of Life" clearly demonstrates. Landon had also begun to contribute poems to the Gift Books and Annuals, the literary venue that had rapidly grown throughout the 1820s and 1830s to become a key mode of verse production. The style she developed in writing commodity-poems for the *Gazette* was perfectly suited to the steel-engraved subjects that dominated these remarkable and popular volumes. Landon contributed hundreds of amatory lyrics to at least fifteen of these publications, including *The Keepsake* and *The Amulet.* She edited two annuals, *Fishers Drawing Room Scrap Book* (1832–39) and *Heath's Book of Beauty* (1833), and contributed poems and short stories to *The New Monthly Magazine* from 1832 until her death. Eventually she also wrote several "Silver Fork" novels, that most popular mode of fiction, at once moral and decadent, so well-suited to the period. These were her triple-decker novels *Romance and Reality* (1831), *Francesca Carrera* (1834), and *Ethel Churchill* (1837).

Around the close of 1834 Landon became engaged to John Forster, literary reviewer for the *Examiner* and the future biographer of Dickens. The event stirred up malicious rumours about Landon's character. These involved her not only with Jerdan but also with Edward Bulwer-Lytton, with the portrait painter Daniel Maclise, and with William Maginn, who wrote for *Fraser's Magazine*. Maginn's wife seized some letters addressed from Landon to her husband and showed them to Forster, who demanded an explanation from his fiancée. Both Forster and Mrs. Maginn were soon persuaded of the innocence of the letters. Forster tried to make amends, but Landon broke off the engagement.[3]

Landon published a sixth volume of poetry, *The Vow of the Peacock and Other Poems*, in 1835, and a collection of short stories for children, *Traits and Trials of Early Life*, in 1836. The final story, "The History of a Child," was widely reputed to be an autobiographical account, and Landon herself encouraged this interpretation.[4] In 1837, she wrote her only play, *The Triumph of Lucca*, which was published posthumously by Blanchard.

In October 1836 Landon met George Maclean, governor of Cape Coast Castle, the principal English settlement on the Gold Coast, West Africa. They were engaged by the end of the year, when Maclean returned to his home in Scotland. Upon hearing the recurrent slanders on Landon's character, Maclean began to retreat from the engagement. He broke off correspondence during the winter. Landon also reconsidered his proposal upon hearing reports that Maclean kept a native mistress in Africa. However, the two reconciled, Maclean having been persuaded of Landon's innocence, and insisting, for his part, that the affair with the African woman had ended long before. The two were married on 7 June 1838 in a private ceremony and departed England on 5 July, arriving at Cape Coast Castle (in what is now Ghana) on 15 August.

Landon would live in Africa for only two months. On the morning of 15 October she was discovered by a servant on the floor of her bedroom, near death, holding an empty bottle of diluted prussic (hydrocyanic) acid, a medicine she had been taking to relieve peri-odic spasmatic attacks. The attending physician was unable to revive her. At the inquest conducted the same day, the cause of death was determined to be death by accidental overdose, though no post-mortem was performed.

If Landon was the focus of attention during her life, her shocking death set the seal on her mythic stature. Shortly after the London papers announced her death on 1 January 1839 rumours began to spread about the event. Several of Landon's friends had opposed her marriage, and suspicions that George Maclean or his African mistress had poisoned her led to public accusations. Samuel Carter Hall, whose wife had been Landon's close friend for a decade, maintained to the last: "For my part, that unhappy 'L.E.L.' was murdered I never had a doubt." (Hall 1883: 396). Others suggested that Landon had committed suicide, a possibility that took its strength from her poet-ry, where many of her heroines met such an end.

The first biographers were quick to clear Landon's name. Emma Roberts, in a biography prefaced to Landon's posthumously pub-lished volume *The Zenana and Minor Poems* (1839), assured the read-ing public that the poet's death had been accidental. Laman Blanchard's two-volume *Life and Literary Remains of L.E.L.*, pub-lished two years later, denounced rumours about suicide or murder as well as all slanderous rumours about Landon's character. Both Roberts and Blanchard were friends of the late poet, and both want-ed to clear Landon's name, even to the extent of censoring passages of her letters, as Blanchard does. In 1843, after Roberts' death, William Howitt encouraged the suicide hypothesis by publishing an anecdote which he claimed he had from Roberts, in which Landon showed Roberts a vial of prussic acid, declaring it to be her "reme-dy" if the accusations about her character should ever be published in the press (161).

Richard Robert Madden, biographer of the Countess of Blessing-ton, also surmised that Landon had taken her own life. Katherine and Antony Todd Thomson supported the theory that Landon had been murdered when they averred that shortly before Landon's mys-terious death "a little native boy" had given Landon a cup of coffee, a fact which does not appear in the deposition or in statements given by any witness.

The most careful examination of the evidence surrounding Landon's death would not come until 1942. In a shrewd and badly neglected study, Anne Ethel Wyly determined that the cause of Landon's death was not an overdose of prussic acid, which had always been assumed, but a fatal epileptic seizure.[5] Wyly based her conclusion on statements made by the physician and other witnesses at the deposition on Landon's death. She argues that the death is inconsistent with symptoms of death by hydrocyanic acid poisoning. Furthermore, she points out that none of the deposition statements, even that of William Cobbold, the attending physician, mention smelling the strong and noxious odour of hydrocyanic acid on Landon's body or in the room. Wyly bases her alternative hypothesis on statements by numerous biographers that Landon suffered from convulsions resembling epileptic seizures, and on the fact that several of the medications in Landon's medicine chest were prescribed remedies for epilepsy in the nineteenth century.

The tendency to mythologize "L.E.L." is evident in the numerous poems written for and about her, both during her lifetime and long after her death. Writing a poem to L.E.L. became a rite of passage for numerous early nineteenth-century readers and writers, women and men alike. As the century proceeded this rite became a female devotion, although no less intense or significant for that reason. The poems to Landon written by Elizabeth Barrett Browning and Christina Rossetti are among their best. Indispensable cultural documents, they explicate the myth of L.E.L., whose worldly "heart was breaking for a little love," as Rossetti wrote. Punning shrewdly on the preposition, she reads Landon's life in the same spirit that the author had once written her celebrated poetry.

In the twentieth century, however, Landon's work became all but completely forgotten. Even the sympathetic imagination of Virginia Woolf seems baffled by Landon; and after Woolf comes the desert. Her once celebrated life sank into three dismal and factually unreliable biographical fictions: D.E. Enfield's *L.E.L., A Mystery of the Thirties* (1928), Helen Ashton's *Letty Landon* (1951), and Clyde Chantler's *Eight Weeks: A Novel* (1965). Only in the past ten years have we seen a notable shift in cultural attitudes and with it a renewed interest in the great sentimental myth that became focused with such intensity in Landon's life and works.

II

Like Poe in America, Letitia Elizabeth Landon can scarcely be understood apart from a distinctive and shared literary context. Both writers established their reputations in the world of the 1820s and 1830s, in a period when the institutions of literary production were undergoing drastic change. We date the change – for both countries – from two signal events: the founding of *Blackwood's Edinburgh Magazine* in 1817, and the publication of the *Forget Me Not* in 1822. These two works inaugurated an important shift in the way literature, especially poetry, essay, and short fiction, would be written for the rest of the century.

The period opens the aftermath of almost thirty years of desperate military struggle in Europe. These are the years of the Wars with France, as the protracted conflict that began with the French Revolution was called in England. The military climax came with the defeat of Napoleon at Waterloo, and the political and economic consequences flowing from that event would dominate the European scene for the next one hundred years. Landon's career spans the first, decisive phase of that period, when England assumed her all but absolute imperial presence in the world. The fruits of the victory over France were great material wealth and political power, but they were not uniformly distributed. While the working class realized few benefits, for the middle and upper classes "Bliss was it in that dawn to be alive." Or so at least it might appear on the luxurious surface of things, which is where Landon's work firmly, or fragilely, established itself.

Even as England's success over France began to seem a likely outcome, dark interpreters began to emerge. The year 1812, when Napoleon suffered his great defeat in Russia, brought the most notorious of those bleak prophets to prominence: Lord Byron. With *Childe Harold's Pilgrimage. A Romaunt* he opened a broad-ranging critique of English politics and culture. Neither patriot nor Jacobin, Byron cast a cold eye across the actions of all the thrones and principalities of his day. When he altered the focus and interrogated the English cultural scene, he drew similar mordant conclusions. The period of the Napoleonic Wars also defines what cultural historians call the period of English Romanticism. Nourished in the success of both, Byron emerged as their most prominent critic. For this reason his work became the bar sinister across what he called, in a letter to his publisher in 1817, the "wrong revolutionary poetical system" of romanticism.

Byron's critical posture is important for understanding Landon's work because his life and writings were the dominant influence on her own work and career. She inherited the scepticism for which his name would be the byword. But we want to remember that Byron did not invent this sceptical view of things; he simply brought it into sharp focus. The same year that saw the appearance of Byron's *Childe Harold's Pilgrimage. A Romaunt* brought a new book by one of England's oldest and most revered authors, *Eighteen Hundred and Eleven* by Anna Letitia Barbauld. Byron's poem caused a great sensation, Barbauld's a small scandal. That difference – a highly significant one, as we shall see – measures a kind of paradox, for both poems meditate darkly on current events. Like Byron's, Barbauld's poem imagines a world at war with itself. To Barbauld, the torments of contemporary civilization are not tares among the new spring wheat; they are a function of the presiding "Genius" of the European world in general:

> There walks a Spirit o'er the peopled earth,
> Secret his progress is, unknown his birth;
> Moody and viewless as the changing wind,
> No force arrests his foot, no chain can bind. (61–64)

Seen from a contemporary vantage, this is the spirit of what Mary Shelley would call "The Modern Prometheus," here imagined raising up "the human brute" (65) from ignorance and darkness. Like Shelley's *Frankenstein*, Barbauld's Prometheus is a figure of severest contradiction – as one sees in the startling conjunction of "Moody" with the Miltonic poeticism "viewless." A spirit of grandeur, beauty, and great power, he is a "destroyer and preserver" in a sense far more darkly imagined than Percy Shelley's West Wind. According to Barbauld, "Arts, arms, and wealth destroy the fruits they bring" (161).

Barbauld's is a root and branch critique of a systemic malaise. The most disturbing thought of all is that a demonic force can be traced as easily in the "Arts" as in any other feature of civilization. The (romantic) imagination that art is not among the ideologies is dismissed in Barbauld's text as it was not in Byron's famous poem of the same year, as it typically would not be in most romantic texts. Whereas Byron's despair held out a secret romantic (i.e., personal) hope, Barbauld's final hope – the poem ends with a vision of freedom for America – can only suggest an unnerving question: if spring comes, can winter be far behind?

Comparable to *Childe Harold's Pilgrimage. A Romaunt* in so many ways, Barbauld's poem differs from Byron's in one crucial respect: it genders the issues. The "capricious" (88) Promethean Genius is gendered male; the knowledge of suffering, female. To note this is not to suggest that the poem is arguing a moral equation of men with evil and women with good. It *is* to suggest, however, that a new way of seeing may emerge when an alienated imagination comes to consciousness.

The fact that Barbauld's poem – unlike Byron's – was denounced and then forgotten as soon as it appeared is telling, particularly given the respect and fame that Barbauld's work enjoyed. To her contemporaries, Barbauld's poem seemed grotesque and anomalous from a writer who had come to define the proprieties of the feminine imagination for almost fifty years.

In this respect her poem would prove a song before the dark sunrise of the poetry of the 1820s and 1830s. Literary history has all but forgotten this interregnum because its work is marked with the sign of a bourgeois Cain. With the emergence of Gift Books and literary Annuals as the dominant outlets for poetry, the arts appeared to have scattered the high altars of the imagination. Landon's is a fast world dominated by a self-conscious trade in art and a studious pursuit of cultural fashion in every sense. In the face of it twentieth-century readers have learned to avert their eyes and await the coming of the authoritative poetical voices of Tennyson and Browning.

Two women – both of whom wrote for money, to support themselves and their families – preside over the poetry scene that developed with the deaths of Keats, Shelley, and Byron. One was Felicia Hemans, who would prove the most published English poet of the nineteenth century. The other was Landon. In certain respects the two writers could not be more different. Hemans' work focuses on domestic issues and a Wordsworthian ideology of "the country," whereas Landon, distinctly an urban writer, explores the treacherous cross currents of love. Because each moves within a clearly defined female imagination of the world, however, their work independently establishes new possibilities for poetry.

Most immediately, they deepen *our understanding of romanticism*. Not even John Clare makes such a difference in this respect, though his class position and his madness both supplied him with an advantageous view of his social context. Hemans and Landon are just as important because their cultural alienation, if less apparent, is no less extreme. Each in her way pursued and accommodated the social order they knew well to distrust.

The cultural change involved here is very great, and the poets rather than the fiction writers found it most difficult to manage. Those difficulties, in fact, give the poetry its peculiar edge and expository power. From Byron's mordant and clotted satire *The Age of Bronze* (1823) through Tennyson's obliquely troubled "The Lady of Shalott" (1832), we observe a broad range of conscious poetical reflection on the commerce of letters. In these events Hemans' work is central and runs a parallel course with that of the "later Wordsworth." Like Wordsworth, Hemans preserved a fastidious distance from the fast literary world that was emerging as the twilight of the romantic movement. That is to say, she did not locate herself in London or even in Edinburgh. Nevertheless, literary entrepreneurs like William Blackwood grasped and exploited the cultural capital of her poetry.

The draining melancholy of Hemans' verse carries special force exactly because of its domesticity. What is most unstable, most threatened, is what she most values: the child and its immediate world, the family unit (centred in the mother). Hemans' governing myth represents a home where the father is, for various reasons, absent. This loss turns the home to a precarious scene dominated by the mother. As in Wordsworth, one of Hemans' most important precursors, the mother's protective and conserving imagination presides over a scene of loss. But whereas Wordsworth's (male) myth of (feminine) nature licenses what he called a "strength in what remains behind," Hemans' is an imagination of disaster because her mothers are so conscious of their fragile quotidian state.

The disaster is clearly displayed in a poem like "The Image in Lava." Theatrical by modernist conventions, the verse deploys a muted Byronic extravagance as a vehicle for measuring social catastrophe and domestic loss. "The Image in Lava" studies the epic destruction of Pompeii in a bizarre silhouette of a mother cradling her child. The artist of the end of the world is here imagined not on a grand scale — as a Blakean "history painter" — but rather as a miniaturist. For Hemans, catastrophe is finally what Byron famously called "home desolation," and world-historical events are important only because they help to recall that fact.

> Babe! wert thou brightly slumbering
> Upon thy mother's breast,
> When suddenly the fiery tomb
> Shut round each gentle guest?

Hemans' poem is imagining a new burning babe and a new sacred heart. The events at Pompeii comprise a mere figure for the "impassioned grasp" that bonds child to mother. Burning in the fire of their relationship — setting their fires against "the cities of reknown/ Wherein the mighty trust" — mother and child transcend the Pompeiian world. As Blake might have said, they "go to Eternal Death" (*Jerusalem* 39.16), which now reveals itself in and as the poem Hemans is writing, what she calls a "print upon the dust."

III

Mrs. Hemans, born Felicia Browne, had a cultivated upbringing. Her youthful poetry, praised by family and friends, was put in print by her close admirers in three books before she was married (in 1812). She thus entered the literary world in protective custody. So did Landon. Unlike Browne, however, Landon was ushered into a volatile cultural arena, the highly public and journalistic scene centred in London. Landon lived and worked in this world throughout her years of fame and she was swept up in many of its controversies. Hemans stayed away, and when her poems appeared in *Blackwood's*, as they often did in the 1820s, they signalled a region of cultivated domestic retirement by which to measure and judge the (imperial) controversies being played out in the other parts of the magazine. That removed domestic vantage became the mythic core of her writing – the feature of her work that her readers, both in and out of London, most wanted to experience.

The domestic and maternal love infusing so much of Hemans' work gets replaced in Landon with the subject of erotic love. By that choice of subject Landon gave an immediately provocative edge to her work. For one thing, it placed her writing in a direct relation to the problematic verse of the 1790s, i.e., to the poetry of the Della Cruscan line with its republican sympathies, urban orientation, and its array of "unsex'd females," as Richard Polwhele named the women associated with the movement. Landon's published volumes would only underscore her Della Cruscan inheritance. Whereas the Della Cruscans' troubador and *stil novisti* conventions function in mostly non-explicit ways in their writing, Landon's books plainly declare her allegiances: *The Troubadour, The Improvisatrice, The Golden Violet*. In works like these, the subject of poetry and erotic love, and of the relation between the two, is being unequivocally announced.

Because Landon chose to work and publish in London, and to become intimately involved with its volatile life (both personally and professionally), her position as a writer was far more fragile and even perilous than, say, that of Hemans. Landon had to negotiate her way with great care and deliberation. The consequence is a socially self-conscious style of writing that often – especially in the later work –

comes inflected with a disturbing mood or tone of bad faith. Again and again the poetry seems oblique, or held in reserve, or self-censored. Its romantic subjects lack altogether the fresh and "naive" quality of the work of Burns, Wordsworth, and Coleridge, or the disturbed features of belated works like Byron's *The Giaour* or Keats's "On First Looking Into Chapman's Homer." In Landon there is little new under the sun, although there is much that is novel. Her poetry recreates a factitious world and she is shrewd enough, and cursed enough, to see that her own perceptions are part of that world, as is the language in which she speaks of it.

Landon approaches writing from the same angle, if not in exactly the same spirit, that Poe does. She rehearses established forms and ideas, she echoes and alludes to recognized authors and styles. Byronic tags and phrases recur throughout her work because Byron's writing is well-known; as such, its signs may be effectively deployed as second-order signs of the presence of a poetical discourse of personal disillusionment.

Organized in these terms, Landon's self-consciously quotational writing works to demystify the ancient authority of poetry. This result obtains because Landon, like Poe, implicitly argues that "authority" and "tradition" can only be, in an immediate frame of reference, what is more or less popular. In the end Landon replays the battle of the Ancients and the Moderns not to argue the case for one side or the other but to expose the struggle as a Blakean Orc Cycle of reciprocating engines. What evolves through her writing is not an "Art of Allusion," as Reuben Brower once called the poetry of Pope, but an Art of Disillusion.

IV

Landon executes her disillusions in a number of ways. Often she proceeds in an oblique and circumspect style, as in a poem like "Lady, thy face is very beautiful" or in the "Six Songs" she published in the 10 November 1821 issue of the *Literary Gazette*.[6] At other times her candour is shocking, as works like "Lines of Life," "Revenge" or her many poems for pictures show. "The Enchanted

Island," for instance (after Danby's painting of the same title), implodes upon its own "dream of surpassing beauty." Itself enchanted by that equivocal and double-meaning fantasy, Landon's poem brings an antithetical reading to proverbial romantic ideas like "A thing of beauty is a joy for ever" and "Beauty is truth, truth beauty." The truth that Landon discovers in beauty, including the beauty of art, is death. Keats of course had begun to make similar discoveries, but Landon's more intimate, feminized knowledge of the institutions and machineries of beauty gave a special privilege to her work. Whereas Keats, like Byron, imagined a transcendent power coming from sorrow's knowledge, Landon's knowledge is like Eve's original and cursed discovery of the cruel fantasy grounding the ideal of transcendent power.

Landon's imaginative authority rests in what she is able to fashion from her experience of passivity. The dynamic of love and courtship – Landon's great subject – supplies the (female) object of the enchanted (male) gaze with special insight. The women in Landon's poems are shrewd observers of their spectacular society – cold spectators of a colder spectacle repeatedly masked in the warm colours of dissimulating love. In such a world the distinction between a woman and a thing of beauty is continually collapsing, as one sees in the flat splendours of Landon's "Lady, thy face is very beautiful," where we are never sure if the text is addressing a mirror, a painting, or a woman.

A poet of *dis*enchantments, Landon works by putting the vagaries of imagination on full display:

> Ay, gaze upon her rose-wreathed hair,
>   And gaze upon her smile;
> Seem as you drank the very air
>   Her breath perfumed the while.
>
> ("Revenge," 1-4; 1829)

The enchanted i(s)land is equally under the spell of the romantic "I," the assenting "Ay," and the gazing eye. Wordplays that call attention to the relations among the three are recurrent in Landon's verse.

Ay, moralize, – is it not thus
   We've mourn'd our hope and love?
Alas! there's tears for every eye,
   A hawk for every dove!
   ("A Child Screening a Dove from a Hawk, 9-12; 1825)

Here Landon muses on a painting by Stewardson, which is triangu-
lated by two fearful eyes (dove, child) and one cold eye (hawk).
Studying the aesthetics of the painter's moralizing and sympathetic
eye, the poem succeeds through its ironic appropriation of the
hawk's point of view. The cruelty of the poem – not to be separated
from its sentimental sympathies – anticipates the equally cruel drama
displayed in "Revenge," which retraces Blake's "torments of love and
jealousy":

   But this is fitting punishment,
      To live and love in vain, –
   Oh my wrung heart, be thou content,
      And feed upon his pain. (25-28)

In this world, love's "yes" is joined to the spectacular eye ("Ay, gaze
...") and the coupling proves disastrous. Landon succeeds by entering
fully into the terms of the relationship. Identifying with both her
rival and her false lover, the speaker overgoes Keats' *voluptas* of pain
by an act of incorporation. The poem thus inverts Keats' "Ode to
Melancholy," a work Landon seems specifically to recall. Feeding on
the pain Keats misimagined in a pair of "peerless eyes," Landon's
speaker becomes a "cloudy trophy" hung in the atrocity exhibition
of her own poem.

                              V

If it is true, as has been said, that women have a special knowledge of
imaginary worlds – having lived so long in mirrors and as visionary
objects – one understands the source of Landon's poetic authority.
An imagination like hers has few illusions about illusory worlds, and

least of all about that supreme Land of Cockayne, the romantic imagination. Small wonder that her work, like her spectacular and mythic life, was banished from our high-minded cultural memories. For institutions committed to maintaining kings' treasuries and queens' gardens, she is a dangerous writer. She knows too much about those institutions, and in late work such as "The Fairy of the Fountains" she casts her knowledge into a broad-ranging and summary form.

The poem is an impressive rewriting of Keats's "La Belle Dame sans Merci" and *Lamia* – and through those works, of the long tradition of "femme fatale" studies spun out of the myth of Melusine. Nor had any woman before Landon attempted to retell this foundational European chivalric myth. As Landon well knew, the myth encodes a history of European orientalism that originates in the Crusades and that Scott brilliantly named, in *Ivanhoe*, "the fantastic chivalry of the Nazarenes." In Landon's poem Melusine and her mother are the objects of imperious desires, and if Landon leaves no doubt about the political issues at stake, she subordinates them to the psycho-sexual struggles that are repeated through two generations. The subordination is, however, purely thematic, for the Gift Books and Annuals, in text and image alike, traverse in exhaustive and quite material ways the close relation between imperial and sexual politics. These are the books of a culture that knows what it means to own and administer other lands, people, and cultures. Djouni, Pulo Penang, The Caves of Elephanta, Borro Boedoor: Landon's poetry and its related illustrations play out tales of disastered love across a world-map of exotic places. Where else should Landon have died but in a fortified British outpost in remote West Africa? Tunis? Sbietlah? Kursalee? She knew them all already.

Landon never went to any of those romantic places, nor did she have to. She knew them in another reality, as the fantasy locales for dark and tragic tales of the homes of England: tales telling of love's bad or betrayed faith, of women's inter-generational conflicts and blindnesses, and of the dark fatalities that seem to evolve from such circumstances. These are the main themes of "The Fairy of the Fountains," and if they have clear connections to Landon's own life, Landon depersonalizes her subjects. Which is not to say that she erases the crucial gender issues. On the contrary, her conception of the story pivots on those issues and forces the legend's contemporary applications. Political questions are not engaged directly, although the gendered and historicist treatment of Christianity comes very close to doing so. The focus is rather on the alienation of women and the desire that women both represent and pursue.

That frame of reference supplies the poem with its politics of imagination. Figures of art dominate the textual scene of Landon's work, where men and women regularly appear in marble and stone – as statuary, beautiful but dead.

> Sits the fairy ladye there,
> Like a statue, pale and fair. (369-370)

The world of art, enveloping Landon's own work, thus emerges in troubled forms that trouble its patrimony. As an explicit rewriting of a central male legend, "The Fairy of the Fountains" makes the subject of art and imagination its problematic centre.

> Once that ladye, dark and tall,
> Stood upon the castle wall;
> And she marked her daughter's eyes
> Fix'd upon the glad sunrise,
> With a sad yet eager look,
> Such as fixes on a book
> Which describes some happy lot,
> Lit with joys that we have not.
> And the thought of what has been,
>   And the thought of what might be,
> Makes us crave the fancied scene,
>   And despise reality.
> 'Twas a drear and desert plain
> Lay around their own domain;
> But, far off, a world more fair
> Outlined on the sunny air.... (97-112)

A first person (plural) slips into the text to underscore the contemporary relevance of the ballad tale. The passage constructs an allegory of the impasse revealed to Landon in and through the romantic imagination. Reading it one thinks immediately of Blake's "Auguries of Innocence:"

> God Appears & God is Light
> To those poor Souls who dwell in Night,
> But does a Human Form display
> To those who Dwell in Realms of day.

Landon's souls do not display human forms. They pose in stone, or they walk in beauty, like the night they inhabit. The daughter Melusine dreams toward an ideal future in the gloom of her mother's palatial prison. The figure of the book, which locates her dream, says only that fantasy rules the imagined "sunrise" of her unencountered homeland. Revelatory truth is held within the ineffectual reserves of her mother's "dark eye's funeral flame" (90). Melusine's mother warns her against her driving desires because she foresees only nightwood futurities. She possesses a darkened imagination of the truth that Landon knows too well in and as the garish daylight of a contemporary despised reality.

The poem deserves to be better known, as Christina Rossetti's "Goblin Market" has now come to be. Particularly notable is its verbal texture. Because Landon focuses on secondary and evacuated worlds, her atmospheres are as thin as her cartoon characters. Later poets — one thinks immediately of Tennyson and D.G. Rossetti — create palaces of art from such ruined realities, purely linguistic worlds that are, however, richly elaborated. Landon works differently, and a later poem like "The Fairy of the Fountains" makes an impressive display of the style she evolved. It is a style characterized by emblematic shapes and actions. Landon will isolate for special service certain key words and figural forms. In this poem the words "ring" and "scale" and their cognates are particularly important. But she has preferred depositories to draw upon: the discourse of art, for instance, as we have seen. When Melusine's "world more fair" rises to her imagination, it comes as an aesthetic object "Outlined on the sunny air." Because the lines involve a romantic commonplace, one is struck by the odd grammatical usage. But these kinds of aberrations are not infrequent in her work. They become a general feature of her otherwise flat style, as if customary forms of expression were subject to unmotivated deviance that then brings surprising insight. Here the verb's transitive voice defines the imaginary world as self-generating. But the power thus formally coded is exposed at the semantic level as thin and attenuated: as if a spectacular Turner sunrise had been analytically reduced to an engraving.

This is not a style that would be appreciated by most twentieth-century readers. It is cold and sentimental at the same time, flat and intense, like the photographs of Cindy Sherman. We once thought Beauty shouldn't know so much, that it would lose its aura in gaining this kind of knowledge. And so it does: for all her romantic materials, Landon is a notably unspectacular writer, easily – too easily – forgotten. But for those who like poets writing under the sign "Beauty is truth, truth beauty," Landon ought to have a special attraction.

VI

There is a letter from Elizabeth Barrett to Mary Russell Mitford that ought to be recalled when we read Landon's poetry. The two women argued the relative merits of the poetry of Hemans and Landon, Mitford preferring the former, Barrett the latter. To Mitford, Landon's poetry seemed crude and incompetent beside the finished works of the older poet. When Barrett meditates on this judgement in a letter of 15 July 1841, she cannot withhold her assent to the justice of Mitford's thought. But neither can she be persuaded from her preference:

> I feel all you say of the material unworked! – She might indeed have achieved a greatness which her fondest admirers can scarcely consider achieved now. And do you know (ah! – I know that you won't agree with me!) I have sometimes thought to myself that if I had those two powers to choose

from ... Mrs. Hemans' and Miss Landon's ... I mean the raw bare powers ... I would choose Miss Landon's. I surmise that it was more elastic, more various & of a stronger web.... As it is, Mrs. Hemans has left the finer poems. Of that there can be no question. But perhaps ... & indeed I do say it very diffidently ... there is a sense of sameness which goes with the sense of excellence, – while we read her poems – a satiety with the satisfaction.... (Raymond and Sullivan, I: 235)

The image of choice, "the raw bare powers," is telling. Barrett cannot bring herself to argue that Landon's less finished work might exhibit "the finer poems," but it is clear that she *feels* this to be the case. She ends her comment by posing and answering the following question: "If [Hemans] had lived longer wd. she have been greater? 'I trow not.'" The Keatsian implication tells Barrett's whole mind on the subject of the two poets' comparative worth. Both Hemans and Landon deal in exquisite subjects, but Landon's stylistic indiscretions seem to Barrett more equal to those subjects, and a longer life would have proven her powers. Indeed, though she does not say so, Barrett plainly senses in the unsuccess of Landon's style an adequate vehicle for what would be Landon's greatest subject: *dis*satisfaction with her epoch's satieties and satisfactions. It was Robert Browning, not Alfred Tennyson, that Miss Barrett fell in love with.

Notes

1   This was in fact her second book of verse. Her first book, *The Fate of Adelaide* (1821), was a juvenile effort published before her success in *The Literary Gazette*, and went virtually unnoticed by the reading public.

2   Glennis Stephenson argues that a series of anonymous articles published in *The Wasp* in 1826 were the first public slander of Landon's reputation (35-36). This contradicts Grace and Philip Wharton (Katherine and Antony Todd Thomson), who claim that "the first attempt to injure her character was made in the

'Sun' newspaper" about the time of the publication of *The Trou-badour* (174). Other biographical accounts remain silent on the source of the slander.

3   Apart from the anonymous slander, only two contemporary published sources argue that rumours of Landon's sullied reputation were true. Grantley Berkeley, in *My Life and Recollections*, claimed that Landon confided in him that Maginn had seduced her and was threatening her with blackmail. Miriam Thrall has challenged the credibility of Berkeley's account (Thrall 216-22). The other contemporary source is William Charles Macready, a friend of Forster's, whose assertion that Landon carried on an affair with Maginn is based solely on hearsay (Toynbee 1: 262). According to Michael Sadleir, Rosina Bulwer-Lytton in her later years accused her husband of having carried on an affair with Landon. However, as Michael Sadleir points out, by the 1850s Rosina had become "so obsessed with loathing for her husband that actuality and propaganda had become inextricably confused in her mind," a fact which casts serious doubt on the truth of her statements (435).

4   In answer to a request for an autobiographical sketch, Landon wrote a letter to S.C. Hall in which she claimed that her child-hood served as the basis for "The History of a Child" (Hall 1871: 269). Her brother and cousin denied the story's basis in fact. (See Blanchard 1: 24-26.)

5   In *Letitia Elizabeth Landon: Her Career, Her "Mysterious" Death, and Her Poetry* (unpublished thesis, Duke University, 1942). Brodie Cruickshank, the only eyewitness to publish an account of Landon's death, provides evidence that supports Wyly's thesis: see Cruickshank, I 221-229.

6   For a discussion of this set of poems see McGann, 147-149.

Letitia Elizabeth Landon: A Brief Chronology

1802 L. born, 14 August, to John and Katherine Landon.

1807 Attends Frances Rowden's school for young women.

1815 Napoleon defeated at Waterloo; John Landon's army agency, Adair & Co., suffers as a result.

1816 Landon family moves to Old Brompton, residing near William Jerdan, editor of *The Literary Gazette.*

1820 Jerdan publishes L.'s first poem, "Rome," in the 11 March issue of the *Gazette.*

1821 *The Fate of Adelaide* published. Dissolution of Adair & Co.

1822 First English annual, the *Forget Me Not,* published.

1824 Death of Byron (19 April). Publication of *The Improvisatrice and Other Poems,* July. L. begins contributing poems to annuals. Death of John Landon, 18 November.

1825 L. moves in with her grandmother. Publication of *The Troubadour,* July. First anonymous slanders linking L. and Jerdan begin about this time.

1826 Slanderous articles about L. published anonymously in *The Wasp,* October–November. Publication of *The Golden Violet,* December. L. moves into an attic apartment of her former schoolhouse.

1829 Publication of *The Venetian Bracelet,* October.

1831 Publication of *Romance and Reality.* L. begins editing *Fishers Drawing Room Scrap Book.*

1832 Publication of *The Easter Gift*, a short book of Christian poems. L. begins contributing to *New Monthly Magazine*, and edits *Heath's Book of Beauty for 1833*.

1834 Publication of *Francesca Carrera*. L. visits Paris, summer. Becomes engaged to John Forster, reviewer for *The Examiner*; L. breaks off engagement after slanderous rumors resurface.

1835 Death of Felicia Hemans (16 May). Publication of *The Vow of the Peacock*, a collection of poems.

1836 Publication of *Traits and Trials of Early Life*. L. meets George Maclean, governor of Gold Coast, October; engaged shortly afterward.

1837 Publication of long poem *A Birthday Gift to Princess Victoria*, May; final novel, *Ethel Churchill*, published in September. L. completes her only play, *The Triumph of Lucca or Castruccio Castrucani*.

1838 Marries George Maclean, 7 June. Coronation of Victoria (27 June). L. sails to Gold Coast, July–August. Death, 15 October.

WORKS

FROM *THE LITERARY GAZETTE*

SIX SONGS OF LOVE, CONSTANCY, ROMANCE, INCONSTANCY, TRUTH, AND MARRIAGE.[1]

OH! yet one smile, tho' dark may lower
Around thee clouds of woe and ill,
Let me yet feel that I have power,
Mid Fate's bleak storms, to soothe thee still.

Tho' sadness be upon thy brow,
Yet let it turn, dear love, to me,
I cannot bear that thou should'st know
Sorrow I do not share with thee.

True love's wreath is of mountain flowers,
They stand the storm and brave the blast,   10
And blossom on, so love like ours
Is sweetest when all else is past.

Too well I know what storms have frowned,
And now frown on life's troubled tide;
Still darker let them gather round,
They have no power on hearts so tried.

Then say not that you may not bear,
To shadow spirit light as mine;

I shall not shrink, or fear to share
20   The darkest fate if it be thine!

————

OH! say not love was never made
For heart so light as mine;
Must love then seek the cypress shade,
Rear but a gloomy shrine.

Oh! say not, that for me more meet
The revelry of youth;
Or that my wild heart cannot beat
With deep devoted truth.

Tho' mirth may many changes ring,
10   'Tis but an outward show,
Even upon the fond dove's wing
Will varying colours glow.

Light smiles upon my lip may gleam
And sparkle o'er my brow,
'Tis but the glisten of the stream
That hides the gold below.

'Tis love that gilds the mirthful hour,
That lights the smile for me,
Those smiles would instant lose their power,
20   Did they not glance on thee!

————

OH! come to my slumber
Sweet dreams of my love,
I have hung the charmed wreath
My soft pillow above.

The roses are linked
In a chain pure and white;
And the rose-leaves are wet
With the dew drops of night.

The moon was on high
As I gather'd each flower;   10
The dew that then falls
Has a magical power.

The Spirit of slumber
Those roses has blest;
And sweet are the visions
They'll bring to my rest.

Be their spell on my soul,
So they let me but see
His dark eyes flash in love
And his smile glance on me.   20

Let sleep bring the image
Of him far away;
'Tis worth all the tears
I shed for him by day.

I have hung the charmed wreath
My soft pillow above;
Then come to my slumber,
Sweet dreams of my love!

————

How vain to cast my love away
On bosom false as thine;
The floweret's bloom, that springs in May
Would be a safer shrine

To build my fondest hopes upon,
Tho' fragile it may be.
That flower's smile is not sooner gone
Than love that trusts to thee. a torn

Love asks a calm, a gentle home,
10   Or else its life is o'er;
If once you let its pinions roam,
Oh! then 'tis love no more.

The aspin's changeful shade can be
No shelter for the dove;
And hearts as varying as that tree,
Are sure no place for love.

Hope linger'd long and anxiously,
O'er failing faith, but now
I give thee back each heartless sigh,
20   Give back each broken vow.

I'll trust the stay of tulip dyes,
The calm of yon wild sea,
The sunshine of the April skies,
But never more to thee!

———

OH! would that love had power to raise
A little isle for us alone,
With fairy flowers, and sunny rays,
The blue sea wave its guardian zone.

No other step should ever press
This hidden Eden of the heart,
And we would share its loveliness,
From every other thing apart.

The rose and violet should weep,
Whene'er our leafy couch was laid,   10
The lark should wake our morning sleep
The bulbul[2] sing our serenade.

And we would watch the starry hours,
And call the moon to hear our vows,
And we would cull the sweetest flowers,
And twine fresh chaplets for our brows.

———

I thought thus of the flowers, the moon,
This fairy isle for you and me;
And then I thought how very soon
How very tired we should be.

We become tired of love. 20

———

MATRIMONIAL CREED.

HE must be rich whom I could love,
His fortune clear must be,
Whether in land or in the funds,
'Tis all the same to me.

He must be old whom I could love,
Then he'll not plague me long;
In sooth 'twill be a pleasant sight,
To see him borne along

To where the croaking ravens lurk,
And where the earth worms dwell: 10
A widow's hood will suit my face,
And black becomes me well.

And he must make a settlement,
I'll have no man without;
And when he writes his testament,
He must not leave me out.

Oh! such a man as this would suit
Each wish I here express;
If he should say, — Will you have me?
I'll very soon say — Yes!

FROM *MEDALLION WAFERS.*[3]

[The hint for this series of Poems (to be continued occasionally) has been taken from the account of the Medallion Wafers in the *Literary Gazette.* These slight things preserve many of the most beautiful forms of antiquity; and they are here devoted to verse, on the supposition that they have been employed as seals to lovers' correspondence.]

INTRODUCTION.

I DO so prize the slightest thing
   Touched, looked, or breathed upon by thee,
That all or aught which can but bring
   One single thought of thine to me,
Is precious as a pilgrim's gift
Upon the shrine he most loves left.

And if, like those charmed caves that weep,
   Preserving tears of crystal dew,
My lute's flow has a power to keep
   From perishing what it shrines too —   10
It only shall preserve the things
Bearing the bright print of Love's wings.

Here's many a youth with radiant brow
   Darkened by raven curls like thine,
Beauty, whose smile burns even now,
   And love-tales made by song divine:
And these have been the guardian powers
To words as sweet as summer flowers.

I'll tell thee now the history
   Of these sweet shapes: they are so dear,   20
Each has been on a scroll from thee;
   Thy kiss, thy sigh, are glowing here:

They'll be the spirit of each tone
I fain would wake from chords long gone.

Just glimpses of the fairest dreams
    I've had when in a hot noon sleeping,
Or those diviner, wilder gleams
    When I some starry watch was keeping;
And sometimes those bright waves of thought
Only from lips like thine, Love, caught.

Oh dear, these lights from the old world,
    So redolent with love and song!
Those radiant gods, now downward hurled
    From the bright thrones they held so long!
But they have power that cannot die
Over the heart's eternity.

CONCLUSION.

ALL, all forgotten! Oh, false Love!
    I had not deemed that this could be,
That heart and lute, so truly thine,
    Could both be broken, and by thee.

I did not dream, when I have loved
    To dwell on Sorrow's saddest tone,
That its reality would soon
    Be but the echo of mine own.

Farewell! I give thee back each vow,
    Vows are but vain when love is dead;
What boot the trammels, when the bird
    They should have kept so safe, is fled?

But go! be happy and be free,
    My heart is far too warm for thine;

Go! and 'mid Pleasure's lights and smiles,
    Heed not what tears and clouds are mine.

But I, — oh, how can I forget
    What has been more than life to me!
Oh wherefore, wherefore was I taught
    So much of passion's misery!   20

Thy name is breathed on every song —
    How can I bid those songs depart?
The thoughts I've treasur'd up of thee
    Are more than life-blood to my heart.

But I may yet learn to forget;
    I am too proud for passion's chain;
I yet may learn to wake my lute —
    But never at Love's call again.

I will be proud for you to hear
    Of glory brightening on my name;   30
Oh vain, oh worse than vanity!
    Love, love is all a woman's fame.

Then deepest silence to the chords
    Which only wakened for thy sake;
When love has left both heart and harp,
    Ah what can either do but break!

RICH the crimson curtains fell, *a*
Coloured with the hues that dwell *a*
In the Tyrian's purple shell — *a*
That bright secret which is known *b*
To the mighty past alone. *b*
Forty pillars rose between, *c*
   In that fine Corinthian mould *d*
When a life's whole task has been *c*
   How to work the burning gold — *d*
Gold which some young conqueror's hand *e*
Brought from many a vanquish'd land; *e*
Then bade genius raise a shrine — *f*
Thus profaning the divine — *f*
Till his rapine and his crime *f*
Grew in that false light sublime. *f*

Azure was the roof, and light *a*
   Pour'd down from the crystal dome; *b*
Clear the crystal was and bright *a*
   As in its own ocean home. *b*

Polish'd like a warrior's shield, *a*
Black (for such the quarries yield *a*
Where the sun hath never shone, *b*
Which night only rests upon,) *b*
Was the marble floor, which gave *c*
Mirror like some clear dark wave. *c*

Silent was that hall around, *a*
Moved no step and stirred no sound; *a*
Yet the shapes of life were there, *b*
Spiritual, calm, and fair — *b*
Statues to whose rest seem'd given *c*
Not the life of earth but heaven; *c*
For each statue here enshrined *d*

10

20

30

What in the immortal mind
Makes its beauty and its power —
Genius's eternal dower:
Those embodyings of thought
Which within the spirit wrought
In its most ethereal time,
Of its own and earlier clime
Ere the shade and soil of earth   40
Tainted an immortal birth.

Thankful should we be to those
Who disdain a dull repose —
Who have head and heart on fire
With unquenchable desire
Of those higher hopes which spring
Heavenward on an eager wing —
Those wide aims which seek to bind
Man the closer with his kind —
By earth's most unearthly ties,   50
Praises, hopes, and sympathies;
And call beauty, like a dream,
Up from life's most troubled stream.

From that mighty crystal dome,
Clear and cold the sunbeams roam
Over th' ethereal band
Which beside the column stand.

God of the West Wind, awake!
See who fain thy sleep would break* —
She, the morning's gracious power,   60
Born in its most lovely hour,
When the stars retire in night
For the mighty fates to write
On their rays the word and sign

---

* Mr. Hollins' Aurora waking Zephyrus.[5]

Only prophets may divine;
When the blushing clouds are breaking,
As if Love himself were waking —
When the sun first turns the mist
Into melted amethyst —
70   She hath bade the north wind keep
In his caverns dark and deep —
Told the south wind, that his breath
Fades too soon the morning wreath —
Sent the east wind where the sands
Sweep around the pilgrim bands —
Her sweet hand is on thy brow —
Wake thee, gentle West Wind, now.
She doth want thy wings to bear
Morning's messages through air,
80   Where the dewy grass is keeping
Watch above the skylark's sleeping;
Stir the clover with thy wing,
Send him 'mid the clouds to sing.
Thou must go and kiss the rose,
Crimson with the night's repose;
She will sigh for coming day,
Bear thou that sweet sigh away;
On the violet's sleepy eyes
Pour the azure of the skies;
90   From the rich and purple wreath
Steal the fragrance of its breath;
Wake the bees to the sweet spoil
Which rewards their summer toil;
Shake the bough, and rouse the bird,
Till one general song is heard;
Fling aside the glittering leaves,
Till the darkest nook receives
Somewhat of the morning beam;
Stir the ripples of the stream,
100   Till it flash like silver back
In the white swan's radiant track.

Rouse thee for Aurora's sake —
God of the West Wind, awake!
    Close beside 's a child,[†] whose hand
O'er a lute holds sweet command:
Like a spirit is that child —
For his gentle lip is mild,
And his smile like those which trace
Sunshine on an angel's face:
But upon that brow is wrought   110
Evidence of deeper thought,
Higher hopes, and keener fears,
Than should mark such infant years.
Childhood should have laughing eye,
Where tears pass like showers by —
When the sky becomes more bright,
For a moment's shadowed light.
Childhood's step should be as gay
As the sunbeam on its way:
There will come another hour,   120
When fate rules with harsher power —
When the weary mind is worn
By the sorrow it hath borne —
When desire sits down to weep
Over hope's unbroken sleep —
When we know our care and toil
Cultures an ungrateful soil —
When in our extremest need
Only grows the thorn and weed —
Well the face may be o'ercast   130
By the trouble it has past.
Ah, fair child! I read it now
By the meaning on thy brow —
By thy deep and thoughtful eyes,
Where the soul of genius lies;
Even now the shade is o'er thee

---

†   Mr. Lough's Child playing a Lyre.[6]

Of the path which lies before thee;
For thy hand is on the lyre,
And thy lip is living fire,
140 And before thee is the wreath
Which the poet wins by death.
Brief and weary life is thine —
But thy future is divine.

Near it kneels a maid in prayer,[‡]
Fair as the white rose is fair —
With a sad and chastened look,
As the spirit early took
Bitter lessons, how on earth
Flowers perish in their birth,
150 Blossoms fall before they bloom,
And the bud is its own tomb.
Once she dreamed a gentle dream —
Such, alas! love's ever seem —
Whence she only waked to know
Every thing is false below.
Soon the warm heart has to learn
Lessons of despair, and turn
From a world whose charm is o'er
When its hope deceives no more.
160 Maiden, thy young brow is cold —
'Tis because thy heart is old;
And thine eyes are raised above,
For earth hath betrayed thy love.

Dark the shades of evening fall —
Night is gathering o'er that hall;
All seems indistinct and pale —
Thick falls the shadowy veil;
All the shapes I gazed upon,
Like the dream that raised them, gone.

[‡] Mr. Macdonald's Supplicating Virgin.[7]

FROM *THE IMPROVISATRICE AND OTHER POEMS.*[8]

from *THE IMPROVISATRICE*

ADVERTISEMENT.

POETRY needs no Preface: if it do not speak for itself, no comment can render it explicit. I have only, therefore, to state that *The Improvisatrice* is an attempt to illustrate that species of inspiration common in Italy, where the mind is warmed from earliest childhood by all that is beautiful in Nature and glorious in Art. The character depicted is entirely Italian, — a young female with all the loveliness, vivid feeling, and genius of her own impassioned land. She is supposed to relate her own history; with which are intermixed the tales and episodes which various circumstances call forth.

Some of the minor poems have appeared in *The Literary Gazette.*

L.E.L.

I AM a daughter of that land,
Where the poet's lip and the painter's hand
Are most divine, — where the earth and sky,
Are picture both and poetry —
I am of Florence. 'Mid the chill
Of hope and feeling, oh! I still
Am proud to think to where I owe
My birth, though but the dawn of woe!

My childhood passed 'mid radiant things,
Glorious as Hope's imaginings;
Statues but known from shapes of the earth,
By being too lovely for mortal birth;
Paintings whose colours of life were caught
From the fairy tints in the rainbow wrought;
Music whose sighs had a spell like those
That float on the sea at the evening's close;
Language so silvery, that every word
Was like the lute's awakening chord;
Skies half sunshine, and half starlight;
Flowers whose lives were a breath of delight;
Leaves whose green pomp knew no withering;
Fountains bright as the skies of our spring;
And songs whose wild and passionate line
Suited a soul of romance like mine.

My power was but a woman's power;
Yet, in that great and glorious dower
Which Genius gives, I had my part:
I poured my full and burning heart
In song, and on the canvass made
    My dreams of beauty visible;
I knew not which I loved the most —
    Pencil or lute, — both loved so well.

Oh, yet my pulse throbs to recall,
When first upon the gallery's wall
Picture of mine was placed, to share
Wonder and praise from each one there!
Sad were my shades; methinks they had
    Almost a tone of prophecy —
I ever had, from earliest youth,
    A feeling what my fate would be.

My first was of a gorgeous hall,
Lighted up for festival;
Braided tresses, and cheeks of bloom,

Diamond agraff,[9] and foam-white plume;
Censers of roses, vases of light,
Like what the moon sheds on a summer night.
Youths and maidens with linked hands,
Joined in the graceful sarabands,
Smiled on the canvass; but apart
   Was one who leant in silent mood
As revelry to his sick heart   50
   Were worse than veriest solitude.
Pale, dark-eyed, beautiful, and young,
   Such as he had shone o'er my slumbers,
When I had only slept to dream
   Over again his magic numbers.

Divinest Petrarch! he whose lyre,
Like morning light, half dew, half fire,
To Laura and to love was vowed —
He looked on one, who with the crowd
Mingled, but mixed not; on whose cheek   *Painting Petrarch*
   There was a blush, as if she knew   60
Whose look was fixed on her's. Her eye,
   Of a spring-sky's delicious blue,
Had not the language of that bloom,
But mingling tears, and light, and gloom,
Was raised abstractedly to Heaven: —
No sign was to her lover given.
I painted her with golden tresses,
Such as float on the wind's caresses
When the laburnums wildly fling   70
Their sunny blossoms to the spring.
A cheek which had the crimson hue
   Upon the sun touched nectarine;
A lip of perfume and of dew;
   A brow like twilight's darkened line.
I strove to catch each charm that long
Has lived, — thanks to her lover's song!
Each grace he numbered one by one,

That shone in her of Avignon.

I ever thought that poet's fate
Utterly lone and desolate.
It is the spirit's bitterest pain
To love, to be beloved again;
And yet between a gulf which ever
The hearts that burn to meet must sever.
And he was vowed to one sweet star,
Bright yet to him, but bright afar.

O'er some, Love's shadow may but pass
As passes the breath-stain o'er glass;
And pleasures, cares, and pride combined,
Fill up the blank Love leaves behind.
But there are some whose love is high,
Entire, and sole idolatry;
Who, turning from a heartless world,
   Ask some dear thing, which may renew
Affection's severed links, and be
   As true as they themselves are true.
But Love's bright fount is never pure;
And all his pilgrims must endure
All passion's mighty suffering
Ere they may reach the blessed spring.
And some who waste their lives to find
   A prize which they may never win:
Like those who search for Irem's groves,[10]
   Which found, they may not enter in.
Where is the sorrow but appears
In Love's long catalogue of tears?
And some there are who leave the path
In agony and fierce disdain;
But bear upon each cankered breast
   The scar that never heals again.

My next was of a minstrel too,
   Who proved what woman's hand might do,

When, true to the heart pulse, it woke
   The harp. Her head was bending down,
As if in weariness, and near,
   But unworn, was a laurel crown.
She was not beautiful, if bloom
And smiles form beauty; for, like death,   120
Her brow was ghastly; and her lip
Was parched, as fever were its breath.
There was a shade upon her dark,
Large, floating eyes, as if each spark
Of minstrel ecstacy was fled,
Yet leaving them no tears to shed;
Fixed in their hopelessness of care,
And reckless in their great despair.
She sat beneath a cypress tree,
   A little fountain ran beside,   130
And, in the distance, one dark rock
   Threw its long shadow o'er the tide;
And to the west, where the nightfall
Was darkening day's gemm'd coronal,
Its white shafts crimsoning in the sky,
Arose the sun-god's sanctuary.
I deemed, that of lyre, life, and love
   She was a long, last farewell taking; —
That, from her pale and parched lips,
   Her latest, wildest song was breaking.   140

SAPPHO'S SONG.

FAREWELL, my lute! — and would that I
   Had never waked thy burning chords!
Poison has been upon thy sigh,
   And fever has breathed in thy words.

Yet wherefore, wherefore should I blame
   Thy power, thy spell, my gentlest lute?
I should have been the wretch I am,

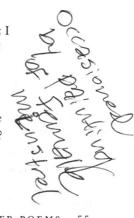

Had every cord of thine been mute.

It was my evil star above,
    Not my sweet lute, that wrought me wrong:
It was not song that taught me love,
    But it was love that taught me song.

If song be past, and hope undone,
    And pulse, and head, and heart, are flame;
It is thy work, thou faithless one!
    But, no! — I will not name thy name!

Sun-god! lute, wreath are vowed to thee!
    Long be their light upon my grave —
My glorious grave — yon deep blue sea:
    I shall sleep calm beneath its wave!

———

FLORENCE! with what idolatry
    I've lingered in thy radiant halls,
Worshipping, till my dizzy eye
    Grew dim with gazing on those walls,
Where Time had spared each glorious gift
By Genius unto Memory left!
And when seen by the pale moonlight,
More pure, more perfect, though less bright,
What dreams of song flashed on my brain,
Till each shade seemed to live again;
And then the beautiful, the grand,
The glorious of my native land,
In every flower that threw its veil
Aside, when wooed by the spring gale;
In every vineyard, where the sun,
His task of summer ripening done,
Shone on their clusters, and a song
Came lightly from the peasant throng; —

[handwritten margin note: Apostrophe to Florence]

In the dim loveliness of night,
In fountains with their diamond light, 180
In aged temple, ruined shrine,
And its green wreath of ivy twine; —
In every change of earth and sky,
Breathed the deep soul of poesy.

As yet I loved not; — but each wild,
High thought I nourished raised a pyre
For love to light; and lighted once
By love, it would be like the fire
The burning lava floods that dwell
In Etna's cave unquenchable. 190

One evening in the lovely June,
    Over the Arno's waters gliding,
I had been watching the fair moon
    Amid her court of white clouds riding; —
I had been listening to the gale,
    Which wafted music from around,
(For scarce a lover, at that hour,
    But waked his mandolin's light sound), —
And odour was upon the breeze,
Sweet thefts from rose and lemon trees. 200

They stole me from my lulling dream,
    And said they knew that such an hour
Had ever influence on my soul,
    And raised my sweetest minstrel power.
I took my lute, — my eye had been
Wandering round the lovely scene,
Filled with those melancholy tears,
Which come when all most bright appears,
And hold their strange and secret power,
Even on pleasure's golden hour. 210
I had been looking on the river,
Half-marvelling to think that ever

Wind, wave, or sky, could darken where
All seemed so gentle and so fair:
And mingled with these thoughts there came
   A tale, just one that Memory keeps —
Forgotten music, till some chance
   Vibrate the chord whereon it sleeps!

★   ★   ★   ★

FROM many a lip came sounds of praise,
   Like music from sweet voices ringing;
For many a boat had gathered round,
   To list the song I had been singing.
There are some moments in our fate
   That stamp the colour of our days;
As, till then, life had not been felt, —
   And mine was sealed in the slight gaze
420   Which fixed my eye, and fired my brain,
And bowed my heart beneath the chain.
'Twas a dark and flashing eye,
Shadows, too, that tenderly,
With almost female softness, came
O'er its mingled gloom and flame.
His cheek was pale; or toil, or care,
Or midnight study, had been there,
Making its young colours dull,
Yet leaving it most beautiful.
430   Raven curls their shadow threw,
Like the twilight's darkening hue,
O'er the pure and mountain snow
Of his high and haughty brow:
Lighted by a smile, whose spell
Words are powerless to tell.
Such a lip! — oh, poured from thence
Lava floods of eloquence
Would come with fiery energy,
Like those words that cannot die.

Words the Grecian warrior spoke   440
When the Persian's chain he broke;
Or that low and honey tone,
Making women's heart his own;
Such as should be heard at night,
In the dim and sweet starlight;
Sounds that haunt a beauty's sleep,
Treasures for her heart to keep.
Like the pine of summer tall;
Apollo, on his pedestal
In our own gallery, never bent   450
More graceful, more magnificent;
Ne'er look'd the hero, or the king,
    More nobly than the youth who now,
As if soul-centred in my song,
    Was leaning on a galley's prow.
He spoke not when the others spoke,
    His heart was all too full for praise;
But his dark eyes kept fixed on mine,
    Which sank beneath their burning gaze.
Mine sank — but yet I felt the thrill   460
Of that look burning on me still.
I heard no word that others said —
    Heard nothing, save one low-breathed sigh.
My hand kept wandering on my lute,
    In music, but unconsciously
My pulses throbbed, my heart beat high,
A flush of dizzy ecstasy
    Crimsoned my cheek; I felt warm tears
Dimming my sight, yet was it sweet,
My wild heart's most bewildering beat,   470
    Consciousness, without hopes or fears,
Of a new power within me waking,
Like light before the morn's full breaking.
I left the boat — the crowd: my mood
Made my soul pant for solitude.

Amid my palace halls was one,
The most peculiarly my own:
The roof was blue and fretted gold,
The floor was of the Parian stone,[11]
480   Shining like snow, as only meet
For the light tread of fairy feet;
And in the midst, beneath a shade
Of clustered rose, a fountain played,
Sprinkling its scented waters round,
With a sweet and lulling sound, —
O'er oranges, like Eastern gold,
Half hidden by the dark green fold
Of their large leaves; — o'er hyacinth bells,
Where every summer odour dwells,
490   And, nestled in the midst, a pair
Of white wood-doves, whose home was there:
And like an echo to their song,
At times a murmur past along;
A dying tone, a plaining fall,
So sad, so wild, so musical —
As the wind swept across the wire,
And waked my lone Æolian lyre,
Which lay upon the casement, where
The lattice wooed the cold night air,
500   Half hidden by a bridal twine
Of jasmine with the emerald vine.
And ever as the curtains made
A varying light, a changeful shade,
As the breeze waved them to and fro,
Came on the eye the glorious show
Of pictured walls where landscape wild
Of wood, and stream, or mountain piled,
Or sunny vale, or twilight grove,
Or shapes whose every look was love;
510   Saints, whose diviner glance seemed caught
From Heaven, — some whose earthlier thought
Was yet more lovely, — shone like gleams

Of Beauty's spirit seen in dreams.
I threw me on a couch to rest,
   Loosely I flung my long black hair;
It seemed to soothe my troubled breast
   To drink the quiet evening air.
I looked upon the deep-blue sky,
And it was all hope and harmony.
Afar I could see the Arno's stream   520
Glorying in the clear moonbeam;
And the shadowy city met my gaze,
Like the dim memory of other days;
And the distant wood's black coronal
Was like oblivion, that covereth all.
I know not why my soul felt sad;
   I touched my lute, — it would not waken,
Save to old songs of sorrowing —
   Of hope betrayed — of hearts forsaken:
Each lay of lighter feeling slept,   530
I sang, but, as I sang, I wept.

THE CHARMED CUP.

AND fondly round his neck she clung;
Her long black tresses round him flung, —
Love chains, which would not let him part;
And he could feel her beating heart,
The pulses of her small white hand,
The tears she could no more command,
The lip which trembled, though near his,
The sigh that mingled with her kiss; —
Yet parted he from that embrace.
He cast one glance upon her face: 540
His very soul felt sick to see
Its look of utter misery;
Yet turned he not; one moment's grief,
One pang, like lightning, fierce and brief,
One thought, half pity, half remorse,

Passed o'er him. On he urged his horse;
Hill, ford, and valley spurred he by,
And when his castle-gate was nigh,
550   White foam was on his 'broider'd rein,
And each spur had a blood-red stain.
But soon he entered that fair hall:
His laugh was loudest there of all;
And the cup that wont one name to bless,
Was drained for its forgetfulness.
The ring, once next his heart, was broken;
The gold chain kept another token.
Where is the curl he used to wear —
The raven tress of silken hair?
560   The winds have scattered it. A braid
Of the first spring day's golden shade,
Waves with the dark plumes on his crest.
Fresh colours are upon his breast:
The slight blue scarf, of simplest fold,
Is changed for one of woven gold.
And he is by a maiden's side,
Whose gems of price, and robes of pride,
Would suit the daughter of a king;
And diamonds are glistening
570   Upon her arm. There's not one curl
Unfastened by a loop of pearl.
And he is whispering in her ear
Soft words that ladies love to hear.

Alas! — the tale is quickly told —
His love hath felt the curse of gold!
And he is bartering his heart
For that in which it hath no part.
There's many an ill that clings to love;
But this is one all else above; —
580   For love to bow before the name
Of this world's treasure: shame! oh, shame!
Love, be thy wings as light as those

That waft the zephyr from the rose, —
This may be pardoned — something rare
In loveliness has been thy snare!
But how, fair Love, canst thou become
A thing of mines — a sordid gnome?

And she whom JULIAN left — she stood
A cold white statue; as the blood
Had, when in vain her last wild prayer,   590
Flown to her heart, and frozen there.
Upon her temple, each dark vein
Swelled in its agony of pain.
Chill, heavy damps were on her brow;
Her arms were stretched at length, though now
Their clasp was on the empty air:
A funeral pall — her long black hair
Fell over her; herself the tomb
Of her own youth, and breath, and bloom.

Alas! that man should ever win   600
So sweet a shrine to shame and sin
As woman's heart! — and deeper woe
For her fond weakness, not to know
That yielding all but breaks the chain
That never reunites again!

It was a dark and tempest night —
No pleasant moon, no blest starlight;
But meteors glancing o'er the way,
Only to dazzle and betray.
And who is she that, 'mid the storm,   610
Wraps her slight mantle round her form?
Her hair is wet with rain and sleet,
And blood is on her small snow feet.
She has been forced a way to make
Through prickly weed and thorned brake,
Up rousing from its coil the snake;

And stirring from their damp abode
The slimy worm and loathsome toad:
And shuddered as she heard the gale
620   Shriek like an evil spirit's wail;
When followed, like a curse, the crash
Of the pines in the lightning flash: —
A place of evil and of fear —
Oh! what can JULIAN'S love do here?

On, on the pale girl went. At last
The gloomy forest depths are past,
And she has reached the wizard's den,
Accursed by God and shunned by men.
And never had a ban been laid
630   Upon a more unwholesome shade.
There grew dank elders, and the yew
Its thick sepulchral shadow threw;
And brooded there each bird most foul,
The gloomy bat and sullen owl.

But IDA entered in the cell,
Where dwelt the wizard of the dell.
Her heart lay dead, her life-blood froze
To look upon the shape which rose
To bar her entrance. On that face
640   Was scarcely left a single trace
Of human likeness: the parched skin
Showed each discoloured bone within;
And, but for the most evil stare
Of the wild eyes' unearthly glare,
It was a corpse, you would have said,
From which life's freshness long had fled.
Yet IDA knelt her down and prayed
To that dark sorcerer for his aid.
He heard her prayer with withering look;
650   Then from unholy herbs he took
A drug, and said it would recover

The lost heart of her faithless lover.
She trembled as she turned to see
His demon sneer's malignity;
And every step was winged with dread,
To hear the curse howled as she fled.

It is the purple twilight hour,
And JULIAN is in IDA'S bower.
He has brought gold, as gold could bless
His work of utter desolateness!   660
He has brought gems, as if Despair
Had any pride in being fair!
But IDA only wept, and wreathed
Her white arms round his neck; then breathed
Those passionate complaints that wring
A woman's heart, yet never bring
Redress. She called upon each tree
To witness her lone constancy!
She called upon the silent boughs,
The temple of her JULIAN'S vows   670
Of happiness too dearly bought!
Then wept again. At length she thought
Upon the forest-sorcerer's gift —
The last, lone hope that love had left!
She took the cup, and kissed the brim,
Mixed the dark spell, and gave it him
To pledge his once dear IDA'S name!
He drank it. Instantly the flame
Ran through his veins: one fiery throb
Of bitter pain — the gasping sob   680
Of agony — the cold death-sweat
Is on his face — his teeth are set —
His bursting eyes are glazed and still:
The drug has done its work of ill.
Alas! for her who watched each breath,
The cup her love had mixed bore — death.

———

LORENZO! — when next morning came
For the first time I heard thy name!
LORENZO! — how each ear-pulse drank
   The more than music of that tone!
690 LORENZO! — how I sighed that name,
   As breathing it, made it mine own!
I sought the gallery: I was wont
   To pass the noontide there, and trace
Some statue's shape of loveliness —
   Some saint, some nymph, or muse's face.
There, in my rapture, I could throw
   My pencil and its hues aside,
And, as the vision past me, pour
   My song of passion, joy, and pride.
700 And he was there, — LORENZO there!
   How soon the morning past away,
With finding beauties in each thing
   Neither had seen before that day!
Spirit of Love! soon thy rose-plumes wear
The weight and the sully of canker and care:
Falsehood is round thee; Hope leads thee on;
Till every hue from pinion is gone.

But one bright moment is all thine own,
710 The one ere thy visible presence is known;
When, like the wind of the south, thy power,
Sunning the heavens, sweetening the flower,
Is felt, but not seen. Thou art sweet and calm
As the sleep of a child, as the dew-fall of balm.
Fear has not darkened thee; Hope has not made
The blossoms expand, it but opens to fade.
Nothing is known of those wearing fears
Which will shadow the light of thy after years.
Then art thou bliss: — but once throw by
720 The veil which shrouds thy divinity;
Stand confessed, — and thy quiet is fled!
Wild flashes of rapture may come instead,

But pain will be with them. What may restore
The gentle happiness known before?
I owned not to myself I loved, —
    No word of love LORENZO breathed;
But I lived in a magic ring,
    Of every pleasant flower wreathed.
A brighter blue was on the sky,
A sweeter breath in music's sigh;   730
The orange shrubs all seemed to bear
Fruit more rich, and buds more fair.
There was a glory on the noon,
A beauty in the crescent moon,
A lulling stillness in the night,
A feeling in the pale starlight.
There was a charmed note on the wind,
    A spell in Poetry's deep store —
Heart-uttered words, passionate thoughts,
    Which I had never marked before.   740
'Twas as my heart's full happiness
Poured over all its own excess.

One night there was a gorgeous feast
    For maskers in COUNT LEON'S hall;
And all of gallant, fair, and young,
    Were bidden to the festival.
I went, garbed as a Hindoo girl;
    Upon each arm an amulet,
And by my side a little lute
    Of sandal-wood with gold beset.   750
And shall I own that I was proud
To hear, amid the gazing crowd,
A murmur of delight, when first
    My mask and veil aside I threw?
For well my conscious cheek betrayed
    Whose eye was gazing on me too!
And never yet had praise been dear,
As on that evening, to mine ear.

LORENZO! I was proud to be
760   Worshipped and flattered but for thee!

THE HINDOO GIRL'S SONG.

PLAYFUL and wild as the fire-flies' light,
This moment hidden, the next moment bright,
Like the foam on the dark-green sea,
Is the spell that is laid on my lover by me.
Were your sigh as sweet as the sumbal's[12] sigh,
When the wind of the evening is nigh;
Were your smile like that glorious light,
Seen when the stars gem the deep midnight;
Were that sigh and that smile for ever the same —
770   They were shadows, not fuel, to love's dulled flame.

Love once formed an amulet,
With pearls, and a rainbow, and rose-leaves set.
The pearls were pure as pearls could be,
And white as maiden purity;
The rose had the beauty and breath of soul,
And the rainbow-changes crowned the whole.
Frown on your lover one little while.
Dearer will be the light of your smile;
780   Let your blush, laugh, and sigh ever mingle together,
Like the bloom, sun, and clouds of the sweet spring weather.
Love never must sleep in security,
Or most calm and cold will his waking be.

———

And as that light strain died away,
    Again I swept the breathing strings:
But now the notes I waked were sad
    As those the pining wood-dove sings.

★   ★   ★   ★

68   LETITIA ELIZABETH LANDON

I heard the words of praise, but not
   The one voice that I paused to hear;   890
And other sounds to me were like
   A tale poured in a sleeper's ear.
Where was LORENZO? — He had stood
   Spell-bound; but when I closed the lay,
As if the charm ceased with the song,
   He darted hurriedly away.
I masqued again, and wandered on
   Through many a gay and gorgeous room;
What with sweet waters, sweeter flowers,
   The air was heavy with perfume,   900
The harp was echoing the lute,
Soft voices answered to the flute,
And, like rills in the noontide clear,
Beneath the flame-hung gondolier,
Shone mirrors peopled with the shades
Of stately youths and radiant maids;
And on the ear in whispers came
Those winged words of soul and flame,
Breathed in the dark-eyed beauty's ear
By some young love-touched cavalier;   910
Or mixed at times some sound more gay,
Of dance, or laugh, or roundelay.
Oh, it is sickness to the heart
To bear in revelry its part,
And yet feel bursting: — not one thing
Which has part in its suffering, —
The laugh as glad, the step as light,
The song as sweet, the glance as bright;
As the laugh, step, and glance and song,
Did to young happiness belong.   920

I turned me from the crowd, and reached
   A spot which seemed unsought by all —
An alcove filled with shrubs and flowers,
   But lighted by the distant hall,

With one or two fair statues placed,
　　Like deities of the sweet shrine.
That human art should ever frame
　　Such shapes so utterly divine!
A deep sigh breathed, — I knew the tone;
930　　My cheek blushed warm, my heart beat high; —
One moment more I too was known, —
　　I shrank before LORENZO'S eye.
He leant beside a pedestal.
　　The glorious brow, of Parian stone,
Of the Antinous,[13] by his side,
　　Was not more noble than his own!
They were alike: he had the same
　　Thick-clustering curls the Roman wore —
The fixed and melancholy eye —
940　　The smile which passed like lightning o'er
The curved lip. We did not speak,
But the heart breathed upon each cheek;
We looked round with those wandering looks,
　　Which seek some object for their gaze,
As if each other's glance was like
　　The too much light of morning's rays.

I saw a youth beside me kneel;
I heard my name in music steal;
I felt my hand trembling in his; —
950　Another moment, and his kiss
Had burnt upon it; when, like thought,
　　So swift it past, my hand was thrown
Away, as if in sudden pain.
　　LORENZO like a dream had flown!
We did not meet again: — he seemed
　　To shun each spot where I might be;
And, it was said, another claimed
　　The heart — more than the world to me!

I loved him as young Genius loves,
    When its own wild and radiant heaven   960
Of starry thought burns with the light,
    The love, the life, by passion given.
I loved him, too, as woman loves —
    Reckless of sorrow, sin, or scorn:
Life had no evil destiny
    That, with him, I could not have borne!
I had been nurst in palaces;
    Yet earth had not a spot so drear,
That I should not have thought a home
    In Paradise, had he been near!   970
How sweet it would have been to dwell,
Apart from all, in some green dell
Of sunny beauty, leaves and flowers;
And nestling birds to sing the hours!
Our home, beneath some chestnut's shade,
But of the woven branches made:
Our vesper hymn, the low, lone wail
The rose hears from the nightingale;
And waked at morning by the call
Of music from a waterfall.   980
But not alone in dreams like this,
Breathed in the very hope of bliss,
I loved: my love had been the same
In hushed despair, in open shame.
I would have rather been a slave,
    In tears, in bondage, by his side,
Than shared in all, if wanting him,
    This world had power to give beside!
My heart was withered, — and my heart
    Had ever been the world to me;   990
And love had been the first fond dream,
    Whose life was in reality.
I had sprung from my solitude
    Like a young bird upon the wing
To meet the arrow; so I met

My poisoned shaft of suffering.
And as that bird, with drooping crest
And broken wing, will seek his nest,
But seek in vain: so vain I sought
1000 My pleasant home of song and thought.
There was one spell upon my brain,
Upon my pencil on my strain;
But one face to my colours came;
My chords replied but to one name —
LORENZO! — all seemed vowed to thee,
To passion, and to misery!
I had no interest in the things
    That once had been like life, or light;
No tale was pleasant to mine ear,
1010   No song was sweet, no picture bright.

★ ★ ★ ★

And lays which only told of love
    In all its varied sorrowing,
The echoes of the broken heart,
1070   Were all the songs I now could sing.
Legends of olden times in Greece,
    When not a flower but had its tale:
When spirits haunted each green oak;
    When voices spoke in every gale;
When not a star shone in the sky
    Without its own love history.
Amid its many songs was one
    That suited well with my sick mind.
I sang it when the breath of flowers
1080   Came sweet upon the midnight wind.

She sat her in her twilight bower,
A temple formed of leaf and flower;
Rose and myrtle framed the roof,
To a shower of April proof;
And primroses, pale gems of spring,
Lay on the green turf glistening,
Close by the violet, whose breath
Is so sweet in a dewy wreath.
And oh, that myrtle! how green it grew!
With flowers as white as the pearls of dew   1090
That shone beside; and the glorious rose
Lay like a beauty in warm repose,
Blushing in slumber. The air was bright
With the spirit and glow of its crimson light.

  CYDIPPE had turned from her columned hall,
Where, the queen of the feast, she was worshipped by all:
Where the vases were burning with spices and flowers,
And the odorous waters were playing in showers;
And lamps were blazing — those lamps of perfume
Which shed such a charm of light over the bloom   1100
Of woman, when Pleasure a spell has thrown
Over one night hour and made it her own.
And the ruby wine-cup shone with a ray,
As the gems of the East had there melted away;
And the bards were singing those songs of fire,
That bright eyes and the goblet so well inspire; —
While she, the glory and pride of the hour,
Sat silent and sad in her secret bower!

There is a grief that wastes the heart,
    Like mildew on a tulip's dyes, —   1110
When hope, deferred but to depart,
    Loses its smiles, but keeps its sighs:
When love's bark, with its anchor gone,

Clings to a straw, and still trusts on.
Oh, more than all! — methinks that love
    Should pray that it might ever be
Beside the burning shrine which had
    Its young heart's fond idolatry.
Oh, absence is the night of love!
    Lovers are very children then!
Fancying ten thousand feverish shapes,
    Until their light returns again.
A look, a word, is then recalled,
    And thought upon until it wears,
What is, perhaps, a very shade,
    The tone and aspect of our fears.
And this was what was withering now
The radiance of CYDIPPE's brow.
She watched until her cheek grew pale;
The green wave bore no bounding sail:
Her sight grew dim; 'mid the blue air
No snowy dove came floating there,
The dear scroll hid beneath his wing,
With plume and soft eye glistening,
To seek again, in leafy dome,
The nest of its accustomed home!
Still far away, o'er land and seas,
Lingered the faithless LEADES.

    She thought on the spring days, when she had been,
Lonely and lovely, a maiden queen;
When passion to her was a storm at sea,
Heard 'mid the green land's tranquillity.
But a stately warrior came from afar;
He bore on his bosom the glorious scar
So worshipped by woman — the death-seal of war.
And the maiden's heart was an easy prize,
When valour and faith were her sacrifice.

Methinks, might that sweet season last,
In which our first love-dream is past,
Ere doubts and cares, and jealous pain,   1150
Are flaws in the heart's diamond-chain: —
Men might forget to think on Heaven,
And yet have the sweet sin forgiven.

But ere the marriage-feast was spread,
   LEADES said that he must brook
To part awhile from that best light,
   Those eyes which fixed his every look:
Just press again his native shore,
   And then he would that shore resign
For her dear sake, who was to him   1160
   His household-god! — his spirit's shrine!

   He came not! Then the heart's decay
Wasted her silently away: —
A sweet fount, which the mid-day sun
Has all too hotly looked upon!

   It is most sad to watch the fall
Of autumn leaves! — but worst of all
It is to watch the flower of spring
Faded in its fresh blossoming!
To see the once so clear blue orb   1170
   Its summer light and warmth forget;
Darkening beneath its tearful lid,
   Like a rain-beaten violet!
To watch the banner-rose of health
   Pass from the cheek! — to mark how plain,
Upon the wan and sunken brow,
   Become the wanderings of each vein!
The shadowy hand, so thin, so pale!
   The languid step! — the drooping head!
The long wreaths of neglected hair!   1180
   The lip whence red and smile are fled!

And having watched thus, day by day,
Light, life, and colour, pass away!
To see, at length, the glassy eye
Fix dull in dread mortality;
Mark the last ray, catch the last breath,
Till the grave sets its sign of death!

This was CYDIPPE'S fate! — They laid
The maiden underneath the shade
1190   Of a green cypress, — and that hour
The tree was withered, and stood bare!
The spring brought leaves to other trees,
But never other leaf grew there!
It stood, 'mid others flourishing,
A blighted, solitary thing.

The summer sun shone on that tree,
When shot a vessel o'er the sea —
When sprang a warrior from the prow —
LEADES! by the stately brow.
1200   Forgotten toil, forgotten care,
All his worn heart has had to bear.
That heart is full! He hears the sigh
That breathed 'Farewell!' so tenderly.
If even then it was most sweet,
What will it be that now they meet?
Alas! alas! Hope's fair deceit!
He spurred o'er land, has cut the wave,
To look but on CYDIPPE'S grave.

It has blossomed in beauty, that lone tree,
1210   LEADES' kiss restored its bloom;
For wild he kissed the withered stem —
It grew upon CYDIPPE'S tomb!
And there he dwelt. The hottest ray,
Still dew upon the branches lay
Like constant tears. The winter came;

But still the green tree stood the same.
And it was said, at evening's close,
A sound of whispered music rose;
That 'twas the trace of viewless feet
Made the flowers more than flowers sweet.   1220
At length LEADES died. That day,
Bark and green foliage past away
From the lone tree, — again a thing
Of wonder and of perishing!

$$\star \quad \star \quad \star \quad \star$$

Rust gathered on the silent chords
    Of my neglected lyre, — the breeze
Was now its mistress: music brought
    For me too bitter memories!
The ivy darkened o'er my bower;
Around, the weeds choked every flower.
I pleased me in this desolateness,
As each thing bore my fate's impress.   1320

At length I made myself a task —
    To paint that Cretan maiden's fate,[14]
Whom Love taught such deep happiness,
    And whom Love left so desolate.
I drew her on a rocky shore: —
Her black hair loose, and sprinkled o'er
With white sea-foam: — her arms were bare
Flung upwards in their last despair.
Her naked feet the pebbles prest;
The tempest-wind sang in her vest: 1330
A wild stare in her glassy eyes;
White lips, as parched by their hot sighs;
And cheek more pallid than the spray,
Which, cold and colourless, on it lay: —
Just such a statue as should be
    Placed ever, Love! beside thy shrine:

Warning thy victims of what ills —
    What burning tears, false god! are thine.
Before her was the darkling sea:
    Behind the barren mountains rose —
A fit home for the broken heart
    To weep away life, wrongs, and woes!

I had now but one hope: — that when
    The hand that traced these tints was cold —
Its pulse but in their passion seen —
    LORENZO might these tints behold,
And find my grief; — think — see — feel all
    I felt, in this memorial!

* * * *

Oh, mockery of happiness!
    Love now was all too late to save.
False Love! oh, what had you to do
    With one you had led to the grave?
A little time I had been glad
    To mark the paleness on my cheek;
To feel how, day by day, my step
    Grew fainter, and my hand more weak;
To know the fever of my soul
    Was also preying on my frame:
But now I would have given worlds
    To change the crimson hectic's flame[15]
For the pure rose of health; to live
For the dear life that Love could give.
— Oh, youth may sicken at its bloom,
And wealth and fame pray for the tomb; —
But can love bear from love to part,
And not cling to that one dear heart?
I shrank away from death, — my tears
Had been unwept in other years: —
But thus, in love's first ecstacy,
Was it not worse than death to die?

1340

1490

1500

LORENZO! I would live for thee!
But thou wilt have to weep for me!
That sun has kissed the morning dews, —
    I shall not see its twilight close!
That rose is fading in the noon,
    And I shall not outlive that rose!   1510
Come, let me lean upon thy breast,
My last, best place of happiest rest!
Once more let me breathe thy sighs —
Look once more in those watching eyes!
Oh! but for thee, and grief of thine,
And parting, I should not repine!
It is deep happiness to die,
Yet live in Love's dear memory.
Thou wilt remember me, — my name
Is linked with beauty and with fame.   1520
The summer airs, the summer sky,
The soothing spell of Music's sigh, —
Stars in their poetry of night,
The silver silence of moonlight, —
The dim blush of the twilight hours,
The fragrance of the bee-kissed flowers; —
But, more than all, sweet songs will be
Thrice sacred unto Love and me.
LORENZO! be this kiss a spell!
My first! — my last! FAREWELL! — FAREWELL!   1530

———

THERE is a lone and stately hall, —
Its master dwells apart from all.
A wanderer through Italia's land,
    One night a refuge there I found.
The lightning flash rolled o'er the sky,
    The torrent rain was sweeping round: —
These won me entrance. He was young,
    The castle's lord, but pale like age;

His brow, as sculpture beautiful,
1540   Was wan as Grief's corroded page,
He had no words, he had no smiles,
      No hopes: — his sole employ to brood
Silently over his sick heart
      In sorrow and in solitude.
I saw the hall where, day by day,
He mused his weary life away; —
It scarcely seemed a place for woe,
      But rather like a genie's home.
Around were graceful statues ranged,
1550   And pictures shone around the dome.
But there was one — a loveliest one! —
      One picture brightest of all there!
Oh! never did the painter's dream
      Shape thing so gloriously fair!
It was a face! — the summer day
      Is not more radiant in its light!
Dark flashing eyes, like the deep stars
      Lighting the azure brow of night;
A blush like sunrise o'er the rose;
1560   A cloud of raven hair, whose shade
Was sweet as evening's, and whose curls
      Clustered beneath a laurel braid.
She leant upon a harp: — one hand
      Wandered, like snow, amid the chords;
The lips were opening with such life,
      You almost heard the silvery words.
She looked a form of light and life, —
      All soul, all passion, and all fire;
A priestess of Apollo's, when
1570   The morning beams fall on her lyre;
A Sappho, or ere love had turned
The heart to stone where once it burned.
But by the picture's side was placed
A funeral urn, on which was traced
The heart's recorded wretchedness; —

And on a tablet, hung above,
Was 'graved one tribute of sad words —
     'LORENZO TO HIS MINSTREL LOVE.'

LINES
WRITTEN UNDER A PICTURE OF A GIRL
BURNING A LOVE-LETTER.

The lines were filled with many a tender thing,
All the impassioned heart's fond communing.

I TOOK the scroll: I could not brook
     An eye to gaze on it, save mine;
I could not bear another's look
     Should dwell upon one thought of thine.
My lamp was burning by my side,
     I held thy letter to the flame,
I marked the blaze swift o'er it glide,
     It did not even spare thy name.
Soon the light from the embers past,
     I felt so sad to see it die,   10
So bright at first, so dark at last,
     I feared it was love's history.

WHEN SHOULD LOVERS BREATHE
THEIR VOWS?[16]

WHEN should lovers breathe their vows?
    When should ladies hear them?
When the dew is on the boughs,
    When none else are near them;
When the moon shines cold and pale,
    When the birds are sleeping,
When no voice is on the gale,
    When the rose is weeping;
When the stars are bright on high,
10   Like hopes in young Love's dreaming,
And glancing round the light clouds fly,
    Like soft fears to shade their beaming.

The fairest smiles are those that live
    On the brow by starlight wreathing;
And the lips their richest incense give
    When the sigh is at midnight breathing.
Oh, softest is the cheek's love-ray
    When seen by moonlight hours,
Other roses seek the day,
20   But blushes are night-flowers.
Oh, when the moon and stars are bright,
    When the dew-drops glisten,
Then their vows should lovers plight,
    Then should ladies listen.

FROM *THE TROUBADOUR*

A CHILD SCREENING A DOVE FROM A HAWK. [17]

By Stewardson.

Ay, screen thy favourite dove, fair child,
    Ay, screen it if you may, —
Yet I misdoubt thy trembling hand
    Will scare the hawk away.

That dove will die, that child will weep, —
    Is this their destinie?
Ever amid the sweets of life
    Some evil thing must be.

Ay, moralize, — is it not thus
    We've mourn'd our hope and love?   10
Alas! there's tears for every eye,
    A hawk for every dove!

THE ENCHANTED ISLAND. [18]

By Danby.

AND there the island lay, the waves around
Had never known a storm; for the north wind
Was charm'd from coming, and the only airs
That blew brought sunshine on their azure wings,
Or tones of music from the sparry caves,
Where the sea-maids make lutes of the pink conch.
These were sea breezes, — those that swept the land
Brought other gifts, — sighs from blue violets,
Or from June's sweet Sultana, the bright rose,
10   Stole odours. On the silver mirror's face
Was but a single ripple that was made
By a flamingo's beak, whose scarlet wings
Shone like a meteor on the stream: around,
Upon the golden sands, were coral plants,
And shells of many colours, and sea weeds,
Whose foliage caught and chain'd the Nautilus,
Where lay they as at anchor. On each side
Were grottoes, like fair porticoes with steps
Of the green marble; and a lovely light,
20   Like the far radiance of a thousand lamps,
Half-shine, half-shadow, or the glorious track
Of a departing star but faintly seen
In the dim distance, through those caverns shone,
And play'd o'er the tall trees which seem'd to hide
Gardens, where hyacinths rang their soft bells
To call the bees from the anemone,
Jealous of their bright rivals' golden wealth.
— Amid those arches floated starry shapes,
Just indistinct enough to make the eye
30   Dream of surpassing beauty; but in front,
Borne on a car of pearl, and drawn by swans,
There lay a lovely figure, — she was queen
Of the Enchanted Island, which was raised

From ocean's bosom but to pleasure her:
And spirits, from the stars, and from the sea,
The beautiful mortal had them for her slaves.

She was the daughter of a king, and loved
By a young Ocean Spirit from her birth, —
He hover'd o'er her in her infancy,
And bade the rose grow near her, that her cheek   40
Might catch its colour, — lighted up her dreams
With fairy wonders, and made harmony
The element in which she moved; at last,
When that she turn'd away from earthly love,
Enamour'd of her visions, he became
Visible with his radiant wings, and bore
His bride to the fair island.

The Enchanted Island, by Francis Danby

[handwritten margin annotations: "PURPLE! Reflect on Romantic Women Legitimizing themselves through Praise of their predecessors? R who they see as Geniuses encompass all forms of artistry"]

[handwritten: "Prop. Rossi the past lyre"]

FROM *THE GOLDEN VIOLET* (1826)

ERINNA.[19]

INTRODUCTORY NOTICE.

AMONG the obligations I owe to "The Brides of Florence,"[20] and to the information contained in its interesting notes, I must refer particularly for the origin of the present poem. In one of those notes is the first, indeed the only account I ever met with of Erinna. The following short quotation is sufficient for my present purpose: — "Erinna was a poetess from her cradle, and she only lived to the completion of her eighteenth year. — Of Erinna very little is known; there is in the Grecian Anthology a sepulchral epigram by Antipater[21] on this young poetess." A poem of the present kind had long floated on my imagination; and this gave it a local habitation and a name.[22] There seemed to me just enough known of Erinna to interest; and I have not attempted to write a classical fiction; feelings are what I wish to narrate, not incidents: my aim has been to draw the portrait and trace the changes of a highly poetical mind, too sensitive perhaps of the chill and bitterness belonging even to success. The feelings which constitute poetry are the same in all ages, they are acted upon by similar causes. Erinna is an ideal not a historical picture, and as such I submit it less to the judgment than to the kindness of my friends.

[handwritten margin note: "allows fiction"]

[handwritten margin note: "Slowly coming into terms w/ concept of fame becomes less sustaining"]

WAS she of spirit race, or was she one
Of earth's least earthly daughters, one to whom

A gift of loveliness and soul is given,
Only to make them wretched?

———

There is an antique gem, on which her brow
Retains its graven beauty even now.
Her hair is braided, but one curl behind
Floats as enamour'd of the summer wind;
The rest is simple. Is she not too fair
Even to think of maiden's sweetest care?
The mouth and brow are contrasts. One so fraught
With pride, the melancholy pride of thought
Conscious of power, and yet forced to know
How little way such power as that can go;
Regretting, while too proud of the fine mind,
Which raises but to part it from its kind:
But the sweet mouth had nothing of all this;
It was a mouth the rose had lean'd to kiss
How soft an echo it was to the lute.
The one spoke genius, in its high revealing;
The other smiled a woman's gentle feeling.
It was a lovely face: the Greek outline
Flowing, yet delicate and feminine;
The glorious lightning of the kindled eye,
Raised, as it communed with its native sky.
A lovely face, the spirit's fitting shrine;
The one almost, the other quite divine.

———

My hand is on the lyre, which never more
With its sweet commerce, like a bosom friend,
Will share the deeper thoughts which I could trust
Only to music and to solitude.
It is the very grove, the olive grove,
Where first I laid my laurel crown aside,
And bathed my fever'd brow in the cold stream;
As if that I could wash away the fire
Which from that moment kindled in my heart.
I well remember how I flung myself,   10
Like a young goddess, on a purple cloud
Of light and odour — the rich violets
Were so ethereal in bloom and breath:
And I, — I felt immortal, for my brain
Was drunk and mad with its first draught of fame.
'T is strange there was one only cypress tree,
And then, as now, I lay beneath its shade.
The night had seen me pace my lonely room,
Clasping the lyre I had no heart to wake,
Impatient for the day: yet its first dawn   20
Came cold as death; for every pulse sang down,
Until the very presence of my hope
Became to me a fear. The sun rose up;
I stood alone mid thousands: but I felt
Mine inspiration; and, as the last sweep
Of my song died away amid the hills,
My heart reverberate the shout which bore
To the blue mountains and the distant heaven
ERINNA'S name, and on my bended knee,
Olympus, I received thy laurel crown.   30

    And twice new birth of violets have sprung,
Since they were first my pillow, since I sought
In the deep silence of the olive grove
The dreamy happiness which solitude
Brings to the soul o'erfill'd with its delight:
For I was like some young and sudden heir

[handwritten annotations: "Religious calling to poetry"; "set aside talents, praise"; "Sense of being god-like"; "afraid to hope"; "Other's shout"; "Celebratory, Religious!"; "Erinna as Muse"; "Inspired in nature"; "overflow of emotion"]

Of a rich palace heap'd with gems and gold,
Whose pleasure doubles as he sums his wealth
And forms a thousand plans of festival;
40   Such were my myriad visions of delight.
The lute, which hitherto in Delphian shades
Had been my twilight's solitary joy,
Would henceforth be a sweet and breathing bond
Between me and my kind. Orphan unloved,
I had been lonely from my childhood's hour,
Childhood whose very happiness is love:
But that was over now; my lyre would be
My own heart's true interpreter, and those
To whom my song was dear, would they not bless
50   The hand that waken'd it? I should be loved
praise/   For the so gentle sake of those soft chords
Fame   Which mingled others' feelings with mine own.

Vow'd I that song to meek and gentle thoughts.
To tales that told of sorrow and of love,
To all our nature's finest touches, all
That wakens sympathy: and I should be
Alone no longer; every wind that bore,
And every lip that breathed one strain of mine,
Henceforth partake in all my joy and grief.
60   Oh! glorious is the gifted poet's lot,
Power of   And touching more than glorious: 't is to be
Poetry   Companion of the heart's least earthly hour;
The voice of love and sadness, calling forth
Tears from their silent fountain: 't is to have
Share in all nature's loveliness; giving flowers
A life as sweet, more lasting than their own;
And catching from green wood and lofty pine
Language mysterious as musical;
Making the thoughts, which else had only been
Like colours on the morning's earliest hour,
70   Immortal, and worth immortality;
Yielding the hero that eternal name

For which he fought; making the patriot's deed
A stirring record for long after time;
Cherishing tender thoughts, which else had pass'd
Away like tears; and saving the loved dead
From death's worst part — its deep forgetfulness.

From the first moment when a falling leaf,
Or opening bud, or streak of rose-touch'd sky,
Waken'd in me the flush and flow of song,   80
I gave my soul entire unto the gift
I deem'd mine own, direct from heaven; it was
The hope, the bliss, the energy of life;
I had no hope that dwelt not with my lyre,
No bliss whose being grew not from my lyre,
No energy undevoted to my lyre.
It was my other self, that had a power;
Mine, but o'er which I had not a control.
At times it was not with me, and I felt
A wonder how it ever had been mine:
And then a word, a look of loveliness,
A tone of music, call'd it into life;
And song came gushing, like the natural tears,
To check whose current does not rest with us.

Had I lived ever in the savage woods,
Or in some distant island, which the sea
With wind and wave guards in deep loneliness;
Had my eye never on the beauty dwelt
Of human face, and my ear never drank
The music of a human voice; I feel   100
My spirit would have pour'd itself in song,
Have learn'd a language from the rustling leaves,
The singing of the birds, and of the tide.
Perchance, then, happy had I never known
Another thought could be attach'd to song
Than of its own delight. Oh! let me pause
Over this earlier period, when my heart

[handwritten margin note near line 80:] When became she the poet entirely became personality power like 2nd child a mothers power

[handwritten margin note near line 100:] a/ at would sing a short. and musical a/

Mingled its being with its pleasures, fill'd
With rich enthusiasm, which once flung
110   Its purple colouring o'er all things of earth,
And without which our utmost power of thought
But sharpens arrows that will drink our blood.
Like woman's soothing influence o'er man,
Enthusiasm is upon the mind;
Softening and beautifying that which is
Too harsh and sullen in itself. How much
I loved the painter's glorious art, which forms
A world like, but more beautiful than this;
Just catching nature in her happiest mood!
120   How drank I in fine poetry, which makes
The hearing passionate, fill'd with memories
Which steal from out the past like rays from clouds!
And then the sweet songs of my native vale,
Whose sweetness and whose softness call'd to mind
The perfume of the flowers, the purity
Of the blue sky; oh, how they stirr'd my soul! —
Amid the many golden gifts which heaven
Has left, like portions of its light on earth,
None hath such influence as music hath.
130   The painter's hues stand visible before us
In power and beauty; we can trace the thoughts
Which are the workings of the poet's mind:
But music is a mystery, and viewless
Even when present, and is less man's act,
And less within his order; for the hand
That can call forth the tones, yet cannot tell
Whither they go, or if they live or die,
When floated once beyond his feeble ear;
And then, as if it were an unreal thing,
The wind will sweep from the neglected strings
140   As rich a swell as ever minstrel drew.

A poet's word, a painter's touch, will reach
The innermost recesses of the heart,

Making the pulses throb in unison
With joy or grief, which we can analyse;
There is the cause for pleasure and for pain:
But music moves us, and we know not why;
We feel the tears, but cannot trace their source.
Is it the language of some other state,
Born of its memory? For what can wake   150
The soul's strong instinct of another world,
Like music? Well with sadness doth it suit,
To hear the melancholy sounds decay,
And think (for thoughts are life's great human links,
And mingle with our feelings,) even so
Will the heart's wildest pulses sink to rest.

How have I loved, when the red evening fill'd
Our temple with its glory, first, to gaze
On the strange contrast of the crimson air,
Lighted as if with passion, and flung back,   160
From silver vase and tripod rich with gems,
To the pale statues round, where human life
Was not, but beauty was, which seemed to have
Apart existence from humanity:
Then, to go forth where the tall waving pines
Seem'd as behind them roll'd a golden sea,
Immortal and eternal; and the boughs,
That darkly swept between me and its light,
Were fitting emblems of the worldly cares
That are the boundary between us and heaven;   170
Meanwhile, the wind, a wilful messenger
Lingering amid the flowers on his way,
At intervals swept past in melody,
The lutes and voices of the choral hymn
Contending with the rose-breath on his wing!
Perhaps it is these pleasures' chiefest charm,
They are so indefinable, so vague.
From earliest childhood all too well aware
Of the uncertain nature of our joys,

180   It is delicious to enjoy, yet know
No after consequence will be to weep.
Pride misers with enjoyment, when we have
Delight in things that are but of the mind:
But half humility when we partake
Pleasures that are half wants, the spirit pines
And struggles in its fetters, and disdains
The low base clay to which it is allied.
But here our rapture raises us: we feel
What glorious power is given to man, and find
190   Our nature's nobleness and attributes,
Whose heaven is intellect; and we are proud
To think how we can love those things of earth
Which are least earthly; and the soul grows pure
In this high communing, and more divine.
This time of dreaming happiness pass'd by,
Another spirit was within my heart;
I drank the maddening cup of praise, which grew
Henceforth the fountain of my life; I lived
Only in others' breath; a word, a look,
200   Were of all influence on my destiny:
If praise they spoke, 't was sunlight to my soul;
Or censure, it was like the scorpion's sting.

     And a yet darker lesson was to learn —
The hollowness of each: that praise, which is
But base exchange of flattery; that blame,
Given by cautious coldness, which still deems
'T is safest to depress; that mockery,
Flinging shafts but to show its own keen aim;
That carelessness, whose very censure 's chance;
210   And, worst of all, the earthly judgment pass'd
By minds whose native clay is unredeem'd
By aught of heaven, whose every thought falls foul
Plague spot on beauty which they cannot feel,
Tainting all that it touches with itself.
O dream of fame, what hast thou been to me

But the destroyer of life's calm content!
I feel so more than ever, that thy sway
Is weaken'd over me. Once I could find
A deep and dangerous delight in thee;
But that is gone. I am too much awake.   220
Light has burst o'er me, but not morning's light;
'T is such light as will burst upon the tomb,
When all but judgment 's over. Can it be,
That these fine impulses, these lofty thoughts,
Burning with their own beauty, are but given
To make me the low slave of vanity,
Heartless and humbled? O my own sweet power,
Surely thy songs were made for more than this!
What a worst waste of feeling and of life
Have been the imprints on my roll of time,   230
Too much, too long! To what use have I turn'd
The golden gifts in which I pride myself?
They are profaned; with their pure ore I made
A temple resting only on the breath
Of heedless worshippers. Alas! that ever
Praise should have been what it has been to me —
The opiate of my heart. Yet I have dream'd
Of things which cannot be; the bright, the pure,
That all of which the heart may only dream;
And I have mused upon my gift of song,   240
And deeply felt its beauty, and disdain'd
The pettiness of praise to which at times
My soul has bow'd; and I have scorn'd myself
For that my cheek could burn, my pulses beat
At idle words. And yet, it is in vain
For the full heart to press back every throb
Wholly upon itself. Ay, fair as are
The visions of a poet's solitude,
There must be something more for happiness;
They seek communion. It had seem'd to me   250
A miser's selfishness, had I not sought
To share with others those impassion'd thoughts,

FROM THE GOLDEN VIOLET 95

Like light, or hope, or love, in their effects.
When I have watch'd the stars write on the sky
In characters of light, have seen the moon
Come like a veiled priestess from the east,
While, like a hymn, the wind swell'd on mine ear,
Telling soft tidings of eve's thousand flowers,
Has it not been the transport of my lute
To find its best delight in sympathy?
Alas! the idols which our hopes set up,
They are Chaldean ones, half gold, half clay;
We trust, we are deceived, we hope, we fear,
Alike without foundation; day by day
Some new illusion is destroyed, and life
Gets cold and colder on towards its close.
Just like the years which make it, some are check'd
By sudden blights in spring; some are dried up
By fiery summers; others waste away
In calm monotony of quiet skies,
And peradventure these may be the best:
They know no hurricanes, no floods that sweep
As a God's vengeance were upon each wave;
But then they have no ruby fruits, no flowers
Shining in purple, and no lighted mines
Of gold and diamond. Which is the best, —
Beauty and glory, in a southern clime,
Mingled with thunder, tempest; or the calm
Of skies that scarcely change, which, at the least,
If much of shine they have not, have no storms?
I know not: but I know fair earth or sky
Are self-consuming in their loveliness,
And the too radiant sun and fertile soil
In their luxuriance run themselves to waste,
And the green valley and the silver stream
Become a sandy desert. Oh! the mind,
Too vivid in its lighted energies,
May read its fate in sunny Araby.
How lives its beauty in each Eastern tale,

260

270

280

Its growth of spices, and its groves of balm!   290
They are exhausted; and what is it now?
A wild and burning wilderness. Alas!
For such similitude. Too much this is
The fate of this world's loveliest and best.

    Is there not a far people, who possess
Mysterious oracles of olden time,
Who say that this earth labours with a curse,
That it is fallen from its first estate,
And is now but the shade of what it was?   *a shade of eden*
I do believe the tale. I feel its truth   300
In my vain aspirations, in the dreams
That are revealings of another world,
More pure, more perfect than our weary one,
Where day is darkness to the starry soul.

    O heart of mine! my once sweet paradise
Of love and hope! how changed thou art to me!
I cannot count thy changes: thou hast lost
Interest in the once idols of thy being;
They have departed, even as if wings
Had borne away their morning; they have left   310
Weariness, turning pleasure into pain,
And too sure knowledge of their hollowness.

    And that too is gone from me; that which was
My solitude's delight! I can no more
Make real existence of a shadowy world.
Time was, the poet's song, the ancient tale,   *Recognition*
Were to me fountains of deep happiness,   *of*
For they grew visible in my lonely hours,   *failed powers*
As things in which I had a deed and part;
Their actual presence had not been more true: 320
But these are bubbling sparkles, that are found
But at the spring's first source. Ah! years may bring
The mind to its perfection, but no more

Will those young visions live in their own light;
Life's troubles stir life's waters all too much,
Passions chase fancies, and, though still we dream,
The colouring is from reality.

Farewell, my lyre! thou hast not been to me
All I once hoped. What is the gift of mind,
But as a barrier to so much that makes
Our life endurable, — companionship,
Mingling affection, calm and gentle peace,
Till the vex'd spirit seals with discontent
A league of sorrow and of vanity,
Built on a future which will never be!

And yet I would resign the praise that now
Makes my cheek crimson, and my pulses beat,
Could I but deem that when my hand is cold,
And my lip passionless, my songs would be
Number'd mid the young poet's first delights;
Read by the dark-eyed maiden in an hour
Of moonlight, till her cheek shone with its tears;
And murmur'd by the lover when his suit
Calls upon poetry to breathe of love.
I do not hope a sunshine burst of fame,
My lyre asks but a wreath of fragile flowers.
I have told passionate tales of breaking hearts,
Of young cheeks fading even before the rose;
My songs have been the mournful history
Of woman's tenderness and woman's tears;
I have touch'd but the spirit's gentlest chords, —
Surely the fittest for my maiden hand; —
And in their truth my immortality.

Thou lovely and lone star, whose silver light,
Like music o'er the waters, steals along
The soften'd atmosphere; pale star, to thee
I dedicate the lyre, whose influence

I would have sink upon the heart like thine.

Just pensive time, thinking about Erinna

In such an hour as this, the bosom turns
Back to its early feelings; man forgets   360
His stern ambition and his worldly cares,
And woman loathes the petty vanities
That mar her nature's beauty; like the dew,
Shedding its sweetness o'er the sleeping flowers
Till all their morning freshness is revived,
Kindly affections, sad, but yet sweet thoughts
Melt the cold eyes, long, long unused to weep.
O lute of mine, that I shall wake no more!
Such tearful music linger on thy strings,
Consecrate unto sorrow and to love;   370
Thy truth, thy tenderness, be all thy fame!

To be remembered for truth & tenderness places fame in lute rather than self

SONG.[23]

M Y heart is like the failing hearth
   Now by my side,
One by one its bursts of flame
   Have burnt and died.
There are none to watch the sinking blaze,
   And none to care,
Or if it kindle into strength,
   Or waste in air.
My fate is as yon faded wreath
   Of summer flowers;   10
They've spent their store of fragrant health
   On sunny hours,
Which reck'd them not, which heeded not
   When they were dead;
Other flowers, unwarn'd by them,

Will spring instead.
And my own heart is as the lute
  I now am waking;
Wound to too fine and high a pitch
20   They both are breaking.
And of their song what memory
  Will stay behind?
An echo, like a passing thought,
  Upon the wind.
Silence, forgetfulness, and rust,
  Lute, are for thee:
And such my lot; neglect, the grave,
  These are for me.

SONG. [24]

WHERE, oh! where's the chain to fling,
One that will bind CUPID's wing,
One that will have longer power
Than the April sun or shower?
Form it not of Eastern gold,
All too weighty it to hold;
Form it neither all of bloom,
Never does Love find a tomb
Sudden, soon, as when he meets
10 Death amid unchanging sweets:
But if you would fling a chain,
And not fling it all in vain,
Like a fairy form a spell
Of all that is changeable,
Take the purple tints that deck,
Meteor-like, the peacock's neck;
Take the many hues that play
On the rainbow's colour'd way;
Never let a hope appear
20 Without its companion fear;

Only smile to sigh, and then
Change into a smile again;
Be to-day as sad, as pale,
As minstrel with his lovelorn tale;
But to-morrow gay as all
Life had been one festival.
If a woman would secure
All that makes her reign endure,
And, alas! her reign must be
Ever most in phantasy,   30
Never let an envious eye
Gaze upon the heart too nigh;
Never let the veil be thrown
Quite aside, as all were known
Of delight and tenderness,
In the spirit's last recess;
And, one spell all spells above,
Never let her own her love.

FROM *THE VENETIAN BRACELET*

PREFACE [TO *THE VENETIAN BRACELET.*][25]

DIFFIDENCE of their own abilities, and fear, which heightens the anxiety for public favour, are pleas usually urged by the youthful writer: may I, while venturing for the first time to speak of myself, be permitted to say they far more truly belong to one who has had experience of both praise and censure. The feelings which attended the publication of the "Improvisatrice" are very different from those that accompany the present volume. I believe I *then* felt little beyond hope, vague as the timidity which subdued it, and that excitement which every author must know: *now* mine is a "farther looking hope;"[26] and the timidity which apprehended the verdict of others, is now deepened by distrust of my own powers. Or, to claim my poetical privilege, and express my meaning by a simile, I should say, I am no longer one who springs forward in the mere energy of exercise and enjoyment; but rather like the Olympian racer, who strains his utmost vigour, with the distant goal and crown in view. I have devoted my whole life to one object: in society I have but sought the material for solitude. I can imagine but one interest in existence, — that which has filled my past, and haunts my future, — the perhaps vain desire, when I am nothing, of leaving one of those memories at once a good and a glory. Believing as I do in the great and excellent influence of poetry, may I hazard the expression of what I have myself sometimes trusted to do? A highly-cultivated state of society must ever have for concomitant evils, that selfishness, the result of indolent indulgence; and that heartlessness attendant on refinement, which too often hardens while it polishes. Aware that to elevate I must first soften, and that if I wished to purify I must first touch, I have ever endeavoured to bring forward grief, disappointment, the fallen leaf, the faded flower, the broken heart, and the early grave. Surely we must be less worldly, less interested, from this sympathy with the sorrow in which our unselfish feelings alone can take part. And now a few words on a subject, where the variety of the opinions offered have left me somewhat in the situation of the prince in the fairy tale, who, when in the vicinity of the magic fountain, found himself so distracted by the multitude of voices that directed his way, as to be quite incapable of deciding which was the right path. I allude to the blame and eulogy which have been equally bestowed on my frequent choice of Love as my source of song. I can only say, that for a woman, whose influence and whose sphere must be in the affections, what subject can be more fitting than one which it is her peculiar province to refine, spiritualise, and exalt? I have always sought to paint it self-denying, devoted, and making an almost religion of its truth; and I must add, that such as I would wish to draw her, woman actuated by an attachment as intense as it is true, as pure as it is deep, is not only more admirable as a heroine, but also in actual life, than one whose idea of love is that of light amusement, or at worst of vain mortification. With regard to the frequent application of my works to myself, considering that I sometimes pourtrayed love unrequited, then betrayed, and again destroyed by death — may I hint the conclusions are not quite logically drawn, as assuredly the same mind cannot have suffered such varied modes of misery. However, if I must have an unhappy passion, I can only console myself with my own perfect unconsciousness of so great a misfortune. I now leave the following Poems to their fate: they must speak for themselves. I could but express my anxiety, an anxiety only increased by a popularity beyond my most sanguine dreams.

With regard to those whose former praise encouraged, their best recompense is the happiness they bestowed. And to those whose differing opinion expressed itself in censure, I own, after the first chagrin was past, I never laid down a criticism by which I did not benefit, or trust to benefit. I will conclude by apostrophising the hopes and fears they excited, in the words of the Mexican king — "Ye have been the feathers of my wings."

A SUMMER EVENING'S TALE.

Come, let thy careless sail float on the wind;
Come, lean by me, and let thy little boat
Follow like thee its will; come, lean by me.
Freighted with roses which the west has flung,
Over its waters on the vessel glides,
Save where the shadowy boughs shut out the sky,
And make a lovely darkness, while the wind
Stirs the sad music of their plaining leaves.
The sky grows paler, as it burnt away
10 Its crimson passion; and the falling dew
Seems like the tears that follow such an hour.
I'll tell thee, love, a tale, — just such a tale
As you once said my lips could breathe so well;
Speaking as poetry should speak of love,
And asking from the depths of mine own heart
The truth that touches, and by what I feel
For thee, believe what others' feelings are.
There, leave the sail, and look with earnest eyes;
Seem not as if the worldly element
20 In which thou movest were of thy nature part,
But yield thee to the influence of those thoughts
That haunt thy solitude; — ah, but for those
I never could have loved thee; I, who now
Live only in my other life with thee;
Out on our beings' falsehood! — studied, cold,
Are we not like that actor of old time,
Who wore his mask so long, his features took
Its likeness? — thus we feign we do not feel,
Until our feelings are forgotten things,
30 Their nature warp'd in one base selfishness;
And generous impulses, and lofty thoughts,
Are counted folly, or are not believed:
And he who doubts or mocks at excellence
(Good that refines our nature, and subdues),
Is riveted to earth by sevenfold chains.

Oh, never had the poet's lute a hope,
An aim so glorious as it now may have,
In this our social state, where petty cares
And mercenary interests only look
Upon the present's littleness, and shrink   40
From the bold future, and the stately past, —
Where the smooth surface of society
Is polish'd by deceit, and the warm heart
With all its kind affections' early flow,
Flung back upon itself, forgets to beat,
At least for others; — tis the poet's gift
To melt these frozen waters into tears,
By sympathy with sorrows not our own,
By wakening memory with those mournful notes,
Whose music is the thoughts of early years,   50
When truth was on the lip, and feelings wore
The sweetness and the freshness of their morn.
Young poet, if thy dreams have not such hope
To purify, refine, exalt, subdue,
To touch the selfish, and to shame the vain
Out of themselves, by gentle mournfulness,
Or chords that rouse some aim of enterprise,
Lofty and pure, and meant for general good;
If thou hast not some power that may direct
The mind from the mean round of daily life,   60
Waking affections that might else have slept,
Or high resolves, the petrified before,
Or rousing in that mind a finer sense
Of inward and external loveliness,
Making imagination serve as guide
To all of heaven that yet remains on earth, —
Thine is a useless lute: break it, and die.
    Love mine, I know my weakness, and I know
How far I fall short of the glorious goal
I purpose to myself; yet if one line   70
Has stolen from the eye unconscious tears,
Recall'd one lover to fidelity

Which is the holiness of love, or bade
One maiden sicken at cold vanity,
When dreaming o'er affection's tenderness,
The deep, the true, the honour'd of my song, —
If but one worldly soil has been effaced,
That song has not been utterly in vain.
All true deep feeling purifies the heart.
80   Am I not better by my love for you?
At least, I am less selfish; I would give
My life to buy you happiness: — Hush, hush!
I must not let you know how much I love, —
So to my tale. — 'Twas on an eve like this,
When purple shadows floated round, and light,
Crimson and passionate, o'er the statues fell,
Like life, for that fair gallery was fill'd
With statues, each one an eternity
Of thought and beauty: there were lovely shapes,
90   And noble ones; some which the poet's song
Had touch'd with its own immortality;
Others whose glory flung o'er history's page
Imperishable lustre. There she stood,
Forsaken A R I A D N E ; [27] round her brow
Wreathed the glad vine-leaves; but it wore a shade
Of early wretchedness, that which once flung
May never be effaced: and near her leant
E N D Y M I O N , [28] and his spiritual beauty wore
The likeness of divinity; for love
Doth elevate to itself, and she who watch'd
100   Over his sleeping face, upon it left
The brightness of herself. Around the walls
Hung pictures, some which gave the summer all
Summer can wish, a more eternal bloom;
And others in some young and lovely face
Embodied dreams into reality.
There hung a portrait of St. R O S A L I E , [29]
She who renounced the world in youth, and made
Her heart an altar but for heavenly hopes —

Thrice blessed in such sacrifice. Alas!
The weakness, yet the strength of earthly ties!
Who hath not in the weariness of life
Wish'd for the wings of morning or the dove,
To bear them heavenward, and have wish'd in vain?
For wishes are effectual but by will,
And that too much is impotent and void
In frail humanity; and time steals by
Sinful and wavering, and unredeem'd.
    Bent by a casement, whence her eye could dwell
Or on the countenance of that sweet saint,
Or the fair valley, where the river wound
Like to a fairy thing, now light, now shade,
Which the eye watches in its wandering,
A maiden pass'd each summer eve away.
Life's closing colour was upon her cheek,
Crimson as that which marks the closing day:
And her large eyes, the radiant and the clear,
Wore all the ethereal beauty of that heaven
Where she was hastening. Still her rosebud mouth
Wore the voluptuous sweetness of a spring
Haunted by fragrance and by melody.
Her hair was gather'd in a silken net,
As if its luxury of auburn curls
Oppress'd the feverish temples all too much;
For you might see the azure pulses beat
In the clear forehead painfully; and oft
Would her small hands be press'd upon her brow,
As if to still its throbbing. Days pass'd by,
And thus beside that casement would she spend
The summer evenings. Well she knew her doom,
And sought to linger with such loveliness:
Surely it soothed her passage to the grave.
    One gazed upon her, till his very life
Was dedicate to that idolatry
With which young Love makes offering of itself.
In the vast world he only saw her face.

The morning blush was lighted up by hope, —
The hope of meeting her; the noontide hours
Were counted for her sake; in the soft wind,
When it had pass'd o'er early flowers, he caught
150   The odour of her sigh; upon the rose
He only saw the colour of her cheek.
He watch'd the midnight stars until they wore
Her beauty's likeness — love's astrology.
His was the gifted eye, which grace still touch'd
As if with second nature; and his dreams,
His childish dreams, were lit by hues from heaven —
Those which make genius. Now his visions wore
A grace more actual, and one worshipp'd face
Inspired the youthful sculptor, till like life
160   His spirit warm'd the marble. Who shall say
The love of genius is a common thing,
Such as the many feel — half selfishness,
Half vanity? — for genius is divine,
And, like a god, doth turn its dwelling-place
Into a temple; and the heart redeem'd
By its fine influence is immortal shrine
For love's divinity. In common homes
He dies, as he was born, in nothingness;
But love, inspiring genius, makes the world
170   Its glorious witness; hence the poet's page
Wakens its haunting sympathy of pain;
And hence the painter with a touch creates
Feelings imperishable. 'Twas from that hour
CANOVA[30] took his inspiration: love
Made him the sculptor of all loveliness;
The overflowing of a soul imbued
By most ideal grace, the memory
Which lingers round first passion's sepulchre.
— Why do I say first love? — there is no second.
180   Who asks in the same year a second growth
Of spring leaves from the tree, corn from the field? —
They are exhausted. Thus 'tis with the heart: —

'Tis not so rich in feeling or in hope
To bear that one be crush'd, the other faded,
Yet find them ready to put forth again.
It does not always last; man's temper is
Often forgetful, fickle, and throws down
The temple he can never build again;
But when it does last, and that asks for much, —
A fix'd yet passionate spirit, and a mind   190
Master of its resolves, — when that love lasts,
It is in noblest natures. After years
Tell how C A N O V A felt the influence.
They never spoke: she look'd too spiritual,
Too pure for human passion; and her face
Seem'd hallow'd by the heaven it was so near.
And days pass'd on: — it was an eve in June —
How ever could it be so fair a one? —
And she came not: hue after hue forsook
The clouds, like Hope, which died with them, and night   200
Came all too soon and shadowy. He rose,
And wander'd through the city, o'er which hung
The darkness of his thoughts. At length a strain
Of ominous music wail'd along the streets:
It was the mournful chanting for the dead,
And the long tapers flung upon the air
A wild red light, and show'd the funeral train:
Wreaths — O what mockeries! — hung from the bier;
And there, pale, beautiful, as if in sleep,
Her dark hair braided graceful with white flowers,   210
She lay, — his own beloved one!

    No more, no more! — love, turn thy boat to land, —
I am so sorrowful at my own words.
Affection is an awful thing! — Alas!
We give our destiny from our own hands,
And trust to those most frail of all frail things,
The chances of humanity.
— The wind hath a deep sound, more stern than sweet;
And the dark sky is clouded; tremulous,

220 A few far stars — how pale they look to-night! —
Touch the still waters with a fitful light.
There is strange sympathy between all things,
Though in the hurrying weariness of life
We do not pause to note it: the glad day,
Like a young king surrounded by the pomp
Of gold and purple, sinks but to the shade
Of the black night: — the chronicle I told
Began with hope, fair skies, and lovely shapes,
And ended in despair. Even thus our life
230 In these has likeness; with its many joys,
Its fears, its eagerness, its varying page,
Mark'd with its thousand colours, only tends
To darkness, and to silence, and the grave!

LINES OF LIFE.[31]

————

Orphan in my first year's, I early learnt
To make my heart suffice itself, and seek
Support and sympathy in its own depths.

————

WELL, read my cheek, and watch my eye, —
  Too strictly school'd are they,
One secret of my soul to show,
  One hidden thought betray.

I never knew the time my heart
  Look'd freely from my brow;
It once was check'd by timidness,
  'Tis taught by caution now.

I live among the cold, the false,   10
  And I must seem like them;
And such I am, for I am false
  As those I most condemn.

I teach my lip its sweetest smile,
  My tongue its softest tone;
I borrow others' likeness, till
  Almost I lose my own.

I pass through flattery's gilded sieve,
  Whatever I would say;
In social life, all, like the blind,   20
  Must learn to feel their way.

I check my thoughts like curbed steeds
  That struggle with the rein;
I bid my feelings sleep, like wrecks
  In the unfathom'd main.

I hear them speak of love, the deep,
    The true, and mock the name;
Mock at all high and early truth,
    And I too do the same.

I hear them tell some touching tale,
    I swallow down the tear;
I hear them name some generous deed,
    And I have learnt to sneer.

I hear the spiritual, the kind,
    The pure, but named in mirth;
Till all of good, ay, even hope,
    Seems exiled from our earth.

And one fear, withering ridicule,
    Is all that I can dread;
A sword hung by a single hair
    For ever o'er the head.

We bow to a most servile faith,
    In a most servile fear;
While none among us dares to say
    What none will choose to hear.

And if we dream of loftier thoughts,
    In weakness they are gone;
And indolence and vanity
    Rivet our fetters on.

Surely I was not born for this!
    I feel a loftier mood
Of generous impulse, high resolve,
    Steal o'er my solitude!

I gaze upon the thousand stars
   That fill the midnight sky;
And wish, so passionately wish,
   A light like theirs on high.

I have such eagerness of hope
   To benefit my kind;
And feel as if immortal power
   Were given to my mind.   60

I think on that eternal fame,
   The sun of earthly gloom,
Which makes the gloriousness of death,
   The future of the tomb —

That earthly future, the faint sign
   Of a more heavenly one;
— A step, a word, a voice, a look, —
Alas! my dream is done.

And earth, and earth's debasing stain,
   Again is on my soul;   70
And I am but a nameless part
   Of a most worthless whole.

Why write I this? because my heart
   Towards the future springs,
That future where it loves to soar
   On more than eagle wings.

The present, it is but a speck
   In that eternal time,
In which my lost hopes find a home,
   My spirit knows its clime.   80

Oh! not myself, — for what am I? —
    The worthless and the weak,
Whose every thought of self should raise
    A blush to burn my cheek.

But song has touch'd my lips with fire,
    And made my heart a shrine;
For what, although alloy'd, debased,
    Is in itself divine.

I am myself but a vile link
    Amid life's weary chain;
But I have spoken hallow'd words,
    Oh do not say in vain!

My first, my last, my only wish,
    Say will my charmed chords
Wake to the morning light of fame,
    And breathe again my words?

Will the young maiden, when her tears
    Alone in moonlight shine —
Tears for the absent and the loved —
    Murmur some song of mine?

Will the pale youth by his dim lamp,
    Himself a dying flame,
From many an antique scroll beside,
    Choose that which bears my name?

Let music make less terrible
    The silence of the dead;
I care not, so my spirit last
    Long after life has fled.

A HISTORY OF THE LYRE.

_____

Sketches indeed, from that most passionate page,
A woman's heart, of feelings, thoughts, that make
The atmosphere in which her spirit moves;
But, like all other earthly elements,
O'ercast with clouds, now dark, now touch'd with light,
With rainbows, sunshine, showers, moonlight, stars,
Chasing each other's change. I fain would trace
Its brightness and its blackness; and these lines
Are consecrate to annals such as those,
That count the pulses of the beating heart.

_____

'T IS strange how much is mark'd on memory,
In which we may have interest, but no part;
How circumstance will bring together links
In destinies the most dissimilar.
This face, whose rudely-pencill'd sketch you hold,
Recalls to me a host of pleasant thoughts,
And some more serious. — This is E U L A L I E,
Once the delight of Rome for that fine skill
With which she woke the lute when answering
With its sweet echoes her melodious words.   10
She had the rich perfection of that gift,
Her Italy's own ready song, which seems
The poetry caught from a thousand flowers;
The diamond sunshine, and the lulling air,
So pure, yet full of perfume; fountains tuned
Like natural lutes, from whispering green leaves;
The low peculiar murmur of the pines:
From pictured saints, that look their native heaven —
Statues whose grace is a familiar thing;
The ruin'd shrine of mournful loveliness;   20
The stately church, awfully beautiful;

Their climate, and their language, whose least word
Is melody — these overfill the heart
Till, fountain-like, the lips o'erflow with song,
And music is to them an element.
  — I saw EULALIA: all was in the scene
Graceful association, slight surprise,
That are so much in youth. It was in June,
Night, but such night as only is not day, —
30   For moonlight, even when most clear, is sad:
We cannot but contrast its still repose
With the unceasing turmoil in ourselves.
  — We stood beside a cypress, whose green spire
Rose like a funeral column o'er the dead.
Near was a fallen palace — stain'd and gray
The marble show'd amid the tender leaves
Of ivy but just shooting; yet there stood
Pillars unbroken, two or three vast halls,
Entire enough to cast a deep black shade;
40   And a few statues, beautiful but cold, —
White shadows, pale and motionless, that seem
To mock the change in which they had no part, —
Fit images of the dead. Pensive enough,
Whatever aspect desolation wears;
But this, the wrecking work of yesterday,
Hath somewhat still more touching; here we trace
The waste of man too much. When years have past
Over the fallen arch, the ruin'd hall,
It seems but course of time, the one great doom,
50   Whose influence is alike upon us all;
The gray tints soften, and the ivy wreath
And wild flowers breathe life's freshness round: but here
We stand before decay; scarce have the walls
Lost music left by human step and voice;
The lonely hearth, the household desolate,
Some noble race gone to the dust in blood;
Man shames of his own deeds, and there we gaze,
Watching the progress not of time, but death.

— Low music floated on the midnight wind,
A mournful murmur, such as opes the heart 60
With memory's key, recalling other times,
And gone by hopes and feelings, till they have
An echo sorrowful, but very sweet.
"Hush!" said my comrade, — "it is EULALIE;
"Now you may gaze upon the loneliness
"Which is her inspiration." Soft we pass'd
Behind a fragment of the shadowy wall.
— I never saw more perfect loveliness.
It ask'd, it had no aid from dress: her robe
Was white, and simply gather'd in such folds 70
As suit a statue: neck and arms were bare;
The black hair was unbound, and like a veil
Hung even to her feet; she held a lute,
And, as she paced the ancient gallery, waked
A few wild chords, and murmur'd low sweet words,
But scarcely audible, as if she thought
Rather than spoke: — the night, the solitude,
Fill'd the young Pythoness with poetry.
— Her eyes were like the moonlight, clear and soft,
That shadowy brightness which is born of tears, 80
And raised towards the sky, as if they sought
Companionship with their own heaven; her cheek, —
Emotion made it colourless, that pure
And delicate white which speaks so much of thought,
Yet flushes in a moment into rose;
And tears like pearls lay on it, those which come
When the heart wants a language; but she pass'd,
And left the place to me a haunted shrine,
Hallow'd by genius in its holiest mood.
— At Count ZARIN'S pallazzo the next night 90
We were to meet, and expectation wore
Itself with fancies, — all of them were vain.
I could not image aught so wholly changed.
Her robe was Indian red, and work'd with gold,
And gold the queen-like girdle round her waist.

Her hair was gather'd up in grape-like curls;
An emerald wreath, shaped into vine leaves, made
Its graceful coronal. Leant on a couch
The centre of a group, whose converse light
100 Made a fit element, in which her wit
Flash'd like the lightning: — on her cheek the rose
Burnt like a festal lamp; the sunniest smiles
Wander'd upon her face. — I only knew
EULALIA by her touching voice again.
— They had been praying her to wake the lute:
She would not, wayward in her mood that night;
When some one bade her mark a little sketch
I brought from England of my father's hall;
Himself was outlined leaning by an oak,
110 A greyhound at his feet. "And is this dog
Your father's sole companion?" — with these words
She touch'd the strings: — that melancholy song,
I never may forget its sweet reproach.
— She ask'd me how I had the heart to leave
The old man in his age; she told how lorn
Is solitude; she spoke of the young heart
Left in its loneliness, where it had known
No kindness but from strangers, forced to be
Wayfarer in this bleak and bitter world,
120 And looking to the grave as to a home.
— The numbers died in tears, but no one sought
To stay her as she pass'd with veiled face
From the hush'd hall. — One gently whisper'd me,
EULALIA is an orphan! ⋆ ⋆ ⋆
Yet still our meetings were mid festival,
Night after night. It was both sad and strange,
To see that fine mind waste itself away,
Too like some noble stream, which, unconfined,
Makes fertile its rich banks, and glads the face
130 Of nature round; but not so when its wave
Is lost in artificial waterfalls,
And sparkling eddies; or coop'd up to make

The useless fountain of a palace hall.
— One day I spoke of this; her eager soul
Was in its most unearthly element.
We had been speaking of the immortal dead.
The light flash'd in her eyes. "'Tis this which makes
The best assurance of our promised heaven:
This triumph intellect has over death —
Our words yet live on others' lips; our thoughts   140
Actuate others. Can that man be dead
Whose spiritual influence is upon his kind?
He lives in glory; and such speaking dust
Has more of life than half its breathing moulds.
Welcome a grave with memories such as these,
Making the sunshine of our moral world!"
"This proud reward you see, and yet can leave:
Your songs sink on the ear, and there they die,
A flower's sweetness, but a flower's life.
An evening's homage is your only fame;   150
'Tis vanity, EULALIA." — Mournfully
She shook the raven tresses from her brow,
As if she felt their darkness omen-like.
"Speak not of this to me, nor bid me think;
It is such pain to dwell upon myself;
And know how different I am from all
I once dream'd I could be. Fame! stirring fame!
I work no longer miracles for thee.
I am as one who sought at early dawn
To climb with fiery speed some lofty hill: 160
His feet are strong in eagerness and youth;
His limbs are braced by the fresh morning air,
And all seems possible: — this cannot last.
The way grows steeper, obstacles arise,
And unkind thwartings from companions near.
The height is truer measured, having traced
Part of its heavy length; his sweet hopes droop.
Like prison'd birds that know their cage has bars,
The body wearies, and the mind is worn —

170 That worst of lassitude: — hot noon comes on;
There is no freshness in the sultry air,
There is no rest upon the toilsome road;
There is the summit, which he may not reach,
And round him are a thousand obstacles.
    "I am a woman: — tell me not of fame.
The eagle's wing may sweep the stormy path,
And fling back arrows, where the dove would die.
Look on those flowers near yon acacia tree —
The lily of the valley — mark how pure
180 The snowy blossoms, — and how soft a breath
Is almost hidden by the large dark leaves.
Not only have those delicate flowers a gift
Of sweetness and of beauty, but the root —
A healing power dwells there; fragrant and fair,
But dwelling still in some beloved shade.
Is not this woman's emblem? — she whose smile
Should only make the loveliness of home —
Who seeks support and shelter from man's heart,
And pays it with affection quiet, deep, —
190 And in his sickness — sorrow — with an aid
He did not deem in aught so fragile dwelt.
Alas! this has not been my destiny.
Again I'll borrow Summer's eloquence.
Yon Eastern tulip — that is emblem mine;
Ay! it has radiant colours — every leaf
Is as a gem from its own country's mines.
'Tis redolent with sunshine; but with noon
It has begun to wither: — look within,
It has a wasted bloom, a burning heart;
200 It has dwelt too much in the open day,
And so have I; and both must droop and die!
I did not choose my gift: — too soon my heart,
Watch-like, had pointed to a later hour
Than time had reach'd: and as my years pass'd on,
Shadows and floating visions grew to thoughts,
And thoughts found words, the passionate words of song,

And all to me was poetry. The face,
Whose radiance glided past me in the dance,
Awoke a thousand fantasies to make
Some history of her passing smile or sigh.   210
The flowers were full of song: — upon the rose
I read the crimson annals of true love;
The violet flung me back on old romance;
All was association with some link
Whose fine electric throb was in the mind.
I paid my price for this — 'twas happiness.
My wings have melted in their eager flight,
And gleams of heaven have only made me feel   *Icarus*
Its distance from our earth more forcibly.
My feelings grow less fresh, my thoughts less kind: 220
My youth has been too lonely, too much left
To struggle for itself; and this world is
A northern clime, where ev'ry thing is chill'd.
I speak of my own feelings — I can judge
Of others but by outward show, and that
Is falser than the actor's studied part.   *Recognition*
We dress our words and looks in borrow'd robes: *of need*
The mind is as the face — for who goes forth   *to be*
In public walks without a veil at least?   *theatrical*
'Tis this constraint makes half life's misery.   230
'Tis a false rule: we do too much regard
Others' opinions, but neglect their feelings;
Thrice happy if such order were reversed.
Oh why do we make sorrow for ourselves,
And, not content with the great wretchedness
Which is our native heritage — those ills
We have no mastery over — sickness, toil,
Death, and the natural grief which comrades death —
Are not all these enough, that we must add
Mutual and moral torment, and inflict   240
Ingenious tortures we must first contrive?
I am distrustful — I have been deceived
And disappointed — I have hoped in vain.

I am vain — praise is opium, and the lip
Cannot resist the fascinating draught,
Though knowing its excitement is a fraud —
Delirious — a mockery of fame.
I may not image the deep solitude
In which my spirit dwells. My days are past
250   Among the cold, the careless, and the false.
What part have I in them, or they in me?
Yet I would be beloved; I would be kind;
I would share others' sorrows, others' joys;
I would fence in a happiness with friends.
I cannot do this: — is the fault mine own?
Can I love those who but repay my love
With half caprice, half flattery; or trust,
When I have full internal consciousness
They are deceiving me? I may be kind,
260   And meet with kindness, yet be lonely still;
For gratitude is not companionship. —
We have proud words that speak of intellect;
We talk of mind that magnifies the world,
And makes it glorious: much of this is true, —
All time attests the miracles of man:
The very elements, whose nature seems
To mock dominion, yet have worn his yoke.
His way has been upon the pathless sea;
The earth's dark bosom search'd; bodiless air
270   Works as his servant; and from his own mind
What rich stores he has won, the sage, the bard,
The painter, these have made their nature proud:
And yet how life goes on, its great outline
How noble and ennobling! — but within
How mean, how poor, how pitiful, how mix'd
With base alloy; how Disappointment tracks
The steps of Hope; how Envy dogs success;
How every victor's crown is lined with thorns,
And worn mid scoffs! Trace the young poet's fate:
280   Fresh from his solitude, the child of dreams,

His heart upon his lips, he seeks the world,
To find him fame and fortune, as if life
Were like a fairy tale. His song has led
The way before him; flatteries fill his ear,
His presence courted, and his words are caught;
And he seems happy in so many friends.
What marvel if he somewhat overrate
His talents and his state? These scenes soon change.
The vain, who sought to mix their name with his;
The curious, who but live for some new sight;   290
The idle, — all these have been gratified,
And now neglect stings even more than scorn.
Envy has spoken, felt more bitterly,
For that it was not dream'd of; worldliness
Has crept upon his spirit unaware;
Vanity craves for its accustom'd food;
He has turn'd sceptic to the truth which made
His feelings poetry; and discontent
Hangs heavily on the lute, which wakes no more
Its early music: — social life is fill'd   300
With doubts and vain aspirings; solitude,
When the imagination is dethroned,
Is turn'd to weariness. What can he do
But hang his lute on some lone tree, and die?
    "Methinks we must have known some former state
More glorious than our present, and the heart
Is haunted with dim memories, shadows left
By past magnificence; and hence we pine
With vain aspirings, hopes that fill the eyes
With bitter tears for their own vanity.   310
Remembrance makes the poet; 'tis the past
Lingering within him, with a keener sense
Than is upon the thoughts of common men
Of what has been, that fills the actual world
With unreal likenesses of lovely shapes,
That were and are not; and the fairer they,
The more their contrast with existing things,

The more his power, the greater is his grief.
— Are we then fallen from some noble star,

CULTURAL
MEMORY

320   Whose consciousness is as an unknown curse,
And we feel capable of happiness
Only to know it is not of our sphere?
   "I have sung passionate songs of beating hearts;
Perhaps it had been better they had drawn
Their inspiration from an inward source.
Had I known even an unhappy love,
It would have flung an interest round life
Mine never knew. This is an empty wish;
Our feelings are not fires to light at will

330   Our nature's fine and subtle mysteries;
We may control them, but may not create,
And love less than its fellows. I have fed
Perhaps too much upon the lotos fruits
Imagination yields, — fruits which unfit
The palate for the more substantial food
Of our own land — reality. I made
My heart too like a temple for a home;
My thoughts were birds of paradise, that breathed
The airs of heaven, but died on touching earth.

340   — The knight whose deeds were stainless as his crest,
Who made my name his watchword in the field;
The poet with immortal words, whose heart
I shared with beauty; or the patriot,
Whose eloquence was power, who made my smile
His recompense amid the toil which shaped
A nation's destiny: these, such as these,
The glorified — the passionate — the brave —
In these I might have found the head and heart
I could have worshipp'd. Where are such as these?

350   — Not mid gay cavaliers, who make the dance
Pleasant with graceful flatteries; whose words
A passing moment might light up my cheek,
But haunted not my solitude. The fault
Has been my own; perhaps I ask'd too much: —

Yet let me say, what firmly I believe,
Love can be — ay, and is. I held that Love
Which chooseth from a thousand only one,
To be the object of that tenderness
Natural to every heart; which can resign
Its own best happiness for one dear sake;   360
Can bear with absence; hath no part in Hope, —
For Hope is somewhat selfish, Love is not, —
And doth prefer another to itself.
Unchangeable and generous, what, like Love,
Can melt away the dross of worldliness;
Can elevate, refine, and make the heart
Of that pure gold which is the fitting shrine
For fire, as sacred as e'er came from Heaven?
No more of this: — one word may read my heart,
And that one word is utter weariness!   370
Yet sometimes I look round with vain regret,
And think I will restring my lute, and nerve
My woman's hand for nobler enterprise;
But the day never comes. Alas! we make
A ladder of our thoughts, where angels step,
But sleep ourselves at the foot: our high resolves
Look down upon our slumbering acts."
   I soon left Italy: it is well worth
A year of wandering, were it but to feel
How much our England does outweigh the world.   380
A clear cold April morning was it, when I first
Rode up the avenue of ancient oaks,
A hundred years upon each stately head.
The park was bright with sunshine, and the deer
Went bounding by; freshness was on the wind,
Till every nerve was braced; and once the air
Came with Arabian sweetness on its wing, —
It was the earliest growth of violets.
A fairy foot had left its trace beside, —
Ah, EMILY had nursed my favourite flowers.   390
Nearer I came, I heard familiar sounds —

They are the heart's best music; saw the blaze
Through the wide windows of the dear old hall.
One moment more, my eager footsteps stood
Within my father's home, beside his hearth.
— Three times those early violets had fill'd
Their urns with April dew, when the changed cheek
Of E MILY wore signs of young decay.
The rose was too inconstant, and the light
400 Too clear in those blue eyes; but southern skies
Might nurse a flower too delicate to bear
The winds of March, unless in Italy.
I need not tell thee how the soothing air
Brought tranquil bloom that fed not on itself
To E MILY 'S sweet face; but soon again
We talk'd of winter by our own wood fire,
With cheerful words, that had no tears to hide.
— We pass'd through Rome on our return, and there
Sought out E ULALIA . Graceful as her wont
410 Her welcome to my bride; but oh, so changed!
Her cheek was colourless as snow; she wore
The beauty of a statue, or a spirit
With large and radiant eyes: — her thrilling voice
Had lost its power, but still its sweetness kept.
One night, while seated in her favourite hall,
The silken curtains all flung back for air,
She mark'd my E MILY , whose idle gaze
Was fix'd on that fair garden. "Will you come
And wander in the moonlight? — our soft dew
420 Will wash no colour from thine island cheek."
She led the way by many a bed, whose hues
Vied with the rainbow, — through sweet-scented groves
Golden with oranges: at length the path
Grew shadowy with darker, older trees,
And led us to a little lonely spot.
There were no blossoming shrubs, but sweeping pines
Guarded the solitude; and laurel boughs
Made fitting mirrors for the lovely moon,

With their bright shining leaves; the ivy lay
And trail'd upon the ground; and in the midst 430
A large old cypress stood, beneath whose shade
There was a sculptured form; the feet were placed
Upon a finely-carved rose wreath; the arms
Were raised to Heaven, as if to clasp the stars
EULALIA leant beside; 'twas hard to say
Which was the actual marble: when she spoke,
You started, scarce it seem'd a human sound;
But the eyes' lustre told life linger'd still;
And now the moonlight seem'd to fill their depths.
"You see," she said, "my cemetery here: — 440
Here, only here, shall be my quiet grave.
Yon statue is my emblem: see, its grasp
Is raised to Heaven, forgetful that the while
Its step has crush'd the fairest of earth's flowers
With its neglect." ——
        Her prophecy was sooth:
No change of leaf had that green valley known,
When EULALIE lay there in her last sleep.

  Peace to the weary and the beating heart,
That fed upon itself!

[handwritten annotation: Eulalia's new emblem of scenes / pleasures / life forgotten for the / less tangible / less reachable / the ideal]

FANTASIES,

INSCRIBED TO T. CROFTON CROKER, ESQ.[32]

1.

I'm weary, I'm weary, — this cold world of ours;
I will go dwell afar, with fairies and flowers.
Farewell to the festal, the hall of the dance,
Where each step is a study, a falsehood each glance;
Where the vain are displaying, the vapid are yawning;
Where the beauty of night, the glory of dawning,
Are wasted, as Fashion, that tyrant, at will
Makes war on sweet Nature, and exiles her still.

2.

I'm weary, I'm weary, — I'm off with the wind:
Can I find a worse fate than the one left behind?
— Fair beings of moonlight, gay dwellers in air,
O show me your kingdom! O let me dwell there!
I see them, I see them! — how sweet it must be
To sleep in yon lily! — is there room in 't for me?
I have flung my clay fetters; and now I but wear
A shadowy seeming, a likeness of air.

3.

Go harness my chariot, the leaf of an oak;
A butterfly stud, and a tendril my yoke.
Go swing me a hammock, the poles mignonette;
I'll rock with its scent in the gossamer net.
Go fetch me a courser: yon reed is but slight,
Yet far is the distance 'twill bear me to-night.
I must have a throne, — ay, yon mushroom may stay,
It has sprung in a night, 'twill be gather'd next day:
And fit is such throne for my brief fairy reign;
For, alas! I'm but dreaming, and dreams are but vain.

REVENGE.

Ay, gaze upon her rose-wreathed hair,
    And gaze upon her smile;
Seem as you drank the very air
    Her breath perfumed the while:

And wake for her the gifted line,
    That wild and witching lay,
And swear your heart is as a shrine,
    That only owns her sway.

'Tis well: I am revenged at last, —
    Mark you that scornful cheek, —   10
The eye averted as you pass'd,
    Spoke more than words could speak.

Ay, now by all the bitter tears
    That I have shed for thee, —
The racking doubts, the burning fears, —
    Avenged they well may be —

By the nights pass'd in sleepless care,
    The days of endless woe;
All that you taught my heart to bear,
    All that yourself will know.   20

I would not wish to see you laid
    Within an early tomb;
I should forget how you betray'd,
    And only weep your doom:

But this is fitting punishment,
    To live and love in vain, —
Oh my wrung heart, be thou content,
    And feed upon his pain.

Go thou and watch her lightest sigh, —
    Thine own it will not be;
And bask beneath her sunny eye, —
    It will not turn on thee.

'Tis well: the rack, the chain, the wheel,
    Far better had'st thou proved;
Ev'n I could almost pity feel,
    For thou art not beloved.

STANZAS

TO THE

AUTHOR OF "MONT BLANC," "ADA," &C. [33]

THY hands are fill'd with early flowers,
    Thy step is on the wind;
The innocent and keen delight
    Of youth is on thy mind; —
That glad fresh feeling that bestows
Itself the pleasure which it knows,
    The pure, the undefined;
And thou art in that happy hour
Of feeling's uncurb'd, early power.

Yes, thou art very young, and youth,
    Like light, should round thee fling
The sunshine thrown round morning's hour,
    The gladness given to spring:
And yet upon thy brow is wrought
The darkness of that deeper thought,
    Which future time should bring.
What can have traced that shadowy line
Upon a brow so young as thine?

'Tis written in thy large dark eyes,
      Fill'd with unbidden tears;   20
The passionate paleness on thy cheek,
      Belying thy few years.
A child, yet not the less thou art
One of the gifted hand and heart,
      Whose deepest hopes and fears
Are omen-like: the poet's dower
Is even as the prophet's power.

Thy image floats before my eyes,
      Thy book is on my knee;
I'm musing on what now thou art,   30
      And on what thou wilt be.
Dangerous as a magic spell,
Whose good or evil none may tell,
      The gift that is with thee;
For Genius, like all heavenly light,
Can blast as well as bless the sight.

Thou art now in thy dreaming time:
      The green leaves on the bough,
The sunshine turning them to gold,
      Are pleasures to thee now;   40
And thou dost love the quiet night,
The stars to thee are a delight;
      And not a flower can grow,
But brings before thy haunted glance
The poet days of old romance.

With thine "own people" dost thou dwell,
      And by thine own fireside;
And kind eyes keep o'er thee a watch,
      Their darling and their pride.
I cannot choose but envy thee;   50
The very name of home to me
      Has been from youth denied;

But yet it seems like sacred ground,
By all earth's best affections bound.

'Tis well for thee! thou art not made
    Struggle like this to share;
Ill might that gentle, loving heart
    The world's cold conflict bear;
Where selfish interest, falsehood, strife,
Strain through their gladiatorial life;
    Save that the false ones wear
Seeming and softness and a smile,
As if guilt were effaced by guile.

I dare not speak to thee of fame,
    That madness of the soul,
Which flings its life upon one cast,
    To reach its desperate goal.
Still the wings destined for the sky
Will long their upward flight to try,
    And seek to dare the whole,
Till, space and storm and sunshine past,
Thou find'st thou art alone at last.

But love will be thy recompense,
    The love that haunts thy line;
Ay, dream of love, but do not dream
    It ever will be thine.
His shadow, not himself, will come;
Too spiritual to be his home,
    Thy heart is but his shrine;
For vainest of all earthly things
The poet's vain imaginings.

Go, still the throbbing of thy brow,
    The beating of thy heart;
Unstring thy lute, and close thy page,
    And choose an humbler part;

60

70

80

Turn not thy glistening eyes above,
Dwell only in thy household love,
    Forgetting what thou art;
And yet life like what this must be
Seems but a weary lot for thee.   90

Or trust thee to thy soaring wing,
    Awake the gifted lay;
Fling life's more quiet happiness
    For its wild dreams away.
'Tis a hard choice: on either side
Thy heart must with itself divide,
    Be thy doom what it may.
Life's best to win, life's best to lose, —
The lot is with thee, maiden, — choose.

Georgiana, Duchess of Bedford, by Landseer

FROM *THE KEEPSAKE FOR 1829*

VERSES. [34]

LADY, thy face is very beautiful,
A calm and stately beauty: thy dark hair
Hangs as the passing winds paid homage there;
And gems, such gems as only princes cull
From earth's rich veins, are round thy neck and arm;
Ivory, with just one touch of colour warm;
And thy white robe floats queen-like, suiting well
A shape such as in ancient pictures dwell!
  If thou hadst lived in that old haunted time,
When sovereign Beauty was a thing sublime,   10
For which knights went to battle, and her glove
Had even more of glory than of love; —
Hadst thou lived in those days, how chivalrie,
With brand and banner, would have honour'd thee!
Then had this picture been a chronicle,
Of whose contents might only poets tell
What king had worn thy chains, what heroes sigh'd,
What thousands nameless, hopeless, for thee died.
But thou art of the Present — there is nought
About thee for the dreaming minstrel's thought,   20
Save vague imagination, which still lives
Upon the charmed light all beauty gives.
What hath romancing lute, or fancied line,
Or colour'd words to do with thee or thine?

No, the chords sleep in silence at thy feet,
They have no measures for thy music meet;
The poet hath no part in it, his dream
Would too much idleness of flattery seem;
And to that lovely picture only pays
30   The wordless homage of a lingering gaze.

THE ALTERED RIVER. [35]

THOU lovely river, thou art now
    As fair as fair can be,
Pale flowers wreathe upon thy brow,
    The rose bends over thee.
Only the morning sun hath leave
    To turn thy waves to light,
Cool shade the willow branches weave
    When noon becomes too bright.
The lilies are the only boats
10   Upon thy diamond plain,
The swan alone in silence floats
    Around thy charm'd domain.
The moss bank's fresh embroiderie,
    With fairy favours starr'd,
Seems made the summer haunt to be
    Of melancholy bard.
Fair as thou art, thou wilt be food
    For many a thought of pain;
For who can gaze upon thy flood,
20   Nor wish it to remain
The same pure and unsullied thing
    Where heaven's face is as clear
Mirror'd in thy blue wandering
    As heaven's face can be here.
Flowers fling their sweet bonds on thy breast,
    The willows woo thy stay,

In vain, — thy waters may not rest,
    Their course must be away.
In yon wide world, what wilt thou find?
    What all find — toil and care: 30
Your flowers you have left behind
    For other weight to bear.
The heavy bridge confines your stream,
    Through which the barges toil,
Smoke has shut out the sun's glad beam,
    Thy waves have caught the soil.
On — on — though weariness it be,
    By shoal and barrier cross'd,
Till thou hast reach'd the mighty sea,
    And there art wholly lost.   40
Bend thou, young poet, o'er the stream —
    Such fate will be thine own;
Thy lute's hope is a morning dream,
    And when have dreams not flown?

FROM *ROMANCE AND REALITY* (1831)

ROMANCE AND REALITY.[36]

CHAPTER I.

"It was an ancient venerable hall."[37] — CRABBE.

"This is she,
Our consecrated Emily,"[38] — WORDSWORTH.

SUCH a room as must be at least a century's remove from London, large, white, and wainscoted; six narrow windows, red curtains most ample in their dimensions, an Indian screen, a present in which expectation had found "ample space and verge enough"[39] to erect theories of their cousin the nabob's rich legacies, ending, however, as many such expectations do, in a foolish marriage and a large family; a dry-rubbed floor, only to have been stepped in the days of hoops and handings; and some dozen of large chairs covered with elaborate tracery, each chair cover the business of a life spent in satin-stitch. On the walls were divers whole-length portraits, most pastoral-looking grandmammas, when a broad green sash, a small straw hat, whose size the very babies of our time would disdain, a nosegay somewhat larger than life, a lamb tied with pink riband, concocted a shepherdess just stepped out of an ecologue into a picture. Grandpapas by their side, one hand, or rather three fingers, in the bosom of each flowered waistcoat, the small three-cornered hat under each arm; two sedate-looking personages in gowns and wigs, and one — the fine gentleman of the family — in a cream-coloured coat extending a rose for the benefit of the company in general. Over the chimney-piece was a glass, in a most intricate frame of cut crystal within the gilt one, which gave you the advantage of seeing your face in square, round, oblong, triangular, or all shapes but its natural one. On each side the fire-place was an arm chair; and in them sat, first, Mr. Arundel, reading the county newspaper as if he had been solving a problem; and, secondly, his lady dozing very comfortably over her knitting: while the centre of the rug was occupied by two white cats, — one worked in worsted, and surrounded by a wreath of roses — the other asleep, with a blue riband round her neck; and all as still and quiet as the Princess Nonchalante — who, during her lover's most earnest supplication, only begged he would not hurry himself — could have wished.

The quiet was not very lasting, for the fire was stirred somewhat suddenly, the chairs pushed aside somewhat hastily, the cat disturbed, but without any visible notice from either reader or sleeper. "My aunt asleep — my uncle as bad!" exclaimed Emily Arundel, emerging from the corner, where she had been indulging in one of those moods which may be called melancholy or sullen, out of temper or out of spirits, accordingly as they are spoken of in the first or second person; and Emily was young, pretty, and spoilt enough to consider herself privileged to indulge in any or all of them.

The course of life is like the child's game — "here we go round by the rule of contrary" — and youth, above all others, is the season of united opposites, with all its freshness and buoyancy. At no period of our existence is depression of the spirits more common or more painful. As we advance in life our duties become defined; we act more from necessity and less from impulse; custom takes the place of energy, and feelings, no longer powerfully excited, are proportionally quiet in reaction. But youth, balancing itself upon hope, is for ever in extremes; its expectations are continually aroused only to be baffled; and disappointment, like a summer shower, is violent in proportion to its brevity.

Young she was — but nineteen, that pleasantest of ages, just past the blushing, bridling, bewildering coming out, when a courtesy and a compliment are equally embarrassing; when one half of the evening is spent in thinking what to do and say, and the other half in repenting what has been said and done. Pretty she was — very pretty: a profusion of dark, dancing ringlets, that caught the sun-beams and then kept them prisoners; beautiful dark grey eyes with large black pupils, very mirrors of her meaning; that long curled eye-lash, which gives a softness nothing else can give; features small, but Grecian in their regularity; a slight delicate figure, an ankle fit for a fairy, a hand fit for a duchess, — no marvel Emily was the reigning beauty of the county. Sprung from one of its oldest families, its heiress too, the idol of her uncle and aunt, who had brought her up from infancy; accustomed to be made much of, that most captivating kind of flattery, — it may be pardoned if her own estimate was a very pleasant one. Indeed, with the exception of young gentlemen she had refused, and young ladies she had rivalled, Emily was universally liked: kind, enthusiastic, warm, and affectionate, her good qualities were of a popular kind; and her faults — a temper too hasty, a vanity too cultivated — were kept pretty well in the background by the interest or affection, by the politeness or kindness, of her usual circle. To conclude, she was very much like other young ladies, excepting that she had neither lover nor confidante: a little romance, a little pride, and not a little good taste, had prevented the first, so that the last was not altogether indispensable.

Her father had been the youngest brother, and, like many other younger brothers, both unnecessary and imprudent; a captain in a dragoon regiment, who spent his allowance on his person, and his pay on his horse. He was the last man in the world who ought to have fallen in love, excepting with an heiress, yet he married suddenly and secretly the pretty and portionless Emily Delawarr, and wrote home to ask pardon and cash. The former was withheld on account of the latter, till his elder brother's unexceptionable marriage with Miss Belgrave, and her estate, gave him an interest in the family which he forthwith exerted in favour of Captain Arundel. But a few short years, and the officer died in battle, and his widow only survived to place their orphan girl in Mr. and Mrs. Arundel's care, to whom Emily had ever been even as their own.

Mr. Arundel was a favourable specimen of the old school, when courtesy, though stately, was kind, and, though elaborate, yet of costly *matériel*; a well-read, though not a literary man — every body did not write in his day — generous to excess; and if proud, his consciousness of gentlemanlike descent was but shown in his strictness of gentlemanlike feelings. The last of a very old family, an indolent, perhaps an over-sensitive temper — often closely allied — had kept him a quiet dweller on his own lands; and though, from increasing expenses without increasing funds, many an old manor and ancient wood had developed those aërial propensities which modern times have shown to be inherent in their nature, and had made themselves wings and flown away, yet enough remained for dignity, and more than enough for comfort: and in a county where people had large families, Emily was an heiress of considerable pretension.

His lady was one of those thousand-and-one women who wore dark silk dresses and lace caps — who, after a fashion of their own, have made most exemplary wives; that is to say, they took to duties instead of accomplishments, and gave up music when they married — who spent the mornings in the housekeeper's room, and the evenings at the tea-table, waiting for the guests who came not — who rose after the first glass of wine — whose bills and calls were paid punctually, and whose dinners were a credit to them. In addition to this, she always knitted Mr. A's worsted stockings with her own hands, was good-natured, had a whole book of receipts, and loved her husband and niece as parts of herself.

Few families practised more punctuality and propriety, and perhaps in few could more happiness, or rather content, be found. Occasionally, Mr. Arundel's temper might be ruffled by pheasants and poachers, and his wife's by some ill-dressed dish; but then there were the quarter sessions to talk of, and other and faultless dinners to redeem aught of failure in the last. Sometimes Emily might think it was rather dull, and lay down the Morning Post with a sigh, or close her novel with a hope; but in general her spirits were buoyant as her steps, and the darling of the household was also its life and delight. But to-night, the third rainy evening of three rainy days, every flower in the divers china bowls, cups, vases, was withered; the harp was out of tune with the damp; and Emily betook herself to the leafy labyrinth of a muslin flounce, *la belle alliance* of uselessness and industry.

Corinne at the Cape of Misena, by François Gérard

FROM *THE AMULET FOR 1832*

CORINNE AT THE CAPE OF MISENA.[40]

How much of mind is in this little scroll,
Whereon the artist's skill has bodied forth
The shapes which genius dreamed! — The quiet sea
Sleeps in the distance, with that happy sleep
Which, in the human world, but childhood knows —
Childhood, whose hope is present! Pale with light,
For colour has departed with the sun,
The moon has risen in the faint grey sky,
Bearing a clear young beauty on her brow,
Which has been turned to earth too short a while   10
To wear its shadow. With a darker hue
Than when the sun is on their shining leaves
The myrtles spread their branches to the night,
Whose dews are falling. By the moonlight touched
With silvery softness and with gentle shade,
The fair city seems as if repose
And sleep alone were in its quiet walls.
Silence was made for such a night, or song,
And song has just been floating o'er the waves;
The lute is yet within its mistress' hand,   20
Though now the music from its chords is gone
To wander o'er the waters, and to perish:
Ay, perished long the music of those chords,
They had but life from sweetness, so they died.

Not so the words! — for, even as the wind,
That wafts the seeds which afterwards spring up
In a perpetual growth, and then subsides,
The song was only minister to words
Which have the immortality of pain.

30   A lady leans upon that silent lute,
With large dark eyes, like the eternal night,
So spiritual and so melancholy —
The exquisite Corinne!

                 There is a power
Given to some minds to fashion and create,
Until the being present on the page
Is actual as our life's vitality!
Such was Corinne — and such the mind that gave
Its own existence to its work. Corinne
Is but another name for her who wrote,
40   Who felt, and poured her spirit on her lay.
What are the feelings but her own? The hope
Which in the bleak world finds no resting-place,
And, like the dove, returns unsatisfied,
But bringing no green leaf, it seeks its ark
With wearied wing, and plumes whose gloss is gone.
Here, too, is traced that love which hath too much
Of heaven in its fine nature for the earth —
Where love pines for a home and finds a grave;
The eagerness which turns to lassitude;
50   The thirst of praise which ends in bitterness;
Those high aspirings which but rise to find
What weight is on their wings; and that keen sense
Of the wide difference between ourselves
And those who are our fellows; and which marks
A withered ring around all confidence:
We cannot soothe the pain we do not know.
The heart is sacrificed upon the shrine
Of mental power — at least its happiness.

A whole life's bitterness is in the song
Whose words, too truly, are the singer's own.   60

     Fragment of Corinne's Song at Naples.

"Thus, shrinking from the desert spread around,
Doth Genius wander through the world, and finds
No likeness to himself — no echo given
By Nature: and the common crowd but hold
As madness that desire of the rapt soul
Which finds not in this world enough of air,
Of high enthusiasm, or of hope!
For Destiny compels exalted minds;
The poet whose imagination draws
Its power from loving and from suffering,   70
They are the banished of another sphere:
For the Almighty goodness might not frame
All for a few — th' elect or the proscribed.
Why spoke the ancients with such awe of Fate?
What had this terrible Fate to do with them,
The common and the quiet, who pursue
The seasons, and do follow timidly
The beaten track of ordinary life?
But she, the priestess of the oracle,
Shook with the presence of a cruel power.   80
I know not what the involuntary force
That plunges Genius into misery.
Genius doth catch that music of the spheres
Which mortal ear was never meant to know;
Genius can penetrate the mysteries
Of feeling all unknown to other hearts; —
A Power hath entered in his inmost soul,
Whose presence he may not contain."*

---

* The part marked as quotation is translated literally from Corinne's song. Its only
merit is its exactness, for I have scarcely permitted myself to alter a word. This
brief passage is chosen as having less reference to the story than other parts equally
beautiful. There occurs, soon afterwards, one of those almost startling remarks

Such were the words of one who felt those words
90   With all the truth of sorrow. In this world,
Grief and life go together; 'neath the tent,
The palace, and the cottage, woe is heard,
Speaking with suffering's universal voice.
But of the many who at night are glad
To lay their common burden down and rest,
Surely the mind endowed with gifts from heaven
Must be most glad, for it foresees its home,
And saith, in its rejoicing orison,
Thank God, thank God, there is a grave; and hope
100   That looks beyond to heaven!

which give such peculiarity of thoughtfulness to Madame de Stael's writings.
Corinne says, "Perhaps it is what we shall do to-morrow that will decide our fate;
perhaps even yesterday have we said some word that nothing can recal." I know
not what may be the effect on others, but I could never read this short, but true,
remark without a feeling of terror.

L.E.L.

FROM *TRAITS AND TRIALS OF EARLY LIFE* (1836)

THE HISTORY OF A CHILD.[41]

How well I remember it, that single and lonely laurel tree, it was my friend, my confidant. How often have I sat rocking on the one long, pendant branch which dropped even to the grass below. I can remember the strange pleasure I took in seeing my tears fall on the bright shining leaves, often while observing them have I forgotten the grief that led to their falling. I was not a pretty child, and both shy and sensitive; I was silent, and therefore not amusing. No one loved me but an old nurse — why she should have been fond of me I know not, for I gave her much trouble; night after night has she wakened with my crying — but she only wakened to soothe me. She was far advanced in years, but was still strikingly handsome. Her face, with its bold Roman profile, its large black eyes, is still before me as I used to see it bending over my crib, and singing, or rather crooning me to sleep with the old ballad of "Barbara Allen."[42] Never will the most finished music, that ever brought the air and perfume of an Italian summer upon its melody — never will it be sweet in my ears as that untaught and monotonous tone: my first real sorrow was her departure; life has been to me unhappy enough, but never has it known a deeper desolation than that first parting. It is as present as yesterday; she had married, and was now about to go to a home of her own. How I hated her husband; with the rest of the nursery he was a popular person, for he had been a sailor, and his memory was stored with wild histories of the Buccaneers; nor was he without his own perils; he had been shipwrecked on the coast of Cornwall, and was once prisoner of war, though rescued before the French vessel made harbor. From any one else with what rapt attention should I have listened to these narratives, but to him I always turned a reluctant ear. Whenever he came, which he often did, into the large old nursery, where the hearth would have sufficed for ten fire-places of these degenerate days; I used to draw my stool close to my nurse, and, leaning my head on her knee, keep fast hold of her hand — she encouraged this, and used to tell me she would never go away.

The time of her departure was kept a secret, but I knew it; the coach past the road at the end of the horse-chestnut avenue, and one night, they thought that I was asleep, I heard that two days after she was there to meet the coach, and go to London, to go there forever. I buried my face in my pillow that my crying might not be heard. I slept, and my dreams brought the old avenue, the coach stopping, as vividly as when I really saw them.

I awoke the next morning, pale and heavy eyed, but I was subject to violent head-aches, and all passed off as their effects. Not a word passed my lips of the previous night's discourse. For the first time I felt the bitterness of being deceived; I could have better brooked the approaching separation, had I been trusted with it. But the secrecy made me feel so unworthy and so helpless; young as I was, I should have been proud of my nurse's confidence; at length, after three miserable silent days, the last night came. My nurse gave us all some little keep-sake, though without telling her immediate departure. To me she gave a book, for I was, to use her own expression, "a great scholar." That is, I had not the bodily strength for more active amusement, and was therefore very fond of reading; but to-night I had not the heart to look into the pages which at another time would have been greedily devoured. She was hurt at my seeming indifference, and took my brother on her knee, who was all rapture with his windmill; I was very wrong, I could not bear to see him carest, and pushing him violently aside, entreated her with a passionate burst of tears, to love me, and only me.

We slept in a sort of gallery off the nursery, and the next morning I was up with the earliest day-break. Taking the greatest care not to awaken my companions, I put on my clothes as well as I could, and stole down stairs. It was scarcely light through the closed windows, and the shadows took all fantastic semblances, and one or two of the chance rays fell upon the pictures in the hall, giving them strange and distorted likenesses. There was one stately lady in black, with a huge white ruff that encircled a face yet paler. The eyes seemed to follow me wherever I moved; cold, glassy, immoveable eyes, which looked upon, as if they hated, the little trembling thing that was creeping along below. Suddenly a noise like thunder, at least such it seemed in my ears, rang through the hall. I clung to the oaken bannisters of the staircase, my very heart died within me, and I could scarcely raise my head from the place in which it had almost unconsciously buried itself, to ascertain the cause of an unusual light: the fact was a shutter had been carelessly fastened, and a gust of wind had caused the iron bar to fall. It was, however, fortunate for me, as in my well arranged plan, I had forgotten one very important point; namely, how I was to leave the house. To unfasten the hall door was utterly beyond my strength; now an obvious method of escape presented itself. I opened the window and sprang out, running thence at full speed till I gained the avenue; there I was secure. Breathless with running, agitated and afraid, it is singular how soon I grew composed, and even cheerful in the clear bright morning; its gladness entered into my heart. For a moment I almost forgot the purpose that had brought me there at such an hour: the mists were rising from the park, rolling away like waves of some silvery sea, such as I ever after fancied the seas in fairy tales to be. The clouds were warming into deeper crimson every moment, till the smallest leaf on the chesnut trees seemed distinct on that bright red sky. How beautifully it was reflected on the lake, and yet it was almost terrible; it seemed to me filled with flame. How huge and dark too rose our two cedars; what a distance did their shadows spread before them; but I then turned to what was brightest. I was delighted to see the dew drops on the pointed speargrass, and the down balls shining with moisture; it is a common superstition in our part of the country that wish and blow away the gossamer round, if it goes at one breath your wish will be granted. I caught one eagerly — I blew with all my strength — alas, only a little of the shining down was displaced; I could scarcely see the remainder for tears; at that moment I heard the horn of the coach. I wonder now that I could distinguish it at such a distance; I stopped my ears not to hear it again; and the moment after held my breath to listen. At last I caught sight of the coach in a winding of the road; how glad I felt to think that there was still the hill between us. I had never before seen it coming, though I had often watched it drive past on a summer evening: I saw it pass rapidly through the windings of the green hedges, till it began slowly to ascend the hill. Here my attention was drawn from it, by the sight of my nurse and one of her fellow servants hurrying up the avenue; years — years have past since then, but even now the pang of that moment is cold at my heart. I was standing with my arm round the slender stem of one of the young trees. I leant my face upon it; but I saw my nurse coming along as distinctly as if I had watched her. The coach stopped at the gate, and the coachman gave a loud and hasty ring, my nurse hurried by without seeing me, another moment and I felt that she was lost to me forever. I sprang forward, I flung my arms around her, I clung to her with the momentary strength of despair; I implored her to take me with her, I said I would work, beg for her, anything, if she would let me go and be her own child. At first she kissed and coaxed me to loose her, but at last the coachman became impatient of waiting; in the fear of the stage going without her, harassed too by all the perplexities which I have since learnt belong to all departures; she exclaimed in the momentary peevishness of not being able to unclasp my arms, —

"What a tiresome child it is, I shall have the coach go without me."

My arms relaxed their tender and passionate clasp, I stood at her side pale, for I felt the color go from my cheek back upon my heart; my eyes drank back their tears, I felt then what I never felt before; the perfect self-control of strong excitement, and I bade her civilly good morning. I walked slowly away from the gate without looking back to see her get into the coach, but hearing the horn echo on the air, I ran to a point of rising ground, I caught the last sight of the horses, and flung myself down on the grass; the words "how tiresome the child is," ringing in my ears, as if another person at my side delighted to repeat them in every possible way.

To know yourself less beloved than you love, is a dreadful feeling — alas, how often has the rememberance of that bitter hour come back again by some following hour too sadly like the one that went before — How often have I since exclaimed, "I am not beloved as I love."

The consequence of my being so long on the dewy grass, aided by the agitation that I had endured, brought on one of those violent colds to which I have always been subject. It was poor consolation, the undeniable fact that it had been brought on by my own fault. I never coughed without a sensation of shame. Of all shapes that illness can take, a cough is the worst. Pain can be endured in silence, but a cough is so noisy, it inevitably attracts attention; the echo of mine from the vaulted roof was a perpetual torment to myself, because I knew that others must hear it as well. My cough brought also what was the severest of punishments, it kept me within doors, it prevented my daily visit to the old laurel, where I used to share my luncheon with a favorite old pointer of my father's.

One day, while I was sitting by the window, forced, alas, to be shut, I heard a whining at the door. I opened it, and in bounded the dog, overwhelming me with its caresses. Its large bright brown eyes were fixed upon me with all the depth of human affection. It was a delicious sensation to think that anything in the world had missed me. Clio was a beautiful creature with a coat of glossy blackness only broken by a few spots of tan. I have since heard a lovely head of hair compared to the "down of darkness"[43] and to the raven's wing, but the highest compliment that ever passes through my mind is to liken it to the dark silkiness of my darling Clio. The weather being very dry, no dirt could be brought into the house, and the visits of the intruder were a permitted pleasure. Another source of enjoyment too opened upon me. I began to read the book that my nurse had given me; at first the very sight of it was insupportably painful, but one long weary morning when the severity of illness had softened into that languor which needs some quiet amusement, I opened its pages. It was an epoch in my life, it is an epoch in every child's life, the first reading of Robinson Crusoe. What entire possession it took of my imagination. Henceforth one half of my time was past on that lovely and lonely island. The only thing that I could not understand were Robinson Crusoe's lamentations over his solitude, to me the most unreasonable things in the world. How little did I share his joy when the English vessel came and bore him once more over the sea to his native England. It was a long time before I had any wish to read the rest. For weeks after reading that book, I lived as if in a dream, indeed I rarely dreamt of anything else at night, I went to sleep with the cave, its parrots and goats, floating before my closed eyes; I wakened in some rapid flight from the savages landing in their canoes. The elms in our own hedges were not more familiar than the prickly shrubs which formed his palisade; and the grapes whose drooping branches made fertile the wild savannahs. When at length allowed to go into the open air, my enjoyment was ten-fold.

We lived in a large, old, and somewhat dilapidated place, only part of the grounds were kept up in their original high order. I used to wander in the almost deserted shrubberies, where the flowers grew in all the luxuriance of neglect over the walks, and the shrubs become trees drooped to the very ground, the boughs heavy with bloom and leaves. In the very heart of one of these was a large deep pond, almost black with the depths of shadow — One bank only was sunny, it had been turf, but one flower after another had taken possession of a situation so favorable. The rododhendron spread its fragile blossom of the softest lilac, beside the golden glories of the Constantinople rose; a variety too of our English roses, had taken root and flourished there. There was the damask, with all its York and Lancaster[44] associations, the white, cold as snow, the little red Ayshire darling, and last but not least, for it grew with a spendthrift's prodigality, the Chinese rose, a delicate frail stranger, yet the last to shed beauty on even our dark November. Below, the pond was covered with water lilies with the large green leaves that support the loveliest of ivory boats, fit for the fairy Queen and her summer court. But these were not the attractions of that solitary pond in my eyes. Its charm was a little island which seemed to float upon the dark water; one side of the pond was covered with ancient willow trees, whose long pendant branches drooped forever over the same mournful mirror. One of these trees, by some natural caprice, shot out direct from the bank, a huge, straight bough that formed a complete bridge to the little island — at least so near that a rapid spring enabled me to gain it. — There was only one tree on this miniature island — a curiously shaped but huge yew tree; it quite rivalled the laurel that used to be my favorite haunt. I would remain hidden in the deep shadows of that gloomy tree, for the whole of my playtime, I was there,

> "Monarch of all I surveyed
> My right there was none to dispute."[45]

How well I recollect the eagerness with which, one morning, I sprang into its shade. The day before I had been to a juvenile ball given in the neighborhood. I was dressed with unusual care — and I am convinced that dress is the universal passion — and turned to leave the nursery with an unusual glow of complacency, one of the servants smoothing down a rebellious curl. As I past I heard the other say "leave well alone" — and unfortunately I heard the rejoinder also — "Leave ill alone, you mean; did you ever see such a little plain thing." This was but the beginning of my mortifications, that evening was but the first of many coming events that cast their shadows before. Still it was my earliest experience of the bitterness of neglect, and of the solitude of a crowd. I had for several hours the melancholy satisfaction of sitting unnoticed in a corner; at length the Lady of the House, in the most cruel kindness, insisted on my dancing — How the first figure of the quadrille was accomplished I know not. I fancied every one was laughing at me, I had to advance by myself, the room swam round, my head became giddy, I left my unfortunate partner, sprang away, and took refuge in a balcony and a burst of tears. The next morning I had to endure reproof, for I had inflicted the mortification I felt, and the unanswerable question of "What use was my being taught anything?" In sad truth, at that time, it might have seemed very little use indeed. I was a clever, very clever child, but my mind was far beyond my years, and it lacked the knowledge which alone can teach how to use its powers. Moreover I was wholly deficient in all showy talents; for music I had no ear, for drawing no eye, and dancing was positively terrible to my timid temper. My sensitiveness made any attempt at display a hopeless endeavor. An hundred times has my book been returned because I was too anxious that I might say my lesson well, the words died on my lips, I became confused, speechless, while the tears that rose too readily into my eyes appeared like sullenness. And yet at that moment my heart almost stopped beating with its eagerness, to repeat what in reality I had thoroughly mastered, and whose spirit had become a part of my mind.

Still the imagination conquers the real. My head ached with crying when I reached my darling island, and yet in half an hour I was sitting in the shadow of the yew tree, my arm round Clio's dark and glossy neck, and fancying the pointer an excellent representation of "my man Friday." There was one time in the day, however, when I could never prevail on Clio to be my companion — about six she regularly disappeared, and all my coaxing to keep her at my side was in vain. One afternoon I watched and followed her. She took her way across the long shadows that were now beginning to sweep over the sunny park. She made her way to a small gate that opened on the road, and there lay down patiently awaiting the arrival of her master. I thought I would wait too, for I knew that my father was in the habit of coming in at that gate, as it saved a long round by the road. I soon heard the sound of his horse's hoofs, and felt half inclined to run away. I was so glad that I did not, for my father took me up in his arms and kissed me with the utmost pleasure, saying, — "So you have been waiting for me;" and taking the horse's bridle in one hand, and me in the other, we walked across the park together. I now went to meet him every day; happy, happy, hours that I past on that gate, with the pointer at my feet, looking up with its large human eyes, as if to read in mine when I first caught sight of my father. How I hated the winter with its cold cutting air, its thick fog, that put an end to this waiting; winter, that left out the happiest hour of the day. But spring came again, spring that covered one bank with the sweet languor of the pale primrose, and another with the purple arabia of the breathing violet. No flower takes upon me the effect of these. Years, long years past away since I have seen these flowers, other than in the sorted bouquet, and the cultivated garden, but those fair fresh banks rise distinct on my mind's eye. They colour the atmosphere with themselves, their breath rises on the yet perfumed air, and I think with painful pleasure over all that once surrounded them, I think of affections gone down to the grave, and of hopes and beliefs which I can trust no more.

It was in the first week of an unusually forward May, that one afternoon, for I had again began my watchings by the Park gate, that my father produced four volumes, and for me. How delicious was the odour of the Russian leather in which they were bound, how charming the glance at the numerous pictures which glanced through the half opened leaves. The first reading of the Arabian Nights was like the first reading of Robinson Crusoe. For a time their world made mine — my little lonely island, dark with the mingled shadow of the yew and the willow, was now deserted, I sought a gayer site, that harmonised better with the bright creations now around me, I found it in a small old fashioned flower garden, where the beds, filled with the richest colours, were confined by small edgings of box into every variety of squares, ovals, and rounds. At one end was the bee house, whence the murmur of myriad insect wings came like the falling of water. Near was a large accacia, now in the prodigality of bloom which comes but every third year; I found a summer palace amid its luxuriant boughs. The delight of reading those enchanted pages, I must even to this day rank as the most delicious excitement of my life. I shall never have courage to read them again, it would mark too decidedly, too bitterly, the change in myself, — I need not. How perfectly I recollect those charming fictions whose fascination was so irresistible! How well I remember the thrill of awe which came over me at the brazen giant sitting alone amid the pathless seas, mighty and desolate till the appointed time came, for the fated arrow at whose touch he was to sink down an unsolved mystery hidden by the eternal ocean!

How touching the history of Prince Agib[46] — when he arrives at the lovely island only inhabited by the beautiful boy who dwelt there in solitude and fear till he came! How in the thoughtlessness of youth, they laughed when sweet confidence had grown up between them, at the prediction which threatened that beloved and gentle child with death at Prince Agib's hand! Fate laughs at human evasion — the fated morning comes one false step, and even in the very act of tender service, the knife enters the heart of the predestined victim. Prince Agib sees from the thick leaves of the tree where he had taken shelter, the anxious father, anxious but hopeful, arrive. He comes with music and rejoicing. What does he take back with him! The dead body of his son.

Again with what all but actual belief did I devour the history of the wondrous lamp, whose possessor had only to wish. For weeks I lived in a world of wishes, and yet it was this dreaming world first led me into contact with the actual. As usual such knowledge began in sorrow.

One morning before the period of leaving the school-room, I heard the report of a gun. In spite of the intricate path of rivers and boundaries I was then tracing, it still occurred to me to wonder what could lead to a gun's being fired at that time of year. Alas, I learnt only too soon. On going to the accacia I was surprised not to find my usual companion waiting. As to reading in any comfort, till I had Clio's soft brown eyes watching me, was impossible. I sent off in search of the truant, perhaps she had been fastened up. I found my way to the stable, and to the dead body of my favourite. She had been bitten by an adder, and they had been obliged to shoot her. It was one of those shocking spectacles which remain with you for your life. Even now my dreams are haunted with the sight. I believe at first that horror pre-dominated over regret. I could not cry, I stood trembling beside the mangled remains of what I had loved so dearly. I prevailed on one of the servants to bury it near my accacia tree. For days afterwards I did nothing but sob on that grave. How desolate the mornings seemed — how the presence of one real sorrow shook to its very foundations my fairy-land. I started from even a moment's forgetfulness as a wrong to the memory of my beloved companion.

At length I began to take an interest in decorating the grave, and planted first one flower and then another. I was not very successful in my gardening attempts, till at length Lucy came to my assistance. Lucy was the grandaughter of an old blind woman who lived near; an aged retainer of some great family, whose small pension had long out-lasted the original donors. I have seen many beautiful faces since, but nothing that rises to my memory to be compared with Lucy's childish but exceeding loveliness. She was delicately fair, though constant exposure to the sun had touched the little hands, and the sweet face with soft brown, through which came the most transparent colour that ever caught its red from the rose, or its changefulness from the rainbow. Her hair was of that pale yet rich gold so rarely seen: with the sunshine upon it, it was positively radiant; it shone as the wind lifted some of the long soft curls. It was a species of beauty too frail, too delicate, and the large blue eyes had that clear sky-like azure, that violet shadow round the orbs which mark an hereditary tendency to decline. She was in the habit of coming into our gardens to gather roses for distillation. Accustomed from her cradle to strangers and exertion, making friends by a manner whose sweetness was as natural as the smile to her face, Lucy was not the least shy: if she had been, we should never have become acquainted. But when she frankly offered her services to assist in ornamenting the little plot of ground on which my shrubs were drooping, and round which my flowers always made a point of dying; they were accepted on my part with equal surprise and gratitude. Under her more judicious management, the ground was soon covered with leaf and bloom, and every blossom that put forth was a new link in our intimacy.

"I wish I could do anything to oblige you," was my exclamation at the sight of my first carnation.

"Oh," exclaimed she, the soft colour warming into her cheek with eagerness, "you are a great reader, would you sometimes come and read to my grandmother?" This I easily obtained permission to do, and that evening I went with Lucy to Mrs. Selby's. The cottage where she lived stood alone in a little nook between our park and the churchyard; yew trees were on the one side, and our cedars on the other, but the garden itself seemed a very fairy-land of sunshine; a jessamine covered the front with its long trailing green branches, and its white delicate blossoms. The porch was enlivened by that rare and odoriferous shrub, the yellow musk rose; it is the only one I have ever seen, but of a summer evening, it covered that little portal with gold, and filled the whole air with its peculiar and aromatic fragrance. We read of the gales that bear from the shores of Ceylon the breathings of the cinnamon groves. I have always fancied that the musk rose resembles them. Inside how cool, clean, and neat was the room with its brick floor and large old fire place, and yet there was only Lucy to do everything; I have often thought since of the difference between the children of the rich, and the children of the poor — the first kept apart, petted, indulged, and useless; — the second with every energy in full exercise from the cradle, actively employed, and earning their daily bread, almost from the hour that they begin to eat it. If there is too much of this in the lower classes, if labour be carried into cruelty, there is infinitely too little of it in the higher. The poor child, as Charles Lamb so touchingly expresses it,[47] is not brought, but "dragged out," and if the wits are sharpened, so too is the soft round cheek. The crippled limb and broken constitution attest the effects of the over-early struggle with penury; but the child of rich parents suffers though in another way; there it is the heart that is crippled, by the selfishness of indulgence and the habit of relying upon others. It takes years of harsh contact with the realities of life to undo the enervating work of a spoilt and over aided childhood. We cannot too soon learn the strong and useful lessons of exertion and self-dependence. Lucy was removed from the heaviest pressure of poverty, but how much did she do that was wonderful in a child of her age! The cottage was kept in the most perfect neatness, and her grandmother's every want watched as only love watches; she was up with the lark, the house was put in order, their own garden weeded, her nosegays collected from all parts, for Lucy was the flower market, the Madeline of our village. Then their dinner was made ready; afterwards, her light song and even lighter step were again heard in the open air, and when evening came on, you saw her in the porch as busily plaiting straw as if the pliant fingers had only just found employment.

That was my time for visiting at the cottage, when the last red shadows turned the old Gothic lattices of the Church into rubies; then on the low bench beside Lucy, I used to sit and read aloud to her grandmother. She was a very remarkable woman, her tall stately figure was unbent by age, and her high and strongly marked features were wonderful in expression for a face where the eyes were closed for ever. She was a north country woman, and her memory was stored with all those traditions which make so large a portion of our English poetry. Lucy was her only link with the present, but for her affection to that beautiful child, she lived entirely with the past. The

old castle where she had chiefly lived, whose noble family had per-
ished from the earth as if smitten by some strange and sudden doom,
the legends connected with their house, — these were her sole topics
of discourse. All these legends were of a gloomy tendency, and I used
to gaze on her pale sightless face, and listen to the hollow tones of
her voice till my heart sank within me for fear. But if by any chance
Lucy left us for a moment, no matter how interesting the narrative,
the old woman would suspend her discourse and question me about
Lucy's appearance. I did not then understand the meaning of her
questions. Alas! how I look back to the hour passed every summer
evening in that little shady porch, reading to that old blind woman,
Lucy thanking me all the time, with her sweet blue eyes. I have rarely
I fear me been so useful since, certainly never so beloved. It was not
to last long; August was now beginning, and it came in with violent
thunder storms. One of Lucy's occupations was to gather wild straw-
berries in a wood at some distance, and nothing could exceed the
natural taste with which she used to arrange the bright scarlet fruit
amid the vine leaves she fetched from our garden. Returning over
the common, she was caught in a tremendous shower, and wet
through. The sudden chill struck to a constitution naturally delicate,
and in four and twenty hours, Lucy was no more — I went to see
her unconscious of what had happened. The house was shut up; I felt
for the first time in my life that vague presentiment of evil which is
its certain forerunner; I thought only of the aged woman, and
entered hastily yet stealthily in. No one was to be seen in the front
room, and I found my way to the one at the back. There were no
shutters to the window, and the light streamed through the thin
white curtain; it fell on the face of the dead. Beside sat the grand-
mother, looking the corpse which she became in the course of that
night. She never spoke after she felt her child's hand grow cold and
stiff in her own. There she lay, that beloved and beautiful girl, her
bright hair shining around her, and her face so pale, but with such
strange sweetness. I bent down to kiss her, but the touch was death.
But why should I go on; I had lost my gentle companion for ever.

I have told the history of my childhood, childhood which images
forth our after life. Even such has been mine — it has but repeated
what it learnt from the first, Sorrow, Beauty, Love and Death.

ON THE ANCIENT AND MODERN INFLUENCE OF POETRY.[48]

I T is curious to observe how little one period resembles another. Centuries are the children of one mighty family, but there is no family-likeness between them. We ourselves are standing on the threshold of a new era, and we are already hastening to make as wide a space, mark as vast a difference as possible, between our own age and its predecessor. Whatever follies we may go back upon, whatever opinions we may re-adopt, they are never those which have gone *immediately* before us. Already there is a wide gulph between the last century and the present. In religion, in philosophy, in politics, in manners, there has passed a great change; but in none has been worked a greater change than in poetry, whether as it regards the art itself, or the general feeling towards it. The decline and fall of that Roman empire of the mind seems now advanced as an historical fact; while we are equally ready to admit that some twenty years since the republic was in its plenitude of power. In the meantime a new set of aspirants have arisen, and a new set of opinions are to be won. But it is from the past that we best judge of the present; and perhaps we shall more accurately say what poetry is by referring to what it has been.

Poetry in every country has had its origin in three sources, connected with the strongest feelings belonging to the human mind —

Religion, War, and Love. The mysteries of the present; the still greater mysteries of the future; the confession of some superior power so deeply felt; higher impulses speaking so strongly of some spiritual influence of a purer order than those of our common wants and wishes; — these all found words and existence in poetry. The vainest fictions of mythology were the strongest possible evidence how necessary to the ignorance of humanity was the belief of a superior power; so entire was the interior conviction, that sooner than believe in nothing no belief was too absurd for adoption. The imagination, which is the source of poetry, has in every country been the beginning as well as the ornament of civilization. It civilizes because it refines. A general view of its influence in the various quarters of the globe will place this in the most striking point of view.

Africa is the least civilized quarter of the globe, not so much from its savage as from its apathetic state; one could almost believe that it had been formed from the dregs of the other parts.[49] Now, the distinguishing mark of its deficiency in that soil of mind wherewith the intellect works, is its total want of imagination. It is the only great portion of the world which is not emphatically made known to us by its own peculiar religion. Her mythology was the earthly immortality of Greece. Greece is indelibly linked with the idea of civilization; but all those fine and graceful beliefs which made its springs holy places, and haunted the fragrant life of every flower and leaf, were the creations of its earliest time. Look from thence to the fierce regions of the North, — how full is the Scandinavian faith of the wild and wonderful! or to the East, how gorgeous their tales of enchantment, with their delicate Peris,[50] and the fallen and fearful spirits in their subterranean caverns! — again, the faith of Brahma, with its thousand deities. Or, to cross the wide Atlantic, there are the vestiges of a terrible creed yet touched with something of spiritual loveliness, in their singing-birds bringing tidings of the departed, and in the green hunting-grounds which made their future hope. Each and all these creeds are the work and wonder of the imagination — but in these Africa has no part. No august belief fills with beauty or terror the depths of her forests, and no fallen temple makes its site sacred though in ruins. Her creeds have neither beauty nor grandeur. The Devil is their principal Deity, and their devotion is born of physical fear. Other nations have had their various faiths, created and coloured by the scenes which gave them birth. The religion of Greece was beautiful as her own myrtle and olive groves. The Scandinavian was like its own wild mountains and snowy wastes, with just gleams of beauty from its starry nights and meteors. The Arabian was glowing and magnificent as the summer earth and radiant sky of its believers; while that of the American Indian was terrible as the huge serpents and the interminable forests which gave shelter to its mysteries. But in Africa the sunny sky, the noble rivers, the woods, splendid in size and foliage, have been without their wonted effect. Slaves from the earliest period, the very superstitions of her sable sons are mean fears caught from their masters; all about them is earthly, utterly unredeemed by those spiritual awakenings which are as lights from another world. We might believe that some great original curse has been said over them, and that they are given over into the hand of man and not of God. And in simple truth that curse has been slavery. The Helots even of Greece were uninspired. "A slave cannot be eloquent;" said Longinus;[51] nor poetical either — the wells of his enthusiasm are dried up. What some ancient writer says of iron may be applied to Poetry — its use is the first step to civilization, and civilization is freedom.[52]

Next to Religion War was the great source of poetry; and the deeds of the brave were sung in that spirit of encouragement which one man will ever receive from the praise bestowed on the deeds of another, when he meditates similar achievements of his own. And here we may be permitted a few words on what we cannot but consider an unjust and erroneous opinion, now much insisted upon, — that poets and conquerors have been equal enemies of the human race — the one but acting what the other praised; and that the sin of encouragement was equal, if not greater, than that of commission. In answer to this we must observe that it is not fair to judge of former actions by our present standard. Our first view of society is always the same: we see the human race dwelling in small dispersed sets, with rude habits, the results of hardships and of dangers. A more favourable situation, or, more commonly, the influence of some superior mind, which from the wonderful effects produced by a single man is often a nation's history: these or similar causes first placed some of the tribes in positions of comparative comfort and advancement. This position would of course be envied by their savage and starving neighbours, who would consider brute force the only means of sharing their advantages. Single motives never last: ambition, aggrandisement, conquest with a view to security, soon gave a thousand motives to warfare that had originally began in want and self-defence. It has required centuries so to consolidate kingdoms that now a breathing space is allowed for reflection on the sin of sacrificing man's most valuable possession — life. But what part has the poet taken in these scenes of bloodshed? One certainly of amelioration. If he has sung of conquerors, the qualities held up to admiration were those of magnanimity and generosity. He has spoken of the love of liberty as holding light the love of life; and the highest eulogium of a warrior was that he died in defence of his native country. But to give our assertion the support of an example. — Perhaps the spirit which animates, the desire which excites, the power which supports, a conqueror, were never more entirely personified than in Xerxes.[53] He possessed to the utmost that grasping ambition, that carelessness of human blood, which characterize the mere conqueror; yet with all the purple pomp of his power, we are not aware of his having been held up otherwise than in reprobation, while the whole world has been filled with the fame of his brave opposers; and the names of those who fell at Marathon are still the watchwords of freedom. Again, in the days of chivalry, what were the qualities the minstrel lauded in the knight? — his valour, certainly, but still more his courtesy, his protection of the weak against the strong, his devotion, his truth; — till the "ungentle knight" was almost as much a phrase of disgrace as that of the "recreant."

Love was the third great fountain of poetry's inspiration; and who that has ever loved will deny the necessity of a language, beyond the working-day tongue of our ordinary run of hopes and fears, to express feelings which have so little in common with them. What has been the most popular love-poetry in all countries? — that which gave expression to its spiritual and better part — constancy kept like a holy thing — blessing on the beloved one, though in that blessing we have ourselves no share; or sad and affectionate regrets in whose communion our own nature grows more kindly from its sympathy. We are always the better for entering into other's sorrow or other's joy.

The whole origin and use of poetry may be expressed in a few brief words: it originates in that idea of superior beauty and excellence inherent in every nature — and it is employed to keep that idea alive; and the very belief in excellence is one cause of its existence. When we speak of poetry as the fountain whence youth draws enthusiasm for its hopes, — where the warrior strengthens his courage, and the lover his faith, — the treasury where the noblest thoughts are garnered, — the archives where the noblest deeds are recorded, — we but express an old belief. One of our great reviews — the "Westminster" — in speaking of the fine arts, &c. says, "The aristocracy do well to encourage poetry: it is by fiction themselves exist — and what is poetry but fiction?"[54] We deny that poetry is fiction; its merit and its power lie alike in its truth: to one heart the aspiring and elevated will come home; to another the simple and natural: the keynote to one will be the voice of memory, which brings back young affections — early confidence, — hill and valley yet glad with the buoyant step which once past over them, — flowers thrice lovely from thoughts indelibly associated with their leaf or breath: such as these are touched by all that restores, while it recalls, days whose enjoyment would have been happiness, could they but have had the knowledge of experience without its weariness. To another, poetry will be a vision and a delight, because the virtue of which he dreams is there realized — and because the "love which his spirit has painted"[55] is to be found in its pages. But in each and all cases the deep well of sympathy is only to be found when the hazel rod is poised by the hand of truth. And, till some moral steam is discovered as potent as that now so active in the physical world, vain will be the effort to regulate mankind like machinery: there will ever be spiritual awakenings, and deep and tender thoughts, to turn away from the hurry and highways of life, and whose place of refuge will still be the green paths and pleasant waters of poesy. That tribes of worse than idle followers have crowded the temple, and cast the dust they brought around the soiled altar, — that many have profaned their high gift to base use — that poetry has often turned aside from its divine origin and diviner end, — is what must be equally admitted and lamented; but who will deny that our best and most popular (indeed in this case best and popular are equivalent terms) poetry makes its appeal to the higher and better feelings of our nature, and not a poet but owes his fame to that which best deserves it? What a code of pure and beautiful morality, applicable to almost every circumstance, might be drawn from Shakspeare!

The influence of poetry has two eras, — first as it tends to civilize; secondly as it tends to prevent that very civilization from growing too cold and too selfish. Its first is its period of action; its second is that of feeling and reflection: it is that second period which at present exists. On the mere principle of utility, in our wide and weary world, with its many sorrows and more cares, how anxiously we ought to keep open every source of happiness! and who among us does not recollect some hour when a favourite poet spread before us a page like that of a magician's; when some expression has seemed like the very echo of our feelings; how often and with what a sensation of pleasure have long-remembered passages sprang to our lips; how every natural beauty has caught a fresh charm from being linked with some associate verse! Who that has these or similar recollections but would keep the ear open, and the heart alive, to the "song that lightens the languid way!"[56]

Why one age should be more productive in poetry than another is one of those questions — a calculation of the mental longitude — likely to remain unanswered. That peculiar circumstances do not create the poet is proved by the fact, that only one individual is so affected: if it were mere circumstance, it would affect alike all who are brought within its contact. What confirmation of this theory (if theory it be) is to be found in the history of all poets! — where are we to seek the cause which made them such, if not in their own minds? We daily see men living amid beautiful scenery; and scenery is much dwelt upon by the advocates of circumstance. Switzerland is a most beautiful country, yet what great poet has it ever produced? The spirit which in ancient days peopled grove and mountain with Dryad and Oread, or, in modern times, with associations, must be in him who sees, not in the object seen. How many there are, leading a life of literary leisure, living in a romantic country, and writing poetry all their days, who yet go down to their unremembered graves no more poets than if they had never turned a stanza! While, on the other hand, we see men with every obstacle before them, with little leisure and less encouragement, yet force their upward way, make their voice heard, and leave their memory in imperishable song. Take Burns for an example: much stress has been laid on the legendary ballads he was accustomed to hear from infancy; but if these were so potent, why did they not inspire his brother as well as himself? Mr. Gilbert Burns is recorded, by every biographer, to have been a sensible, and even a superior man; he dwelt in the same country — he heard the same songs — why was he not a poet too? There can be but one answer, — there was not that inherent quality in his mind which there was in his brother's. Many young men are born to a higher name than fortune — many spend their youth amid the most exciting scenes — yet why do none of these turn out a Byron, but for some innate first cause? What made Milton in old age, — in sickness, in poverty — depressed by all that would have weighed to the very dust an ordinary man — without one of man's ordinary encouragements, — what could have made him turn to the future as to a home, collect his glorious energies, and finish a work, the noblest aid ever given to the immortality of a language? What, but that indefinable spirit, whose enthusiasm is nature's own gift to the poet. *Poeta nascitur non fit*[57] is, like many other old truths, the very truth after all.

We cannot but consider that, though some be still among us, our own great poets belong to another age. Their fame is established, and their horde of imitators have dispersed; those wearying followers who, to use the happy expression of a contemporary writer, "think that breaking the string is bending the bow of Ulysses." We hear daily complaints of the want of present taste and talent for poetry: we are more prepared to admit the latter than the former. In the most sterile times of the imagination, love of poetry has never been lacking; the taste may have been bad, but still the taste existed. Wordsworth truly says, "that, with the young, poetry is a passion;"[58] and there will always be youth in the world to indulge the hopes, and feel the warm and fresh emotions, which their fathers have found to be vain, or have utterly exhausted. To these, poetry will ever be a natural language; and it is the young who make the reputation of a poet. We soon lose that keen delight, which marvels if others share not in it: the faculty of appreciation is the first which leaves us. It is tact rather than feeling which enables experience to foresee the popularity of a new poet. As to the alleged want of taste, we only refer to the editions of established authors which still find purchasers: one has just appeared of Scott, another of Byron. With what enthusiasm do some set up Wordsworth for an idol, and others Shelley! But this taste is quite another feeling to that which creates; and the little now written possesses beauty not originality. The writers do not set their own mark on their property: one might have put forth the work of the other, or it might be that of their predecessors. This was not the case some few years ago. Who could have mistaken the picturesque and chivalric page of Scott for the impassioned one of Byron? or who could for a moment have hesitated as to whether a poem was marked with the actual and benevolent philosophy of Wordsworth, or the beautiful but ideal theory of Shelley? We are now producing no great or original (the words are synonymous) poet. We have graceful singing in the bower, but no voice that startles us into wonder, and hurries us forth to see whose trumpet is awakening the land. We know that when the snow has long lain, warming and fertilizing the ground, and when the late summer comes, hot and clear, the rich harvest will be abundant under such genial influences. Perhaps poetry too may have its atmosphere; and a long cold winter may be needed for its glad and glorious summer. The soil of song, like that of earth, may need rest for renewal. Again we repeat, that though the taste be not, the spirit of the day is, adverse to the production of poetry. Selfishness is its principle, indifference its affectation, and ridicule its commonplace. We allow no appeals save to our reason, or to our fear of laughter. We must either be convinced or sneered into things. Neither calculation nor sarcasm are the elements for poetry. A remark made by Scott to one of his great compeers shows how he knew the age in which he was fated to end his glorious career: — "Ah — it is well that we have made our reputation!"[59] The personal is the destroyer of the spiritual; and to the former everything is now referred. We talk of the author's self more than his works, and we know his name rather than his writings. There is a base macadamizing spirit in literature; we seek to level all the high places of old. But till we can deny that fine "farther looking hope"[60] which gives such a charm to Shakspeare's confessional sonnets; till we can deny that "The Paradise Lost" was the work of old age, poverty, and neglect, roused into delightful exertion by a bright futurity; till we can deny the existence of those redeemers of humanity — we must admit, also, the existence of a higher, more prophetic, more devoted and self-relying spirit than is to be accounted for on the principles either of vanity or of lucre: we shall be compelled to admit that its inspiration is, indeed,

> "A heavenly breath
> Along an earthly lyre."[61]

Methinks there are some mysteries in the soul on whose precincts it were well to "tread with unsandalled foot."[62] Poetry like religion requires faith, and we are the better and happier for yielding it. The imagination is to the mind what life is to the body — its vivifying and active part. In antiquity, poetry had to create, it now has to preserve. Its first effort was against barbarism, its last is against selfishness. A world of generous emotions, of kindly awakenings, those

> "Which bid the perished pleasures move
> In mournful mockery o'er the soul of love;"[63]

a world of thought and feeling, now lies in the guardianship of the poet. These are they who sit in the gate called the beautiful, which leads to the temple. Its meanest priests should feel that their office is sacred. Enthusiasm is no passion of the drawing-room, or of the pence-table: its home is the heart, and its hope is afar. This is too little the creed of our generation; yet, without such creed, poetry has neither present life nor future immortality. As Whitehead finely says in his poem of "The Solitary," —

> "Not for herself, not for the wealth she brings,
> Is the muse wooed and won, but for the deep,
> Occult, profound, unfathomable things, —
> The engine of our tears whene'er we weep,

The impulse of our dreams whene'er we sleep,
    The mysteries that our sad hearts possess,
Which, and the keys whereof, the Muse doth keep, —
    Oh! to kindle soft humanity, to raise,
With gentle strength infused, the spirit bowed;
    To pour a second sunlight on our days,
And draw the restless lightning from our cloud;
To cheer the humble and to dash the proud.
    Besought in peace to live, in peace to die, —
    The poet's task is done — Oh, Immortality!"[64]

He is only a true poet, who can say, in the words of Coleridge, "My task has been my delight; I have not looked either to guerdon or praise, and to me Poetry is its own exceeding great reward."[65]

❦

STANZAS ON THE DEATH OF MRS. HEMANS.[66]

"The rose — the glorious rose is gone." — *Lays of Many Lands.*[67]

BRING flowers to crown the cup and lute, —
    Bring flowers, — the bride is near;
Bring flowers to soothe the captive's cell,
    Bring flowers to strew the bier!
Bring flowers! thus said the lovely song;
    And shall they not be brought
To her who linked the offering
    With feeling and with thought?

Bring flowers, — the perfumed and the pure, —   10
    Those with the morning dew,
A sigh in every fragrant leaf,
    A tear on every hue.
So pure, so sweet thy life has been,
    So filling earth and air
With odours and with loveliness,
    Till common scenes grew fair.

Thy song around our daily path
    Flung beauty born of dreams,
That shadows on the actual world
    The spirit's sunny gleams.
Mysterious influence, that to earth
    Brings down the heaven above,
And fills the universal heart
    With universal love.

Such gifts were thine, — as from the block,
    The unformed and the cold,
The sculptor calls to breathing life
    Some shape of perfect mould,
So thou from common thoughts and things
    Didst call a charmed song,
Which on a sweet and swelling tide
    Bore the full soul along.

And thou from far and foreign lands
    Didst bring back many a tone,
And giving such new music still,
    A music of thine own.
A lofty strain of generous thoughts,
    And yet subdued and sweet, —
An angel's song, who sings of earth,
    Whose cares are at his feet.

And yet thy song is sorrowful,
    Its beauty is not bloom;
The hopes of which it breathes, are hopes
    That look beyond the tomb.
Thy song is sorrowful as winds
    That wander o'er the plain,
And ask for summer's vanished flowers,
    And ask for them in vain.

Ah! dearly purchased is the gift,
   The gift of song like thine;   50
A fated doom is hers who stands
   The priestess of the shrine.
The crowd — they only see the crown,
   They only hear the hymn; —
They mark not that the cheek is pale,
   And that the eye is dim.

Wound to a pitch too exquisite,
   The soul's fine chords are wrung;
With misery and melody
   They are too highly strung.   60
The heart is made too sensitive
   Life's daily pain to bear;
It beats in music, but it beats
   Beneath a deep despair.

It never meets the love it paints,
   The love for which it pines;
Too much of Heaven is in the faith
   That such a heart enshrines.
The meteor wreath the poet wears
   Must make a lonely lot;   70
It dazzles, only to divide
   From those who wear it not.

Didst thou not tremble at thy fame,
   And loathe its bitter prize,
While what to others triumph seemed,
   To thee was sacrifice?
Oh, Flower brought from Paradise
   To this cold world of ours,
Shadows of beauty such as thine   80
   Recall thy native bowers.

Let others thank thee — 'twas for them
    Thy soft leaves thou didst wreathe;
The red rose wastes itself in sighs
    Whose sweetness others breathe!
And they have thanked thee — many a lip
    Has asked of thine for words,
When thoughts, life's finer thoughts, have touched
    The spirit's inmost chords.

How many loved and honoured thee
90   Who only knew thy name;
Which o'er the weary working world
    Like starry music came!
With what still hours of calm delight
    Thy songs and image blend;
I cannot choose but think thou wert
    An old familiar friend.

The charm that dwelt in songs of thine
    My inmost spirit moved;
And yet I feel as thou hadst been
100   Not half enough beloved.
They say that thou wert faint, and worn
    With suffering and with care;
What music must have filled the soul
    That had so much to spare!

Oh, weary One! since thou art laid
    Within thy mother's breast —
The green, the quiet mother-earth —
    Thrice blessed be thy rest!
Thy heart is left within our hearts,
110   Although life's pang is o'er;
But the quick tears are in my eyes,
    And I can write no more.

ON THE CHARACTER OF MRS. HEMANS'S WRITINGS.[68]

"Oh! mes amis, rappellez-vous quelquefois mes vers; mon ame y est empreinte." "Mon ame y est empreinte."[69] Such is the secret of poetry. There cannot be a greater error than to suppose that the poet does not feel what he writes. What an extraordinary, I might say, impossible view, is this to take of an art more connected with emotion than any of its sister sciences. What — the depths of the heart are to be sounded, its mysteries unveiled, and its beatings numbered by those whose own heart is made by this strange doctrine — a mere machine wound up by the clock-work of rhythm! No; poetry is even more a passion than a power, and nothing is so strongly impressed on composition as the character of the writer. I should almost define poetry to be the necessity of feeling strongly in the first instance, and the as strong necessity of confiding in the second.

It is curious to observe the intimate relation that subsists between the poet and the public. "Distance lends enchantment to the view,"[70] and those who would shrink from avowing what and how much they feel to even the most trusted friend, yet rely upon and crave for the sympathy of the many. The belief that it exists in the far off and the unknown is inherent as love or death. Under what pressure of the most discouraging circumstances has it existed, given enjoyment, and stimulated to exertion. The ill-fated and yet gifted being, steeped to the lips in poverty — that bitterest closer of the human heart — surrounded by the cold and the careless — shrinking from his immediate circle, who neglect and misunderstand him, has yet faith in the far away. Suffering discourses eloquent music, and it believes that such music will find an echo and reply where the music only is known, and the maker loved for its sake.

Fame, which the Greeks idealized so nobly, is but the fulfilment of that desire for sympathy which can never be brought home to the individual. It is the essence of such a nature to ask too much. It expects to be divined where it is too shy to express. Praise — actual personal praise — oftener frets and embarrasses than it encourages. It is too small when too near. There is also the fear of mistaking the false Florimel flattery for the true Florimel praise.[71] Hence Hope takes the wings of the morning, and seeks an atmosphere, warm, kindly, and congenial, and where it is not ashamed. Without such timidity, without such irritability, without a proneness to exaggeration, the poetical temperament could not exist. Nor is its reliance on distance and on solitude in vain. We talk, and can never be sure but that our hearers listen as much from kindness as from interest. Their mood may or may not be in unison with our own. If this be the case even in ordinary intercourse, how much more must it be felt where the most shrinking, subtle, and sorrowful ideas are to be expressed. But the poet relies on having his written page opened when the spirit is attuned to its melody. He asks to be read in the long summer-mornings, when the green is golden on the trees, when the bird sings on the boughs, and the insect in the grass; and yet when the weight of the past presses heavily upon the present, when —

> "memory makes the sky
> Seem all too joyous for the shrinking eye."[72]

In such a mood the voice of passionate complaining is both understood and welcome. There is a well of melancholy poetry in every human bosom. We have all mourned over the destroyed illusion and the betrayed hope. We have quarrelled in some embittered moment with an early friend, and when too late lamented the estrangement. We have all stood beside the grave, and asked of the long grass and ever-springing wild flowers why they should have life, while that of the beloved has long since gone down to the dust. How many have

> "laid their youth as in a burial urn,
> Where sunshine may not find it."[73]

I remember to have read of a Hanoverian chorister, who, having lost by an early death the young village girl to whom he was betrothed, rudely carved upon her tomb a rose-bud broken on its stem, with the words beneath, *"C'est ainsi qu'elle fût."*[74] This might be emblem and inscription for all the loveliest emotions of the soul. While such recollections remain garnered, poetry will always have its own appointed hour. Its haunted words will be to us even as our own. Solitude and sorrow reveal to us its secrets, even as they first revealed themselves to those

"Who learnt in suffering what they taught in song."[75]

I believe that no poet ever made his readers feel unless he had himself felt. The many touching poems which most memories keep as favourites originated in some strong personal sensation. I do not mean to say that the fact is set down, but if any feeling is marked in the writing, that feeling has been keenly and painfully experienced. No indication of its existence would probably be shown in ordinary life: first, because the relief of expression has already been found in poetry, and secondly, from that extreme sensitiveness which shrinks from contact with the actual. Moreover, the habit has so grown up with us, — so grown with our growth, and strengthened with our strength, that we scarcely know the extraordinary system of dissimulation carried on in our present state of society.

In childhood, the impetus of conversation is curiosity. The child talks to ask questions. But one of its first lessons, as it advances, is that a question is an intrusion, and an answer a deceit. Ridicule parts social life like an invisible paling; and we are all of us afraid of the other. To this may be in great measure attributed the difference that exists between an author's writings and his conversation. The one is often sad and thoughtful, while the other is lively and careless. The fact is, that the real character is shown in the first instance, and the assumed in the second. Besides the impulses of an imaginative temperament are eager and easily excited, and gaiety has its impulses as well as despondency, but it is less shy of showing them. Only those in the habit of seclusion, occupied with their own thoughts, can know what a relief it is sometimes to spring, as it were, out of themselves. The fertile wit, the sunny vivacity, belong to a nature which must be what the French so happily term *impressionable* to be poetical. The writer of a recent memoir of Mrs. Hemans deems it necessary almost to apologize for her occasional fits of buoyant spirits:[76] —

> "Oh, gentle friend,
> Blame not her mirth who was sad yesterday,
> And may be sad to-morrow."[77]

The most intense sunshine casts the deepest shadow. Such mirth does not disprove the melancholy which belonged to Mrs. Hemans's character. She herself alludes to the times when

> "Sudden glee
> Bears my quick heart along
> On wings that struggle to be free
> As bursts of skylark song."[78]

Society might make her say —

> "Thou canst not wake the spirit
> That in me slumbering lies,
> Thou strikest not forth the electric fire
> Of buried melodies."[79]

But it might very well strike the sparkles from the surface.

I have said that the writer's character is in his writings: Mrs. Hemans's is strongly impressed upon hers. The sensitiveness of the poet is deepened by the tenderness of the woman. You see the original glad, frank, and eager nature

> "Blest, for the beautiful is in it dwelling."[80]

Soon feeling that the weight of this world is too heavy upon it —

> "The shadow of departed hours
> Hangs dim upon its early flowers."[81]

Soon, too, does she feel that

> "A mournful lot is mine, dear friends,
> A mournful lot is mine."[82]

The fate of the pearl-diver is even as her own: —

> "A sad and weary life is thine,
>   A wasting task and lone,
> Though treasure-grots for thee may shine
>   To all beside unknown.
>
> Woe for the wealth thus dearly bought!
>   And are not those like thee
> Who win for earth the gems of thought,
>   Oh wrestler with the sea?
>
> But oh! the price of bitter tears
>   Paid for the lonely power,
> That throws at last o'er desert years
>   A darkly-glorious dower.
>
> And who will think, when the strain is sung,
>   Till a thousand hearts are stirr'd,
> What life-drops from the minstrel wrung
>   Have gush'd at every word."[83]

Imagine a girl, lovely and gifted as Mrs. Hemans was, beginning life, — conscious, for genius must be conscious of itself, — full of hope and of belief; — gradually the hope darkens into fear, and the belief into doubt; one illusion perishes after another, "and love grown too sorrowful,"

> "Asks for its youth again."[84]

No emotion is more truly, or more often pictured in her song, than that craving for affection which answers not unto the call. The very power that she possesses, and which, in early youth, she perhaps deemed would both attract and keep, is, in reality, a drawback. Nothing can stand its test. The love which the spirit hath painted has too much of its native heaven for earth. In how many and exquisite shapes is this vain longing introduced on her page. Some slight incident gives the framework, but she casts her own colour upon the picture. In this consists the difference between painting and poetry: the painter reproduces others, — the poet reproduces himself. We would draw attention especially to one or two poems in which the sentiment is too true for Mrs. Hemans not to have been her own inspiration. Is it not the heart's long-suppressed bitterness that exclaims —

> "Tell me no more — no more
> Of my soul's lofty gifts! are they not vain
> To quench its panting thirst for happiness?
> Have I not tried, and striven, and failed to bind
> One true heart unto me, whereon my own
> Might find a resting-place — a home for all
> Its burden of affections? I depart
> Unknown, though fame goes with me; I must leave
> The earth unknown. Yet it may be that death
> Shall give my name a power to win such tears
> As might have made life precious."[85]

How exquisitely is the doom of a woman, in whose being pride, genius, and tenderness contend for mastery, shadowed in the lines that succeed! The pride bows to the very dust; for genius is like an astrologer whose power fails when the mighty spell is tried for himself; and the tenderness turns away with a crushed heart to perish in neglect. We proceed to mark what appears to bear the deep impress of individual suffering: —

> "One dream of passion and of beauty more:
> And in its bright fulfilment let me pour
> My soul away! Let earth retain a trace
> Of that which lit my being, though its race
> Might have been loftier far .....
> ...... For thee alone, for thee!
> May this last work, this farewell triumph be —
> Thou loved so vainly! I would leave enshrined
> Something immortal of my heart and mind,
> That yet may speak to thee when I am gone,

Shaking thine inmost bosom with a tone
Of best affection — something that may prove
What she hath been, whose melancholy love
On thee was lavished; silent love and tear,
And fervent song that gushed when none were near,
And dream by night, and weary thought by day,
Stealing the brightness from her life away."[86]

"And thou, oh! thou on whom my spirit cast
Unvalued wealth — who knew not what was given
In that devotedness, the sad and deep
And unrepaid farewell! If I could weep
Once, only once, beloved one! on thy breast,
Pouring my heart forth ere I sink to rest!
But that were happiness, and unto me
Earth's gift is fame."[87]

"I have been
Too much alone."[88]

With the same sympathy does she stand beside the grave of the
author of "Psyche"[89] —

"And mournful grew my heart for thee —
Thou in whose woman's mind
The ray that brightens earth and sea,
The light of song was shrined."

"Thou hast left sorrow in thy song,
A voice not loud but deep!
The glorious bowers of earth among
How often didst thou weep!"[90]

Did we not know this world to be but a place of trial — our bit-
ter probation for another and for a better — how strange in its
severity would seem the lot of genius in a woman. The keen feeling
— the generous enthusiasm — the lofty aspiration — and the deli-

cate perception — are given but to make the possessor unfitted for her actual position. It is well; such gifts, in their very contrast to the selfishness and the evil with which they are surrounded, inform us of another world — they breathe of their home, which is Heaven; the spiritual and the inspired in this life but fit us to believe in that which is to come. With what a sublime faith is this divine reliance expressed in all Mrs. Hemans's later writings. As the clouds towards nightfall melt away on a fine summer evening into the clear amber of the west, leaving a soft and unbroken azure whereon the stars may shine through; so the troubles of life, its vain regrets and vainer desires, vanished before the calm close of existence — the hopes of Heaven rose steadfast at last — the light shone from the windows of her home as she approached unto it.

> "No tears for thee, though light be from us gone
> With thy soul's radiance, bright and restless one —
>   No tears for thee.
> They that have loved an exile must not mourn
> To see him parting for his native bourn,
>   O'er the dark sea."[91]

We have noticed this yearning for affection — unsatisfied, but still unsubdued — as one characteristic of Mrs. Hemans's poetry: the rich picturesque was another. Highly accomplished, the varied stores that she possessed were all subservient to one master science. Mistress both of German and Spanish, the latter country appears to have peculiarly captivated her imagination. At that period when the fancy is peculiarly alive to impression — when girlhood is so new, that the eagerness of childhood is still in its delights — Spain was, of all others, the country on which public attention was fixed: victory after victory carried the British flag from the ocean to the Pyrenees; but, with that craving for the ideal which is so great a feature in her writings, the present was insufficient, and she went back upon the past; — the romantic history of the Moors was like a storehouse, with treasures gorgeous like those of its own Alhambra.[92]

It is observable in her minor poems that they turn upon an

incident rather than a feeling. Feelings, true and deep, are developed; but one single emotion is never the original subject. Some graceful or touching anecdote or situation catches her attention, and its poetry is developed in a strain of mourning melody, and a vein of gentle moralizing. I always wish, in reading my favourite poets, to know what first suggested my favourite poems. Few things would be more interesting than to know under what circumstances they were composed, — how much of individual sentiment there was in each, or how, on some incident seemingly even opposed, they had contrived to ingraft their own associations. What a history of the heart would such annals reveal! Every poem is in itself an impulse.

Besides the ideal and the picturesque, Mrs. Hemans is distinguished by her harmony. I use the word harmony advisedly, in contradistinction to melody. Melody implies something more careless, more simple, than belongs to her style: it is song by snatches; our English ballads are remarkable for it. To quote an instance or two. There is a verse in that of "Yarrow Water:"[93] —

> "O wind that wandereth from the south,
>   Seek where my love repaireth,
> And blow a kiss to his dear mouth,
>   And tell me how he fareth."

Nothing can exceed the tender sweetness of these lines; but there is no skill. Again, in "Faire Rosamonde,"[94] the verse that describes the cruelty of Eleanor, —

> "With that she struck her on the mouth,
>   So dyed double red;
> Hard was the heart that gave the blow,
>   Soft were the lips that bled."

How musical is the alliteration; but it is music which, like that of the singing brook, has sprung up of itself. Now, Mrs. Hemans has the most perfect skill in her science; nothing can be more polished than her versification. Every poem is like a piece of music, with its eloquent pauses, its rich combinations, and its swelling chords. Who that has ever heard can forget the exquisite flow of "The Voice of Spring?" —

> "I come! I come! — ye have call'd me long;
> I come o'er the mountains with light and song!
> Ye may trace my step o'er the wakening earth,
> By the winds that tell of the violet's birth,
> By the primrose stars in the shadowy grass,
> By the green leaves opening as I pass."[95]

It is like the finest order of Italian singing — pure, high, and scientific.

I can never sufficiently regret that it was not my good fortune to know Mrs. Hemans personally; it was an honour I should have estimated so highly — a happiness that I should have enjoyed so keenly. I never even met with an acquaintance of hers but once; that once, however, was much. I knew Miss Jewsbury, the late lamented Mrs. Fletcher.[96] She delighted in speaking of Mrs. Hemans: she spoke of her with the appreciation of one fine mind comprehending another, and with the earnest affection of a woman and a friend. She described her conversation as singularly fascinating — full of poetry, very felicitous in illustration by anecdote, happy, too, in quotation, and very rich in imagery; "in short, her own poem on 'The Treasures of the Deep' would best describe it." She mentioned a very striking simile to which a conversation on Mrs. Hemans's own poem of "The Sceptic*" had led: —

"Like Sindbad, the sailor,[97] we are often shipwrecked on a strange shore. We despair; but hope comes when least expected. We pass through the gloomy caverns of doubt into the free air and blessed sunshine of conviction and belief." I asked her if she thought Mrs. Hemans a happy person; and she said, "No; her enjoyment is feverish, and she desponds. She is like a lamp whose oil is consumed by the very light which it yields." What a cruel thing is the weakness of memory! How little can its utmost efforts recall of conversation that

---

*   The Sceptic. Murray.

was once an instruction and a delight!

To the three characteristics of Mrs. Hemans' poetry which have already been mentioned — viz., the ideal, the picturesque, and the harmonious — a fourth must be added, — the moral. Nothing can be more pure, more feminine and exalted, than the spirit which pervades the whole: it is the intuitive sense of right, elevated and strengthened into a principle. It is a glorious and a beautiful memory to bequeath; but she who left it is little to be envied. Open the volumes which she has left, legacies from many various hours, and what a record of wasted feelings and disappointed hopes may be traced in their sad and sweet complainings! Yet Mrs. Hemans was spared some of the keenest mortifications of a literary career. She knew nothing of it as a profession which has to make its way through poverty, neglect, and obstacles: she lived apart in a small, affectionate circle of friends. The high road of life, with its crowds and contention — its heat, its noise, and its dust that rests on all — was for her happily at a distance; yet even in such green nest, the bird could not fold its wings, and sleep to its own music. There came the aspiring, the unrest, the aching sense of being misunderstood, the consciousness that those a thousand times inferior were yet more beloved. Genius places a woman in an unnatural position; notoriety frightens away affection; and superiority has for its attendant fear, not love. Its pleasantest emotions are too vivid to be lasting: hope may sometimes,

> "Raising its bright face,
> With a free gush of sunny tears, erase
> The characters of anguish,"[98]

but, like the azure glimpses between thunder-showers, the clouds gather more darkly around for the passing sunshine. The heart sinks back on its solitary desolation. In every page of Mrs. Hemans's writings is this sentiment impressed; what is the conclusion of "Corinne crowned at the Capitol?"

> "Radiant daughter of the sun!
> Now thy living wreath is won.
> Crown'd of Rome! Oh, art thou not

Happy in that glorious lot?
Happier, happier far than thou
With the laurel on thy brow,
She that makes the humblest hearth
Lovely but to one on earth."

What is poetry, and what is a poetical career? The first is to have an organization of extreme sensibility, which the second exposes bare-headed to the rudest weather. The original impulse is irresistible — all professions are engrossing when once began; and acting with perpetual stimulus, nothing takes more complete possession of its follower than literature. But never can success repay its cost. The work appears — it lives in the light of popular applause; but truly might the writer exclaim —

"It is my youth — it is my bloom — it is my glad free heart
I cast away for thee — for thee — ill fated as thou art."[99]

If this be true even of one sex, how much more true of the other. Ah! Fame to a woman is indeed but a royal mourning in purple for happiness.

———

NOTE. — I have alluded to Miss Jewsbury (Mrs. Fletcher), and cannot resist a brief recollection of one who was equally amiable and accomplished. I never met with any woman who possessed her powers of conversation. If her language had a fault, it was its extreme perfection. It was like reading an eloquent book — full of thought and poetry. She died too soon; and what noble aspirings, what generous enthusiasm, what kindly emotions went down to the grave with her unfulfilled destiny. There is no word that will so thoroughly describe her as "high-minded;" she was such in every sense of the word. There was no envy, no bitterness about her; and it must be a lofty nature that delights in admiration. Greatly impressed as I was with her powers, it surprised me to note how much she desponded over them.

"Day by day,
Gliding, like some dark mournful stream away,
My silent youth flows from me."[100]

Alas! it was the shadow of the early grave that rested upon her. Her
letters were very brilliant, and I believe her correspondence was
extensive; what a pity that they should not be collected. Speaking of
Wordsworth she said, "There is about him a grand and noble plain-
ness, a dignified simplicity — a something of high ideal Paganism,
that I never saw in any one else. He is not so much a rock covered
with flowers, as a rock crowned with a castle. He is a dweller on the
heights — he would have made a friend for Phocion.[101] He reminds
me of the Druidical oaks, strong and sacred." Again, while discussing
the intercourse of society, — "You consider society something like a
honeycomb — sweet, but hollow; so do I. But you seemed also to
consider it expedient for every one by right or courtesy termed 'dis-
tinguished' to play truant — laying aside all habits of thought or
feeling by which such distinction had been acquired. As if the
earnestness of genius were less endurable than the heartlessness of
the world; nay, as if the polished chain-mail of the latter were the
only garb fit to be worn by the former. Personally speaking, I should
be sorry to go into public with any other disposition than one anx-
ious to give and willing to receive pleasure. Very high or very deep
conversation, anything like communion of heart, would be out of
place; but I do not see that we are called upon to pay so costly a
compliment to society, as to assume a character diametrically
opposed to our real world; to utter sentiments we secretly disbelieve
— to be as angry with our better nature for their bursting from
restraint, as at other times with our inferior nature for refusing sub-
mission. I think that wisdom may wear 'motley,' and truth, unlike
man, be born laughing; and that until we go into society thus deter-
mined to seek for more than mere amusement in pleasure, we must
not be surprised to find ourselves living in Thalaba's palace of the
desert[102] — a creation of clouds. Genius ought everywhere to be
true to itself — to its origin, the divine mind — to its home, the
undying spirit — to its power, that of being a blessing — to its

reward, that of being remembered. If genius be not true to itself, if in reckless sport it flings around the flowers and tendrils, how are we ever to look for a fruitage time?"

I need not dwell on the eloquence and beauty of such passages, and her letters were filled with them. Mrs. Fletcher went to India, full of hope and belief — she thought she might do much good. These anticipations were fated to disappointment. The tomb has closed upon her warm and kindly heart. Better it should be thus.

> "Where couldst thou fix on mortal ground
>   Thy tender thoughts and high?
> Now peace the woman's heart hath found,
>   And joy the poet's eye*."[103]

---

* It is almost needless to say, that all the poetical quotations are from Mrs. Hemans's own writings.

FIRST LOVE; OR, CONSTANCY IN THE NINETEENTH CENTURY. [104]

THE assertion that "What is everybody's business is nobody's," is true enough; but the assertion that "What is nobody's business is everybody's," is still truer. Now, a love affair, for example, is, of all others, a thing apart — an enchanted dream, where "common griefs and cares come not." It is like a matrimonial quarrel — never to be benefited by the interference of others: it is a sweet and subtle language, "that none understand but the speakers;" and yet this fine and delicate spirit is most especially the object of public curiosity. It is often supposed before it exists: it is taken for granted, commented upon, continued and ended, without the consent of the parties themselves; though a casual observer might suppose that they were the most interested in the business.

All love affairs excite the greatest possible attention; but never was so much attention bestowed as in the little town of Allerton, upon that progressing between Mr. Edward Rainsforth and Miss Emily Worthington. They had been a charming couple from their birth — were called the little lovers from their cradle; and even when Edward was sent to school, his letter home once a quarter always contained his love to his little wife. Their course of true love seemed likely to run terribly smooth, their fathers having maintained a friendship as regular as their accounts. Mr. Worthington's death, however, when Emily was just sixteen, led to the discovery that his affairs were on the verge of bankruptcy. Mr. Rainsforth now proved himself a true friend; he said little, but did everything. Out of his own pocket he secured a small annuity to the orphan girl, placed her in a respectable family, and asked her to dine every Sunday. With his full sanction, "the little" became "the young lovers;" and the town of Allerton, for the first time in its life, had not a fault to find with the conduct of one of its own inhabitants.

The two old friends were not destined to be long parted, and a few months saw Mr. Rainsforth carried to the same churchyard whither he had so recently followed the companion of his boyhood. A year passed away, and Edward announced his intention of (pray let us use the phrase appropriated to such occasions) becoming a votary of the saffron god.[105] The whole town was touched by his constancy, and felt itself elevated into poetry by being the scene of such disinterested affection. But, for the first time in his life, Edward found there was another will to be consulted than his own. His trustees would not hear of his marrying till he was two-and-twenty, the time that his father's will appointed for his coming of age. The rage and despair of the lover were only to be equalled by the rage and despair of the whole town of Allerton. Every body said that it was the cruellest thing in the world; and some went so far as to prophesy that Emily Worthington would die of a consumption before the time came of her lover's majority. The trustees were declared to have no feeling, and the young people were universally pitied. The trustees would not abate one atom of their brief authority; they had said that their ward ought to see a little of the world, and they were both of them men of their word.

Accordingly, it was settled that Edward should go to London for the next three months, and see how he liked studying the law. He certainly did not like the prospect at all; and his only consolation was, that he should not leave his adored Emily exposed to the dissipations of Allerton. She had agreed to go and stay with an aunt, some forty miles distant, where there was not even a young curate in the neighbourhood. The town of Allerton was touched to the heart by the whole proceeding; no one spoke of them but as that romantic and that devoted young couple. I own that I have known greater misfortunes in life than that a young gentleman and lady of twenty should have to wait a twelve-month before they were married; but every person considers their own the worst that ever happened, and Edward and Emily were miserable to their hearts' content. They exchanged locks of hair; and Emily gave him a portfolio, embroidered by herself, to hold the letters that she was to write. He saw her off first, under the care of an old servant, to the village where she was to stay. She waved her white handkerchief from the window as long as she could see her lover, and a little longer, and then sank back in a flood of "falling pearl, which men call tears."[106]

Edward was as wretched, and he was also exceedingly uncomfortable, which helps wretchedness on very much. It was a thorough wet day — all his things were packed up — for he himself was to start in the afternoon when the mail passed through — and never was young gentleman more utterly at a loss what to do with himself. In such a case an affair of the heart is a great resource; and young Rainsforth got upon the coach-box looking quite unhappy enough to satisfy the people of Allerton. It must be owned that he and the weather equally brightened up in the course of a couple of stages. To be sure, a cigar has a gift of placidity peculiarly its own. If I were a woman I should insist upon my lover's smoking: if not of much consequence before, it will be an invaluable qualification after, the happiest day of one's life.

In these days roads have no adventurers — they might exclaim, with the knife-grinder,[107] "Story! Lord bless you, I have none to tell!" — we will therefore take our hero after he was four days in London. He is happy in a lover's good conscience, for that very morning he had written a long letter to his beloved Emily — the three first days having been "like a teetotum all in a twirl,"[108] he had been forced to neglect that duty so sweet and so indispensable to an absent lover. He had, however, found time to become quite domesticated in Mr. Alford's family. Mr. Alford was of the first eminence in his profession, and had two or three other young men under his charge; but it was soon evident that Edward was a first-rate favourite with the mother and two daughters at all events. They were fine-looking girls, who understood how to look their best. They were well dressed, and it is wonderful how much the hair "done to a turn," ribands which make a complexion, and an exquisite *chaussure*,[109] set off a young woman. Laura taught him to waltz, and Julia began to sing duets with him. Now, these are dangerous employments for a youth of one-and-twenty. The heart turns round, as well as the head sometimes, in a *sauteuse*,[110] and then it is difficult to ask these tender questions appropriated to duets, such as "Tell me, my heart, why wildly beating?" "Canst thou teach me to forget?"[111] &c., without some emotion.

A week passed by, and the general postman's knock, bringing with it letters from his trustee, who, as an item in his accounts, mentioned that he had just heard that Miss Emily Worthington was quite well, put him in mind that he had not heard from her himself. Oh!

how ill-used he felt; he had some thoughts of writing to overwhelm her with reproaches for her neglect; but, on second thoughts, he resolved to treat her with silent disdain. To be sure, such a method of showing his contempt took less time and trouble than writing four pages to express it would have done. That evening he was a little out of spirits, but Julia showed so much gentle sympathy with his sadness, and Laura rallied him so pleasantly upon it, that they pursued the subject long after there was any occasion for it. The week became weeks — there was not a drawback to the enjoyment of the trio, excepting now and then "some old friends of papa, to whom we must be civil; not," said Laura, "but that I would put up with one and all, excepting that odious Sir John Belmore."

Edward had been in town two months and a fortnight, when one evening Julia — they had been singing "Meet me by moonlight alone"[112] — asked him to breakfast with them. "I have," said she, "some commissions, and papa will trust me with you." He breakfasted, and attended the blue-eyed Julia to Swan and Edgar's. "Now I have some conscience!" exclaimed she, with one of her own sweet languid smiles. Julia had an especially charming smile — it so flattered the person to whom it was addressed. It was that sort of smile which it is impossible to help taking as a personal compliment. "I have a little world of shopping to do — bargains to buy — netting silks to choose; and you will never have patience to wait. Leave me here for an hour, and then come back — now be punctual. Let me look at your watch — ah! it is just eleven. Good bye, I shall expect you exactly at twelve."

She turned into the shop with a most becoming blush, so pretty, that Edward had half a mind to have followed her in, and quoted Moore's lines —

> "Oh! let me only breathe the air,
> The blessed air that's breathed by thee;"[113]

but a man has a natural antipathy to shopping, and even the attraction of a blush and a blush especially of that attractive sort, one on your own account — even that was lost in the formidable array of ribands, silks, and bargains —

"Bought because they may be wanted,
Wanted because they may be had."[114]

Accordingly, he lounged into his club, and the hour was almost gone before he arrived at Swan and Edgar's. Julia told him she had waited, and he thought — What a sweet temper she must have not to show the least symptom of dissatisfaction! on the contrary, her blue eyes were even softer than usual. By the time they arrived at her father's door he had also arrived at the agreeable conclusion, that he could do no wrong. They parted hastily, for he had a tiresome business appointment; however, they were to meet in the evening, and a thousand little tender things which he intended to say occupied him till the end of his walk.

When the evening came, and after a toilette of that particular attention which in nine cases out of ten one finds leisure to bestow on oneself, he arrived at Mr. Alford's house. The first object that caught his attention was Laura looking, as the Americans say, "dreadful beautiful." She had on a pink dress direct from Paris, that flung around its own atmosphere *de rose*, and nothing could be more finished than her whole *ensemble*. Not that Edward noted the exquisite perfection of all the feminine and Parisian items which completed her attire, but he was struck by the general effect. He soon found himself, he scarcely knew how, quite devoted to her; and his vanity was flattered, for she was the belle of the evening.

It is amazing how much our admiration takes its tone from the admiration of others; and when to that is added an obvious admiration of ourselves, the charm is irresistible. "Be sure," said Laura, in that low, confidential whisper, which implies that only to one could it be addressed, "if you see me bored by that weariful Sir John Belmore, to come and make me waltz. Really, papa's old friends make me quite undutiful!" There was a smile accompanying the words which seemed to say, that it was not only to avoid Sir John that she desired to dance with himself.

The evening went off most brilliantly; and Edward went home with the full intention of throwing himself at the fascinating Laura's feet the following morning; and, what is much more, he got up with the same resolution. He hurried to Harley-street, and — how propitious the fates are sometimes! — found the *dame de ses pensées*[115] alone. An offer is certainly a desperate act. The cavalier —

> "Longs to speak, and yet shrinks back,
> As from a stream in winter, though the chill
> Be but a moment."[116]

Edward certainly felt as little fear as a gentleman well could do, under the circumstances. He, therefore, lost no time in telling Miss Alford, that his happiness was in her hands. She received the intelligence with a very pretty look of surprise.

"Really," exclaimed she, "I never thought of you but as a friend; and last night I accepted Sir John Belmore! As that is his cabriolet, I must go down to the library to receive him; we should be so interrupted here with morning visiters!"

She disappeared, and at that moment Edward heard Julia's voice singing on the stairs. It was the last duet that they had sang together.

> "Who shall school the heart's affection?
> Who shall banish its regret?
> If you blame my deep dejection,
> Teach, oh, teach me to forget!"[117]

She entered, looking very pretty, but pale. "Ah," thought Edward, "she is vexed that I allowed myself to be so engrossed by her sister last night."

"So you are alone," exclaimed she. "I have such a piece of news to tell you! Laura is going to be married to Sir John Belmore. How can she marry a man she positively despises?"

"It is very heartless," replied Edward, with great emphasis.

"Nay," replied Julia, "but Laura could not live without gaiety. Moreover, she is ambitious. I cannot pretend to judge for her; we never had a taste in common."

"You," said Edward, "would not have so thrown yourself away!"

"Ah! no," answered she, looking down, "the heart is my world."

And Edward thought he had never seen anything so lovely as the deep blue eyes that now looked up full of tears.

> "Ah, too convincing, dangerously dear,
> In woman's eye, th' unanswerable tear."[118]

Whither Edward might have floated on the tears of the "dove-eyed Julia"[119] must remain a question; for at that moment — a most unusual occurrence in a morning — Mr. Alford came into his own drawing-room.

"So, Madam," he exclaimed in a voice almost inarticulate from anger, "I know it all. You were married to Captain Dacre yesterday; and you, Sir," turning to Edward, "made yourself a party to the shameful deception."

"No," interrupted Julia; "Mr. Rainsforth believed me to be in Swan and Edgar's shop the whole time. The fact was, I only passed through it."

Edward stood aghast. So the lady, instead of silks and ribands, was buying, perhaps, the dearest bargain of her life. A few moments convinced him that he was *de trop*; and he left the father storming, and the daughter in hysterics.

On his arrival at his lodgings, he found a letter from his guardians, in which he found the following entered among other items: — "Miss Emily Worthington has been ill, but is now recovering." Edward cared, at this moment, very little about the health or sickness of any woman in the world. Indeed, he rather thought Emily's illness was a judgment upon her. If she had answered his letter, he would have been saved all his recent mortification. He decided on abjuring the flattering and fickle sex for ever, and turned to his desk to look over some accounts to which he was referred by his guardians. While tossing the papers about, half-listless, half-fretful, what should catch his eye but a letter with the seal not broken! He started from his seat in consternation. Why, it was his own epistle to Miss Worthington! No wonder that she had not written; she did not even know his address. All the horrors of his conduct now stared him full in the face. Poor, dear, deserted Emily, what must her feelings have been! — He could not bear to think of them. He snatched up a pen, wrote to his guardians, declaring that the illness of his beloved Emily would, if they did not yield, induce him to take any measure, however desperate; and that he insisted on being allowed permission to visit her. Nothing but his own eyes could satisfy him of her actual recovery. He also wrote to Emily, enclosed the truant letter, and the following day set off for Allerton.

In the meantime what had become of the fair disconsolate? Emily had certainly quite fulfilled her duty of being miserable enough in the first instance. Nothing could be duller than the little village to which was consigned the Ariadne of Allerton. Day after day she roamed — not along the beach, but along the fields towards the post-office, for the letter which, like the breeze in Lord Byron's calm, "came not."[120] A fort-night elapsed, when one morning, as she was crossing the grounds of a fine but deserted place in the neighbourhood, she was so much struck by the beauty of some pink May, that she stopped to gather it; — alas! like most other pleasures, it was out of her reach. Suddenly, a very elegant looking young man emerged from one of the winding paths, and insisted on gathering it for her. The flowers were so beautiful, when gathered, that it was impossible not to say something in their praise, and flowers lead to many other subjects. Emily discovered that she was talking to the proprietor of the place, Lord Elmsley — and, of course, apologised for her intrusion. He equally, of course, declared that his grounds were only too happy in having so fair a guest.

Next they met by chance again, and, at last, the only thing that made Emily relapse into her former languor was — a wet day; for then there was no chance of seeing Lord Elmsley. The weather, however, was, generally speaking, delightful — and they met, and talked about Lord Byron — nay, read him together; — and Lord Elmsley confessed that he had never understood his beauties before. They talked also of the heartlessness of the world; and the delights of solitude in a way that would have charmed Zimmerman.[121] One morning, however, brought Lord Elmsley a letter. It was from his uncle, short and sweet, and ran thus: —

"My dear George,

"Miss Smith's guardians have at last listened to reason — and allow that your rank is fairly worth her gold. Come up, therefore, as soon as you can and preserve your interest with the lady. What a lucky fellow you are to have fine eyes — for they have carried the prize for you! However, as women are inconstant commodities at the best, I advise you to lose no time in securing the heiress.

"Your affectionate uncle,
"E."

"Tell them," said the Earl, "to order post-horses immediately. I must be off to London in the course of half an hour."

During this half hour he dispatched his luncheon, and, — for Lord Elmsley was a perfectly well-bred man, — dispatched the following note to Miss Worthington, whom he was to have met that morning to show her the remains of the heronry: —

"My dear Miss Worthington,

"Hurried as I am I do not forget to return the volume of Lord Byron you so obligingly lent me. How I envy you the power of remaining in the country this delightful season — while I am forced to immure myself in hurried and noisy London. Allow me to offer the best compliments of

"Your devoted servant,
"ELMSLEY."

No wonder that Emily tore the note which she received with smiles and blushes into twenty pieces, and did not get up to breakfast the next day. The next week she had a bad cold, and was seated in a most disconsolate-looking attitude and shawl, when a letter was brought in. It contained the first epistle of Edward's, and the following words in the envelope: —

"My adored Emily,

"You may forgive me — I cannot forgive myself. Only imagine that the inclosed letter has by some strange chance remained in my desk, and I never discovered the error till this morning. You would pardon me if you knew all I have suffered. How I have reproached you! I hope to see you to-morrow, for I cannot rest till I hear from your own lips that you have forgiven

"Your faithful and unhappy

"EDWARD."

That very morning Emily left off her shawl, and discovered that a walk would do her good. The lovers met the next day, each looking a little pale — which each set down to their own account. Emily returned to Allerton, and the town was touched to the very heart by a constancy that had stood such a test.

"Three months' absence," as an old lady observed, "is a terrible trial."[122] The guardians thought so too — and the marriage of Emily Worthington to Edward Rainsforth soon completed the satisfaction of the town of Allerton. During the bridal trip, the young couple were one wet day at an inn looking over a newspaper together, and there they saw — the marriage of Miss Smith with the Earl of Elmsley — and of Miss Alford with Sir John Belmore. I never heard that the readers made either of them any remark as they read. They returned to Allerton, lived very happily, and were always held up as touching instances of first love and constancy — in the 19th century.

THREE EXTRACTS FROM THE DIARY
OF A WEEK.

———

A record of the inward world, whose facts
Are thoughts — and feelings — fears, and hopes, and dreams.
There are some days that might outmeasure years —
Days that obliterate the past, and make
The future of the colour which they cast.
A day may be a destiny; for life
Lives in but little — but that little teems
With some one chance, the balance of all time:
A look — a word — and we are wholly changed.
We marvel at ourselves — we would deny
That which is working in the hidden soul;
But the heart knows and trembles at the truth:
On such these records linger.

———

WE MIGHT HAVE BEEN!

We might have been! — these are but common words,
    And yet they make the sum of life's bewailing;
They are the echo of those finer chords,
    Whose music life deplores when unavailing.
            We might have been!

We might have been so happy! says the child,
    Pent in the weary school-room during summer,
When the green rushes 'mid the marshes wild,
    And rosy fruits attend the radiant comer.   10
            We might have been!

It is the thought that darkens on our youth,
    When first experience — sad experience — teaches

What fallacies we have believed for truth,
   And what few truths endeavour ever reaches.
      We might have been!

Alas! how different from what we are
   Had we but known the bitter path before us;
But feelings, hopes, and fancies left afar,
   What in the wide bleak world can e'er restore us?
20   We might have been!

It is the motto of all human things,
   The end of all that waits on mortal seeking;
The weary weight upon Hope's flagging wings,
   It is the cry of the worn heart while breaking.
      We might have been!

And when warm with the heaven that gave it birth
   Dawns on our world-worn way Love's hour Elysian;
The last fair angel lingering on our earth;
   The shadow of what thought obscures the vision.
30   We might have been!

A cold fatality attends on love,
   Too soon or else too late the heart-beat quickens;
The star which is our fate springs up above,
   And we but say — while round the vapour thickens —
      We might have been!

Life knoweth no like misery, — the rest
   Are single sorrows, — but in this are blended
All sweet emotions that disturb the breast;
   The light that was our loveliest is ended.
40   We might have been.

Henceforth how much of the full heart must be
   A seal'd book at whose contents we tremble?
A still voice mutters 'mid our misery

The worst to hear — because it must dissemble —
    We might have been.

Life is made up of miserable hours,
    And all of which we craved a brief possessing,
For which we wasted wishes, hopes, and powers,
    Comes with some fatal drawback on the blessing.
    We might have been.   50

The future never renders to the past
    The young belief 's intrusted to its keeping;
Inscribe one sentence — life's first truth and last —
    On the pale marble where our dust is sleeping —
    We might have been.

NECESSITY.

In the ancestral presence of the dead
Sits a lone power — a veil upon the head,
Stern with the terror of an unseen dread.

It sitteth cold, immutable, and still,
Girt with eternal consciousness of ill,
And strong and silent as its own dark will.

We are the victims of its iron rule,
The warm and beating human heart its tool;
And man immortal-godlike but its fool.

We know not of its presence, though its power   10
Be on the gradual round of every hour,
Now flinging down an empire, now a flower.

And all things small and careless are its own,
Unwittingly the seed minute is sown, —
The tree of evil out of it is grown.

At times we see and struggle with our chain,
And dream that somewhat we are freed, in vain;
The mighty fetters close on us again.

We mock our actual strength with lofty thought,
And towers that look into the heavens are wrought, —
But after all our toil the task is nought.

Down comes the stately fabric, and the sands
Are scatter'd with the work of myriad hands,
High o'er whose pride the fragile wild flower stands.

Such are the wrecks of nations and of kings,
Far in the desert, where the palm-tree springs,
'Tis the same story in all meaner things.

The heart builds up its hopes, though not addrest
To meet the sunset glories of the west,
But garnered in some still, sweet singing nest.

But the dark power is on its noiseless way,
The song is silent so sweet yesterday,
And not a green leaf lingers on the spray.

We mock ourselves with freedom and with hope
The while our feet glide down life's faithless slope,
And the one has no strength, the other has no scope.

Toys we are flung on Time's tumultuous wave,
Forced there to struggle, but denied to save,
Till the stern tide ebbs — and there is the grave.

MEMORY.

I do not say bequeath unto my soul
   Thy memory, — I rather ask forgetting;
Withdraw, I pray, from me thy strong control,
   Leave something in the wide world worth regretting.

I need my thoughts for other things than thee,
   I dare not let thine image fill them only;
The hurried happiness it wakes in me
   Will leave the hours that are to come more lonely.

I live not like the many of my kind,
   Mine is a world of feelings and of fancies,   10
Fancies whose rainbow empire is the mind,
   Feelings that realize their own romances.

To dream and to create has been my fate,
   Alone, apart from life's more busy scheming;
I fear to think that I may find too late
   Vain was the toil, and idle was the dreaming.

Have I uprear'd my glorious pyre of thought
   Up to the heavens but for my own entombing?
The fair and fragrant thing that years have brought
   Must they be gathered for my own consuming?   20

Oh! give me back the past that took no part
   In the existence it was but surveying;
That knew not then of the awaken'd heart
   Amid the life of other lives delaying.

Why should such be mine own? I sought it not:
   More than content to live apart and lonely,
The feverish tumult of a loving lot,
   Is what I wish'd and thought to picture only.

Surely the spirit is its own free will;
30   What should o'ermaster mine to vain complying
With hopes that call down what they bring of ill,
      With fears to their own questioning replying?

In vain, in vain! Fate is above us all;
      We struggle, but what matters our endeavour?
Our doom is gone beyond our own recall,
      May we deny or mitigate it — never!

And what art thou to me, — thou who dost wake
      The mind's still depths with trouble and repining?
Nothing; — though all things now thy likeness take;
40   Nothing, — and life has nothing worth resigning.

Ah, yes! one thing thy memory — though grief
      Watching the expiring beam of hope's last ember,
Life had one hour, — bright, beautiful, and brief,
      And now its only task is to remember.

◅

THE POLAR STAR. [123]

This star sinks below the horizon in certain latitudes. I watched it sink lower and
lower every night, till at last it disappeared.

A STAR has left the kindling sky —
   A lovely northern light —
How many planets are on high,
   But that has left the night.

I miss its bright familiar face,
   It was a friend to me,
Associate with my native place,
   And those beyond the sea.

It rose upon our English sky,
   Shone o'er our English land,   10
And brought back many a loving eye,
   And many a gentle hand,

It seemed to answer to my thought,
   It called the past to mind,
And with its welcome presence brought
   All I had left behind.

The voyage it lights no longer, ends
   Soon on a foreign shore;
How can I but recall the friends,
   Who I may see no more?   20

Fresh from the pain it was to part —
   How could I bear the pain?
Yet strong the omen in my heart
   That says — We meet again.

Meet with a deeper, dearer love,
   For absence shows the worth

Of all from which we then remove,
　　Friends, home, and native earth.

Thou lovely polar star, mine eyes
　　Still turned the first on thee,
Till I have felt a sad surprise
　　That none looked up with me.

But thou hast sunk below the wave,
　　Thy radiant place unknown;
I seem to stand beside a grave,
　　And stand by it alone.

Farewell! — ah, would to me were given
　　A power upon thy light,
What words upon our English heaven
　　Thy loving rays should write!

Kind messages of love and hope
　　Upon thy rays should be;
Thy shining orbit would have scope
　　Scarcely enough for me.

Oh, fancy vain as it is fond,
　　And little needed too,
My friends! I need not look beyond
　　My heart to look for you!

NIGHT AT SEA. [123]

THE lovely purple of the noon's bestowing
  Has vanished from the waters, where it flung
A royal colour, such as gems are throwing
  Tyrian or regal garniture among.
'Tis night, and overhead the sky is gleaming,
  Thro' the slight vapour trembles each dim star;
I turn away — my heart is sadly dreaming
  Of scenes they do not light, of scenes afar.
      My friends, my absent friends!
          Do you think of me, as I think of you?   10

By each dark wave around the vessel sweeping,
  Farther am I from old dear friends removed,
Till the lone vigil that I now am keeping,
  I did not know how much you were beloved.
How many acts of kindness little heeded,
  Kind looks, kind words, rise half reproachful now!
Hurried and anxious, my vexed life has speeded,
  And memory wears a soft accusing brow.
      My friends, my absent friends!
          Do you think of me, as I think of you?   20

The very stars are strangers, as I catch them
  Athwart the shadowy sails that swell above;
I cannot hope that other eyes will watch them
  At the same moment with a mutual love.
They shine not there, as here they now are shining,
  The very hours are changed. — Ah, do ye sleep?
O'er each home pillow, midnight is declining,
  May some kind dream at least my image keep!
      My friends, my absent friends!
          Do you think of me, as I think of you?   30

Yesterday has a charm, to-day could never
  Fling o'er the mind, which knows not till it parts

How it turns back with tenderest endeavour
    To fix the past within the heart of hearts.
Absence is full of memory, it teaches
    The value of all old familiar things;
The strengthener of affection, while it reaches
    O'er the dark parting, with an angel's wings.
        My friends, my absent friends!
40   Do you think of me, as I think of you?

The world with one vast element omitted —
    Man's own especial element, the earth,
Yet, o'er the waters is his rule transmitted
    By that great knowledge whence has power its birth.
How oft on some strange loveliness while gazing
    Have I wished for you, — beautiful as new,
The purple waves like some wild army raising
    Their snowy banners as the ship cuts thro'.
        My friends, my absent friends!
50   Do you think of me, as I think of you?

Bearing upon its wing the hues of morning,
    Up springs the flying fish, like life's false joy,
Which of the sunshine asks that frail adorning
    Whose very light is fated to destroy.
Ah, so doth genius on its rainbow pinion,
    Spring from the depths of an unkindly world;
So spring sweet fancies from the heart's dominion, —
    Too soon in death the scorched up wing is furled.
        My friends, my absent friends!
60   Whate'er I see is linked with thoughts of you.

No life is in the air, but in the waters
    Are creatures, huge and terrible and strong,
The sword-fish and the shark pursue their slaughters,
    War universal reigns these depths along.
Like some new island on the ocean springing,
    Floats on the surface some gigantic whale,

From its vast head a silver fountain flinging
   Bright as the fountain in a fairy tale.
      My friends, my absent friends!
           I read such fairy legends while with you.   70

Light is amid the gloomy canvass spreading,
   The moon is whitening the dusky sails,
From the thick bank of clouds she masters, shedding
   The softest influence that o'er night prevails.
Pale is she like a young queen pale with splendour,
   Haunted with passionate thoughts too fond, too deep,
The very glory that she wears is tender,
   The eyes that watch her beauty fain would weep.
      My friends, my absent friends!
           Do you think of me, as I think of you?   80

Sunshine is ever cheerful, when the morning
   Wakens the world with cloud-dispelling eyes;
The spirits mount to glad endeavour, scorning
   What toil upon a path so sunny lies.
Sunshine and hope are comrades, and their weather
   Calls into life the energies of earth;
But memory and moonlight go together,
   Reflected in the light that either brings.
      My friends, my absent friends!
           Do you think of me then? I think of you.   90

The busy deck is hushed, no sounds are waking
   But the watch pacing silently and slow;
The waves against the sides incessant breaking,
   And rope and canvass swaying to and fro.
The topmast sail seems some dim pinacle
   Cresting a shadowy tower amid the air;
While red and fitful gleams come from the binacle,
   The only light on board to guide us — where?
      My friends, my absent friends!
           Far from my native land, and far from you.   100

On one side of the ship the moonbeams shimmer
   In luminous vibration sweeps the sea,
But where the shadow falls, a strange pale glimmer
   Seems glow-worm like amid the waves to be.
All that the spirit keeps of thought and feeling,
   Takes visionary hues from such an hour;
But while some fantasy is o'er me stealing,
   I start, remembrance has a keener power.
     My friends, my absent friends,

        From the fair dream I start to think of you!

A dusk line in the moonlight I discover,
   What all day long vainly I sought to catch;
Or is it but the varying clouds that hover
   Thick in the air, to mock the eyes that watch?
No! well the sailor knows each speck appearing,
   Upon the tossing waves, the far-off strand
To that dusk line our eager ship is steering.
   Her voyage done — to-morrow we shall land.

August 15.

FROM *FISHER'S DRAWING ROOM SCRAP BOOK*[124]

SKELETON GROUP IN THE RAMESWUR, CAVES OF ELLORA.[125]

SUPPOSED TO REPRESENT THE NUPTIALS OF SIVA AND PARVATI.

HE comes from Kilas,[126] earth and sky,
Bright before the deity;
The sun shines, as he shone when first
His glory over ocean burst.
The vales put forth a thousand flowers,
Mingling the spring and summer hours;
The Suras* fill with songs the air,
The Genii and their lutes are there;
By gladness stirred, the mighty sea
Flings up its waves rejoicingly;   10
And Music wanders o'er its tide,
For Siva comes to meet his bride.

THE above lines are a paraphrase of a translation from the Siva-Pooraun. It goes on to mention, besides the signs of rejoicing I have enumerated, that "The dwellers upon earth stocked the casket of their ideas with the jewels of delight;" also, that "the eyes of the devotees flamed like torches," and that "Siva set off like a garden in full blow." Among the guests who attended his wedding were "Brahma, who came on his goose" — "the Kerokee and other serpents all drest in

---

* Good spirits.

Skeleton Group in the Rameswur, Caves of Ellora

habits of ceremony." Query, What habits of ceremony did the serpents wear? Vide Maurice. Captain Sykes[127] mentions, that one of the compartments represents Siva and Parvati playing at dice, her attitude expressing "unsuccess or denial." May not this allude to their celebrated quarrel, so often mentioned by Hindoo writers. The tale is as follows. Siva and Parvati parted, owing to a quarrel at dice. They severally performed rigid acts of devotion; but the fires they kindled blazed so vehemently as to threaten a general conflagration. The other deities in great alarm supplicated him to recall his consort, but the angry god answered, that she must come of her own free choice. The river goddess prevailed on Parvati to return, on condition that his love for her was restored. Camdeo, the Indian Cupid, then wounded Siva with one of his arrows, and, for his pains, was reduced to ashes by a flash from Siva's eye. The shaft, however, had lost none of its honied craft. Parvati, as the daughter of a mountaineer, appeared before her immediately enamoured husband; her conquest once secured, she assumed her natural form. Siva, in the joy of reconciliation, decreed, that Camdeo should be known again as the son of Crishna. *Asiatic Researches.*

A LEGEND OF TINTAGEL CASTLE. [128]

ALONE in the forest, Sir Lancelot rode,
O'er the neck of his courser the reins lightly flowed,
And beside hung his helmet, for bare was his brow
To meet the soft breeze that was fanning him now.

And "the flowers of the forest"[129] were many and sweet,
Which, crushed at each step by his proud courser's feet,
Gave forth all their fragrance, while thick over-head
The boughs of the oak and the elm-tree were spread.

The wind stirred the branches, as if its low suit
Were urged, like a lover who wakens the lute,   10
And through the dark foliage came sparkling and bright,
Like rain from the green leaves, in small gems of light.

There was stillness, not silence, for dancing along,
A brook went its way like a child with a song:
Now hidden, where rushes and water-flags grow;
Now clear, while white pebbles were glistening below.

Lo, bright as a vision, and fair as a dream,
The face of a maiden is seen in the stream;
With her hair like a mantle of gold to her knee,
Stands a lady as lovely as lady can be.   20

Short speech tells a love-tale; — the bard's sweetest words
Are poor, beside those which each memory hoards: *expanded*
Sound of some gentle whisper, the haunting and low,
Such as love may have murmured — ah, long, long ago.

She led him away to an odorous cave,
Where the emerald spars shone like stars in the wave,
And the green moss and violets crowded beneath,
And the ash at the entrance hung down like a wreath.

They might have been happy, if love could but learn
30   A lesson from some flowers, and like their leaves turn
Round their own inward world, their own lone fragrant nest,
Content with its sweetness, content with its rest.

But the sound of the trumpet was heard from afar,
And Sir Lancelot rode forth again to the war;
And the wood-nymph was left as aye woman will be,
Who trusts her whole being, oh, false love, to thee.

For months, every sun-beam that brightened the gloom,
She deemed was the waving of Lancelot's plume;
She knew not of the proud and the beautiful queen,
40   Whose image was treasured as her's once had been.

There was many a fair dame, and many a knight,
Made the banks of the river like fairy-land bright;
And among those whose shadow was cast on the tide,
Was Lancelot kneeling near Genevra's side.

With purple sails heavily drooping around,
The mast, and the prow, with the vale lily bound;
And towed by two swans, a small vessel drew near
But high on the deck was a pall-covered bier.

They oared with their white wings, the bark thro' the flood,
50   Till arrived at the bank where Sir Lancelot stood:
A wind swept the river, and flung back the pall,
And there lay a lady, the fairest of all.

But pale as a statue, like sunshine on snow,
The bright hair seemed mocking the cold face below:
Sweet truants, the blush and the smile both are fled —
Sir Lancelot weeps as he kneels by the dead.

And these are love's records; a vow and a dream,
And the sweet shadow passes away from life's stream:
Too late we awake to regret — but what tears
Can bring back the waste to our hearts and our years!   60

❧

LINMOUTH. [130]

O h lone and lovely solitude,
    Washed by the sounding sea!
Nature was in a poet's mood,
    When she created thee.

Created by nature

How pleasant in the hour of noon
    To wander through the shade;
The soft and golden shade which June
    Flings o'er thy inland glade:

The wild rose like a wreath above,
    The ash-tree's fairy keys,   10
The aspen trembling, as if love
    Were whispered by the breeze;

These, or the beech's darker bough,
    For canopy o'er head,
While moss and fragile flowers below
    An elfin pillow spread.

Here one might dream the hours away,
    As if the world had not
Or grief, or care, or disarray,
    To darken human lot.   20

Yet 'tis not here that I would dwell,
   Tho' fair the place may be,
The summer's favourite citadel: —
   A busier scene for me!

[handwritten annotation: not in Solitude, but earlier attributes to poets]

I love to see the human face
   Reflect the human mind,
To watch in every crowded place
   Their opposites combined.

There's more for thought in one brief hour
30   In yonder busy street,
Than all that ever leaf or flower
   Taught in their green retreat.

Industry, intellect, and skill
   Appear in all their pride,
The glorious force of human will
   Triumphs on every side.

Yet touched with meekness, for on all
   Is set the sign and seal
Of sorrow, suffering, and thrall,
40   Which none but own and feel:

The hearse that passes with its dead,
   The homeless beggar's prayer,
Speak words of warning, and of dread,
   To every passer there.

Aye beautiful the dreaming brought
   By valleys and green fields;
But deeper feeling, higher thought,
   Is what the city yields.

POPE's hackneyed line[131] of "An honest man's the noblest work of God," has a
companion in Cowper's "God made the country, but man made the town;"[132]

both are the perfection of copy-book cant. I am far from intending to deprecate that respectable individual, "an honest man," but surely genius, intellectual goodness and greatness, are far nobler emanations of the Divine Spirit than mere honesty. This is just another branch of that melodramatic morality which talks of rural felicity, and unsophisticated pleasures. Has a wife been too extravagant, or a husband too gay, all is settled by their agreeing to reform, and live in the country. Is a young lady to be a pattern person; forsooth, she must have been brought up in the country. Your philosophers inculcate it, your poets rave about it, your every-day people look upon it as something between a pleasure and a duty — till poor London has its merits as little understood as any popular question which every body discusses. I do own I have a most affectionate attachment for London — the deep voice of her multitudes "haunts me like a passion."[133] I delight in observing the infinite variety of her crowded streets, the rich merchandise of the shops, the vast buildings, whether raised for pomp, commerce, or charity, down to the barrel-organ, whose music is only common because it is beautiful. The country is no more left as it was originally created, than Belgrave Square[134] remains its pristine swamp. The forest has been felled, the marsh drained, the enclosures planted, and the field ploughed. All these, begging Mr. Cowper's pardon, are the works of man's hands; and so is the town — the one is not more artificial than the other. Both are the result of God's good gifts — industry and intelligence exerted to the utmost. Let any one ride down Highgate Hill[135] on a summer's day, see the immense mass of buildings spread like a dark panorama, hear the ceaseless and peculiar sound, which has been likened to the hollow roar of the ocean, but has an utterly differing tone; watch the dense cloud that hangs over all — one perpetual storm, which yet bursts not — and then say, if ever was witnessed hill or valley that so powerfully impressed the imagination with that sublime and awful feeling which is the epic of poetry.

HEBE. [136]

YOUTH! thou art a lovely time,
  With thy wild and dreaming eyes;
Looking onwards to their prime,
  Coloured by their April skies.
Yet I do not wish for thee,
Pass, oh! quickly pass from me.

Thou hast all too much unrest,
  Haunted by vain hopes and fears;
Though thy cheek with smiles be drest,
10   Yet that cheek is wet with tears.
Bitter are the frequent showers,
Falling in thy sunny hours.

Let my heart grow calm and cold,
  Calm to sorrow, cold to love;
Let affections loose their hold,
  Let my spirit look above.
I am weary — youth, pass on,
All thy dearest gifts are gone.

She in whose sweet form the Greek
20   Bade his loveliest vision dwell;
She of yon bright cup and cheek,
  From her native heaven fell:
Type of what may never last,
Soon the heaven of youth is past.

Oh! farewell — for never more
  Can thy dreams again be mine;
Hope and truth and faith are o'er,
  And the heart which was their shrine
Has no boon of thee to seek,
30   Asking but to rest or break.

THE plate represents a temple to Mahadeo, surrounded by inferior shrines. The Hindoos usually place some religious building at the confluence of two streams: and when the accompanying view was taken, there were some cultivated gardens, and groves of beautiful trees. Still, I believe, few Indian residents but will admit the truth of the feeling which the following lines endeavour to express.

> IT is Christmas, and the sunshine
>   Lies golden on the fields,
> And flowers of white and purple,
>   Yonder fragrant creeper yields.
>
> Like the plumes of some bold warrior,
>   The cocoa tree on high,
> Lifts aloft its feathery branches,
>   Amid the deep blue sky.
>
> From yonder shadowy peepul, [138]
>   The pale fair lilac dove,   10
> Like music from a temple,
>   Sings a song of grief and love.
>
> The earth is bright with blossoms,
>   And a thousand jewelled wings,
> Mid the green boughs of the tamarind
>   A sudden sunshine flings.
>
> For the East, is earth's first-born,
>   And hath a glorious dower,
> As Nature there had lavished
>   Her beauty and her power.   20
>
> And yet I pine for England,
>   For my own — my distant home;

My heart is in that island,
　　Where'er my steps may roam.

It is merry there at Christmas —
　　We have no Christmas here;
'Tis a weary thing, a summer
　　That lasts throughout the year.

I remember how the banners
　　Hung round our ancient hall,
Bound with wreaths of shining holly,
　　Brave winter's coronal.

And above each rusty helmet
　　Waved a new and cheering plume,
A branch of crimson berries,
　　And the latest rose in bloom.

And the white and pearly misletoe
　　Hung half concealed o'er head,
I remember one sweet maiden,
　　Whose cheek it dyed with red.

The morning waked with carols,*
　　A young and joyous band
Of small and rosy songsters,
　　Came tripping hand in hand.

---

* This is one of those pretty customs that yet remain at a due distance from London
— London, that Thalaba[139] of all observances. I remember once being awakened
by a band of children coming up the old beech avenue, singing carols with all
their heart. The tune was monotonous enough, and as to time, I will say nothing
on the subject. Still the multitude of infant voices, and the open air, and the dis-
tance, gave a singularly wild and sweet effect to the chant of the childish company.
The words, which I subjoin, had a practical tendency.

　　　　"Ivy, holly, and misletoe,
　　　　Give me a penny, and let me go."

And sang beneath our windows,
　Just as the round red sun
Began to melt the hoar-frost,
　And the clear cold day begun.

And at night the aged harper
　Played his old tunes o'er and o'er;　　　　　50
From sixteen up to sixty,
　All were dancing on that floor.

Those were the days of childhood,
　The buoyant and the bright;
When hope was life's sweet sovereign,
　And the heart and step were light.

I shall come again — a stranger
　To all that once I knew,
For the hurried steps of manhood
　From life's flowers have dash'd the dew.　　60

I yet may ask their welcome,
　And return from whence I came;
But a change is wrought within me,
　They will not seem the same.

For my spirits are grown weary,
　And my days of youth are o'er,
And the mirth of that glad season
　Is what I can feel no more.

"THE Engraving represents a splendid sculptured Portico of a Temple dedicated to Mahadeo, at Moondheyra in Guzerat. This elaborate and magnificent specimen of the best age of Hindoo architecture, has been in ruins since the invasion of Alla o Deen, surnamed Khoonee, or the Bloody. Tradition inscribes to his intolerant spirit the destruction both of this noble edifice and numerous other religious buildings in Guzerat. This temple is so gigantic that the natives ascribe its erection to a deity, and say, that it was built by Ram some thirty lacks of years ago. The most unpretending insist on an antiquity of five thousand years."

HISTORY hath but few pages — soon is told
    Man's ordinary life,
    Labour, and care, and strife
Make up the constant chronicle of old.

First comes a dream — the infancy of earth,
    When all its untried powers
    Are on the conscious hours
Warm with the light that called them into birth.

'Tis but a dream — for over earth was said
    An early curse — time's flood
    Rolls on in tears and blood;
Blood that upon her virgin soil was shed.

Abel the victim — Cain the homicide,
    Were type and prophecy
    Of times that were to be,
Thus reddened from the first life's troubled tide.

See where in great decay yon temple stands,
    Destruction has began
    Her mockery of man,
Bowing to dust the work of mortal hands.

What are its annals — such as suit all time
     Man's brief and bitter breath,
     Hurrying unwelcome death,
And something too that marks the East's bright clime.

For mighty is the birthplace of the sun,
     All has a vaster scale
     Than climes more cold and pale,
Where yet creation's work is half begun.

Her conquests were by multitudes, — the kings
     Who warred on each vast plain,   30
     Looked on a people slain,
As amid conquest's customary things.

Her wealth — our gold is one poor miser's store,
     Her pomp was as the night,
     With glittering myriads bright,
Her palace floors with gems were covered o'er.

Her summer's prodigality of hues,
     Trees like eternal shrines,
     Where the rich creeper twines,
And all lit up with morn's most golden dews.   40

'Tis a past age — the conqueror's banner furled,
     Droops o'er the falling tower;
     Yet was the East's first hour
The great ideal of the material world.

The beautiful — the fertile and the great,
     The terrible — and wild,
     Were round the first-born child
Of the young hour of earth's imperial state.

And yet the mind's high tones were wanting there,
     The carved and broken stone   50

Tells glories overthrown;
Religions, empires, palaces are — where?

Such annals have the tempest's fire and gloom;
   They tell of desperate power,
   Famine and battle's hour,
War, want, disorder, slavery, and the tomb.

Not such the history that half redeems
   The meanness of our clay;
   That intellectual sway
60   Which works the excellence of which it dreams.

Fall, fall, ye mighty temples to the ground;
   Not in your sculptured rise
   Is the real exercise
Of human nature's highest power found.

'Tis in the lofty hope, the daily toil,
   'Tis in the gifted line,
   In each far thought divine,
That brings down heaven to light our common soil.

'Tis in the great, the lovely, and the true,
70   'Tis in the generous thought,
   Of all that man has wrought,
Of all that yet remains for man to do.

"THE north-western portion of Guzerat is inhabited by a warlike and robber race; hence travellers need an escort. This is sometimes given by the native chieftains. More frequently the merchant hires a guard. The annexed plate represents the halt of such a party. The shelter afforded by the ruined temples and tombs, occasion such resting places to be usually made in their vicinity."

I HAVE a steed, to leave behind
The wild bird, and the wilder wind:
I have a sword, which does not know
How to waste a second blow:
I have a matchlock, whose red breath
Bears the lightning's sudden death:
I have a foot of fiery flight,
I have an eye that cleaves the night.
I win my portion in the land
By my high heart and strong right hand.   10

The starry heavens lit up the gloom
That lay around Al Herid's tomb;
The wind was still, you might have heard
The falling leaf, the rustling bird;
Yet no one heard my footstep fall,
None saw my shadow on the wall:
Yet curses came with morning's light,
Where was the gold they hid at night?
Where was the gold they loved so well,
My heavy girdle best could tell?   20

Three travellers crost by yonder shrine;
I saw their polished pistols shine,
And swore they were, or should be mine.
The first, his head was at my feet;
The second I was glad to greet;
He met me like a man, his sword,

Damascus true, deserved its lord;
Yet soon his heart's best blood ran red:
I sought the third — the slave had fled.

30   I have a lovely mountain bower,
Where blooms a gentle Georgian flower;
She was my spear's accustomed prize,
The antelope hath not such eyes.
Now my sweet captive loves her lot.
What has a queen that she has not?
Let her but wish for shawls or pearls,
To bind her brow, to braid her curls;
And I from east to west would fly,
Ere she should ask and I deny.
40   But those rich merchants must be near,
Away, I cannot linger here;
The vulture hovers o'er his prey,
Come, my good steed — away! — away!

THE FAIRY OF THE FOUNTAINS. [142]

THE Legend, on which this story is founded, is immediately taken from Mr. Thoms's most interesting collection. I have allowed myself some licence, in my arrangement of the story: but fairy tales have an old-established privilege of change; at least, if we judge by the various shapes which they assume in the progress of time, and by process of translation.

WHY did she love her mother's so?
It hath wrought her wondrous wo.

Once she saw an armed knight
In the pale sepulchral night;
When the sullen starbeams throw
Evil spells on earth below;
And the moon is cold and pale,
And a voice is on the gale,
Like a lost soul's heavenward cry,
Hopeless in its agony.

He stood beside the castle gate,
The hour was dark, the hour was late;
With the bearing of a king
Did he at the portal ring,
And the loud and hollow bell
Sounded like a Christian's knell.
That pale child stood on the wall,
Watching there, and saw it all.
Then she was a child as fair
As the opening blossoms are:
But with large black eyes, whose light
Spoke of mystery and might.

The stately stranger's head was bound
With a bright and golden round;
Curiously inlaid, each scale
Shone upon his glittering mail;

20

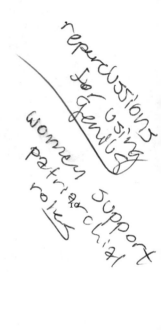

His high brow was cold and dim,
And she felt she hated him.
Then she heard her mother's voice,
Saying, "'Tis not at my choice!
Wo for ever, wo the hour,
When you sought my secret bower,
Listening to the word of fear,
Never meant for human ear.

Thy suspicion's vain endeavour,
Wo! wo! parted us for ever."

Still the porter of the hall
Heeded not that crown'd knight's call.
When a glittering shape there came,
With a brow of starry flame;
And he led that knight again
O'er the bleak and barren plain.
He flung, with an appealing cry,
His dark and desperate arms on high;
And from Melusina's sight
Fled away through thickest night.
Who has not, when but a child,
Treasured up some vision wild;
Haunting them with nameless fear,
Filling all they see or hear,
In the midnight's lonely hour,
With a strange mysterious power?
So a terror undefined
Entered in that infant mind; —
A fear that haunted her alone,
For she told her thought to none.

Years passed on, and each one threw
O'er those walls a deeper hue;
Large and old the ivy leaves
Heavy hung around the eaves,

Till the darksome rooms within
Daylight never entered in.
And the spider's silvery line
Was the only thing to shine.
　　Years past on, — the fair child now
Wore maiden beauty on her brow —
Beauty such as rarely flowers
In a fallen world like ours.
She was tall; — a queen might wear
Such a proud imperial air;   70
She was tall, yet when unbound,
Swept her bright hair to the ground,
Glittering like the gold you see
On a young laburnum tree.
Yet her eyes were dark as night,
Melancholy as moonlight,
With the fierce and wilder ray
Of a meteor on its way.
Lonely was her childhood's time,
Lonelier was her maiden prime;   80
And she wearied of the hours
Wasted in those gloomy towers;
Sometimes through the sunny sky
She would watch the swallows fly,
Making of the air a bath,
　　In a thousand joyous rings;
She would ask of them their path,
　　She would ask of them their wings.
Once her stately mother came,
With her dark eye's funeral flame,   90
And her cheek as pale as death,
And her cold and whispering breath;
With her sable garments bound
By a mystic girdle round,
Which, when to the east she turned,
With a sudden lustre burned.
Once that ladye, dark and tall,

Black eyes golden hair [handwritten marginal note]

Stood upon the castle wall;
And she marked her daughter's eyes
Fix'd upon the glad sunrise,
With a sad yet eager look,
Such as fixes on a book
Which describes some happy lot,
Lit with joys that we have not.
And the thought of what has been,
    And the thought of what might be,
Makes us crave the fancied scene,
    And despise reality.
'Twas a drear and desert plain
Lay around their own domain;
But, far off, a world more fair
Outlined on the sunny air;
Hung amid the purple clouds,
With which early morning shrouds
All her blushes, brief and bright,
Waking up from sleep and night.
    In a voice so low and dread,
As a voice that wakes the dead;
Then that stately lady said:
"Daughter of a kingly line, —
Daughter, too, of race like mine, —
Such a kingdom had been thine;
For thy father was a king,
Whom I wed with word and ring.
But in an unhappy hour,
Did he pass my secret bower, —
Did he listen to the word,
Mortal ear hath never heard;
From that hour of grief and pain
Might we never meet again.
    "Maiden, listen to my rede,
Punished for thy father's deed;
Here, an exile, I must stay,

While he sees the light of day.
Child, his race is mixed in thee,
With mine own more high degree.
Hadst thou at Christ's altar stood,
Bathed in His redeeming flood;
Thou of my wild race had known
But its loveliness alone.   140
Now thou hast a mingled dower,
Human passion — fairy power.
But forefend thee from the last:
Be its gifts behind thee cast.
Many tears will wash away
Mortal sin from mortal clay.
Keep thou then a timid eye
On the hopes that fill yon sky;
Bend thou with a suppliant knee,
And thy soul yet saved may be; —   150
Saved by Him who died to save
Man from death beyond the grave."

Easy 'tis advice to give,
    Hard it is advice to take.
Years that lived — and years to live,
    Wide and weary difference make.
To that elder ladye's mood,
Suited silent solitude:
For her lorn heart's wasted soil
Now repaid not hope's sweet toil.   160
Never more could spring-flowers grow,
On the worn-out soil below;
But to the young Melusine,
Earth and heaven were yet divine.
Still illusion's purple light
    Was upon the morning tide,
And there rose before her sight
    The loveliness of life untried.
Three sweet genii, — Youth, Love, Hope, —
Drew her future horoscope.

Must such lights themselves consume?
Must she be her own dark tomb?
But far other thoughts than these —
Life's enchanted phantasies,
Were, with Melusina now,
Stern and dark, contracts her brow;
And her bitten lip is white,
As with passionate resolve.
Muttered she, — "It is my right;
180   On me let the task devolve:
Since such blood to me belongs;
It shall seek its own bright sphere;
I will well avenge the wrongs
Of my mother exiled here."

★   ★   ★   ★   ★   ★   ★   ★

Two long years are come and past,
And the maiden's lot is cast; —
Cast in mystery and power,
Work'd out by the watching hour,
By the word that spirits tell,
190   By the sign and by the spell.
Two long years have come and gone,
And the maiden dwells alone.
For the deed which she hath done,
Is she now a banished one; —
Banished from her mother's arms,
Banished by her mother's charms,
With a curse of grief and pain,
Never more to meet again.
Great was the revenge she wrought,
200   Dearly that revenge was bought.

When the maiden felt her powers,
Straight she sought her father's towers.
With a sign, and with a word,

Passed she on unseen, unheard.
One, a pallid minstrel born
On Good Friday's mystic morn,
Said he saw a lady there,
Tall and stately, strange and fair,
With a stern and glittering eye,
Like a shadow gliding by.   210
All was fear and awe next day,
For the king had passed away.
He had pledged his court at night,
In the red grape's flowing light.
All his pages saw him sleeping;
Next day there was wail and weeping.
Halls and lands were wandered o'er,
But they saw their king no more.
　　Strange it is, and sad to tell,
What the royal knight befell.   220
Far upon a desert land,
Does a mighty mountain stand;
On its summit there is snow,
While the bleak pines moan below;
And within there is a cave
Opened for a monarch's grave.
Bound in an enchanted sleep
She hath laid him still and deep.
She, his only child, has made
That strange tomb where he is laid: 230
Nothing more of earth to know,
Till the final trumpet blow.
Mortal lip nor mortal ear,
Were not made to speak nor hear
That accursed word which sealed, —
All those gloomy depths concealed.
　　With a look of joy and pride,
Then she sought her mother's side.
Whispering, on her bended knee,
"Oh! my mother, joyous be;   240

For the mountain torrents spring
O'er that faithless knight and king."
Not another word she spoke,
For her speech a wild shriek broke;
For the widowed queen upsprung,
Wild her pale thin hands she wrung.
With her black hair falling round,
Flung her desperate on the ground;
While young Melusine stood by,
250   With a fixed and fearful eye.

　　When her agony was past,
Slowly rose the queen at last;
With her black hair, like a shroud,
And her bearing high and proud;
With the marble of her brow,
Colder than its custom now;
And her eye with a strange light,
Seemed to blast her daughter's sight.
And she felt her whole frame shrink,
260   And her young heart's pulses sink;
And the colour left her mouth,
　　As she saw her mother signing,
One stern hand towards the south,
　　Where a strange red star was shining.
With a muttered word and gaze,
Fixed upon its vivid rays;
Then she spoke, but in a tone,
Her's, yet all alike her own. —
"Spirit of our spirit-line,
270   Curse for me this child of mine.
Six days yield not to our powers,
But the seventh day is ours.
By yon star, and by our line,
Be thou cursed, maiden mine."
Then the maiden felt hot pain
Run through every burning vein.
Sudden, with a fearful cry,

Writhes she in her agony;
Burns her cheek as with a flame,
For the maiden knows her shame.   280

By a lovely river's side,
Where the water-lilies glide,
Pale, as if with constant care
Of the treasures which they bear;
For those ivory vases hold
Each a sunny gift of gold.
And blue flowers on the banks,
Grow in wild and drooping ranks,
Bending mournfully above,
O'er the waters which they love;   290
But which bear off, day by day,
Their shadow and themselves away.
Willows by that river grow
With their leaves half green, half snow,
Summer never seems to be
Present all with that sad tree.
With its bending boughs are wrought
Tender and associate thought,
Of the wreaths that maidens wear
In their long-neglected hair.   300
Of the branches that are thrown
On the last, the funeral stone.
And of those torn wreaths that suit
Youthful minstrel's wasted lute.
    But the stream is gay to-night
With the full-moon's golden light,
And the air is sweet with singing,
And the joyous horn is ringing,
While fair groups of dancers round
Circle the enchanted ground.   310
And a youthful warrior stands

Gazing not upon those bands,
Not upon the lovely scene,
But upon its lovelier queen,
Who with gentle word and smile
Courteous prays his stay awhile.
    The fairy of the fountains, she
A strange and lovely mystery,
320   She of whom wild tales have birth,
When beside a winter hearth,
By some aged crone is told,
Marvel new or legend old.
But the ladye fronts him there,
He but sees she is so fair,
He but hears that in her tone
Dwells a music yet unknown;
He but feels that he could die
For the sweetness of her sigh.
But how many dreams take flight
330   With the dim enamoured night;
Cold the morning light has shone,
And the fairy train are gone,
Melted in the dewy air,
Lonely stands young Raymond there.
Yet not all alone, his heart
Hath a dream that will not part
From that beating heart's recess;
What that dream that lovers guess.

    Yet another year hath flown
340   In a stately hall alone,
Like an idol in a shrine
Sits the radiant Melusine.
It is night, yet o'er the walls,
Light, but light unearthly, falls.
Not from lamp nor taper thrown,
But from many a precious stone,
With whose variegated shade

Is the azure roof inlaid,
And whose coloured radiance throws
Hues of violet and rose. 350
Sixty pillars, each one shining
With a wreath of rubies twining,
Bear the roof — the snow-white floor
Is with small stars studded o'er.
Sixty vases stand between,
Filled with perfumes for a queen;
And a silvery cloud exhales
Odours like those fragrant gales,
Which at eve float o'er the sea
From the purple Araby. 360
Nothing stirs the golden gloom
Of that dim enchanted room.
Not a step is flitting round,
Not a noise, except the sound
Of the distant fountains falling,
With a soft perpetual calling,
To the echoes which reply
Musical and mournfully.

Sits the fairy ladye there,
Like a statue, pale and fair; 370
From her cheek the rose has fled,
Leaving deeper charms instead.
On that marble brow are wrought
Traces of impassioned thought;
Such as without shade or line
Leave their own mysterious sign.
While her eyes, they are so bright,
Dazzle with imperious light.
Wherefore doth the maiden bend?
Wherefore doth the blush ascend, 380
Crimson even to her brow,
Sight nor step are near her now?
Hidden by her sweeping robe,

Near her stands a crystal globe,
Gifted with strange power to show
All that she desires to know.
　　First she sees her palace gate,
With its steps of marble state;
Where two kneeling forms seem weeping
390　　O'er the watch which they are keeping,
While around the dusky boughs
Of a gloomy forest close,
Not for those that blush arose.
But she sees beside the gate,
A young and anxious palmer wait;
Well she knows it is for her,
He has come a worshipper.
For a year and for a day,
Hath he worn his weary way;
400　　Now a sign from that white hand,
And the portals open stand.
But a moment, and they meet,
Raymond kneels him at her feet;
Reading in her downcast eye,
All that woman can reply.
　　Weary, weary had the hours
Passed within her fairy bowers;
She was haunted with a dream
Of the knight beside the stream.
410　　Who hath never felt the sense
Of such charmed influence.
When the shapes of midnight sleep
One beloved object keep,
Which amid the cares of day
Never passes quite away?
Guarded for the sweetest mood
Of our happy solitude,
Linked with every thing we love,
Flower below or star above:
420　　Sweet spell after sweet spell thrown

Till the wide world is its own.
　　Turned the ladye deadly pale,
As she heard her lover's tale,
"Yes," she said, oh! low sweet word,
Only in a whisper heard.
"Yes, if my true heart may be
Worthy, Christian knight, of thee,
By the love that makes thee mine
I am deeply dearly thine.
But a spell is on me thrown,　　　　　　　　　　　　430
Six days may each deed be shown,
But the seventh day must be
Mine, and only known to me.
Never must thy step intrude
On its silent solitude.
Hidden from each mortal eye
Until seven years pass by.
When these seven years are flown
All my secret may be known.
But if, with suspicious eye,　　　　　　　　　　　　440
Thou on those dark hours wilt pry.
Then farewell, beloved in vain,
Never might we meet again."
Gazing on one worshipped brow,
When hath lover spared a vow?
With an oath and with a prayer
Did he win the prize he sought,
Never was a bride so fair,
As the bride that Raymond brought
From the wood's enchanted bowers　　　　　　　　450
To his old ancestral towers.
　　—— Oh, sweet love, could thy first prime
Linger on the steps of time,
Man would dream the unkind skies
Sheltered still a Paradise.
But, alas, the serpent's skill
Is amid our gardens still.

Soon a dark inquiring thought
On the baron's spirit wrought;
460   She, who seemed to love him so,
Had she aught he might not know?
Was it wo, how could she bear
Grief he did not soothe nor share?
Was it guilt? no — heaven's own grace
Lightened in that loveliest face.
Then his jealous fancies rose,
(Our Lady keep the mind from those!)
Like a fire within the brain,
Maddens that consuming pain.
470   Henceforth is no rest by night,
Henceforth day has no delight.
Life hath agonies that tell
Of their late left native hell.
But mid their despair is none
Like that of the jealous one.
    'Tis again the fatal day,
When the ladye must away,
To her lonely palace made
Far within the forest shade,
480   Where the mournful fountains sweep
With a voice that seems to weep.
On that morn Lord Raymond's bride
Ere the daybreak leaves his side.
Never does the ladye speak
But her tears are on his cheek,
And he hears a stifled moan
As she leaves him thus alone.
Hath she then complaint to make,
Is there yet some spell to break?
490   Come what will, or weal or wo,
'Tis the best the worst to know.

He hath followed — wo, for both,
That the knight forgot his oath.

Where the silvery fountains fall,
Stands no more the charmed hall;
But the dismal yew trees droop,
And the pines above them stoop,
While the gloomy branches spread,
As they would above the dead,
In some church-yard large and drear   500
Haunted with perpetual fear.
Dark and still like some vast grave,
Near there yawns a night-black cave.
O'er its mouth wild ivy twines
There the daylight never shines.
Beast of prey or dragon's lair,
Yet the knight hath entered there.
   Dimly doth the distant day
Scatter an uncertain ray,
While strange shapes and ghastly eyes   510
Mid the spectral darkness rise.
But he hurries on, and near
He sees a sudden light appear,
Wan and cold like that strange lamp
Which amid the charnel's damp
Shows but brightens not the gloom
Of the corpse and of the tomb.
With a cautious step he steals
To the cave that light reveals.
'Tis such grotto as might be,   520
Nereïd's[143] home beneath the sea.
Crested with the small bright stars
Of a thousand rainbow spars.
And a fountain from the side
Pours beneath its crystal tide,
In a white and marble bath
Singing on its silvery path;
While a meteor's emerald rays
O'er the lucid water plays. —
Close beside, with wild flowers laid,   530

Is a couch of green moss made.
There he sees his lady lie;
Pain is in her languid eye,
And amid her hair the dew
Half obscures its golden hue;
Damp and heavy, and unbound,
Its wan clusters sweep around.
On her small hand leans her head, —
See the fevered cheek is red,
540   And the fiery colour rushes
To her brow in hectic blushes. —
What strange vigil is she keeping!
He can hear that she is weeping. —
He will fling him at her feet,
   He will kiss away her tears.
Ah, what doth his wild eyes meet,
   What below that form appears?
Downwards from that slender waist,
By a golden zone embraced,
550   Do the many folds escape,
Of the subtle serpent's shape. —
Bright with many-coloured dyes
All the glittering scales arise,
With a red and purple glow
Colouring the waves below!
At the strange and fearful sight,
Stands in mute despair the knight, —
Soon to feel a worse despair,
Melusina sees him there!
560   And to see him is to part
With the idol of her heart,
Part as just the setting sun
Tells the fatal day is done.
Vanish all those serpent rings,
To her feet the lady springs,
And the shriek rings thro' the cell,
Of despairing love's farewell, —

Hope and happiness are o'er,
They can meet on earth no more.

———————

Years have past since this wild tale — 570
Still is heard that lady's wail,
Ever round that ancient tower,
Ere its lord's appointed hour.
With a low and moaning breath
She must mark approaching death,
While remains Lord Raymond's line
Doomed to wander and to pine.
Yet, before the stars are bright,
On the evening's purple light,
She beside the fountain stands 580
Wringing sad her shadowy hands.
May our Lady, as long years
Pass with their atoning tears,
Pardon with her love divine
The fountain fairy — Melusine!*

❦

———————————————————————————

* Raymond, first Lord of Lusignan, died as a hermit, at Monserrat. Melusina's was a
yet harsher doom: fated to flit over the earth, in pain and sorrow, as a spectre.
Only when one of the race of Lusignan were about to die, does she become visi-
ble, — and wanders wailing around the Castle. Tradition also represents her shad-
ow as hovering over the Fountain of Thirst. — *Thoms's Lays and Legends.*

IMMOLATION OF A HINDOO WIDOW. [144]

GATHER her raven hair in one rich cluster,
Let the white champac [145] light it, as a star
Gives to the dusky night a sudden lustre,
      Shining afar.

Shed fragrant oils upon her fragrant bosom,
Until the breathing air around grows sweet;
Scatter the languid jasmine's yellow blossom
      Beneath her feet.

Those small white feet are bare — too soft are they
To tread on aught but flowers; and there is roll'd
Round the slight ankle, meet for such display,
      The band of gold.

Chains and bright stones are on her arms and neck;
What pleasant vanities are linked with them,
Of happy hours, which youth delights to deck
      With gold and gem.

She comes! So comes the Moon, when she has found
A silvery path wherein thro' heaven to glide.
Fling the white veil — a summer cloud — around;
      She is a bride!

And yet the crowd that gather at her side
Are pale, and every gazer holds his breath.
Eyes fill with tears unbidden, for the bride —
      The bride of Death!

She gives away the garland from her hair,
She gives the gems that she will wear no more;
All the affections, whose love-signs they were,
      Are gone before.

The red pile blazes — let the bride ascend,
And lay her head upon her husband's heart,   30
Now in a perfect unison to blend —
                    No more to part.

&

SCENES IN LONDON: — PICCADILLY.

THE sun is on the crowded street,
    It kindles those old towers;
Where England's noblest memories meet,
    Of old historic hours.

Vast, shadowy, dark, and indistinct,
    Tradition's giant fane,
Whereto a thousand years are linked,
    In one electric chain.

So stands it when the morning light
    First steals upon the skies;   10
And shadow'd by the fallen night,
    The sleeping city lies.

It stands with darkness round it cast,
    Touched by the first cold shine;
Vast, vague, and mighty as the past,
    Of which it is the shrine.

'Tis lovely when the moonlight falls
    Around the sculptured stone,
Giving a softness to the walls,
    Like love that mourns the gone.   20

Then comes the gentlest influence
   The human heart can know,
The mourning over those gone hence
   To the still dust below.

The smoke, the noise, the dust of day,
   Have vanished from the scene;
The pale lamps gleam with spirit ray
   O'er the park's sweeping green.

Sad shining on her lonely path,
30   The moon's calm smile above,
Seems as it lulled life's toil and wrath
   With universal love.

Past that still hour, and its pale moon,
   The city is alive;
It is the busy hour of noon,
   When man must seek and strive.

The pressure of our actual life
   Is on the waking brow;
Labour and care, endurance, strife,
40   These are around him now.

How wonderful the common street,
   Its tumult and its throng,
The hurrying of the thousand feet
   That bear life's cares along.

How strongly is the present felt,
   With such a scene beside;
All sounds in one vast murmur melt
   The thunder of the tide.

All hurry on — none pause to look
50   Upon another's face:

The present is an open book
   None read, yet all must trace.

The poor man hurries on his race,
   His daily bread to find;
The rich man has yet wearier chase,
   For pleasure's hard to bind.

All hurry, though it is to pass
   For which they live so fast —
What doth the present but amass,
   The wealth that makes the past.   60

The past is round us — those old spires
   That glimmer o'er our head;
Not from the present is their fires,
   Their light is from the dead.

But for the past, the present's powers
   Were waste of toil and mind;
But for those long and glorious hours
   Which leave themselves behind.

THE sail from Penang to Singapore presents the loveliest succession of scenery which ocean can produce. The sea is studded with tracts of fairy-land, glittering like emeralds in the golden sun, where the waving trees dip their long branches into the water; where the smooth sands are covered with shells, sparkling with all the hues of the prism. Birds, too, of Orient plumage, skim over the surface of the silver sea, or glance in and out from groves laden with fruit and flowers. The ocean-land, locked by these flowery labyrinths, retains its tranquillity even during the summer tempests.

NEVER — that fairy isle can be
   No lengthened resting-place of mine;
I love it dearest when I see
   Its shadow lengthen on the brine:
And then my heart with softness fills;
   I think upon its palmy groves,
I hear the murmur of its rills,
   I hear the singing of its doves.

I see the white catalpa bend,
   As when beneath thy whiter hand,
The buds in snowy showers descend,
   To wreath for thy dark hair a band:
And then I sigh to be on shore,
   To linger languid at thy side,
I think that I will part no more
   From thee, my own, my idol bride.

Oh, only those who part can know
   How dear the love that absence brings;
O'er wind and wave my fancies go,
   As if my very heart had wings:
And yet, when listless on the land,
   Impatient in my happiness,

I long again to grasp my brand,
    Again I long the deck to press.

I love to see my red flag sweep;
    I love to see my sabre shine;
Almost as much I love the deep
    As I love those sweet eyes of thine.
I bring thee treasures from afar;
    For thy dear sake I sweep the sea;   30
But for the honour won in war,
    I should be too unworthy thee.

THE YOUNG DESTRUCTIVE.

    I N truth, I do not wonder
        To see them scatter'd round;
    So many leaves of knowledge —
        Some fruit must sure be found.

    The Eton Latin Grammar[147]
        Has now its verbs declin'd;
    And those of Lindley Murray
        Are not so far behind.

    Oh! days of bread and water —
        How many I recall,   10
    Past — sent into the corner;
        Your face towards the wall.

    Oh! boundaries of Europe!
        Oh! rivers great and small!
    Oh! islands, gulfs, and capitals!
        How I abhorr'd ye all!

And then those dreadful tables
    Of shillings, pence, and pounds!
Tho' I own their greater trouble
    In after life abounds.

'Tis strange how memory lingers
    About those early hours;
And we talk of happy childhood,
    As if such had been ours.

But distance lends enchantment
    To all we suffer'd then;
Thank Heaven, that I never
    Can be a child again!

EXPECTATION.

SHE looked from out the window
With long and asking gaze,
From the gold clear light of morning
    To the twilight's purple haze.
Cold and pale the planets shone,
Still the girl kept gazing on.
From her white and weary forehead
    Droopeth the dark hair,
Heavy with the dews of evening,
    Heavier with her care;
Falling as the shadows fall,
Till flung round her like a pall.

When from the carved lattice
    First she leant to look,
Her bright face was written

Like some pleasant book;
Her warm cheek the red air quaffed,
And her eyes looked out and laughed.
She is leaning back now languid
    And her cheek is white,   20
Only on the drooping eyelash
    Glistens tearful light.
Colour, sunshine hours are gone,
Yet the Lady watches on.

Human heart this history
    Is thy fated lot,
Even such thy watching
    For what cometh not.
Till with anxious waiting dull
Round thee fades the beautiful.   30
Still thou seekest on though weary,
    Seeking still in vain;
Daylight deepens into twilight,
    What has been thy gain?
Death and night are closing round,
All that thou hast sought unfound.

FELICIA HEMANS.

No more, no more — oh, never more returning,
    Will thy beloved presence gladden earth;
No more wilt thou with sad, yet anxious, yearning
    Cling to those hopes which have no mortal birth.
Thou art gone from us, and with thee departed,
    How many lovely things have vanished too:
Deep thoughts that at thy will to being started,
    And feelings, teaching us our own were true.
Thou hast been round us, like a viewless spirit,
10   Known only by the music on the air;
The leaf or flowers which thou hast named inherit
    A beauty known but from thy breathing there:
For thou didst on them fling thy strong emotion,
    The likeness from itself the fond heart gave;
As planets from afar look down on ocean,
    And give their own sweet image to the wave.

And thou didst bring from foreign lands their treasures,
    As floats thy various melody along;
We know the softness of Italian measures,
20   And the grave cadence of Castilian song.
A general bond of union is the poet,
    By its immortal verse is language known,
And for the sake of song do others know it —
    One glorious poet makes the world his own.
And thou — how far thy gentle sway extended!
    The heart's sweet empire over land and sea;
Many a stranger and far flower was blended
    In the soft wreath that glory bound for thee.
The echoes of the Susquehanna's waters
30   Paused in the pine-woods words of thine to hear;
And to the wide Atlantic's younger daughters
    Thy name was lovely, and thy song was dear.

Was not this purchased all too dearly? — never
    Can fame atone for all that fame hath cost.
We see the goal, but know not the endeavour
    Nor what fond hopes have on the way been lost.
What do we know of the unquiet pillow,
    By the worn cheek and tearful eyelid prest,
When thoughts chase thoughts, like the tumultuous billow,
    Whose very light and foam reveals unrest?   40
We say, the song is sorrowful, but know not
    What may have left that sorrow on the song;
However mournful words may be, they show not
    The whole extent of wretchedness and wrong.
They cannot paint the long sad hours, passed only
    In vain regrets o'er what we feel we are.
Alas! the kingdom of the lute is lonely —
    Cold is the worship coming from afar.

Yet what is mind in woman but revealing
    In sweet clear light the hidden world below,   50
By quicker fancies and a keener feeling
    Than those around, the cold and careless, know?
What is to feed such feeling, but to culture
    A soil whence pain will never more depart?
The fable of Prometheus and the vulture,
    Reveals the poet's and the woman's heart.
Unkindly are they judged — unkindly treated —
    By careless tongues and by ungenerous words;
While cruel sneer, and hard reproach, repeated,
    Jar the fine music of the spirit's chords.   60
Wert thou not weary — thou whose soothing numbers
    Gave other lips the joy thine own had not.
Didst thou not welcome thankfully the slumbers
    Which closed around thy mourning human lot?

What on this earth could answer thy requiring,
    For earnest faith — for love, the deep and true,

The beautiful, which was thy soul's desiring,
   But only from thyself its being drew.
How is the warm and loving heart requited
70   In this harsh world, where it awhile must dwell.
Its best affections wronged, betrayed, and slighted —
   Such is the doom of those who love too well.
Better the weary dove should close its pinion,
   Fold up its golden wings and be at peace,
Enter, O ladye, that serene dominion,
   Where earthly cares and earthly sorrows cease.
Fame's troubled hour has cleared, and now replying,
   A thousand hearts their music ask of thine.
Sleep with a light the lovely and undying
80   Around thy grave — a grave which is a shrine.

THE TOMBS OF THE KINGS OF GOLCONDA. [148]

Morning is round the shining palace,
   Mirrored on the tide,
Where the lily lifts her chalice,
   With its gold inside,
        Like an offering from the waves.
Early wakened from their slumbers,
   Stand the glittering ranks;
Who is there shall count the numbers
   On the river's banks?
10   Forth the household pours the slaves
        Of the kings of fair Golconda,
        Of Golconda's ancient kings.

Wherefore to the crimson morning
   Are the banners spread,

Daybreak's early colours scorning
    With a livelier red?
                    Pearls are wrought on each silk fold.
Summer flowers are flung to wither
    On the common way.
Is some royal bride brought hither   20
    With this festival array,
                    To the city's mountain-hold
                    Of the kings of old Golconda,
                    Of Golconda's ancient kings.

From the gates the slow procession,
    Troops and nobles come.
This hour takes the king possession
    Of an ancient home —
                    One he never leaves again.
Musk and sandal-wood and amber   30
    Fling around their breath:
They will fill the murky chamber
    Where the bride is Death.
                    Where the worm hath sole domain
                    O'er the kings of old Golconda,
                    O'er Golconda's ancient kings.

Now the monarch must surrender
    All his golden state,
Yet the mockeries of splendour
    On the pageant wait   40
                    That attends him to the tomb.
Music on the air is swelling,
    'Tis the funeral song,
As to his ancestral dwelling,
    Is he borne along.
                    They must share life's common doom,
                    The kings of fair Golconda,
                    Golconda's ancient kings.

What are now the chiefs that gather?
50   What their diamond mines?[149]
What the heron's snowy feather
    On their crest that shines?
                        What their valleys of the rose?
For another is their glory,
    And their state, and gold;
They are a forgotten story,
    Faint and feebly told —
                        Breaking not the still repose
                        Of the kings of fair Golconda,
60   Of Golconda's ancient kings.

Glorious is their place of sleeping,
    Gold with azure wrought,
And embroidered silk is sweeping,
    Silk from Persia brought,
                        Round the carved marble walls.*
Not the less the night-owl's pinion
    Stirs the dusky air,
Not the less is the dominion
    Of the earth-worm there.
70   Not less deep the shadow falls
                        O'er the kings of fair Golconda,
                        O'er Golconda's ancient kings.

Not on such vain aids relying,
    Can the human heart
Triumph o'er the dead and dying,
    It must know its part
                        In the glorious hopes that wait
The bright openings of the portal,
    Far beyond the sky —

---

*   Thevenot[150] gives a splendid description of these tombs. In addition to their archi-
tectural decoration, they were hung with embroidered satin.

Faith, whose promise is immortal,
   Life, that cannot die. 80

        These, and stronger than the state
        Of the kings of fair Golconda,
        Of Golconda's ancient kings.

◄੨

CAPTAIN COOK. [151]

Do you recall the fancies of many years ago,
When the pulse danced those light measures that again it cannot
    know?
Ah! we both of us are altered, and now we talk no more
Of all the old creations that haunted us of yore.

Then any favourite volume was a mine of long delight,
From whence we took our future, to fashion as we might.
We lived again its pages, we were its chiefs and kings,
As actual, but more pleasant, than what the day now brings.

It was an August evening, with sunset in the trees,
When home you brought his Voyages who found the fair South
    Seas. 10
We read it till the sunset amid the boughs grew dim;
All other favourite heroes were nothing beside him.

For weeks he was our idol, we sailed with him at sea,
And the pond amid the willows the ocean seemed to be.
The water-lilies growing beneath the morning smile,
We called the South Sea islands, each flower a different isle.

No golden lot that fortune could draw for human life,
To us seemed like a sailor's, mid the storm and strife.
Our talk was of fair vessels that swept before the breeze,
And new-discovered countries amid the Southern Seas. 20

Within that lonely garden what happy hours went by,
While we fancied that around us spread foreign sea and sky.
Ah! the dreaming and the distant no longer haunt the mind;
We leave, in leaving childhood, life's fairy land behind.

There is not of that garden a single tree or flower;
They have ploughed its long green grasses, and cut down the lime-
    tree bower.
Where are the Guelder roses, whose silver used to bring,
With the gold of the laburnums, their tribute to the Spring.

They have vanished with the childhood that with their treasures
    played;
30 The life that cometh after, dwells in a darker shade.
Yet the name of that sea-captain, it cannot but recall
How much we loved his dangers, and how we mourned his fall.

ॐ

THE CHURCH OF ST. JOHN, AND THE RUINS OF LAHNECK CASTLE,

FORMERLY BELONGING TO THE TEMPLARS.[152]

ON the dark heights that overlook the Rhine,
    Flinging long shadows on the watery plains,
Crowned with grey towers, and girdled by the vine,
    How little of the warlike past remains!

The castle walls are shattered, and wild flowers
    Usurp the crimson banner's former sign.
Where are the haughty Templars and their powers?
    Their forts are perished — but not so their shrine.

Like Memory veiled, Tradition sits and tells
    Her twilight histories of the olden time.   10
How few the records of those craggy dells
    But what recall some sorrow or some crime.

Of Europe's childhood was the feudal age,
    When the world's sceptre was the sword; and power,
Unfit for human weakness, wrong, and rage,
    Knew not that curb which waits a wiser hour.

Ill suited empire with a human hand,
    Authority needs rule, restraint, and awe;
Order and peace spread gradual through the land,
    And force submits to a diviner law.   20

A few great minds appear, and by their light
    The many find their way; truth after truth
Rise starlike on the depths of moral night,
    Though even now is knowledge in its youth.

Still as those ancient heights, which only bore
    The iron harvest of the sword and spear,
Are now with purple vineyards covered o'er,
    While corn-fields fill the fertile valleys near.

Our moral progress has a glorious scope,
    Much has the past by thought and labour done;   30
Knowledge and Peace pursue the steps of Hope,
    Whose noblest victories are yet unwon.

THE PORTRAIT OF LORD BYRON
AT NEWSTEAD ABBEY. [153]

INSCRIBED TO LORD BYRON'S SISTER, MRS. GEORGE LEIGH.

IT is the face of youth — and yet not young;
    The purple lights, the ready smiles have vanished;
The shadows by the weary forehead flung,
    The gayer influences of life have banished.

'Tis sad, and fixed — yet we can fancy gleams
    Of feverish spirits, suddenly awaking.
Flinging aside doubts, fancies, fears, and dreams,
    Like some red fire on startled midnight breaking.

'Tis an uncertain thing — a mind so framed,
10   Glorious the birthright which its powers inherit,
Mingling the loved — the feared — the praised — the blamed —
    The constant struggle of the clay and spirit.

————————

HIS name is on the haunted shade,
    His name is on the air;
We walk the forest's twilight glade,
    And only he is there.
The ivy wandering o'er the wall,
The fountain falling musical,
    Proclaim him everywhere,
20   The heart is full of him, and flings
Itself on all surrounding things.

The youthful poet! here his mind
    Was in its boyhood nurst;
All that impatient soul enshrined
    Was here developed first.

What feelings and what thoughts have grown
Amid those cloisters, deep and lone!
   Life's best, and yet its worst:
For fiery elements are they,
That mould and make such dangerous clay.   30

A thousand gifts the poet hath
   Of beauty and delight;
He flingeth round a common path,
   A glory never common sight
Would find in common hours.
And yet such visionary powers
   Are kin to strife and wrath.
The very light with which they glow
But telleth of the fire below.

Such minds are like the heated earth   40
   Of southern soils and skies;
Care calls not to laborious birth
   The lavish wealth that lies
Close to the surface; some bright hour
Upsprings the fruit, unfolds the flower,
   And inward wonders rise:
A thousand colours glitter round,
The golden harvest lights the ground.

But not the less there lurks below
   The lava's burning wave;   50
The red rose and the myrtle grow
   Above a hidden grave.
The life within earth's panting veins
Is fire, which silently remains
   In each volcanic cave.
Fire that gives loveliness and breath,
But giveth, in one moment, death!

So framed is such a mind, it works
     With dangerous thoughts and things;
Beneath, the fiery lava lurks,
     But on the surface springs
A prodigality of bloom,
A thousand hues that might illume
     Even an angel's wings!
Thrice beautiful the outward show,
Still the volcano is below.

It is the curse of such a mind
     That it can never rest,
Ever its wings upon the wind
     In some pursuit are prest;
And either the pursuit is vain,
Or, if its object it attain,
     It was not worth the quest,
Yet from the search it cannot cease,
And fold its plumes, and be at peace.

And what were that boy-poet's dreams,
     As here he wont to stray,
When evening cast her pensive gleams
     Around his forest way?
Came there "thick fancies"[154] 'mid the gloom,
Of war-horse, trumpet, pennant, plume,
     And all the proud array,
When mailed barons, stern and old,
Kept state in Newstead's ancient hold?

Or more — was the boy's fancy won
     By penance and by vow,
When hooded monk and veiled nun,
     The beating heart and brow,
Alike concealed from common eyes,
Revealed, perhaps, to midnight skies,

Dreams that possessed him now?
Dreams of a world, whose influence still
Prevaileth over human will.

Or was it some wild dream of love
    That filled the summer noon,
And saw but one sweet face above,
    What time the maiden moon
Looked on a fairy world beneath,
And waked the hawthorn's sweetest breath,
    The fountain's softest tune?   100
For young love, living on a smile,
Makes its own Eden for a while.

The ancient hall, when winter came,
    Gave fantasies to night,
Light by some old lamp's flickering flame,
    Or the red embers' light.
The shadows, that have little power
Upon the sunshine's cheerful hour,
    Then master mind and sight;
The visionary world appears   110
Girt with fantastic shapes and fears.

Such was his childhood, suited well
    To fashion such a mind;
The feudal sword — the gothic cell,
    Their influence combined.
The old oak-wood — the forest stream,
And love soon wakened from the dream
    It never quite resigned.
His life contained no after hour
O'er which his boyhood had no power.   120

Be after scenes with after years —
    Here only we recall

Whatever soothes, subdues, endears,
   In his ancestral hall.
The deep enchantment we have felt,
When every thought and feeling dwelt
   Beneath his spirit's thrall.
Sad, softened, are the hearts that come
To gaze around his boyish home.

❧

DISENCHANTMENT.

Do not ask me why I loved him,
   Love's cause is to love unknown;
Faithless as the past has proved him,
   Once his heart appeared mine own.
Do not say he did not merit
   All my fondness, all my truth:
Those in whom Love dwells inherit
   Every dream that haunted youth.

He might not be all I dreamed him,
10   Noble, generous, gifted, true,
Not the less I fondly deemed him,
   All those flattering visions drew.
All the hues of old romances
   By his actual self grew dim;
Bitterly I mock the fancies
   That once found their life in him.

From the hour by him enchanted
   From the moment when we met,
Henceforth with one image haunted,
20   Life may never more forget.
All my nature changed — his being

Seemed the only source of mine.
Fond heart, hadst thou no foreseeing
    Thy sad future to divine?

Once, upon myself relying,
    All I asked were words and thought;
Many hearts to mine replying,
    Owned the music that I brought.
Eager, spiritual, and lonely,
    Visions filled the fairy hour,   30
Deep with love — though love was only
    Not a presence, but a power.

But from that first hour I met thee,
    All caught actual life from you.
Alas! how can I forget thee,
    Thou who mad'st the fancied true?
Once my wide world was ideal,
    Fair it was — ah! very fair.
Wherefore hast thou made it real?
    Wherefore is thy image there?   40

Ah! no more to me is given
    Fancy's far and fairy birth;
Chords upon my lute are riven,
    Never more to sound on earth.
Once, sweet music could it borrow
    From a look, a word, a tone;
I could paint another's sorrow —
    Now I think but of mine own.

Life's dark waves have lost the glitter
    Which at morning-tide they wore,   50
And the well within is bitter,
    Nought its sweetness may restore:
For I know how vainly given
    Life's most precious things may be,

Love that might have looked on heaven,
　　Even as it looked on thee.

Ah, farewell! — with that word dying,
　　Hope and love must perish too.
For thy sake themselves denying,
　　What is truth with thee untrue?
Farewell! — 'tis a dreary sentence,
　　Like the death-doom of the grave,
May it wake in thee repentance,
　　Stinging when too late to save!

60

❦

THE VILLAGE BELLS.

"How soft the music of those village bells,
Falling, at intervals, upon the ear
In cadence sweet, — now dying all away,
Now pealing loud again, and louder still,
Clear and sonorous, as the gale comes on!
With easy force it opens all the cells
Where mem'ry slept."

There is a lovely English sound
　　Upon the English air,
It comes when else had silence found
　　Its quiet empire there.

All ordinary signs of life
　　To-day are hushed and still;
No voice of labour or of strife
　　Ascends the upland hill.

The leaves in softer music stir,
    The brook in softer tune;
Life rests, and all things rest with her
    This Sabbath afternoon.

10

How fair it is! how English fair!
    No other land could show
A pastoral beauty to compare
    With that which lies below.

The broad green meadow-lands extend
    Up to the hanging wood,
Where oak and beech together blend,
    That have for ages stood.   20

What victories have left those trees,
    What time the winged mast
Bore foreign shores and foreign seas
    St. George's banner past.

Each oak that left yon inland wood
    In some good ship had part,
And every triumph stirred the blood
    In every English heart.

Hence, each green hedge that winds along
    Filled with the wild flowers small,   30
Round each green field, is safe and strong
    As is a castle wall.

God, in his own appointed time,
    Hath made such tumult cease;
There ringeth now in that sweet chime
    But only prayer and peace.

How still it is! the bee — the bird —
    Float by on noiseless wing.

There sounds no step — there comes no word,
There seems no living thing

But still upon the soft west wind
These bells come sweeping by,
Leaving familiar thoughts behind,
Familiar, and yet high.

Ringing for every funeral knell,
And for the marriage stave;
Alike of life and death they tell,
The cradle and the grave.

They chronicle the hopes and fears
Upon life's daily page;
Familiar to our childish years,
Familiar to our age.

The Sabbath bells upon our path,
Long may their sound endure;
The sweetest music England hath —
The music of the poor.

FROM *FLOWERS OF LOVELINESS* (1838)

THE HYACINTH. [155]

WHERE is the bee its sweetest music bringing, —
  The music living in its busy wings,
Like the small fountain's low perpetual singing,
  Counting the quiet hours that noontide brings?

It is the Hyacinth, whose sweet bells stooping,
  Bend with the odours heavy in their cells;
Amid the shadows of their fragrant drooping,
  Memory, that is itself a shadow, dwells.

Ah! do not wreathe it mid the golden tresses
  That mock the sunshine on that childish head;   10
Bind there the meadow flowers the wind caresses;
  Around a thousand careless blossoms shed.

But not the Hyacinth, whose purple sadness
  To an old world long since gone by appeals:
What hath the child's one hour of eager gladness
  To do with all that haunted flower reveals?

Life gave its first deep colour to that blossom;
  Life, in an evil hour untimely shed;
Down to the earth inclines its fragrant bosom,
  As heavy with the memory of the dead.   20

Deep in the twilight depths of those dark flowers,
   Are mystic characters amid them turled:
Are they the language of ancestral hours, —
   The records of a younger, lovelier world?

What is the secret written in their numbers,
   Strange as the figures on Egyptian shrines?
What marvel of the ancient earth now slumbers
   In the obscurity of those dim lines?

Little we know the secrets that surround us,
30   And much has vanished from our later day;
Nature with many a mystery has bound us,
   And much of our old love has past away.

No ancient voices in the dim woods crying,
   Reveal the hidden world; no prophet's eye
Asks the foreseeing stars for their replying,
   And reads the future in the midnight sky.

Many the lovely things that now are banished
   From our harsh path — the actual and the cold;
The angel and the spirit, each are vanished!
40   Where are the beautiful that were of old?

Vain, tho' so lovely, was this old believing;
   But not thus vain the faith that gave it birth;
It was the beauty of the far off — leaving
   The presence of the spiritual on earth.

The Hyacinth

Notes

Landon's citations of other authors are frequently paraphrases rather than exact quotations of the original source. Unless otherwise noted, all verse epigraphs are Landon's.

Though it is known that Landon wrote many literary and art reviews for the *Literary Gazette*, most reviews are unsigned and their authorship remains unknown. All LG articles relating to the subject matter of the poems in this edition have been cited on the assumption that Landon either wrote or was familiar with the majority of the reviews in LG.

Abbreviations: LG=*The Literary Gazette*; NMM=*The New Monthly Magazine*; ZM=*The Zenana and Minor Poems* (1839).

1. *Six Songs*. Published 10 November 1821.
2. *bulbul*. The Persian nightingale.
3. *Medallion Wafers*. This poetical series was published on 25 January, 8 February, and 1 March 1823. The medallion wafers were sealing wafers depicting engraved reproductions of contemporary art. The Fine Arts column of the LG for 4 January 1823 contains a complimentary account of the wafers:

> We think we are right in classing among the Fine Arts one of the prettiest, and not the least useful inventions of the present period: we allude to what are denominated Medallion Wafers. These are Seals of a particular composition, which, being stuck on letters, perform the office of wax or wafer in a very elegant fashion. They are of all sizes, colours, and devices; many of them beautiful as copies of the finest gems, cameos, and intaglios of the antique. Thus these specimens not only serve an every day purpose with facility, but are calculated to spread abroad an acquaintance and admiration of the most graceful forms of taste and genius. The composition is, we take it for granted, a secret to the inventors, Messrs. Thomson, of Wellington-street. We suspect isenglass and white lead to be ingredients; but however made, they are certainly beautiful, and as fit for love-letters as any thing that could be imagined (11-12).

For further discussion, see Daniel Riess, "Laetitia Landon and the Dawn of English Post-Romanticism," *Studies in English Literature 1500-1900* 36 (Autumn 1996): 807-827.

4. *The Hall of Statues*. Published 25 June 1831.

5. *Mr. Hollins' Aurora waking Zephyrus*: The LG for 14 May 1831 favourably reviewed the Bond Street exhibition of British sculptor Peter Hollins (1800-1886):

> We have been highly gratified by a view of an exhibition of sculpture about to be opened to the public in Bond Street. The several groups of which it consists are the production of Mr. Peter Hollins, an artist who has risen to eminence at Birmingham, and now (with perfect safety) advances his claim to the approbation of London.... The third group, of Aurora waking Zephyrus, is a most lovely design, and exquisitely executed. Alone, it is enough to make the fame of a sculptor. (316)

6. *Mr. Lough's Child playing a Lyre*: Lesser known work by British sculptor John Graham Lough (1806-76).

7. *Mr. Macdonald's Supplicating Virgin*: Scottish sculptor Lawrence Macdonald's (1799-1878) 1831 Pall Mall Exhibition was reviewed in LG for 5 and 19 March 1831. The latter review states:

> We have paid another visit to Mr. Macdonald's gallery, in Pall Mall, and the result is a confirmation of the opinions of his powers which we originally formed and expressed. He promises to be — or, rather, he already is — one of the most distinguished ornaments of the British school of sculpture.... "The supplicating Virgin," and "The youthful Slinger," are exceedingly elegant and beautiful (187).

8. *The Improvisatrice*. The text is the fifth edition (London: Hurst, 1825). An improvisatrice is a female poet who recites verses composed on the spur of the moment without previous preparation. "Improvisatore," the masculine form, became recognized as an English word in the mid-18th century and is first used in English literature by Smollett, whose works Landon read in childhood, in Letter XXVIII of *Travels Through France and Italy* (1766). Thomas Lovell Beddoes published *The Improvisatore* in 1821. Landon's use of the term connects her heroine to the medieval tradition of Provençal love poets, the

subjects of her long poems "The Troubadour" and "The Golden Violet," but the plot and the Florentine setting explicitly connects her work to de Staël's controversial novel *Corinne, or Italy* (1807). See note to "Corinne at the Cape of Misena." The Petrarch and Laura section is indebted to Jacques François Paul Aldonce de Sade's *The Life of Petrarch* (London, 1775), which Landon read as a child.

9. *agraff:* Type of hook used as a clasp.

10. *Irem's groves:* Irem (or Iram), one of the paradises named in the Koran.

11. *Parian stone:* Type of white marble highly valued by sculptors.

12. *subul.* A medicinal plant whose aroma is a commonplace figure in Persian and Indian verse.

13. *Antinous* (A.D. 110-130): Lover of Roman emperor Hadrian. Many temples and sculptures survive depicting him as a beautiful youth.

14. *Cretan maiden's fate:* Landon must be thinking of Ariadne, daughter of Minos, King of Crete, whom Theseus loved and then abandoned.

15. *crimson hectic's flame:* I.e., the flush signalling consumption, which was a conventional romantic figure of frustrated or unrequited passion.

16. *When Should Lovers Breathe Their Vows?* This lyric, the concluding poem of *The Improvisatrice and Other Poems*, was later set to music by Thomas Forbes Walmisley (London: Pettet, 1829).

17. *A Child Screening a Dove from a Hawk, by Stewardson.* Thomas Stewardson (1781-1859), a pupil of Romney, served as portrait painter to Caroline Princess of Wales, but in his genre pictures he liked to represent children. Many of his paintings were engraved.

18. *The Enchanted Island, by Danby.* Francis Danby (1793-1861) exhibited "An Enchanted Island" at the British Institution early in 1825. It was reviewed in LG for 5 February:

> In the class of Landscape, we are presented with a novelty (if such a thing be possible in this day of accumulated variety) in No. 59. An Enchanted Island. By F. Danby.—The splendour of this sunlit scene, and the effect thrown into it, are indeed quite enchanting. It is truly a bold experiment to enter thus, into open day, with a subject so visionary.

In scenes of a poetical character, a partial obscurity is of great advantage; and in the Enchanted Island of Claude, this quality of the mysterious and obscure is the charm which sets the imagination at work: and although we think a little more of the romantic, in the form of his (Mr. Danby's) landscape, would have heightened the interest of his subject, the performance is full of talent, and the Painter promises to shed a lustre on the British School of Art. (91)

19. *Erinna.* Greek elegiac poet of the late fourth century BC, believed by some to have been a pupil of Sappho, and supposed to have died at the age of nineteen. In classical antiquity her poetry was as famous as Homer's and Sappho's. In a letter to Katherine Thomson dated October 1826, Landon wrote:

> [The poem "The Golden Violet"] is now complete and I am equally busy with my "Erinna." I shall be so anxious for you and Mr. Thomson to like it. Is there not an old proverb which says "it is ill judging your own bigging?" Still, if I can write up to the idea I have formed, it must be a striking poem. Other poets have painted a very sufficient quantity of poetical miseries; but my aim is not to draw neglected genius, or "mourn a laurel planted on the tomb" — but to trace the progress of a mind highly-gifted, well-rewarded, but finding the fame it won a sting and a sorrow, and finally sinking beneath the shadows of success. (Quoted in Blanchard 1:59-60.)

20. *The Brides of Florence: The Brides of Florence: a play, in five acts: illustrative of the Manners of the Middle Ages, with Historical notes, and Minor Poems* by W. Fraser [Randolph Fitz-Eustace] (London, 1824). Erinna is mentioned on pp. 230-233.

21. *Grecian Anthology ... Antipater.* Antipater of Sidon, Greek poet of the 2nd century B.C., wrote two epigrams about Erinna, both of which are included in Book Seven of the Greek Anthology, a collection of about 3700 short poems, epigrams, songs, and epitaphs in Greek written between the 7th century B.C. and A.D. 1000.

22. *local habitation and a name: A Midsummer Night's Dream* V.1.17.

23. *Song (My heart is like the failing hearth).* Republished as "The Broken Heart" in *The Lady's Magazine* 7 (February 1827): 95-96. Both this and the following piece are songs from "The Golden Violet," a medley poem.

24. *Song (Where oh! where's the chain to fling)*. First published as "Lezione per L'Amore" ("lessons of love") in LG for 14 January 1826: 26. This poem was extensively revised prior to republication in *The Golden Violet*: see Appendix D for the LG text. Both this and the following piece are songs from "The Golden Violet," a medly poem.

25. *Preface to The Venetian Bracelet*. Written partly in response to criticism that her poetry was monotonous. (See, for example, Appendix B, the anonymous review of *The Improvisatrice, and Other Poems* in *The Westminster Review* 3 (April 1825).

26. *"farther looking hope"*: Wordsworth, "The Force of Prayer, or, The Founding of Boulton Priory, A Tradition," l. 47.

27. *ARIADNE*: She fell in love with Theseus and assisted him with his quest to slay the Minotaur. After he abandoned her for another woman, Dionysus wed her and presented her with a crown for a wedding present.

28. *ENDYMION*: The youth beloved by Selene, goddess of the moon, who caused him to fall into an eternal sleep in order that she might enjoy his company undisturbed.

29. *ST. ROSALIE*: According to legend Rosalia, daughter of a Sicilian lord, became a hermit in her youth, living in caves until her death around AD 1160.

30. *CANOVA*: Antonio Canova (1757-1822), celebrated Neo-Hellenic sculptor.

31. *Lines of Life*: Shakespeare, Sonnet 16 line 9.

32. *Fantasies, inscribed to T. Crofton Croker, Esq.* Thomas Crofton Croker (1798-1854) was an Irish writer best known for his *Fairy Legends and Traditions of the South of Ireland* (1827). Croker's books *Daniel O'Rourke* (1828) and *Legends of the Lakes* (1829) were reviewed favourably in LG for 23 February and 20 December 1828.

33. *Stanzas to the Author of "Mont Blanc," "Ada," etc.* Addressed to poet Mary Anne Browne (later Gray) (1812-44), author of *Mont Blanc, and Other Poems* (1827) and *Ada, and Other Poems* (1828). Like Landon's, Browne's poems are often Byronic in tone and stanzaic form, and her poem "Mont Blanc" uses the Spenserian stanza Byron made famous in *Childe Harold's Pilgrimage*. Her poem "The Sky" appears in LG for

5 April 1828, and the review of *Ada, and Other Poems* in LG for 19 April 1828 praises Browne's poems for containing "sweet imagery, much tenderness of feeling, and a fluency of poetic diction wonderful in one so young." It concludes, however, with a warning to the young poet:

> Admiration too often leads to imitation; and there are many tones only "faint echoes of remembered music." We will only remind our fair writer, that the heights of Parnassus, like the passage to the North Pole, are not to be gained by treading in any previous foot-tracks; and we are much deceived if she has not ample resources of her own to rely on, for striking out a more original path. (245)

34. *Verses ("Lady, thy face is very beautiful")*. Written for Charles Heath's engraving of Sir Edwin Landseer's 1823 portrait.

35. *The Altered River*. Landon is probably recalling Wordsworth's "Lines Written Near Richmond, Upon the Thames, at Evening" from *Lyrical Ballads* (later revised and retitled "Remembrance of Collins, Composed upon the Thames Near Richmond").

36. *Romance and Reality*. Landon's first novel, written after the style of the "silver fork" school of novels of the Regency period.

37. *"It was an ancient venerable hall"*: George Crabbe, "Tales of the Hall," I. 43.

38. *"This is she, / Our consecrated Emily"*: Landon misquotes Wordsworth's "The White Doe of Rylstone," ll. 1403-5: "Here is it;—but how? when? must she, / The unoffending Emily, / Again this piteous object see?" Emily is called "consecrated Maid" at l. 591 and l. 999.

39. *"ample space and verge enough"*: Thomas Gray, "The Bard: A Pindaric Ode," 51.

40. *Corinne at the Cape of Misena*. Landon's inspiration for this poem is twofold: (1) the painting "Corinne au cap Misène" (1819) by Francois Gérard (1770-1837), a much-imitated and copied portrait and history painter; and (2), the novel from which Gérard drew his inspiration, Germaine de Staël's *Corinne*, Book 13, Chapter 4. One of Landon's earliest poems is entitled "Corinna," published in *The Fate of Adelaide* (1821). She later translated all the versified portions of de Staël's novel for Isabel Hill's 1833 English translation, in which the "Fragment of Corinne's Song at Naples" was reprinted.

41. *The History of a Child.* This story, the final work in *Traits and Trials of Early Life*, was widely accepted to be autobiographical. Landon encouraged this interpretation, writing to Samuel Carter Hall: "My childhood was passed at Trevor Park, and is the basis of the last tale in *Traits and Trials*" (Hall 1871: 269). Laman Blanchard, however, insisted that while "[s]ome of the incidents of her own childhood are related in it; ... the whole bear the same relation to reality that phantasies bear to facts" (1:24).

42. *old ballad of Barbara Allen:* Scottish broadside ballad relating the story of a young man's death of heartbreak when his love is refused by Barbara Allen.

43. *"down of darkness":* Milton, *Comus* ll. 251-252.

44. The English dynastic houses of York and Lancaster struggled for dominance in the 15th century. Shakespeare's history plays largely centre on these struggles.

45. *"Monarch of all I surveyed / My right there was none to dispute":* William Cowper, "Verses, Supposed to be Written by Alexander Selkirk ...", ll. 1-2.

46. *Prince Agib:* protagonist of a story in the *Arabian Nights.*

47. The quotation from Charles Lamb has not been identified.

48. *On the Ancient and Modern Influence of Poetry.* Published anonymously in NMM 35 (November 1832). Landon's authorship is inferred from a letter dated 19 October 1832 from Bulwer Lytton to Samuel Carter Hall requesting a copy of the article because he disagreed with Landon's essay on modern poets.

49. Landon's views on Africa are characteristic of her age. It would take some 80 years of self-education for Europeans (and Americans) to begin to free themselves from this distinctive type of racist ignorance — what Landon herself called "the depths of moral night" ("The Church of St. John ...", 23).

50. *delicate Peris:* "Peris" are fairy-like beings in Persian mythology, and recur in the Oriental tales of Byron and Moore.

51. *"A slave cannot be eloquent;" said Longinus: On the Sublime* IX.3-4.

52. *"what some ancient writer said of iron ... civilization to freedom"*: unidentified.

53. *Xerxes ... those who fell at Marathon.* In the battle of Marathon (c.490 BC), the Athenians defeated the invading armies of the Persian ruler Darius (not of Xerxes, his son).

54. *"One of our great reviews ... poetry but fiction?"*: unidentified.

55. *"love which his spirit has painted"*: Byron, "Stanzas to Augusta," l. 7.

56. *"song that lightens the languid way!"*: Thomas Moore, "Boat Glee," l. 14.

57. *Poeta nascitur non fit*: "A poet is born and not made." (proverbial).

58. *Wordsworth truly says, "that, with the young, poetry is a passion":* From the "Essay, Supplementary to the Preface" to *Lyrical Ballads* (1815). The actual quotation is: "With the young, of both sexes, Poetry is, like love, a passion."

59. *"A remark made by Scott ... made our reputation!"*: unidentified.

60. *"farther looking hope"*: see note to page 102.

61. *"A heavenly breath / Along an earthly lyre"*: Laman Blanchard, "The Spirit of Poesy," ll. 5-6.

62. *"tread with unsandalled foot"*: Landon is apparently quoting Cowper, "To an Afflicted Protestant Lady in France," line 16: "With unshod feet they yet securely tread"; or perhaps James Hogg, "Mador of the Moor," IV. 32-33: "And light unsandalled foot, o'er wastes so wide / She journeyed far away, with Heaven alone to guide."

63. *"Which bid the perished ... soul of love"*: Landon mixes two sources: ll. 7-8 of Coleridge's "Lines on an Autumnal Evening" ("Ah! rather bid the perish'd pleasures move, / A shadowy train, across the soul of Love!") and l. 227 of Moore's "The Veiled Prophet of Khorassan" ("In mournful mockery, o'er the shining track").

64. *"As Whitehead finely says ... Oh, Immortality!":* Charles Whitehead (1804-1862), *The Solitary*, II. 397-414.

65. *"My task has been ... exceeding great reward"*: from Coleridge's preface to his three-volume *The Poetical Works of S. T. Coleridge* (London: William Pickering, 1828).

66. *Stanzas on the Death of Mrs. Hemans.* Published in NMM 44 (May-August 1835). Hemans died 16 May 1835. Elizabeth Barrett Browning's reply to this poem is printed in Appendix C. The "lovely song" (l. 5) is Hemans's "Bring Flowers," upon which this elegy is modeled.

67. Hemans's "The Nightingale's Death-Song."

68. *On the Character of Mrs. Hemans's Writings.* Published in NMM 44 (May - August 1835). All verse quotations are from Hemans unless otherwise specified.

69. *"Oh! Mes amis ... y est empreinte."* ("Oh! my friends, remember my verses sometimes; my soul is imprinted on them.") Hemans used this quotation from de Staël's *Corinne* as the epigraph to her poem "A Parting Song."

70. *"Distance lends enchantment to the view"*: Thomas Campbell, "The Pleasures of Hope," ll. 7-8.

71. *"false Florimel flattery for the true Florimel praise"*: Book III, Canto 7 of Spenser's *Faerie Queen* relates how a witch creates an evil double of the fair Florimell, whom the braggart Braggadocchio mistakes for the true Florimell.

72. *"memory makes the sky ... shrinking eye"*: "The Lady of the Castle. From The 'Portrait Gallery,' An Unfinished Poem," ll. 35-36.

73. *"laid their youth ... may not find it"*: "Arabella Stuart," ll. 98-99.

74. *"C'est ainsi qu'elle fût"*: This is as she was.

75. *"Who learnt in suffering what they taught in song"*: Shelley, "Julian and Maddalo, A Conversation", l. 546. Hemans had used this line as an epigraph to her poem "The Diver."

76. *"writer of a recent memoir ... buoyant spirits"*: Landon alludes to the anonymous author of *A Short Sketch of the Life of Mrs. Hemans; with Remarks on Her Poetry; and Extracts* (London: James Paul, 1835), who prefaced a series of light-hearted excerpts from Hemans's letters with the following note:

> Many a volume might be written upon the weakness and frivolities of eminent characters: as if to prove that even wisdom itself is mutable, and that no perfection can exist this side of heaven, the greatest minds have engendered the most contemptible foibles and

peculiarities; and we confess that we were filled with sorrow and disappointment, when we found that even Mrs. Hemans was not exempt from these weaknesses (18–19).

77. *"Oh, gentle friend, ... and may be sad tomorrow":* Joanna Baillie, *Orra: A Tragedy in Five Acts* I.3.90–92.

78. *"Sudden glee ... skylark song":* "The Charmed Picture,": ll. 21-24.

79. *"Thou canst not wake the spirit ... Of buried melodies":* "The Lyre's Lament," ll. 5-8.

80. *"Blest, for the beautiful is in it dwelling":* "The Image in the Heart," l. 31.

81. *"The shadow of departed hours / Hangs dim upon its early flowers":* "The Deserted House," ll. 5-6.

82. *"A mournful lot is mine, dear friends / A mournful lot is mine":* "Second Sight," ll. 1-2.

83. *"A sad and weary life is thine, ... every word":* "The Diver," ll. 9-12, 29-32, 41-52.

84. *"and love grown too sorrowful, / Asks for its youth again":* "Come Home!" ll. 27-28.

85. *"Tell me no more—no more ... made life precious":* epigraph to "Properzia Rossi."

86. *"One dream of passion ... her life away":* "Properzia Rossi," ll. 1-18.

87. *"And thou, oh! thou on whom my spirit cast ... gift is fame":* "Properzia Rossi," ll. 103-110.

88. *"I have been / Too much alone":* "Properzia Rossi," ll. 65-66. Cf. Byron, "Mazeppa," ll. 838-9: "while she was gone, / Methought I felt too much alone."

89. *the author of "Psyche":* Mary Tighe (1772-1810).

90. *"And mournful grew my heart ... didst thou weep!":* "The Grave of a Poetess," ll. 13-16, 45-48.

91. *"No tears for thee, ... the dark sea":* "The Requiem of Genius," ll. 1-6.

92. *Alhambra:* The spectacular palace in Granada built in the 13th century for the Moorish kings of Spain.

93. *"Yarrow Water":* Also known as "The Braes o'Yarrow," or "Willy Drowned in Yarrow," a traditional English ballad.

94. *"Faire Rosamonde":* William Warner, *Albion's England* (1602), Book 8, Chap. XLI, ll. 110-111.

95. *"I come! I come! ... as I pass":* ll. 1-6 of "The Voice of Spring."

96. *Miss Jewsbury, the late lamented Mrs. Fletcher.* Maria Jane Jewsbury (1800-33), author of four books and numerous poems in *The Athenaeum* and assorted annuals. She married the Rev. William Fletcher in 1832, and sailed with him to Bombay, where she died of cholera on 4 October 1833.

97. *Sindbad, the sailor.* Sinbad, of the *Arabian Nights.*

98. *"Raising its bright face, ... characters of anguish":* "Arabella Stuart," ll. 37-39.

99. *"It is my youth ... as thou art":* "The Chamois Hunter's Love," ll. 17-18.

100. *"Day by day, ... flows from me":* "Arabella Stuart," ll. 125-127.

101. *Phocion:* Athenian statesman, 402-318 B.C. Famous for his purity of character and wise counsel, he was unjustly condemned for treason by the Greek Assembly and executed.

102. *Thalaba's palace of the desert:* In Book I of Robert Southey's poem "Thalaba the Destroyer" (1801), the proud King Shedad builds an extravagant palace in the Arabian desert, which is destroyed by a magical wind billowing from a black cloud immediately after its completion.

103. *"Where couldst thou fix on mortal ground .... the poet's eye":* "The Grave of a Poetess": ll. 49-52.

104. *First Love; Or, Constancy in the Nineteenth Century.* Published in NMM 48 (1836).

105. *votary of the saffron god:* Saffron was associated with Hymen, Greek god of marriage.

106. *"falling pearl, which men call tears"*: perhaps not a quotation but a poetical commonplace.

107. *knife-grinder*: Quoting George Canning's parody of Southey's "The Widow." The parody appeared in the *Anti-Jacobin* as "The Friend of Humanity and the Knife-Grinder" (1.21).

108. *"like a teetotum all in a twirl"*: Thomas Moore, "Letter V. From Miss Biddy Fudge to Miss Dorothy —," l. 2 (*The Fudge Family in Paris*).

109. *chaussure*: shoes.

110. *sauteuse*: a type of dance.

111. *"Tell me, my heart, ... to forget?"*: "Say, my heart, why wildly beating" and "Teach me, oh! teach me to forget," two popular songs.

112. *"Meet me by moonlight alone"*: Popular ballad by Joseph Augustine Wade (1800-45).

113. *"Oh! let me only breathe ... by thee"*: Moore," Paradise and the Peri," ll. 270-271.

114. *"Bought because they may be wanted, / Wanted because they may be had"*: unidentified.

115. *dame de ses pensées*: lady of his thoughts.

116. *"Longs to speak, ... but a moment."* Byron, *Manfred* II.2.174-6.

117. *"Who shall school the heart's ... to forget!"*: see note to page 189.

118. *"Ah, too convincing ... th' unanswerable tear"*: Byron, *The Corsair*, 1149-1150.

119. *"dove-eyed Julia"*: Barry Cornwall (1787-1874), *Marcian Colonna*, I.194. Like Landon, Cornwall wrote a large quantity of verse for various annuals.

120. *like the breeze in Lord Byron's calm, came not"*: *Don Juan* II. 572.

121. *Zimmerman*: Recalling Johann Georg von Zimmerman's *On Solitude* (1756).

122. *"Three months' absence,"* as an old lady observed, *"is a terrible trial"*: L alludes to her short story 'An Old Lady of the Last Century,' NMM 46 (April 1836)."

123. *The Polar Star* and *Night at Sea.* Published in NMM 55 (January 1839). Landon sailed to West Africa with her husband from 5 July - 16 August 1838. She sent these two poems from Africa to Henry Colburn, editor of NMM, and they were published shortly after notices of her death appeared in English newspapers on 1 January 1839. Brodie Cruikshank, who visited the newly married couple on 15 October 1838, the night before Landon's death, wrote of her:

> She was much struck with the beauty of the heavens in those latitudes at night, and said it was when looking at the moon and the stars that her thoughts oftenest reverted to home. She pleased herself with thinking that the eyes of some beloved friend might be turned in the same direction, and that she had thus established a medium of communication for all that her heart wished to express. (1:222)

Angela Leighton notes that the refrain to "Night at Sea" is an adaptation of the refrain to Hemans's "A Parting Song" ("When will ye think of me, my/kind/sweet friends? / When will ye think of me?") (Leighton 72).

124. From *Fisher's Drawing Room Scrap Book.* All poems in this edition from *Fisher's* were originally written for engraved illustrations, except "The Fairy of the Fountains," "The Young Destructive," "Expectation," and "Disenchantment."

125 *Skeleton Group in the Rameswur, Caves of Ellora.* The Caves of Ellora, India, a popular tourist attraction during the nineteenth century, are temples which were cut from stone between AD 320-540. Many are carved with sculptures of figures from Hindu mythology. Despite her citation, Landon's source for the story of Siva and Parvati, a major Hindu god and goddess, is Thomas Maurice's *The History of Hindostan* (London, 1795; 3 vols. Rptd. New York and London: Garland, 1984). Maurice includes a prose translation of a portion of the Siva-Purana, an ancient Hindu religious text, in vol. 2, pp. 18-22, 104-116. Landon probably consulted Sir Charles Warre's article "Description of the Caves, &c. on the Mountains to the Eastward of Ellora," on pp. 382-423 of *Asiatic Researches* 6 (1809) for information about the Caves of Ellora. Warre describes the skeleton group in the cave-temple of

Ramishwur on p. 402: "a curious group of skeleton figures said to represent a miser, his wife, son, and daughter, all praying in vain for food, while two thieves are carrying off his wealth."

126. *Kilas*: the cave-temple of Keylas (Kailasanatha) is considered the most remarkable of the excavated temples of Ellora. Carved with numerous sculptures of Hindu deities, it is nicknamed "the paradise of the gods."

127. *William Henry Sykes* (1790-1872), naturalist and soldier in the East India Company, and author of the two-volume *A Catalogue of the Mammalia and Birds Observed in Dukhun, East Indies* (London: R. Taylor, 1832). The source of Landon's quotation from Sykes has not been identified.

128. *A Legend of Tintagel Castle.* Landon's sources were probably either Louisa Stuart Costello's poem "The Funeral Boat," published in the 1829 *Forget Me Not*, or Thomas Roscoe's translation of Novella LXXXI of the medieval Italian *Cento Novelle Antiche*, in his collection *The Italian Novelists* (1824):

> A daughter of the great Barbassoro became passionately attached to Launcelot of the Lake; but so far from returning her love, he bestowed all his affections on the fair Queen Genevra. To such a degree did her unhappy attachment arise, that she at length fell a victim to it, and died, leaving a bequest that, as soon as her soul had departed, her body should be transported on board a barge fitted up for the purpose, with a rich couch, and adorned with velvet stuffs and precious stones and ornaments; and thus arrayed in her proudest attire, with a bright golden crown upon her brows, she was to be borne alone to the place of residence of her beloved. Beneath her silver zone was found a letter to the following tenor; but we must first mention what ought to precede the letter itself. Everything was exactly fulfilled as she had appointed, respecting the vessel without a sail or oars, helmsman, or hands to guide her; and so, with its lifeless freight, it was launched upon the open waves. Thus she was borne along by the winds, which conveyed her directly to Camalot[sic], where the barge rested of itself upon the banks. A rumour immediately spread through the court, and a vast train of barons and cavaliers ran out of the palace, followed soon by King Arthur himself. They stood mute with astonishment on observing the strange vessel there, without a voice or a hand to stir her out of the dead calm in which she lay. The king was the first to set his foot upon her side, and he there beheld the gentle lady surrounded with the pomp of death. He too first

unclasped the zone, and cast his eye over the letter, directed —
"To all the Knights of the Round Table, greeting, from the poor
lady of Scalot, who invokes long health and fortune for the proud-
est lances of the world. Do they wish to learn how I am thus fear-
fully brought before them? Let my last hand witness that it was at
once for the sake of the noblest and vilest of the cavaliers of the
land—for the proud knight, Launcelot of the Lake. For neither
tears nor sighs of mine availed with him to have compassion on
my love. And thus, alas! you behold me dead,—fallen a victim
only for loving too true.

The *Cento Novelle Antiche* was also Tennyson's source for "The Lady
of Shalott." See Roger Simpson, "Landon's 'A Legend of Tintagel
Castle': Another Analogue of Tennyson's 'The Lady of Shalott,' *Ten-
nyson Research Bulletin* 4.4 (November 1985): 179-185.

129.   *"the flowers of the forest":* Title of an old Scots song.

130.   *Linmouth.* Republished as "The Country Retreat" in ZM.

131.   *Pope's hackneyed line:* Pope's "Epistle IV. Of the Nature and State of
Man, with respect to Happiness," ll. 237-238: "A Wit's a feather, and a
Chief a rod; / An honest man's the noblest work of God."

132.   *"God made the country, but man made the town":* Cowper, *The Task,*
Book 1 (The Sofa), l. 749.

133.   *"haunts me like a passion":* Wordsworth, "Tintern Abbey," l. 78.

134.   *Belgrave Square:* Prior to 1825-8, when Belgrave Square was designed
and built, the land was bare marshy ground.

135.   *Highgate Hill:* Site of many beautiful Georgian homes in greater Lon-
don.

136.   *Hebe.* Hebe was the daughter of Zeus and Hera, and the goddess of
youth and spring. She is represented in the Homeric epics as the cup-
bearer of Olympus. Her shame at falling down in the presence of the
gods while serving their wine made her desire never to appear before
them again, and she was replaced by Ganymede. Landon appears to
find in her mythology a significance peculiarly appropriate to women
who function in a dominantly male society.

137.   *Sassoor, in the Deccan.* Republished as "Thoughts on Christmas Day in

India" in ZM. The Deccan is the southern peninsula of India. Landon never visited India.

138. *peepul:* Also spelled "pipal," an Indian species of fig-tree, regarded as sacred; also known as the bo-tree.

139. *Thalaba:* see note to page 185.

140. *Hindoo and Mahommedan Buildings.* The source of the epigraph has not been identified.

141. *Scene in Kattiawar.* The source of the epigraph has not been identified. The Kathiawar Peninsula, in the state of Gujarat (Guzerat), in west-central India, did not fall under British control until 1820.

142. *The Fairy of the Fountains.* Landon's source is "The Story of Melusine," the last of sixteen tales in William J. Thoms's *Lays and Legends of France* (London, 1834), v. 2 of *Lays and Legends of Various Nations* (5 vols; London, 1834). *Lays and Legends of France* was reviewed favourably in LG for 31 May 1834, though the Melusina story was not mentioned.

STORY OF MELUSINE.

Elinas, king of Albania, to divert his grief for the death of his wife, amused himself with hunting. One day, at the chase, he went to a fountain to quench his thirst; as he approached it he heard the voice of a woman sing, and on coming to it he found there the beautiful fay Pressine.

After some time the fay bestowed her hand upon him, on the condition that he should never visit her in her lyings-in.

Pressine had three daughters at a birth: Melusine, Melior, and Palatine. Nathas, the king's son by a former wife, hastened to convey the joyful tidings to his father, and who, without reflection, flew to the chamber of the queen, and entered as she was bathing her daughters. Pressine, on seeing him, cried out that he had broken his word, and she must depart; and taking up her three daughters, she disappeared.

She retired to the Lost Island; so called, because it was only by chance, any, even those who had repeatedly visited it, could find it. Here she reared her children, taking them every morning to a high mountain, whence Albania might be seen, and telling them that but for their father's breach of promise they might have lived happily in the distant land they beheld.

When they were fifteen years of age, Melusine asked her mother of what their father had been guilty. On being informed of it, she conceived the idea of being revenged on him. Engaging her sisters to join in her plans, they set out for Albania: arrived there, they took the king and all his wealth, and, by a charm, inclosed him in a high mountain, called Brandelois.

On telling their mother what they had done, she to punish them for the unnatural action, condemned Melusine to become every Saturday a serpent, from the waist downwards, till she should meet a man who would marry her under the condition of never seeing her on a Saturday, and should keep his promise. She inflicted other judgments on her two sisters, less severe in proportion to their guilt.

Melusine now went rambling through the world in search of the man who was to deliver her. She passed through the Black Forest, and that of Ardennes, and at last she arrived in the forest of Colombiers, in Poitou, where all the fays of the neighbourhood came before her, telling her they waited for her to reign in that place.

Raymond having accidentally killed the count, his uncle, by the glancing aside of his boar-spear, was wandering by night in the forest of Colombiers. He arrived at a fountain that rose at the foot of a high rock. This fountain was called by the people the Fountain of Thirst, or the Fountain of the Fays, on account of the many marvellous things that had happened at it.

At the time, when Raymond arrived at the fountain, three ladies were diverting themselves by the light of the moon, the principal of whom was Melusine. Her beauty and her amiable manners quickly won his love: she soothed him, concealed the deed he had done, and married him, he promising on his oath never to desire to see her on a Saturday. She assured him that a breach of his oath would for ever deprive him of her whom he so much loved, and be followed by the unhappiness of both for life. Out of her great wealth, she built for him, in the Fountain of Thirst, where he first saw her, the castle of Lusignan. She also built Larochelle, Cloitre Malliers, Mersent, and other places.

But destiny, that would have Melusine single, was incensed against her. The marriage was made unhappy by the deformity of the children born of one that was enchanted; but still Raymond's love for the beauty that ravished both heart and eyes remained unshaken.

Destiny now renewed her attacks. Raymond's cousin had excited him to jealousy and to secret concealment, by malicious suggestions of the purport of the Saturday retirement of the countess. He hid himself, and then saw how the lovely form of Melusine ended below in a snake, gray and sky-blue, mixed with white. But it was not horror that seized him at the sight, it was infinite anguish at the reflection that through his breach of faith he might lose his lovely wife for ever. Yet this misfortune had not speedily come on him, were it not that his son, Geoffroi with the tooth,* had burned his brother Freimund, who would stay in the abbey of Malliers, with the abbot and a hundred monks. At which the afflicted father, count Raymond, when his wife Melusine was entering his closet to comfort him, broke out into these words against her: —

Out of my sight thou pernicious snake and odious serpent! thou contaminator of my race!

Melusine's former anxiety was now verified, and the evil that had lain so long in ambush had now fearfully sprung on him and her. At these reproaches she fainted away; and when at length she revived, full of the profoundest grief, she declared to him that she must now part from him, and, in obedience to a decree of destiny, fleet about the earth in pain and suffering, as a spectre, until the day of doom: and that only when one of her race was to die at Lusignan would she become visible.

Her words at parting were these:

"But one thing will I say unto thee before I part, that thee, and those who for more than a hundred years shall succeed thee, shall know that whenever I am seen to hover over the fair castle of Lusignan, then will it be certain that in that very year the castle will get a new lord; and though people may not perceive me in the air, yet they will see me by the Fountain of Thirst; and thus shall it be so long as the castle stands in honour and flourishing—especially on the Friday before the lord of the castle shall die."

She immediately, with wailing and loud lamentation, left the castle of Lusignan,† and has ever since existed as a spectre of the night. Raymond died as a hermit on Monserrat.

[*A boar's tusk projected from his mouth. According to Brantome, a figure of him, cut in stone, stood at the portal of Melusine tower, which was destroyed in 1574.]

[†At her departure she left the mark of her foot on the stone of one of the windows, where it remained till the castle was destroyed.]

Thoms's version of the tale is based on Thomas Keightley, *The Fairy Mythology* (London: Bell, 1828). Jean d'Arras first wrote down the history of Melusine as a prose romance in 1387 as *Chronique de la princesse* (first printed in Geneva, 1478).

143. *Nereid*: The Nereids were daughters of the sea god Nereus; they inhabited the seas and were friendly towards humankind.

144. *Immolation of a Hindoo Widow*. Republished as "A Suttee" in ZM. A suttee is a Hindu widow who immolates herself on the funeral pile with her husband's body. The custom was abolished by authority in British India in 1829.

145. *champac*: Indian tree with bright orange flowers, related to the magnolia.

146. *Pulo Penang*. Epigraph quoted from Emma Roberts, *Views in India, China, and on the Shores of the Red Sea* (London: Fisher, 1835), v. 2, p. 39. Pulau Penang is an island in present-day Malaysia; it came under the control of the East India Company in 1786.

147. *Eton Latin Grammar*. Also known as *An Introduction to the Latin Tongue* (1795); *Lindley Murray*: author of *English Grammar Adapted to the Different Classes of Learners* (1795). Both were popular grammar school textbooks.

148. *The Tombs of the Kings of Golconda*. Republished as "The Kings of Golconda" in ZM. Now a ruined city, Golconda, in southern India, was the capital of the Qutb Shahi kingdom in the sixteenth and seventeenth centuries.

149. *diamond mines*: Because of its famous diamond mines, the name of Golconda is synonymous with fabulous wealth in the works of many poets, including Hemans, Keats, Moore, and Browning.

150. *Thevenot*: Jean de Thevenot (1633-1667), French explorer and author of the five-volume *Voyages de M. de Thevenot tant en Europe qu'en Asia et en Afrique* (Paris, 1689). In Part III, Book II, Chapter VI ("Of the Castle of Golconda") Thevenot describes the tombs of the kings of Golconda. See Surendranath Sen, trans., *Indian Travels of Thevenot and Careri* (New Delhi: National Archives of India, 1949): 139-40.

151. *Captain Cook*. Republished as "To My Brother" in ZM. James Cook's *A Voyage Round the World* (1777) was a favourite book of the young Letitia Landon and her younger brother, Whittington.

152. *The Church of St. John, and the Ruins of Lahneck Castle, Formerly Belonging to the Templars*. Republished as "A Ruined Castle on the Rhine" in ZM. Lahneck Castle, near Coblenz, Germany, was built in 1244 and destroyed in 1688.

153. *The Portrait of Lord Byron, at Newstead Abbey.* Written for an engraving of an 1813 portrait of Byron by Richard Westall (1765-1836). Presently exhibited at the National Portrait Gallery, London, the portrait was formerly on display at Newstead Abbey, Nottinghamshire, the ancestral home of Byron's family.

154. "thick fancies": Lady Emmeline Stuart-Wortley (1806-1855), "Stanzas Written on Finishing the Maiden of Moscow," ll. 57-58: "Oft, like bright shattered mirrors, too, seemed, / Those thick fancies, that thronged through my mind!"

155. *The Hyacinth.* The flower is named for Hyacinthus, a youth beloved by Apollo, and slain by him accidentally. The flower sprang up from the dead youth's blood, its petals inscribed with the "mystic characters" (l.22) "Ai" ("woe").

Appendix A: Contemporary Reviews

The following selection of reviews of Landon's poetry and novels is intended to provide the reader with a glimpse into the first stage of her reception history. Though her work was noticed by periodicals such as *The Athenaeum* and *The Westminster Review*, other major literary reviews completely ignored her, including *The Edinburgh Review* and *The Quarterly Review*. As one might expect, *The Literary Gazette* and *The New Monthly Magazine*, whose popularity owed much to the frequent submission of poems, essays, and stories signed "L.E.L.," produced very flattering reviews of Landon's volumes, which led to frequent accusations of "puffery" by other leading journals.

Most of the reviews are anonymous: if an unsigned reviewer has been identified through the use of *The Wellesley Index* or a similar source, his name is provided in brackets. Brackets within the text of the reviews indicate editorial commentary, and a set of ellipses indicate that part of the text has been omitted. For a listing of critical reviews of Landon's major works, see Glennis Stephenson, *Letitia Landon: The Woman Behind L.E.L.*, (Manchester and New York: Manchester UP, 1995): 205-207.

1. *The Literary Gazette*, no. 389 (3 July 1824): 417-20. [Anonymous, but almost certainly William Jerdan. The omitted portion consists of excerpts of the title poem interspersed with minimal commentary.]

The Improvisatrice; and other Poems. By L.E.L. 12mo. pp. 327. London 1824. Hurst, Robinson, & Co.; Edinburgh, Constable & Co.

It will be expected from us that we speak of this volume in terms of the warmest admiration; because, if we had not thought very highly of the genius of its author, the pages of the *Literary Gazette* would not have been enriched with so many of her compositions. But indeed we are enthusiastic in this respect; and as far as our poetical taste and critical judgment enable us to form an opinion, we can adduce no instance, ancient or modern, of similar talent and excellence. That the *Improvisatrice* is the work of a young female, may, at the outset, lessen its importance in the eyes of those who judge by analogy, without fairly examining individual merits; but it will ultimately enhance the value and augment the celebrity of this delightful production.[*]

If true poetry consist in originality of conception, fineness of imagination, beautiful fitness and glow of expression, genuine feeling, and the outpourings of fresh and natural thoughts in all the force of fresh and natural language, it is pre-eminently conspicuous in the writings of L.E.L. Neither are her subjects nor mode of treating them, borrowed from others; but simplicity, gracefulness, fancy, and pathos, seem to gush forth in spontaneous and sweet union, whatever may be the theme. And, especially for a youthful author, her poems possess one rare and almost peculiar quality — their style is purely English. In the whole volume before us we do not meet with one ambitious word, one extraneous idiom, or one affected phrase. The effect is correspondingly great; and never did accustomed English words more distinctly prove their high poetical powers. It seems as if by some magic touch mean and household things were changed into the rarest and most brilliant ornaments; and in reality it is that the spell of native genius throws a splendour over the common, and imparts a new degree of energy and beauty to the simple and plain.

Having offered these general remarks, we shall proceed to illustrate them by a view of the principal poem — *The Improvisatrice*, which would, alone, entitle the fair author to the name of the English Sappho. It is an exquisite story of unfortunate love; and extremely ingenious in its frame or construction. The *Improvisatrice* is an impassioned daughter of sunny Italy, gifted with those powers of

---

[*] Our contemporaries of the periodical press, both in London and the country, will, we are sure, excuse our hinting to them the propriety of acknowledging whatever extracts they may choose to select from this publication. The compositions of L.E.L., as they have appeared in the *Literary Gazette*, have been most universally copied to adorn their pages; and while our Journal alone was concerned, we were not over-desirous that they should quote the original: but now, when the writer comes forward in her own person, justice, gallantry, and honour, demand that tribute which we are confident will be generally and cheerfully paid. — *Ed.*

song which the name implies, and supposed to utter her extemporaneous effusions, as occasions are presented in her chequered life. Her career is represented as alternately bright and clouded; her perceptions are always vivid, and her feelings intense. All fire, and heart, and soul, the chords of her existence vibrate to the slightest impressions, and send forth tones of various and striking melody when swept by the stronger impulses of her excitable and sensitive nature. Endowed with all the characteristic tenderness, fragility, and loveliness of woman, she is the very creature of inspiration; and her being may be said to be divided between the finest sense of external beauty and the deepest consciousness of moral emotions....

It has lately been repeated by several of our critical guides, that our epoch of poetry has closed. They have taken up a fanciful theory; and because the minstrel harp of the Border has been hushed, and the light of Childe Harolde's flame extinguished, they rashly venture to decree, that a number of silent years must elapse before the birth of another era of song. We will not pay them so ill a compliment as to believe that they will maintain this opinion after they have read *The Improvisatrice*. We doubt not the ability to discover some of the faults of youthful composition in her strains; but we would most sincerely pity the person who could notice them amid the transcendant beauties of thought, expression, imagery, and fervent genius, with the blaze of which they are surrounded and illuminated. For ourselves, discarding every idea of such prescribed Augustan ages, we do not hesitate to say, that in our judgment this volume forms itself an era in our country's bright cycle of female poetical fame. What may spring from the continued cultivation of such promise, it is not easy to predicate; but if the author never excels what she has already done, we can confidently give her the assurance of what the possessor of such talents must most earnestly covet — *Immortality*.

[Besides the chief poem upon which we have dwelt with so much pleasure, there is a sequel of about double the extent of miscellaneous pieces, of which we have only at present room to say, that they are devoted to subjects entirely differing in sentiment and subject from each other, and altogether worthy of L.E.L.]

2. *The Literary Magnet* 2 (1824): 106–109.

The IMPROVISATRICE, and other POEMS. By L.E.L. 12mo. pp. 327. London. Hurst, Robinson, and Co. Edinburgh. Constable and Co. 1824.

We have seldom had occasion, in our critical capacity, to question the judgment of our contemporary Reviewers; because, however they may differ in opinion with respect to the merits of particular works, their comments are, in general, remarkable for fairness and candour, and they appear to be influenced only by a wish to afford to their readers a just estimate of the value of such works as have come within their notice: but when we see an instance of open, bare-faced puffing, and undisguised partiality, we cannot too strongly condemn, or too openly expose it. And we feel that this condemnation and exposure are the more incumbent on us, as the critic to whom we shall allude, by some accident or other, stands high in the estimation of the public, and conducts a Literary Journal of talent and celebrity.

The task, which has thus devolved upon us, is not of a very pleasing nature; but, in justice to the public, we shall endeavour to fulfil it. Without farther preamble, we will merely state, that the *Literary Gazette* is the work to which we allude, and that the review, which we cannot sufficiently condemn, will be found in one of its recent numbers, and is occasioned in consequence of the appearance of a poem, called *The Improvisatrice*, which is said to be the production of a very young lady, who has written a vast number of love-sick Sonnets under the initials L.E.L. which, from time to time, have appeared in the pages of the above-named Journal.

Let it not be supposed, however, that we have sat down to pass a sweeping censure on The Improvisatrice, and its fair Author; far be it from us to wish to repress the outpourings of a fond and youthful fancy, or to check the impassioned accents of a Muse, whose strains are devoted to Love, and all his soft endearments. We are no hermits, nor have we reached that sober decline of life, when the heyday of the blood attends upon the judgment; and, indeed, if we had, the verses of our "English Sappho" would go far in heating us again. Her descriptions are sufficiently warm and luxurious: she appears to be the very creature of passionate inspiration; and the wild and romantic being whom she describes as the Improvisatrice, seems to be the very counterpart of her sentimental self. Her poetical breathing appears to proceed from a soul, whose very essence is love; and seared hearts — withered hopes — broken lutes — blighted flowers — music and moonlight, sing their melancholy changes through all her verses. The Improvisatrice, like the Corinne of Madame De Stael, is an Italian female, who is supposed to be endued with the power of uttering her feelings and fancies in extemporaneous rhyme. Born in Florence, her childhood

> Passed mid radiant things,
> Glorious as Hope's imaginings:
> Statues, but known from shapes of the earth,
> By being too lovely for mortal birth;
> Paintings, whose colours of life were caught
> From the fairy tints in the rainbow wrought;
> Music, whose sighs had a spell like those,
> That float on the sea at the evening's close;
> Language so silvery, that every word
> Was like the lute's awakening chord;
> Skies half sunshine, and half star-light;
> Flowers, whose lives were a breath of delight;
> Leaves, whose green pomp knew no withering;
> Fountains, bright as the skies of our spring;
> And songs, whose wild and passionate line,
> Suited a soul of romance. [ll. 9-24]

Surrounded with such beauty and harmony, she becomes naturally a painter and poet, and breathes in song the emotions of her full heart, or pictures on the canvas her dreams of ideal beauty. As yet, however, love had not crossed her visions:

> but each wild
> High thought she nourished, raised a pyre
> For love to light, — [ll. 185-87]

and the young god accordingly soon sets it on fire. Lorenzo is the happy youth who fills her fond heart with a passion as boundless and extravagant as might have been expected from the combustible materials of which her affections were composed. Under the influence of this passion, she sings her improvised songs with new vehemence and vigour. And many episodes are introduced, all of a melancholy tendency, and leading, by a natural sympathy, to the fate which awaited the fair songstress herself. Lorenzo, while he confesses his love for her, is forced to give his hand in marriage to another, and the Improvisatrice, after witnessing the nuptials of her lover with her more fortunate rival, utters a few farewell verses, and is supposed to die of a broken heart. These are the chief incidents which compose the Poem of the Improvisatrice. The volume, which is neatly got up, and prettily embellished, in addition to the principal Poem, is filled up with a number of Miscellaneous Pieces, of which we shall merely remark, that they are all in the same strain of sad monotony, although the critic in the Literary Gazette takes pains to assure his readers, that they totally differ from each other in sentiment and subject. In fact, the chief fault which pervades the poetry of L.E.L. is its unbroken sameness. Her Muse is always in mourning, and sighs and tears are the food on which she loves to banquet. Her harp has but one note, and that wakes to sorrow only. Stanzas on a Withered Flower, Lines to a Deserted Harp, or Verses to a Faithless Lover, are the chief subjects of her song.

We regret that our space will not permit us to give lengthened extracts from the poem before us. The Death Song of Sappho, however, we will take the liberty to extract entire, not only as it affords a good specimen of the author's peculiar talent, and of the monotonous melancholy which runs through all her poetry, but from the high commendation which the Reviewer in the Literary Gazette bestows upon it. "We are acquainted," says he, "with nothing more beautiful in our language."

[here the reviewer prints "Sappho's Song"]

Now, admitting, as we cheerfully do, that these verses are pretty, we will confidently ask, do they merit a higher eulogium? Are they not, in fact, another version of fifty similar songs, to which we could point in the back numbers of the *Literary Gazette*? the inference is easily drawn, and the motive for this Editorial puff is sufficiently obvious. L.E.L. as we have before stated, supplies the poetical department of that journal, and thus, in praising her productions, the wily Editor is not unmindful of himself. But this is not the first occasion for our friend in the Gazette to puff his fair correspondent. We remember that sometime since, a report was spread of the premature death of this same interesting young lady, and the *Literary Gazette* joined in the solemn foolery, lamenting her timeless decease, as if it really happened. How far the humbug succeeded, we have little means of ascertaining, but every honourable mind must despise such a pitiable resort.

We shall now select a few of the extravagant encomiums lavished on the *Improvisatrice* in the Review, to which we have so often alluded, and regretting that our limits will not permit us to draw more copious extracts from the work itself, we refer it to our readers; and when they have considered its contents, we will ask them in sober seriousness, was the grave Editor of the *Literary Gazette* in his right senses when he sent the following passages to be printed? "As far," says the Critic, "as our poetical taste and judgment enable us to form an opinion, we can adduce no instance *ancient* or *modern* of similar talent and excellence;" and again, in his concluding paragraph, "this volume forms an era in our country's bright cycle of female poetical fame — we can give her the assurance of what the possessor of such talents must most earnestly covet — IMMORTALITY!!!"

In concluding our notice of the *Improvisatrice*, we hope that, in offering the foregoing remarks, we may not be misunderstood. We love poetry, and we respect the name of poet, as ardently, perhaps, as any of our brother critics; and, whether the lyre is swept by a male or female hand, matters not to us, so as we are affected by the music of its chords: indeed, we are inclined to feel that, in the latter case, we should be more disposed to be soothed and delighted. Of L.E.L. therefore, we cannot but speak in terms of praise. She possesses taste, sweetness, and a high poetical feeling; and we only regret she should have fallen into interested hands, by which her talents are premature-

[handwritten margin note:] All press is good press.

ly thrust upon the world, and rated so far beyond their merits. We will ask this question, and we believe there are few persons who will not give to it a ready answer. Had the *Improvisatrice* been published anonymously, that is, had its author been *entirely unknown*, would it have been lauded as it has been by the Editor of the *Literary Gazette*? We love to give merit its due: we love to advance timid and retiring genius, and most strongly do we feel the claim, which a young and gifted female advances to our favour and protection. But we despise the despicable artifices of literary men to advance their own interest. And in our estimation of the works of others we shall always remember that there is an unerring standard by which merit may be judged, independently of self-interest, favour, or affection.

3. [John G. Lockhart.] "Noctes Ambrosianae, no. XVI." *Blackwood's Magazine* 16 (August 1824): 237-38.

ODOHERTY.

Literary Gazettes! — What a rumpus all that fry have been keeping up about Miss Landon's poetry — the Improvisatrice, I mean.

NORTH.

Why, I always thought you had been one of her greatest admirers, Odoherty. Was it not you that told me she was so very handsome? — A perfect beauty, I think you said.

ODOHERTY.

And I said truly. She is one of the sweetest little girls in the world, and her book is one of the sweetest little books in the world; but Jerdan's extravagant trumpetting has quite sickened everybody; and our friend Alaric has been doing rather too much in the same fashion. This sort of stuff plays the devil with any book. Sappho! and Corinna, forsooth! Proper humbug!

NORTH.

I confess you are speaking pretty nearly my own sentiments. I ran over the book — and I really could see nothing of the originality, vigour, and so forth, they all chatter about. Very elegant, flowing verses they are — but all made up of Moore and Byron.

ODOHERTY.

Nay, nay, when you look over the Improvisatrice again, I am sure you will retract this. You know very well that I am no great believer in female genius; but nevertheless, there is a certain feminine elegance about the voluptuousness of this book, which, to a certain extent, marks it with an individual character of its own.

NORTH.

I won't allow you to review this book, my dear Standard-bearer for I perceive you are half in love with the damsel concerned; and under such circumstances, a cool and dispassionate estimate is what nobody could be expected to give — least of all you, you red-hot monster of Munster.

ODOHERTY.

No abuse, my old Bully-rock.

4. *The Westminster Review* 3 (April 1825): 537-39. [Landon's preface to The Venetian Bracelet was written largely in response to this and the following reviews.]

The Improvisatrice: and other Poems. By L.E.L. 12mo. p.p. 227. Longman and Co. 1824.

We imagine very few of our readers know, that, within the last twelvemonths, there has appeared a volume of poetry, on which the following decision has been pronounced: "as far as our poetical taste and critical judgment enable us to form an opinion, we can adduce no instance ancient or modern, of similar talent and excellence." The ancients are out done, and the moderns are surpassed by an English poet of the year of our Lord 1824, and this is the first moment that the news has come to our ears! That poet, too, the same critic informs us, is "a young female."

Our readers, no doubt, are restless with curiosity to learn the name of the critic, and the name of the poet: when we mention the London Literary Gazette, as the work in which the criticism appeared, probably we have given to all, who are acquainted with this weekly journal, a sufficient criterion of the worth of the criticism.

We are afraid that having informed our readers that "the poetical taste and critical judgment" which pronounce the eulogium upon this poet, are those of the Literary Gazette, we shall have entirely quenched their curiosity to learn any thing about the writings of the young female; and most probably have excited a strong prejudice against them. Assuredly few have more reason to apply the Italian proverb to themselves, than she has:

> Da chi mi fido, mi guarda Dio:
> Da chi non mi fido, mi guarderò Io.

thus rendered in homely language by a writer of the 16th century:

> From him I trust God help me at my neede:
> Of him I trust not, myself will take heede.

As we may have done harm, therefore, to L.E.L. (for she is the poetess to the talent and excellence of whose Improvisatrice and other poems, the critic of the Literary Gazette can find no parallel ancient or modern), by quoting the eulogium of her panegyrist, we will endeavour to atone for it, by assuring our readers, that her poems are better than such a criticism from such a critic might lead them to expect.

If we are to trust the Literary Gazette and common gossip, authorities pretty much on a par on this subject, poets are as plenty as mushrooms, and start up, in the present day, as rapidly as they do after a shower. We cannot walk the streets of London without jostling a poet; and our provincial towns and country places equally abound in them. There appeared at Christmas last, at least half a dozen Literary Pocket Books, and each of those boasted of having at least a dozen poets on their establishment: what a contrast between the year 1825, when Britain alone could boast of nearly one hundred poets, and the 2500 years or thereabouts that elapsed between Homer and Milton, when the whole world could not boast of half that number.

Every body talks, and judges about poetry; most people write what they call poetry some time in their lives; and yet not two persons agree what poetry really is. We certainly are not going, at present, to define it, or inquire into its essential elements, but we may just remark, that the highest and rarest kind of poetry is that of thought: this, no language can deprive of its essential and intrinsic excellence, though language may set it off to advantage. A second and very inferior species of poetry consists in thoughts not poetical in themselves, but expressed in language, which, by the associations connected with it, excites the imagination or feelings, and carries them out of this world of reality, into a world of their own. Their abode there, however, is not nearly so undisturbed, pleasurable, or permanent, as when they are transported thither by the magic power of the poetry of thought and language united. Besides these, we know of no other kind of poetry: what in general passes for such, is nothing else but an assemblage of metaphors, similes, and poetical words, often destitute of any meaning, and never possessed of more than is barely sufficient to preserve it from falling into absolute nonsense.

All languages have metaphors and similes: the English language is also very rich in poetical terms; words, that, having always been set apart for poetry, have, as mere words, poetical associations, and no associations connected with common life, conversation, or literature. To a real poet, one who has poetical thoughts, such a language affords great facilities and advantages: it enables him to transmit, in their undiminished sublimity, beauty, or pathos, all that his imagination or his feelings create in his own breast. But, to a person who is not a poet in thought, the English language is an evil, not a blessing; its richness in poetical terms conceals from him his own poverty in poetical thought; and because he has at command a string of poetical expressions he foolishly imagines himself a poet.

L.E.L. has, with multitudes of others at all times, and more especially in the present day, fallen into this mistake: and she has fallen into it the more readily and deeply, because nearly all her poetry relates to love, a topic, for every thing connected with which there are nearly as many forms of expression and words as there are in Arabic for a lion; and on which we would engage to manufacture a poet out of any young person, particularly a female, by supplying her with a dictionary of love phrases, similes, &c., with as little exertion of intellect, as is employed in manufacturing a stocking in the loom.

That our authoress is capable of better things, that, amidst very much that is mere verbiage, and pages filled with puny and sickly thoughts clothed in glittering language that draws the eye off from their real character and value, there are indications of poetical talent, the following quotation, from one of the minor poems, proves: premising that the heroine of it had deserted her widowed mother, gone off with a lover; had been, in her turn, deserted by him, and is returning to her parent:

> 'She reached her mother's cottage; by that gate
> She thought how her once lover wont to wait
> To tell her honied tales! — and then she thought
> On all the utter ruin he had wrought!
> The moon shone brightly, as it used to do
> Ere youth, and hope, and love, had been untrue;
> But it shone o'er the desolate! The flowers
> Were dead; the faded jessamine, unbound,
> Trailed, like a heavy weed upon the ground.
> She entered in the cottage. None were there!
> The hearth was dark, — the walls looked cold and bare!
> All — all spoke poverty and suffering!
> All — all was changed; and but one only thing
> Kept its old place! ROSALIE'S mandolin
> Hung on the wall, where it had ever been.

There was one other room — and R O S A L I E
Sought for her mother there. A heavy flame
Gleamed from a dying lamp; a cold air came
Damp from the broken casement. There one lay,
Like marble seen but by the moonlight ray!
And R O S A L I E drew near. One withered hand
Was stretched, as it would reach a wretched stand
Where some cold water stood! And by the bed
She knelt — and gazed — and saw her mother — dead!'
["Rosalie," ll. 277-91.]

To conclude; our serious and well-meant advice to L.E.L. is, to free herself as much as possible from her poetical vocabulary, to nurse her poetical thoughts, to avoid the subject of love, a topic so full of words and so barren of thought, and, above all not to be elated by the praise, or guided by the "poetical taste and critical judgment" of the Literary Gazette, if she wish that her reputation as a poet should rest on a solid and permanent foundation.

5. [John Arthur Roebuck.] "The Poetry of L.E.L." *The Westminster Review* 7 (January 1827): 50-67.

1. *The Troubadour, a Poem.* By L.E.L. Hurst, Robinson, and Co. 1825.
2. *The Golden Violet, a Poem.* By L.E.L. Hurst, Robinson, and Co. 1826.

The attention we shall bestow upon the poems of L.E.L. will not be commensurate with our own opinion of their merits, but rather with the admiration universally bestowed on them by the class of readers to whom they are addressed; viz. the younger part of the fair sex, and those members of our's who deem it interesting to be sentimentally melancholy. As we feel a deep concern in the welfare of the former class of readers, and some pity for the situation of the latter, we shall consider our time well spent if we succeed in laying before them a correct estimate of these extravagantly applauded productions.

One word, however, by way of preface, concerning the authoress. Men are generally accustomed to treat women much in the same manner in which a superstitious votary treats the image of his saint; they approach them with reverence, bestow upon them, in words, great homage and adoration, and invariably manifest, by their actions, a most contemptuous opinion of their intellect. It is our intention to pursue a different course. We shall not shrink from a fair and complete criticism of the present works because they are the works of a woman; but this criticism will be written in the belief, and with a wish to impress the belief, that the authoress is equally capable with ourselves of comprehending the reasons we shall assign for the hardest of our strictures. Though our language be very remote from the extravagant flattery she has experienced, and by which it is scarcely possible that she should not have been intoxicated, it will not be the language of flippancy or invective; it will be addressed to her reason. We shall state no opinions without the arguments on which they are grounded; and however unsparing may be our critique, it will express no disrespect, will assume no fancied superiority. We shall address the authoress as an equal, because we consider her an equal; we shall repress nothing out of regard to her weakness, because we do not consider her weak: in short, we shall be perfectly candid in declaring our opinions, which, though far from favourable, are neither inspired by personal ill-will, nor by the still more contemptible desire of rendering any of our readers merry at her expense. Let the authoress fairly weigh our reasons, and we have little doubt that her good sense will at once acknowledge the justness of the conclusions to which they lead.

We shall endeavour as well to point out the practical tendency of L.E.L.'s productions, as to discuss their poetical merits. But as we well know that the influence exercised by a poem depends chiefly upon the estimation in which its poetical merits are held, we shall first proceed to estimate the value of L.E.L.'s writings considered merely as poetry. If we succeed in establishing our opinions on this point, the observations we shall afterwards promulge regarding their tendency will be received with greater attention, and acquiesced in with greater readiness.

L.E.L.'s poems are, for the most part, metrical romances; generally sentimental descriptions of sentimental loves: it is nothing wonderful, therefore, that they have attracted the admiration of her female readers. Love is the great business of a woman's life; and any one who discourses with but ordinary ability on this all-important topic, finds in a woman a ready, patient, and admiring listener. Such facile judges, however, are not to be implicitly relied on; they but too often confound the attraction of the matter with the manner in which it is treated, and erroneously attribute to the mode in which the subject is discussed, the pleasure which arises solely from the inherent interest of the subject itself. We are inclined to believe that such has been the mistake in the present instance; and that L.E.L. has acquired a degree of fame by writing on love, which she by no means deserves, and which her readers would not have awarded had she chosen a less seductive theme.

It is generally believed, that to render a metrical romance entertaining, requires less ability than to create equal interest in a poem of any other description. This, however, is only partially true. The reader, indeed, finds mediocrity less irksome when his attention is somewhat occupied by a story, than when he has to depend for amusement solely on the poetical beauties of the production: but if mediocrity be more irksome in a poem without a narrative, perfection is more easy. The poetical novelist must not only possess the ordinary poetical excellencies, a fund of striking and original ideas, with the capacity of expressing them in powerful and melodious language, but must also possess powers of a totally distinct, and still more rare description — the powers requisite to imagine, and to unfold an interesting fable: he must know as well what incidents will create vivid emotions in his reader's mind, as the manner in which those incidents should be related to produce their full effect. To acquire this knowledge, he must study human nature profoundly. It is not surprising, that few should soar above mediocrity in a pursuit requiring qualifications that few have perseverance or capacity to acquire.

Concerning the narrative parts of L.E.L.'s poems there can hardly be two opinions. That the incidents of her tales have by others been a hundred times repeated is a matter of fact about which there can be no dispute; that even when new they were exceedingly puerile and uninteresting, is a matter of opinion, to which few, we believe, who have read her poems, will refuse their assent.

A youthful pair invariably find themselves, at the commencement of the romance, in that ecstatic state of feeling usually termed being in love. The heroine is uniformly represented as perfectly beautiful; sometimes, indeed, she is a blonde, flushed with health, possessing "clouds of fair hair," laughing blue eyes, and rosy lips: at other times she is a darker and more pensive beauty, whose brilliant eyes "flash darkly beautiful;" whose glossy curls surpass the raven's wing in the darkness of their hue, and whose pale and lofty brow speaks of exalted and melancholy musings. These engaging qualities are judiciously varied to suit different tastes, but at every change the heroine still is beautiful. The hero also possesses his share of personal attractions: he is always tall, straight, well-proportioned, and valorous; he may be either slender, or stoutly built, brown or fair, possessing dark eyes or blue, fair or black hair, a warrior or a bard. As the romance proceeds, this engaging pair are crossed in their loves: to bear up against this misfortune, the gentleman rushes to war, and consoles himself by slaughtering his fellow-creatures; the lady, with more humanity, manifests her constancy by rendering only herself unhappy: she gradually pines away, and because deprived of one pleasure, ceases to enjoy every other. These untoward circumstances having detained the denouement for the established time, the romance is at length brought to a pleasant or fatal conclusion, by overcoming the cross accidents, or rendering them insuperable.

Such being the dramatis personë, the next question is, where to place them. It is evident that such heavenly beings could only be the production of a heavenly country: we accordingly find them amidst bowers of roses, jasmines, honeysuckles; always wandering by the banks of some fair river; inhaling the odours of the above-mentioned flowers, and lulled to slumber by the gurgling of some sparkling streamlet; cooing turtles attend them by day, and plaintive nightingales by night. The air of this delicious country is ever mild and balmy, the sun ever bright, and the moon always at full. Such are the narrations invariably found in the poems of our authoress: of the talent requisite to concoct them, of their novelty and their interest when concocted, the reader is capable of judging without our assistance.

We believe, however, that L.E.L. would prefer to rest her claims to admiration upon her poetical excellencies, rather than upon her merits as the contriver of a romantic fiction. These excellencies we will now examine.

We shall not attempt in this place to enumerate all the requisites to good poetry; we shall select only those particulars necessary for our present purpose. It may be said, without any great deviation from accuracy, that the excellence of any poetry, considered merely as poetry, depends upon the reflections or descriptions it contains, and the language in which those reflections and descriptions are expressed.

Reflections in poetry, as elsewhere, should at least be just: it would be an additional merit if they were new; and in all cases they should, at any rate, be pertinent, arising naturally from the objects supposed to suggest them, and illustrating, in some manner, the matter then actually in question.

To reflection, however, L.E.L. seems little disposed: all that we have met with in her poems, which comes under that denomination, are some few, yet trite, remarks on the fickleness of fortune, the instability of human happiness, and the cruelty of the world. Her complaints are usually of the following description: — *

> 'The first, the very first; oh! none
> Can feel again as they have done.'

> 'Alas! that every lovely thing
> Lives only but for withering;
> That Spring rainbows, and Summer shine
> End but in Autumn's pale decline.'

---

* Our quotations, in this article, are almost entirely extracted from the Troubadour. The observations, however, which they illustrate, apply equally to the Golden Violet, which is merely a repetition in different words of the ideas contained in the Troubadour.

The fleeting existence of rainbows is indeed an interesting and original subject of complaining; but the wisdom of such sorrow, or the pertinence of the remark, we are at a loss to discover: neither can we perceive what rational cause of rejoicing would exist, even if rainbows became everlasting. Moreover, although it be true as to Summer, that it ends when Autumn begins, Spring rainbows end somewhat earlier: this is an instance of the incorrectness always attendant on hasty writing. We would advise L.E.L. to trust in future less to her reader's ear, and more to his understanding.

The triteness of the following remark is only equalled by its incorrectness.

> 'She led him to the lonely cot,
> And almost Amirald wish'd his lot
> Had been cast in *that humble life,*
> *Over whose peace the hour of strife*
> *Passes but like the storm at sea,*
> *That wakes not earth's tranquillity.'*

The day-dreams of Arcadian happiness have long since vanished: that poverty is rarely a state of enjoyment or content, is a proposition that no one above fifteen years of age now thinks of denying. We would ask also what is meant by the hour of strife passing over peace? peace is destroyed by strife; but we never before heard it made (even by metaphor), a sort of high road over which strife might occasionally travel.

A portrait suggests the following lamentation:—

> 'How sad, how strange, to think the shade,
> The copy faint of beauty made,
> Should be the only wreck that death
> Shall leave of so much bloom and health.
> The cheek, long since the earth-worm's prey,
> Beside the lovely of to-day,
> Here smiles as bright, as fresh, as fair,
> As if of the same hour it were.'

Whatever fame L.E.L. has acquired, however, is owing chiefly to her descriptions; to her descriptions of love, heroes, heroines, and landscapes.

Descriptions, as well as reflections, if intended to be worth reading, should be original: it is not requisite, indeed, that the objects described be different from those which other men have described, but the description should at least put them in a novel light. Moreover, as the object of a description is to present to the mind not only a vivid picture, but a picture of the very thing described, no epithet or illustration should be used that does not directly or indirectly contribute to this end. It is not by crowding epithet on epithet, image on image, that we raise this vivid conception, but by enumerating in the fewest words possible those few leading particulars that are sufficient to suggest all the remaining ideas requisite to a complete conception of the object we wish to represent to the imagination. We cannot better explain our meaning than by adducing the following example. It is the description of Andromache receiving her child from the arms of Hector, whose departure creates in her bosom the most anxious alarm. The tenderness of the mother, and the anxiety of the wife, are thus beautifully, yet simply described: —

> "He spoke, and fondly gazing on her charms,
> Restored the pleasing burthen to her arms;
> Soft on her fragrant breast the babe was laid,
> Hush'd to repose, and with a smile survey'd;
> The troubled pleasure soon chastised by fear,
> She mingled with the smile a tender tear."
>
> [Pope's *Iliad* 6. 616-621.]

It would be difficult by any number of words to raise a more vivid conception of Andromache's feelings than is created by this simple narrative. The reason is obvious. The laying the child on her bosom, hushing it to repose, and smiling over its slumbers, are all actions expressive of maternal affection; these indications are sufficient to suggest the idea of that state of mind which constitutes a tender and affectionate parent, while the sorrow that immediately succeeds or rather mingles with her joy, suggests with equal certainty the ideas of all those painful emotions which an affectionate wife would experience upon the departure of her husband to battle. Thus Cowper, in his admirable description of crazy Kate, conveys to the imagination a more vivid feeling of a wandering intellect by describing her as "begging an idle pin of all she meets," and hoarding it in her sleeve, than the most laboured enumeration of her extravagancies could have created. What more evident and striking proof of imbecillity, than supplicating only for a pin, when destitute of every thing requisite for the preservation of life?

We will adduce one other illustration of these observations. Virgil, in describing the effects of a pest amongst the herds, gives the following example: —

> "Ecce autem duro fumans sub vomere taurus
> Concidit, et mixtum spumis vomit ore cruorem.
> Extremos ciet gemitus. It tristis arator
> Mœrentem abjungens fraternâ morte juvencum;
> Atque opere in medio defixa relinquit aratra."
>
> [*Georgics*, 3. 515-519.]

Every object here mentioned serves to heighten the picture of misery. The ox dropping suddenly down, and dying; the sad husbandman loosing from the yoke the yet remaining ox, sorrowing for the death of his fellow, and the plough stayed in mid-furrow, are images that immediately create a strong and definite conception of the misery and desolation attendant on the pestilence the poet is describing.

The poems of L.E.L. furnish new instances of descriptions in consonance with the rules we are endeavouring to illustrate.

The conventional language of poetry, as distinguished from prose, after it has been made the vehicle of fine poetry, retains in some degree the power of calling up poetical ideas, even when it is thrown together without form, order, or meaning. A dictionary of such words, if printed in lines of ten syllables, might be mistaken for poetry by many who fancy themselves ardent admirers of poetic genius; and would in truth have as much claim to the title as nine tenths of the verses which are commonly read and admired. Trusting to these poetical associations, and being pleased herself with the words, L.E.L. has crowded epithets and similes into her verses without regard either to poetical numbers or to reason. In many of her lines, consequently, it would be difficult to find sense, and still more difficult to find correct prosody. She evidently describes from the descriptions of others, and not from the observation and study of nature itself. Her descriptions therefore never bring the whole object definitely before our view: scattered and unconnected particulars are enumerated, and epithet added to epithet, without any determinate end. We thus find suggested to our imagination only a confused mass of single images, destitute of connection, or any particular adaption to the subject. The following description of a battle from Byron, when compared with one extracted from the Troubadour, will fully illustrate our meaning: —

> "As rolls the river into ocean,
>   In sable torrent widely streaming;
>   As the sea-tide's opposing motion,
>   In azure column proudly gleaming,
> Beats back the current many a rood
> In curling foam and mingling flood,
> While eddying whirl, and breaking wave,
> Roused by the blast of winter rave;
> Through sparkling spray, in thundering clash
> The lightnings of the waters flash
> In awful whiteness o'er the shore,
> That shines and shakes beneath the roar,
> Thus — as the stream and ocean greet
> With waves that madden as they meet —
> Thus join the bands whom mutual wrong,
> And fate and fury drive along."

[The Girour 620-635.]

A river dashing into ocean, and a rushing tide impetuously repelling the headlong torrent, are magnificent illustrations of the furious charge of hostile armies; and the uproar created by the elemental strife is an awful picture of human warfare. From the commencement to the end of this description there is one definite comparison strictly adhered to; and every epithet used, every circumstance alluded to, serves to heighten the similarity. But this apt similitude and determinate purpose are not to be found in the following passage: —

> 'One silent gaze, as if each band
> Could slaughter both with eye and hand.
> Then peals the war-cry! then the dash
> Amid the waters! and the crash
> Of spears — the falchion's iron ring,
> The arrow hissing from the string,
> Tell they have met. *Thus from the height*
> *The torrent rushes in his might.*
> *With lightning's speed, the thunder's peal,*
> *Flashes the lance, and strikes the steel.*
> "Many a steed to earth is borne,
> Many a banner trampled and torn,"*
> †*Or ever its brand* could strike a blow,
> Many a gallant arm lies low:
> Many a scarf and many a crest,
> Float with the leaves on the river's breast.'

This is merely a confused enumeration of a few unconnected particulars, many of which, from the vague and general manner in which they are described, might with equal propriety belong to a tournament, a chase, and to a battle. The fury and the headlong madness of *combatants* are no where depicted. The torrent rushes in his might, but is a pacific torrent; meeting with no opponent, it is not an illustration of a combatant. Moreover, the arrow hissing from the string is no indication of the combatants having met, but is rather a proof that they are yet distant from each other. Neither is there any thing compared with "the torrent rushing in his might." The word "thus" is used, but is neither referred nor referrible to any preceding

---

* Almost verbatim from the two bad lines in the speech of Marmion to king James.
† "Or ever" is not English, at least not grammatical English.

part of the description. "Lightning's speed," and "thunder's peal," are the common-places of a school-boy; and moreover the couplet in which they occur is almost without a meaning. Does the lance flash with the thunder's peal, or with lightning's speed; and if flashing with lightning's speed, what object is attained by describing the *rapidity* of its gleamings? It is evident that the circumstances have been enumerated without any definite end, and the epithets applied without any consideration of the pertinence of their application. Whether a particular epithet serves to illustrate the object to be described, is a question that never suggests itself to L.E.L.'s mind: if a word sound prettily, and possess the proper number of *syllables (feet* never being thought of), no further qualification appears to be required; it is placed in juxta position with certain other syllables, and thus contributes its quota to the formation of a line. L.E.L.'s vocabulary, though so indiscriminately brought to bear upon every subject, is nevertheless exceedingly scanty, and her stock of imagery still more scanty than her vocabulary. Her printed works amount to more than three octavo volumes; yet we seriously believe that these volumes would be reduced to less than fifty pages, if her poetry were stripped of roses, violets, bees, rainbows, suns, and moons; for these elements enter into all her descriptions, and compose, by their various combinations, almost every line of her poetry. The number and dissimilitude of the objects, however, which they are made to illustrate, bespeak a boldness and ingenuity in the application of scanty materials, that few poets have had the power or the opportunity of manifesting. Love, for instance, is like the smell of the rose; lovers are like the rose-trees (love is also like the morning sun, like wine, like a palace, like a lion's den). Dreams, smiles, and eyes, are like sunshine; dreams are also like violet's breath, a rainbow, music, and mirth. A blush is like the inside of a white violet; a turban, a lamp, a lady's blandishments are all like a rainbow; and the lady herself like the moon. We cannot give a more characteristic specimen of L.E.L.'s poetry, than the following fragments of a song from the Troubadour:
—

'In some valley, low and lone,
Where I was the only one

Of the human dwellers there,
Would I dream away my care;
I'd forget how in the world,
Snakes lay amid roses curl'd.'

If this idea be not novel, the mode of expressing it is not more so;
and it is tame enough at best.

'I'd forget at once distress,
For young love's insidiousness;
False foes, and falser friends,
Serving but for their own ends.'

This idea, too, is equally original, and the expression equally appro-
priate, elegant, and new.

'I will fly like these away,
To some lonely solitude,
Where the nightingale's young brood
Lives amid the shrine of leaves,
Which the wild rose round them weaves.
And my dwelling shall be made
Underneath the beech-tree's shade.
Twining ivy for the walls,
Over which the jasmine falls,
Like a tapestry work of gold,
And pearls around each emerald fold.'

Is the image of jasmine and ivy twined together, rendered more
definite and vivid by the simile of the tapestry? The illustration itself
would be unintelligible without the light reflected on it by the sub-
ject it is meant to illustrate.

'And my couches shall be set
With the purple violet;
And the white ones too, inside
Each a blush to suit a bride.'

This collocation of words appears remarkably agreeable to our authoress: in the same poem she has,

> 'And the gold-spotted moss was set
> With crowds of the white violet.'

Again —

> 'With a moss-seat, and its turf set
> With crowds of the white violet.'

Again —

> 'The blush should be like the one,
> White violets hide from the sun.'

We will be a little more methodical, and range the example under particular heads.

Roses and other flowers: —

> 'The lady sits in her lone bower,
> With cheek wan as the white-rose flower.'

> 'And she was nurtured as a flower,
> The favourite bud of a Spring bower.'

> 'Look on the cheek, the rose might own
> The smile around, like sunshine, thrown.'

> 'I will dwell with Summer flowers,
> Fit friends for the Summer hours;
> My companions honey-bees,
> And birds, and buds, and leaves, and trees.'

> 'Beneath the garden lay fill'd with rose-trees,
> Whose sighings came like passion or the breeze.'

'And underneath its shelter stood,
Leant like a beauty o'er the food,
Watching each tender bud unclose,
A beautiful white Provence rose;
Yet wan and pale, as that it knew
What changing skies and sun could do;
As that it knew, and knowing sigh'd,
The vanity of Summer pride.'

Moon-shine and sun-shine: —

'I thought how upon the moon-lit hour,
The minstrel hymn'd his maiden's bower.

'Music's power
Is little felt in sun-lit hour.'

'When memory, like the moonlight, flings,
A softness o'er its wanderings.'

'Hope and fame
Together on my visions came;
For memory had dipp'd her wings
In honey-dews and sun-lit springs.'

To say nothing of the affectation and obscurity of the phrase "sun-lit springs," we would ask if the alleged cause of the expectations of future fame at all elucidates the matter? We hope for fame: why? Because

'Memory has dipp'd her wings
In honey-dews, and sun-lit springs.'

We fear that whoever has no other reason for his expectations of fame, will live and die in obscurity. Under the head of unintelligible, we could adduce a volume; two examples, however, must suffice: —

> '*Freshness of feeling,* as of flower,
> *That lives not more than Spring's first hour.*'

> 'When comrade of the star and flower
> He watch'd beside his lady's bower;
> And number'd every hope and dream,
> *Like blooms that threw upon life's stream*
> *Colours of beauty.*' ———-

Want of space, not of matter, prevents any further extracts.

The merely writing correct poetical lines, is the easiest part of the poet's task. It is an operation that a schoolboy often performs with accuracy, by the aid of a correct ear and a slight knowledge of prosody. Correct prosody indeed is but one of the requisites to poetical numbers: it is, however, an indispensable one. For the formation of a correct poetical line, there are required a certain number of syllables, and a certain number of *emphatic* syllables. Rhythm in poetry resembles time in music, and its emphatic syllables are like the accented musical notes. Without accented notes there is no music; without emphatic syllables there is no poetry. All polysyllabic words have at least one emphatic syllable: the syllable, however, on which the emphasis falls, is different in different words; but the syllable in a poetical line on which the emphasis must fall, is always determinate. And the art of the writer lies in so arranging his words, that their emphatic syllables shall always coincide with the emphatic syllable in the line. In L.E.L.'s opinion, however, a certain number of syllables is of itself sufficient to form a verse; of the necessity of emphasis to constitute rhythm, her lines prove her to be ignorant. The following, in addition to many already quoted for other purposes, are sufficient evidence of this: —

> 'They parted, but each one that night,
> Thought on the meeting at twilight.'

Here the word "at" and the syllable "light," occupy the place of emphatic syllables; and the line is not verse, unless they be improperly accented in the pronunciation.

Again —

> '*Oh!* where *is* the heart but knows
> Love's first steps are *upon* the rose?'

Again —

> 'I cannot *but* think *of* those years.'

No ingenuity can convert this into poetry. The next example is equally untractable: —

> 'A loved one, *and* yet be forgiven.'

The next, as far as rhythm is concerned, are like a sailor's ditty: —

> 'Their fathers died for thy fa*thers*,
> They would have died for thee.'

> 'Too beautiful to be quite vain,'

is prose, unless we make "full" and "be" emphatic; our reading would then be an exact imitation of the sonorous sing song of a school-boy. We fear that we have tired our reader's patience, and shall therefore close here our remarks on L.E.L.'s poetical merits.

It is now our intention briefly to remark upon the tendency of her writings. We shall not examine how great may be the influence these writings are likely to exercise over the feelings and opinions of her readers; but we fear that if they exercise any, that influence is more likely to be pernicious than useful.

It must be recollected, that the heroes whom L.E.L. describes are the heroes of a woman, and they may therefore be supposed to possess the qualifications requisite to engage a woman's affection. A lady is good authority in these cases, and her beau-ideal of a hero may be fairly taken as the standard to which those men must conform who wish for her admiration. And what greater inducement can be found for men to model themselves after any original, than the known approbation and encouragement of women?

That compound of qualities which constitutes a hero in the opin-
ion of our authoress, is that sort of character commonly called
romantic. He is to love women, and poetry, and fighting: he is to
love women with so much ardour, that the remainder of his life is to
be without comfort either if his love be not returned, or if the
beloved object should die or be married to another during the hey-
day of his affection; poetry he is to love, as a means of eulogizing the
bright eyes of a fair lady, courting her smiles, and deprecating her
frowns; and war, as the only noble and gentlemanly mode of dis-
pelling ennui, as well as the most successful means of obtaining the
admiration of a tender and gentle damsel. All his passions are to be
extreme; feeling and impulse are to be the sole guide of his conduct;
while reason and cold calculation are to be strangers to his counsels.
He is indeed always to act nobly, but solely by an instinctive virtue;
for that virtue which is the result of principle seems of too methodi-
cal and homely a character to belong to high-born knights and gal-
lant gentlemen, whose time is supposed far too valuable to be spent
in so trifling and useless an employment as reflecting on the rule of
life, or the difference between vice and virtue. When a lady's eyes are
to be praised, or a gentleman to be run through the body, it would
be a stain on knighthood to delay the accomplishment of either of
these pleasing tasks, by any impertinent inquiry concerning the pos-
sibility of finding a more beneficial, or more benevolent employ-
ment. In short, a hero must rush to war, heedless of the misery it
creates; glory, the most selfish of all passions except love, being wor-
thy of more consideration than the misery or happiness of millions
of his fellow-creatures; he must despise all useful occupations, and
consider the business of war the only decent employment for a gen-
tleman. He must be proud and arrogant, because he is stronger than
his neighbours; and must cultivate all those intense and vehement
emotions the indulgence of which destroys the taste for the calmer
and only permanent pleasures of life. It seems never to have occurred
to our authoress, that the beings whom she so fondly admires,
because endowed with all these pleasing qualifications, and in the
superlative degree, are purely imaginary; and that if accident should
combine these various qualifications in one individual, he would be

no better than a scourge to his fellow-men, and a curse to himself.

We can see no very good reason why women should always be rendered an instrument to the destruction of all our best sympathies; why they should be induced to bestow their approbation upon men, just in proportion to the efficacy with which they produce, and the zest with which they enjoy bloodshed and misery. Love and war are words that we see but too often connected; and success in love is but too well known to be the reward of valour in war. The savage presents to his mistress the scalps of his enemies, and finds favour in her eyes according to the number of these testimonies of his prowess. The more civilized killer of men, the modern soldier, does not indeed preserve as a trophy the bloody heads of his opponents, but dangles at his button-hole a medal, or hangs round his neck an order or a scarf, and obtains, by these petty yet horrible baubles, the admiration and affection of those gentle beings who are supposed to render men mild and benevolent — of women, who at the sight of human blood would tremble, and shriek, and faint, but who recklessly bestow their admiration on men whose trade is to spill it like water, and to spread desolation and carnage over the globe. The time may come when women will cease to aid in rendering mankind a savage and a brutal race. At present, however, a charm is spread over the disgusting trade of blood; ideas of gaiety, of unspeakable pleasure, of romance, of beauty, and of pomp, of every thing, in short, that is glaring and attractive, are associated with the cruel and heart-rending business of war. A woman imagines only the pleasurable part of this life of butchery — the parade — but never the battle; she sees the young soldier decked out in his gaudy livery; she dreams of plumes and helmets, trumpets, cloaks, sashes, and spurs (for thus far the inventory of a soldier's accoutrements is romantic); but seldom can she see this interesting object of her contemplation worn out, fatigued, cold, and hungry; his "brilliant trappings all besmirched," his limbs perhaps shot off, and himself exposed, in this mangled condition, to a burning sun, thirsty, feverish, and almost mad with agony. Neither does the spectacle of cities stormed, their inhabitants plundered and butchered, present itself to her view, nor apparently even to her imagination: yet wherever war is, these things must be. Did L.E.L. weigh these fatal consequences when she indulged in her fantastic descriptions of war and warriors? When she composed the following lines, did she believe that war was an evil?

> 'Lady, to-night I pledge thy name,
> To-morrow thou shalt pledge mine;
> *Ever the smile of beauty should light*
> *The victor's blood-red wine.*

> 'And rush'd the blood, and flash'd the light
> To Raymond's cheek, from Raymond's eye,
> When he stood forth, and claim'd the fight,
> And spoke of death and victory.
> Those words that thrill the heart when first
> Forth the young warrior's soul has burst.

* * * * * *

> 'And Raymond felt as if a gush
> Of thousand waters, in one rush,
> Were on his heart, as if the dreams
> *Of what, alas! life only seems,*
> *Wild thoughts and noon-tide revelries,*
> *Were turned into realities.*'

That is to say, the gay dreams of his youth were about to be realized by the joys of warfare.

> 'Impatient, restless, first his steed
> Was hurried to its upmost speed,
> And next his falchion's edge was tried,
> Then waved the helmet's plume of pride.'

> 'When will youth feel as he felt,
> When first at beauty's feet he knelt!

* * * * * *

And where the glory that will yield
The flush and glow of his first field,
To the young chief? Will Raymond ever
Feel as he now is feeling? Never.'

In other words, no pleasure in life is equal to the satisfaction of having slaughtered a large number of our fellow-creatures in a field of battle.

'The first, the very first: oh, none
Can feel again as they have done,
In love, in war, in pride, in all
The planets of life's coronal;
However beautiful and bright,
What can be like their first sweet light?'

Here, and by a woman, we have WAR classed as one of the "planets of life's coronal;" and thought also "beautiful and bright." Can any one who believes that human suffering is no fit subject for rejoicing, praise without a blush the feelings of satisfaction derived from desolation and carnage? And can L.E.L. with justice lay claim to the praise of gentleness of disposition, or eulogize with sincerity the beneficent sympathies of our nature, at the distance of a few pages from such passages as the above? Of what use are applauses bestowed on tender feelings, when accompanied by the declarations of sentiments which militate against every interest of humanity?

A few words more, upon L.E.L.'s opinion concerning the reciprocal duties of the sexes, and we have done. To a careless observer it must appear extraordinary that a woman should make a distribution of these duties entirely in favour of the opposite sex. To any one who knows with what servility women are accustomed to follow the opinions of men, any other distribution would appear surprising.

There floats in the imagination of most men a vague notion, that it is the peculiar excellence of a woman to possess a timid and retiring character; in other words, to be diffident of her own judgment, and rely implicitly on that of others. They therefore contrive that all rules for her conduct shall have a tendency to make and keep her this timid character. A love of dominion on the part of men has alone induced them to consider this timidity and helplessness as desirable qualifications. They almost universally believe it conducive to their interests to have women paraded before them, and exhibited like automata; to have them patiently submit to be criticised, to be admired, and to be chosen. To permit a woman to weigh one man's merits against those of another; to keep her judgment in suspense, till she learn their comparative excellencies; to permit her to change her opinion, to own that her preference had been improperly bestowed, would, they fear, be to render women free agents, to make them our equals, and to rob us of those dear prerogatives of domination which our vanity and indolence are so deeply interested in maintaining. It unfortunately happens that the opinions of men in any society are invariably the opinions of women also; no matter whether inimical or not to the interests of women. In the case before us it consequently happens that none are more firm or warmer advocates for the utter helplessness of women, than women themselves; none more ready to punish every attempt to escape from thraldom, every indication of a desire to judge for themselves. A vast number of hard epithets have for this purpose been coined by female indignation, of which unsparing use is made whenever a sister manifests restiveness under control. To such a length has this principle been carried, that the mere circumstance of a woman's endeavouring to provide for herself, because it rescues her from the dominion of men, is considered a derogation from her dignity, and degrades her, if she be a gentlewoman, from her station in the world. Although this may be exceedingly grateful to the vanity of men, we have but too convincing proofs of its baneful effects on the happiness of women.

L.E.L. takes every opportunity of preaching up this perfect subordination, and of bestowing admiration upon those qualities which fit women for being useful and agreeable slaves; while those unfortunate attributes, which render the domination of men precarious, are visited with corresponding reprobation. In the Troubadour we find the hero, Raymond, permitted without censure to rove from beauty to beauty, reckless of the fatal effects of his fascinating arts; while Adeline, because she rejects Raymond's love, and is, like himself, somewhat difficult to please, is accused of cruelty and disdain, and visited with all the indignation our authoress is capable of assuming. She is, it appears, a coquet: that is, she can behold a number of men admiring her beauty without falling in love with any of those admirers; and does actually permit young gentlemen to make flattering speeches on the subject of her charms, without absolutely annihilating them with her frowns. On such slight encouragement it appears that the men fall dangerously in love; so dangerously indeed, that usually their lives are despaired of; at least so says our authoress, who cannot retain her wrath when speaking of those heartless creatures who smile, and have the cruelty to look exceedingly pretty, unmindful of the dreadful consequences attendant on the display of so much beauty as they possess.

> 'But she, alas for her false smile,
> Adeline loved him not the while.
> And is it thus that woman's heart
> Can trifle with its dearest part,
> Its own pure sympathies? Can fling
> The poison'd arrow from the string
> In utter heartlessness around,
> And mock, or think not of the wound!
> And thus can woman barter all
> That makes and gilds her gentle thrall;
> The blush which should be like the one,
> *White violets hide from the sun;*[*]
> The soft low sighs, like those which breathe
> In secret from a twilight wreath;
> The smile, like a bright lamp, whose shine
> Is vow'd but only to one shrine;
> All these sweet spells, and can they be
> Weapons of reckless vanity?
> And woman, in whose gentle heart,
> From all, save its sweet self, apart,
> Love should dwell with that purity,
> Which but in woman's love can be:

---

[*]   Is this verse or prose?

A sacred fire, whose flame was given
To shed on earth the light of heaven;
That she can fling her wealth aside
In carelessness, or sport, or pride!'

Here is an injunction as strict as the lord chancellor's against waste, to restrain young ladies in future from being prodigal of blushes, sighs, smiles, or good-natured glances, in presence of any gentleman, save him whom, by the gift of prophecy, she may discover to be destined, in the fulness of time, to become her lawful husband. We would beg leave, however, to assure L.E.L., that, in these days, men seldom die of love; that she needs feel no further uneasiness on this account, and that the overflowings of her benevolence would be more advantageously directed if employed in sympathizing with the wrongs of her sex, than with the victims of their cruelties.

6. *The Athenaeum*, no. 105 (28 October 1829): 669-70.

The Venetian Bracelet, the Lost Pleiad, a History of the Lyre, and other Poems. By L.E.L. Author of 'The Improvisatrice,' 'The Troubadour,' and 'The Golden Violet.' 12mo. pp. 307. Longman and Co. London, 1829.

We could almost wish that a pleasing and modest preface which is prefixed to this volume of poetry had been suppressed; not because it has not added to our respect for the authoress, but because it shows that she entertains abundantly too much respect for the critics. Now there are few subjects upon which we can speak without considerable bashfulness; but this is one, and we take upon ourselves with great boldness to assure Miss Landon that very little which we or our contemporaries can say to her is at all worthy of her attention. The less she reads us or them, let her take our word for it, the better. If we censure her it is most likely on a wrong ground, and to reform according to our direction would be her ruin. If we praise her, and this we speak with real solemnity, and in a fair conviction strengthened by many passages of her late work that her heart will echo our words, she may have reason to curse us all her life through.

We are the more grieved at this over reverence for periodicals which Miss Landon has displayed, because we fancy two or three faults, (so we call them, but we beseech Miss Landon not to believe that they are so, till she has considered the point herself,) which we discover in these poems are directly owing to it. Some impertinent blockhead in the 'Westminster Review,' informed this young lady that love was a very dull and monotonous subject. It is not probable that Miss Landon would cease to write upon a subject in which she takes an interest, and in which mankind generally, and even the humbler class of animals, all excepting the 'Westminster Reviewer' take an interest, because such a very silly bray as this was uttered by a very silly animal in a very silly book. But though Miss Landon did not absolutely submit to be stopped in her course by the same obstruction which hindered the progress of a celebrated prophet in ancient times, she was, nevertheless, so far startled by the strangeness of the sound, that she began to think if there was no way of making her peace with the creature which she probably mistook for a lion, or some other terrible species of wild fowl. To this end she seems to have considered whether a little variety might not be given to this same passion of love, by describing its eccentricities and wayward-ness, instead of its direct simple self-devotedness. Now we confess, to ourselves, this change is by no means agreeable. We are perfectly satisfied that, in spite of the great improvement which has taken place in Miss Landon's powers, since we last met with her, and a very great improvement we think it is, (though we again entreat Miss Landon not to consider our opinion worthy of the least attention,) she would have found that love which dwelt in Shakspeare's hero-ines, and gives them so much of their loveliness, a sufficiently ample field for those powers to exercise in; and that she had not the least occasion to place them in so many bizarre combinations of out-landish circumstances, to describe so many of the back eddyings of the passion when it meets with the current of society, or to make so many careful analyses of the slime which it contracts from mixing with the current, as are found in this volume. If we might advise — Miss Landon will remark our preposterous inconsistency and will treat us with contempt accordingly — we would recommend her not to trouble herself with a moment's thought about the possibility of love being a dull or an exhaustible subject; but having satisfied herself that it is a most exalted one, one that can only cease to be interesting by being compounded with other worthless elements, to labour that she may present to us, as much as possible, its purest and most essential spirit.

The second charge, which has disturbed Miss Landon's spirit, but which she disposes of very cleverly and prettily, is that of egotism. Now, however stale this accusation may have become, and however much misapplied in the present instance, we cannot think that there is as little general truth in it, as in the one to which we have just alluded. When the author of 'Pelham,' for instance, repels this same charge with much affected indignation, he makes out, it seems, to us, a very poor case for himself. He asks, with an air of assurance, whether he may not write in the first person singular as well as another, and yet be presumed to speak of an imaginary being. No doubt, but unfortunately this has very little to do with the question. That he should like the use of that person is one symptom of his disease, but only one. The true diagnosis of it is a disposition to be constantly dealing with these peculiarities of character, which do not originate in the man himself, which are never even worked *into* human nature, but are merely drawn over it by some accidental arrangement of circumstances, and which, therefore, could have no interest for the writer, except what they derive from his self-love. If, therefore, Miss Landon *were* open to this charge, as the fashionable novelist is, her answer, however ingenious, would not be valid. It would not be enough to say, 'I assure you, dear reader and courteous critic, that, whatever you may think, I was in love with no one but you,' — for though we most potently believe Miss Landon's assertion on this point uttered in our private ear, we are bound, when judging a work of her's, not to hear one word of it, and in case she did really exhibit that disposition which we have spoken of, to convict her of being in love, of being deserted, forsaken, and dead, even though she may be in perfect ignorance that any of these sad events have befall-en her. At the same time we cheerfully and joyfully say, that to any great extent this symptom is not discoverable in her; though, we fear, there are more traces of it in this volume than in those which have preceded it, and that for the very cause to which we have just allud-ed: viz. Miss Landon's too great deference to her critics, and her consequent anxiety to remove the charge of exhibiting the monotony of love, by surrounding it with a great many idle accidents.

We shall now proceed to the agreeable task of quoting a passage from each of the principal poems, to show the advantageous change which has taken place in the language and versification of Miss Landon since the appearance of the 'Improvisatrice,'

7. [Edward Bulwer-Lytton.] *The New Monthly Magazine* 32 (December 1831): 545-51.

ROMANCE AND REALITY. BY L.E.L.

We review this work for two reasons; first, because it is exceedingly clever; secondly, because being exceedingly clever, it is written by a lady. One among the designs in the ambition entertained by the present conductors of this Magazine, is to support that wise and enlarged social policy which would give to one sex the same mental cultivation as to the other. Of all cant in this most canting country, no species is at once more paltry and more dangerous than that which has been made the instrument of decrying female accomplishment. All that execrable twaddle about feminine retirement, and feminine ignorance, which we are doomed so often to hear, has done more towards making women scolds, and flirts, and scandal-mongers, than people are well aware of. All minds, whether of males or females, that are ignorant and empty, can only find delight and occupation in a small circle. "Exactly!" cries our canter, "in the household circle! What larger orbit would you have a woman busy herself in? Is not that her proper sphere?" Fiddledee! Does house-keeping — the suckling of fools and the chronicling of small-beer — take up all the lady's time? Is she never visiting her neighbours, and pulling her friends' characters to pieces? How can she do otherwise than talk scandal? What else can she talk of if she is ignorant? If she knows nothing about things, she must talk about persons; if she cannot converse, she must gossip. The sole species of talk that cottagers have, for instance, is gossip. The same cause that makes poor women gossip applies to rich women also — ignorance! Then as to feminine delicacy — what softens so much as knowledge? Does knowledge make men bad husbands? Why should it make women bad wives? And the most sad part of the business is, that women themselves should repeat and exult in all this insulting jargon; that they should be the chief persons always to talk of the blessings of not being well educated; of knowing only how to make puddings and tea; of having no talk but backbiting, and feeling no horror like that at a blue-stocking. All this is very pitiable. The soul of a woman is as fine an emanation from the Great Fountain of Spirit as that of a man. Why is she to paper it up as carefully as if it were made of silver lace, and the breath of Heaven would tarnish it? If there were anything harsh, or unfeeling, or unmatronly, or unfeminine in being well informed, God knows we would not insist upon it. But if there be any truth in this world it is this; that as it was chiefly empty houses that evil spirits were supposed to haunt, so it is chiefly in empty minds that low passions and unworthy sentiments are to be found. Nothing is so tender as true wisdom, or so selfish as folly; and to instruct the mind is the best method wherewith to elevate the heart. The more fit a woman is to be our companion, the more likely she is to be our soother and our friend; and in proportion as she is worthy of our affection will she be capable herself of feeling the loftier and more lasting order of love.

Thinking, then, that it is so necessary for all who are actuated by the high and pure desire to reform and liberalise our social system, no less than our legislative, to encourage rather than (as hitherto Englishmen have done) dampen and satirise that ambition which directs women to intellectual cultivation and mental eminence, we are disposed, in our capacity of critics, to pay peculiar attention to those works which emanate from the gentler sex. The height of literary distinction may be clombe by all; but to women especially it would seem that the ascent should be rendered smooth and easy. The heart-burnings and jealousies that we feel towards rivals of our own sex, we can scarcely experience towards our emulators in the other. Women can neither jostle us in our political career, nor thwart us in our vainer and more alluring ambition of society. And while it is soothing to our pride, and seems generous in our manhood, to encourage the timid and shrinking steps of female genius, we cannot but feel, with a more selfish policy, that those steps will not cross our own, and that by such aspirers we may be equalled without rivalry, and surpassed without defeat. We would please ourselves by comparing that literary eminence to which we would encourage our countrywomen, not to the harsh and rugged steep, where for us

> "Fame's proud temple shines afar,"

but rather to the soft and haunted "Acidale" which Spenser has so beautifully described: —

> "It is an hill placed in an open plaine,
>   That round about is bordered with a wood
> Of matchless height, that seems th' earth to disdaine;
>
> * * * * * * *
>
> And at the foot thereof a gentle flood
>   His silver waves doth softly tumble down,
> Unmoved with rugged moss or filthy mud:
>   Nor may wild beasts, nor may the ruder clowne
> There to approach ——————
>   But nymphs and faeries by the bankes do sit
> In the wood shade which do the waters crowne,
>   Keeping all noisome things away from it,
>   And to the water's fall tuning their accents fit."

The Author of these volumes is a lady of remarkable genius. We remember well when she first appeared before the public in the pages of "The Literary Gazette." We were at that time more capable than we are now of poetic enthusiasm; and certainly that enthusiasm we not only felt ourselves, but we shared with every second person we then met. We were young, and at college, lavishing our golden years, not so much on the Greek verse and mystic character to which we ought, perhaps, to have been rigidly devoted, as

> "Our heart in passion and our head in rhymes."

At that time, poetry was not yet out of fashion, at least with us of the cloister; and there was always, in the Reading Room of the Union, a rush every Saturday afternoon for "The Literary Gazette," and an impatient anxiety to hasten at once to the corner of the sheet which contained the three magical letters of "L.E.L." And all of us praised the verse, and all of us guessed at the author. We soon learned it was a female, and our admiration was doubled, and our conjectures tripled. Was she young? Was she pretty? and — for there were some embryo fortune-hunters among us — was she rich? We ourselves, who, now staid critics and sober gentlemen, are about coldly to measure to a prose work the due quantum of laud and censure, then only thought of homage, and in verse only we condescended to yield it. But the other day, in looking over some of our boyish effusions, we found a paper superscribed to "L.E.L." and beginning with "Fair Spirit." We need scarcely add that we have burnt the weed that we then intended as an offering, and fancied might be mistaken for a flower. These early proofs of the genius of our Poetess are, indeed, singularly beautiful: they have gone far towards producing a new school — a school, in truth, which we do not admire, and in which the proselytes have done their possible to copy the faults, without the merits of the founder. But, despite the beauty of the poems we refer to, Miss Landon has greatly improved in poetical taste of late. Something more vigorous, staid, and thoughtful than belonged to her early poetry, has dignified the grace and sweetness of that last published. And though we think that severe and stern study is yet wanting to complete the full extent of her powers, those powers have given a promise — more especially in her blank verse ("Erinna," for instance,) and her smaller pieces — which can only be duly kept by performances, not of the soft and gentle only, but of the noblest and most enduring order. And now we come to the volumes on our table.

"Romance and Reality" is a novel of great merit. Its beauties and its faults are those of genius. We shall be just to both.

Our heroine sees the great world, and learns a heroine's first task — love. And here we must find space for a specimen of merits of a very different order from those in the extract we have first quoted: —

"I doubt whether this morning twilight of the affections has the same extent of duration and influence in man that it has in woman: the necessity of exertion for attainment has been early inculcated upon him. He knows, that if he would win, he must woo; and his imagination acts chiefly as a stimulus. But a woman's is of a more passive kind: she has no motive for analysing feelings whose future rests not with herself: more imaginative from early sedentary habits, she is content to dream on, and some chance reveals to herself the secret she would never have learnt from self-investigation. Imbued with all the timidity, exalted by all the romance of a first attach-ment, never did a girl yet calculate on making what is called a conquest of the man she loves. A conquest is the resource of weariness — the consolation of disappointment — a second world of vanity and ambition, sighed for like Alexander's, but not till we have wasted and destroyed the heart's first sweet world of early love.

"Let Lord Byron say what he will of bread and butter, girl-hood is a beautiful season, and its love — its warm, uncalculat-ing, devoted love — so exaggerating in its simplicity — so keen from its freshness — is the very poetry of attachment: after-years have nothing like it. To know that the love which once seemed eternal can have an end, destroys its immortality; and, thus brought to a level with the beginnings and endings — the chances and changes of life's commonplace employ-ments and pleasures — and, alas! from the sublime to the ridiculous there is but a step — our divinity turns out an idol — we are grown too wise, too worldly, for our former faith — and we laugh at what we wept before; such laughter is more bitter — a thousand times more bitter — than tears!"

It is impossible to read this extract without being struck with the grace of the style — the tenderness and the truth of the thought. Few are the persons who could be successful in two classes of com-position so wholly distinct from each other as the extracts we have quoted. The talent to delineate character, and the talent to deduce observation from the portrait, are wholly distinct. In the one lies

Scott's genius; in the other, Godwin's. In the latter faculty, Miss Landon is the more especially felicitous. The whole work abounds with passages of equal eloquence and truth — in aphorisms of pointed originality, in descriptions adorned by a singular richness and power of diction. Yet in the reflexions there is sometimes an affectation of imagery, or of novelty, which we do not like, and which we entreat our Author to avoid for the future. For instance: — "Youth is the French Count, who takes the Yorick of Sterne for that of Shakspeare; it combines better than it calculates; its wishes are prophecies of their own fulfilment." Now the discerning reader will perceive at once that the above image is too strained, "too peregrinate," as Master Holofernes would say; and he will also perceive that the fault is one which no stupid person could commit. It is the fault of youth and fancy — a fault of an order to which true criticism is always lenient. Another fault to which we should be disposed to be less indulgent, were it not of very unfrequent occurrence, is, that instead of aspiring from the level road of genius, our Author sometimes stoops below it, and sullies her wings among the flippancies of a class of writers so immeasurably beneath her, that she ought only to know them in order to avoid. We allude to passages against such harmless vulgarities as "blue coats and brass buttons." All those toilet severities do very well for the "*flunkies*," as "Blackwood" expresses himself, but not for the Poetess of "Erinna."

The story continues through romance and reality, through love, reflection, criticism, ambition, travel, and death. We will not abridge it. The reader must fly to the book itself; and if he read it once for the story, he must read it twice for the wit and the eloquence, for the style, the reflections, and the moral. Miss Landon's prose contains the witness of some faculties not visible in her poetry — acute liveliness, and playful, yet deep observation. It contains also the same one fault, which we shall call the want of art, and on which we shall add a word or two of explanation and advice. When an actor first begins to speak in public, let his voice be ever so full and musical, it is ten to one but that it seems weak and overstrained. Why? Because he has not learnt to manage it. The voices that seem the strongest and the richest, are often the least so by nature. Practice and management are the secrets by which the orator or the actor obtains his effects.

Exactly so in fictitious composition: it is not the power only, but the knowledge of those places in which the power should be cast, that makes the novelist or the poet thrill and command his readers at his will. For instance: — Godwin is a writer of extraordinary genius; Miss Jane Porter is a writer of mediocre talent: but Miss Porter constantly produces effects which, with all his metaphysical knowledge of the passions, Godwin rarely does. And this is because Miss Porter knows those parts of her story from which a stirring scene can be created. She throws all her powers into that scene, and it becomes at once full of animation and interest. Godwin, on the contrary, passes over such scenes with a moral, or a discussion, and selects the most uninteresting passages wherein to lavish his eloquence. His voice is good, but is pitched in the wrong places. He reasons where he should describe, and when he comes to describe, it would often be better if he had reasoned. Common-place critics would cry, this was the fault of the Author's natural temperament. Not at all so: it is the want of art. He has the power to describe, but he misapplies it. Whenever we moralise where we should paint, we may be equally clever — nay, cleverer in a higher order of merit, but we are not equally successful in gaining our end, and enforcing our moral. Thus the Author of the book before us often prefers to tell us the character of a person than to throw the person into scenes in which the character would be far more instantaneously and vividly bodied forth. This, since she has the two faculties chiefly requisite for creating dramatic effect — a ready power to enter into various character, and a great command and variety of language, is a deficiency, not of nature, but of art. How is that deficiency alone to be remedied? By a deep and earnest study of the Drama! Many of the fine old plays that enrich our literature are shut out from a female library. But Shakspeare is open to all — a library in himself. The more we study Shakspeare, the more we are astonished at his art. Art in him was even more wonderfully displayed than genius. The reflections of Macbeth, beginning with "Seyton, I'm sick at heart," a great genius only could have written: but it was the deep and learned Art which introduced them exactly in that part of the play where we now find them. Had Godwin written "Macbeth," those reflections, in all probability, would have occurred where, instead of piercing the heart, they would have fatigued the attention. The trick of the boards, the scenic effect, the life of the stage, is what a novelist possessed of Miss Landon's powers should intently study. It will teach her never to narrate, where she can act, her story; and while as thoughtful, as reflective, as analysing as ever, to be so only in the right moment, and with the most effect. We need not say that we should not have given this advice to a writer of moderate genius; nor should we have given it to a novelist of long standing. It *is* given as a proof that we form from the present performance great hopes for the future. And now, passing over unmentioned, on the one hand, a few slight inaccuracies and petty blemishes, and on the other, a whole host of delicate and subtle beauties of composition, we consign our Author to the popularity she will doubtless obtain, and most richly deserve. When we consider her accomplishments, her versatility, her acute observation, her graceful fancy, her powers both in the actual world and the ideal, her habit of thought, and her command of language; and when we remember also how much she has yet done, and how young she yet is, we speak advisedly when we recommend to her the highest models and the severest study. Such a recommendation could only be given to one capable, if she do justice to herself, of achieving those triumphs which, as her critics, we anticipate, and as her admirers, we predict.

8. *The Athenaeum, Journal of English and Foreign Literature, Science, and the Arts*, no. 215 (10 December 1831): 793-95.

Romance and Reality. By L.E.L., Author of 'The Improvisatrice,' &c. 3 vols. London, 1831. Colburn & Bentley.

We were always of opinion that Miss Landon's poetry failed in giving a just estimate of Miss Landon's powers. Glowing with imagery, radiant with bright words, seductive with fond fancies,

> Full of carving strange and sweet,
> All made out of the carver's brain,
> For a lady's chamber meet, —

picturesque, arabesque, and romanesque, it yet lacked vigour and variety — often abounded in carelessness, and dealt too much in the superficial. It bore too great a resemblance to Thalaba's palace in the desert, a structure that Mr. Canning probably had in his mind when he said of all splendid but unsubstantial creations, "they rose in the mists of the morning, but dissolved in the noonday sun." Sand often contains gold, yet sand makes a sorry foundation, and we have often wished that L.E.L. would dig till she reached the rock. So far from agreeing with the objections brought by many grave and corporate critics against the superabundance of "Love" in her verses, we have wished for more that could really deserve the name, — taking leave to think that the sparkling sentiment which had idleness and self-will for its parents, and an impersonation of moonlight and a serenade for bridesmaids, bore passing small resemblance to intense yet rational feeling; real, yet not ungovernable energy of soul. Again, without going the length of other "robustious periwigged" objections raised against her landscape drawing, we have ventured to wish her on more familiar terms with lady Nature; and, finally, as she has undoubtedly founded a poetic school, we have unfeignedly wished that she would whip some dozen of her scholars. The faults of an original may be merged in the light of his beauties; but the faults of a copyist call for the wet sponge of annihilation. What made us think that Miss Landon possessed "powers that she had never used," were occasional lines and passages manifesting, not merely thought, but a capacity for speculating upon thought — a deeper looking into man's heart and destiny — and loftier aspirations after all "that is very far off," than might beseem troubadours and improvisatrici. 'Erinna,' notwithstanding its incorrect versification, proved that there was iron in the rose; the 'Lines on Life' breathed wisdom born of tears and nursed of truth; whilst the majority of her later poems have proved her in possession not only of the genii of the lamp, but of the master of the genii; not only of fancy, that builds with gold and gems, but of truth and thought, that bring the living spirit to inhabit....

But it was to the prose work intended to proceed from her pen that we looked with most expectation, as the test, trial, and, if the truth must be told, triumph of Miss Landon, and of our own particular opinion of her mind. The work is here; we have read it with as much attention as if it had been theology, and as much excitement as if it had been treason. To call it a novel is incorrect; plot, incident, and narrative of all kinds, would go into a nut, or, to be literally correct, into a walnut-shell. Let no lover of history and mystery, no demander of event and catastrophe, no old-fashioned believer in its being equally the duty of governments to put down plots, and of novelists to purvey them — no person who reads a book merely to know what happens in it, sit down to 'Romance and Reality.' If they inquire of us, "who or what is the Romance?" — "who or what is the Reality?" we cannot answer, for the very primitive reason of not knowing. Those who care little about story, or who can wait for it till the third volume, will find real and delightful occupation in its pages. The correct title of the work would have been 'Maxims and Characters' — for it is composed of essays, criticisms, sketches of life, portraits living and dead, opinions on manners, descriptions of feeling, all served up with so much wit that the authoress might never have been sad, — with so much poetic and moral feeling that she might never have been gay. Perused as a work of fiction, it is too desultory and incorrect to be satisfactory; it must be read as a brilliant, and sometimes profound commentary on the life of this "century of crowds" — as the result of keen and varied observation and reflection: in this view we cannot but esteem it a remarkable evidence of talent. We ask the poetry of the authoress, where, till now, dwelt the brave good sense — the sarcasm bitter with medicine, not poison — the remarks that, beginning in levity, die off into reflection — the *persiflage* that is only a feint to conceal love of the beautiful and longing after the true? and the 'Improvisatrice,' the 'Troubadour,' and the 'Venetian Bracelet,' answer — "Where?" How much there is that poetry cannot or must not convey. As the Ettrick Shepherd says, "Blessings on the man who first invented sleep" — so we say, "Honour to the patriarchs, who undoubtedly all wrote in prose!" But for 'Romance and Reality' in prose, half our island might never have awoke from their dream that L.E.L. was an avatar of blue eyes, flaxen ringlets, and a susceptible heart! The counter conviction, that her genius is infinitely more like an arrow, barbed at one end and feathered at the other, will dismay a thousand fancies, the cherished growth of albums and sixteen....

Certainly, reading the two first volumes of 'Romance and Reality' is exceedingly like reading a volume of Horace Walpole's Letters (only that the names and news are newer), or, if acquainted with literary London, like passing an evening with half your acquaintance. In this respect the book answers to a magazine, saves postage, and, if carried on extensively, might do away with the necessity of newspapers. On this topic we commend the authoress to the fatherly care of that most delightful person, Dr. Folliott, whose opinions, as found in 'Crotchet Castle,' we here transcribe: —

...

"*Mr. Eavesdrop.* — Me, Sir! What have I done, Sir, that I am to be poisoned, Sir?

"*The Rev. Dr. Folliott.* — Sir, you have published a character of your facetious friend, the Rev. Dr. F., wherein you have sketched off me; me, Sir, even to my nose and wig. What business have the public with my nose and wig?

"*Mr. E.* — Sir, it is all good-humoured: all in *bonhommie*: all friendly and complimentary.

"*Rev. Dr. F.* — Sir, you have been very unfacetious. You have dished me up like a savory omelette, to gratify the appetite of the reading rabble for gossip. The next time, Sir, I will respond with the *argumentum baculinum*. Print that, Sir: put it on record as a promise of the Rev. Dr. F. which shall be most faithfully kept with an exemplary bamboo.

"*Mr. E.* — Your cloth protects you, Sir.

"*Rev. Dr. F.* — My bamboo shall protect me, Sir.

"*Mr. Crotchet.* — Doctor, Doctor, you are growing too polemical.

"*Rev. Dr. F.* — Sir, my blood boils. What business have the public with my nose and wig?"

L.E.L.'s "takings" are for the most part "friendly and complimentary" — nevertheless, some are so caustic, that, unless she omits them in a second edition, it might be well to publish a literary copy of the advertisement to Rowland's Kalydor, particularly that part which states its soothing qualities for "gentlemen whose chins are tender after shaving." Against her second edition, too, or, rather against her next work, we would remind her, that what has been said of bag-pipe music may be said of witticisms where too numerous — "the one half would sound better for the other half not being heard." The first volume is as full of points as a packet of needles, and, as the writer says of some one's attitude, fails of being easy by being elaborate. This over-abundance of repartees, similes and epigrams, becomes tiresome to the dull, and teazing to the quick; makes wit look too like hard work, and the author too much resemble a vivacious juggler — a

> Katerfelto, with his hair on end
> At his own wonders, wondering for his bread.

We think we dare read this riddle: to be natural, earnest, and quietly dignified, even as an author, requires no less moral courage than to be so in daily life. Ridicule is society's fear of God, and entertainment its "pearl of great price." An author of the *beau monde* puts wit in his first volume to purchase leave to throw heart, truth, and sentiment into his last. Miss Landon's third volume is exempt from all the faults of the two others; there is no want of story, which is so concentrated in its pages, that, with a little introduction, and the entire smothering of the Higgs' family, it might be printed separately, a perfectly true, pure, pleasant specimen of fiction. It is effective, without effect being strained after, and contains passages full of power, beauty, and simplicity. The epigrammatic style is dropped; the narrative flows sweetly yet sadly along; and the history of the grave and noble Beatrice — of the self-will and repentings of the less firmly strung Emily, would redeem an Almack's of young ladies, and "a wilderness of monkeys."...

9. Review of *Ethel Churchill* [William Makepeace Thackeray.] "Our Batch of Novels for Christmas, 1837." *Fraser's Magazine* 17 (January 1838): 89-92. [Begins with an excerpt (with some gaps) of volume 1, chs. 17 (pp. 178-84) and 18 (pp. 189-93) of the novel.]

Love is as good a material in novels, as a sweetmeat at dinner; but a repast of damson cheese is sickly for the stomach, and a thousand consecutive pages of sentiment are neither pleasant nor wholesome. All the heroes and heroines in this book are either consumptive or crossed in love. There is one who marries a man for whom she cares nothing, and loves a man who cares nothing for her. Her husband discovers her attachment, and she her lover's treason, at one and the same time. My Lady Marchmont gives them both poison, and then goes mad. There is another case, where the husband marries against the grain; his wife, crooked, consumptive, but passionately fond of him, dies under the ice of his neglect. There is Ethel Churchill, who adores the gentleman last mentioned, and a young poet who adores her. Both, of course, are hopelessly miserable: the bard perishes from a complaint in the chest; but Ethel, more happy, marries the widower at the end of the third volume. There are a few historical characters — Pope, Walpole, the fair Lavinia Fenton, and some others. This is the outline of Miss Landon's novel.

But, though an uninteresting tale, no one can read it without admiring the astonishing qualities of the authoress. There are a hundred beautiful poems in it, and a thousand brilliant *mots*, which would have made the reputation of a dozen of the French memoir-writers. The wit of it is really startling; and there are occasional remarks which shew quite a fearful knowledge of the heart — of that particular heart, that is to say, which beats in the bosom of Miss Landon; for she has no idea of a dramatic character, and it is Miss Landon who speaks and feels throughout. She writes a very painful journal of misery, and depression, and despair. We do not know what private circumstances may occasion this despondency, what woes or disappointments cause Miss Landon or Mr. Bulwer to cry out concerning the miseries attendant upon genius; but we would humbly observe that there is no reason why genius should not be as cheerful as dulness, — for it has greater capacities of enjoyment, and no greater ills to endure. It has a world of beauty and of happiness which is invisible to commoner clay, and can drink at a thousand sparkling sources of joy inaccessible to vulgar men. Of the ills of life a genius has no more share than another. Hodge feels misfortune quite as keenly as Mr. Bulwer; Polly Jones's heart is to the full as tender as Miss Landon's. Weep, then, whimper and weep, like our fair poetess, or our sage Pelham, as if their woes were deeper than those of the rest of the world? Oh, for a little manly, honest, God-relying simplicity — cheerful, unaffected, and humble! But it is dull to sermonise in magazines; there are better books where the thing is better done, and where every genius of them all may read and profit too.

10. [William Maginn.] "Preface to Our Second Decade." *Fraser's Magazine* **21 (January 1840): 23-26.** [Note: the review of *Francesca Carrara* mentioned by Maginn is in *Fraser's* II (April 1835): 480. Laman Blanchard's *Life and Literary Remains of L.E.L.* was published in 1841.]

The only member of the gentler sex whose name sorrows our obituary, is — Miss Landon. Our notice accompanying the sketch of this accomplished lady, was written in a gay and good-humoured tone; but her own works, as quoted even in our columns, are full of melancholy presages of untimely death. In our review of her *Francesca Carrara*, after remarking upon her looking upon the world in its gloomiest point of view, we proceed to say, —

> "If there be any possibility of construing an event so as to give it a melancholy character, we may feel certain that it is put into full mourning. The gayest occurrences, the brightest scenes, the most gorgeous parties, are all 'sicklied o'er with the pale cast of thought.' A wedding is as sad as an undertaker's procession. Lord Byron used to date the later events of his life from the year of 'his *funeral* with Miss Milbanke,' and Miss Landon seems to have caught the idea from his lordship. There is, in truth, a tone of sorrow and melancholy diffused through the book amounting at times to complete depression, which

we know not how to account for."...

With her we said, alluding to her novel, "a wedding is as sad as a funeral-procession." Her own wedding but shortly preceded her procession to the grave. She was married in June, 1838; in the October of the same year she was dead. In William Howitt's beautiful preface to Fisher's *Drawing-Room Scrap-Book*, which it had been so long her favourite occupation to edit, and in the last volume of which — this for 1840 — still linger some of her latest writings, he makes these touching observations upon her untimely death: —

"It is a singular fact that, spite of her own really cheerful disposition, and spite of all the advice of her most influential friends, she persisted in this tone from the first to the last of her works, from that hour to the hour of her lamented death. Her poems, though laid in scenes and times capable of any course of events, and though filled to overflowing with the splendours, and gauds, and high-toned sentiments of chivalry, though enriched with all the colours and ornaments of a most fertile and sportive fancy, were still but the heralds and delineations of melancholy misfortune and death. Let any one turn to any or all of her poetical volumes, and say whether this be not so, with few, and in most of them, no exceptions. The very words of her first heroine might have literally been uttered as her own: —

> 'Sad were my shades, methinks they had
> Almost a tone of prophecy;
> I ever had, from earliest youth,
> A feeling what my fate would be.'
>
> *The Improvisatrice*, [ll. 37-40.]

* * * * * * *

"They (some passages in *Ethel Churchill*) are the convictions of 'higher moral responsibility and greater power' which strike us so forcibly in the later writings of L.E.L.

"But what shall we say to the preparation of prussic acid, and its preservation by Lady Marchmont? What of the perpetual creed of L.E.L. that all affection brings wo and death? What of *The Improvvisatrice*, in her earliest work, already quoted: —

> 'I ever had, from earliest youth,
> A feeling what my fate would be?'

"And then the fate itself?

"Whether this melancholy belief in the tendency of the great subject of her writings, both in prose and poetry; this irresistible annunciation, like another Cassandra, of wo and desolation; this evolution of scenes and characters in her last work, bearing such dark resemblance to those of her after-experience; this tendency in all her plots to a tragic catastrophe, and this final tragedy itself; whether these be all mere coincidences or not, they are still but the parts of an unsolved mystery. If they be, they are more than strange, and ought to make us superstitious. But surely if ever

> 'Coming events cast their shadows before,'

they did so in the foreboding tone of this gifted spirit. However these things be, we come from a fresh perusal of her works since her lamented death, with a higher opinion of her intellectual and moral constitution, and with a livelier sense of the peculiar character of her genius."

Whether the mystery alluded to by Howitt will ever be dispelled, is hard to conjecture; it is, to say the least, strange, that, although a year has now elapsed since the tidings of her death arrived in England, not a word beyond the first vague and unsatisfactory communication of her sudden fate has reached us. It is somewhat remarkable, that when we can procure minute accounts of the sufferings of nameless Negroes in the West of Africa, and hear them trumpeted forth in a thousand quarters as matters of interest to the world, nothing can be learned of the death of L.E.L. beyond the confused report of a hasty inquest, destitute of many characteristics indispensably required to stamp a value upon such inquiries held in this country.

Charles Swain has some fine stanzas upon her memory in the last *Friendship's Offering*: —

[quoting Swain's "A Vision of Tombs;" See Appendix B]

The demand for her remains, were it ever so reasonable, is now unavailing. The fairy fingers on which she was wont to pride herself, have long since passed into clay, and the moral remnants of L.E.L. are blended undistinguishably with the tropic-baked and fermenting mould of Cape Coast Castle. She had herself predicted, though speaking in the character of another,—

> "Where my father's bones are lying,
>   There my bones will never lie;
>
> ★ ★ ★ ★
>
> Mine shall be a lonelier ending,
>   Mine shall be a wilder grave,
> Where the shout and shriek are blending,
>   Where the tempest meets the wave;
> Or perhaps a fate more lonely,
>   In some drear and distant ward,
> Where my weary eyes meet only
>   Hiréd nurse, and sullen guard."

It is not to be expected, indeed, that her ashes will be brought home; nor, perhaps, that she will have any enduring memory in our language as a poetess of the loftier class, though she finely hopes that some of the golden ore of her genius has been fashioned into fantastic, perhaps beautiful shapes, and looks forward "with an engrossing and enduring belief that the creative feeling, the ardent thought, have not poured themselves forth in vain." But in her poems there are unquestioned indications of genius, and sometimes the indication is fulfilled by her execution. She had a deep and sweet feeling of affection, and a fine eye for the more ornamental and picturesque beauties of the external world, which she frequently expressed in harmonious verse, suggested by copious reading of varied literature and regulated by a musical and practised ear. With the young she was always a favourite: other ladies — for by ladies it must be done, if at all, — may, but hardly soon, supplant her in that favour. May their career be less burthened by wearisome exertion, their close less sorrowful than hers! At the period of her death, she was rapidly rising in all that could gratify a lady and an authoress — in general estimation, in public honour, in increasing respect — as well as in the more matured developement of her genius, made evident in her prose compositions. *Ethel Churchill* is, indeed, a work of beauty and talent, for which it would be hard to find a parallel in the history of female authorship. And then, when the prospect of her taking a place in her land's language was within her sight — *then* she died. The promise of her life was unfulfilled: —

> "Life is made up of miserable hours;
>   And all of which we craved a brief possessing,
> For which we wasted wishes, hopes, and powers,
>   Comes with some fatal drawback on the blessing —
>   We might have been.
>
> The future never renders to the past
>   The young beliefs intrusted to its keeping.
> Inscribe one sentence — life's first truth and last
>   On the pale marble where our dust is sleeping —
>   We might have been."
>   ["Three Extracts from the Diary of a Week," 46-55]

Who wrote those lines? Miss Landon! What *she* might have been, is now idle to conjecture; but, apart from her literary abilities and her literary industry, she *was*, in every domestic relation of life, honourable, generous, dutiful, self-denying; zealous, disinterested, and untiring in her friendships; and, as an ornament of society, what Miss Jewsbury called her — "a gay and gifted thing." Those who knew her still better would give her higher praise, but this is not the place. Where is the book about her by Blanchard, her literary executor? Has it gone to sleep?

11. William Howitt. "L.E.L." *Fisher's Drawing Room Scrap Book for 1840*: 5-8. [Mary Howitt's poem "L'Envoi" immediately follows this essay: see Appendix B for text.]

As we place these talismanic letters, L.E.L., which have stood so attractively for not less than eight years on the title-page of the DRAWING-ROOM SCRAP BOOK, at the head of a closing article on the genius of the very interesting and gifted creature whom they represented, we feel it to be a circumstance in which the readers of the Scrap-Book must, more than all others, take the deepest interest. Every succeeding year must have given to L.E.L. a more captivating and endearing hold on their minds, for over none of her numerous works had she cast more lavishly the rainbow hues of her genius, and in none had the evidences of her still rapidly growing intellect, and the expanding and deepening scope of her observation and her human sympathies, become more apparent. Every reader of the Drawing-Room Scrap Book would at once respond to Miss Landon's own candid declaration to the publishers, that she had given "a high literary character to it;" and nothing is more true than her assertion to the same party, "Some of my best poems have appeared in the Drawing-Room Scrap Book."

The circumstance, however, which terminated the intercourse of L.E.L. with the readers of this work, was that only which snapped asunder her connexion with the earth itself — death — an early and melancholy death.

We have, within a few years, felt some of the most vivid sensations which the death of popular writers can, under any circumstances, possibly create. We have not forgotten the electric shock which the death of Byron, falling in his prime and in a noble cause, sent through Europe: nor the more expected, but not less solemn and strongly recognized departure of Sir Walter Scott: but neither of these exceeded that with which the news was received of the sudden decease of this still young and popular poetess. The apprehensions which the climate suggested, on the first tidings of her going out to Cape Coast Castle, did not even abate the abrupt effect of the news of her death. The mysterious circumstances attending it, threw a tragic horror around it, and kindled an intense eagerness to penetrate their obscurity. The strange contrast between the youthful and buoy-ant spirit of L.E.L.'s genius, and the sombre tone of her views of life and human nature, were not more startling and stimulant than that between her popularity and her fate.

It is not our intention here to pause over this sudden quenching of so lovely and brilliant a luminary, nor to attempt to dissipate a sin-gle mystery which hangs over it. Her amiable and excellent friend, Emma Roberts, has drawn, in the introduction to "The Zenana, and the Minor Poems of L.E.L." published since her death, an admirable, and admirably just, character of her. Our present object is to take a review of her literary career — rapid, yet sufficiently full to point out some particulars in her writings, which we think too peculiar not to interest strongly her former readers.

The subject of L.E.L.'s first volume was love — a subject which we might have supposed, in one so young, would have been clothed in all the gay and radiant colours of hope and happiness; but, on the contrary, it was exhibited as the most fatal and melancholy of human passions. With the strange wayward delight of the young heart ere it has known actual sorrow, she seemed to riot and revel amid death and wo, laying prostrate hope, life, and affection. Of all the episodical tales introduced into the general design of the principal poem, not one but terminated fearfully or sorrowfully: the heroine herself was the fading victim of crossed and wasted affections. The shorter poems which filled up the volume, and which were, mostly, of extreme beauty, were still based on the wrecks and agonies of humanity.

It might be imagined that this morbid indulgence of so strong an appetite for grief, but was the first dipping of the playful foot in the sunny shallows of that flood of mortal experience, through which all have to pass, and but the dallying, yet desperate pleasure afforded by the mingled chill and glittering eddies of the waters which might hereafter swallow up the passer through, and that the first real pang of actual pain would scare her youthful fancy into the bosom of those hopes and fascinations with which the young mind is com-monly only too much delighted to surround itself. But it is a singular fact, that, spite of her own really cheerful disposition, and spite of all the advice of her most influential friends, she persisted in this tone from the first to the last of her works, from that hour to the hour of her lamented death. Her poems, though laid in scenes and times capable of any course of events, and though filled to overflowing with the splendours and gauds and high-toned sentiments of chivalry, though enriched with all the colours and ornaments of a most fertile and sportive fancy, were still but the heralds and delineations of melancholy, misfortune, and death. Let any one turn to any, or all, of her poetical volumes, and say whether this be not so, with few, and, in most of them, no exceptions. The very words of her first heroine might have literally been uttered as her own.

> "Sad were my shades; methinks they had
> Almost a tone of prophecy —
> I ever had, from earliest youth,
> A feeling what my fate would be."
>
> [*The Improvisatrice*, ll. 37-40.]

This is one singular peculiarity of the poetry of L.E.L.; and her poetry must be confessed to be peculiar. It is entirely her own. It had one prominent and fixed character, and that character belonged solely to itself. The rhythm, the feeling, the style and phraseology of, L.E.L.'s poetry, were such, that you could immediately recognize it, though the writer's name was not mentioned. Love was still the great theme, and misfortune the great doctrine. It was not the less remarkable, that she retained to the last the poetical tastes of her very earliest years. The themes of chivalry and romance, feudal pageants and Eastern splendour, delighted her imagination as much in the full growth as in the budding of her genius.

We should say that it is the young and the ardent who must always be the warmest admirers of the larger poems of L.E.L. They are filled with the faith and the fancies of the young. The very scenery and ornaments are of that rich and showy kind which belongs to the youthful taste — the white rose, the jasmine, the summer garniture of deep grass, and glades of greenest foliage; festal gardens with lamps and bowers; gay cavaliers and jewelled dames, and all that glitters in young eyes and love-haunted fancies. But amongst these, numbers of her smaller poems from the first dealt with subjects and sympathies of a more general kind, and gave glimpses of a nobility of sentiment, and a bold expression of her feeling of the unequal lot of humanity, of a far higher character. Such, in the Improvisatrice, are the Guerilla Chief, St. George's Hospital, The Deserter, Gladesmuir, The Covenanters, The Female Convict, The Soldier's Grave, &c. Such are many that we could point out in every succeeding volume. But it was in her few last years that her heart and mind seemed every day to develope more strength, and to gather a wider range of humanity into their embrace. In the later volumes of the Drawing-Room Scrap Book, many of the best poems of which have been reprinted with the Zenana, nothing was more striking than the steady development of growing intellectual power, and of deep, and generous, and truly philosophical sentiments, tone of thought, and serious experience.

But when L.E.L. had fixed her character as a poet, and the public looked only for poetical productions from her, she suddenly came forth as a prose writer, and with still added proofs of intellectual vigour. Her prose stories have the leading characteristics of her poetry. Their theme is love, and their demonstration, that all love is fraught with destruction and desolation. But there are other qualities manifested in the tales. The prose page was for her a wider tablet, on which she could, with more freedom and ampler display, record her views of society. Of these, Francesca Carrara, and Ethil Churchill, are unquestionably the best works, the latter pre-eminently so. In these she has shown, under the characters of Guido and Walter Maynard, her admiration of genius, and her opinion of its fate; under those of Francesca and Ethil Churchill, the adverse destiny of pure and high-souled woman.

These volumes abound with proofs of a shrewd observation of society, with masterly sketches of character, and the most beautiful snatches of scenery. But what surprise and delight more than all, are the sound and true estimates of humanity, and the honest boldness with which her opinions are expressed. The clear perception of the fearful social condition of this country, and the fervent advocacy of the poor, scattered through these works, but especially the last, do honour to her woman's heart. These portions of L.E.L.'s writings require to be yet more truly appreciated.

There is another characteristic of her prose writings which is peculiar. Never were the feelings and experiences of authorship so cordially and accurately described. She tells us all that she has learned freely. She puts words into the mouth of Walter Maynard, of which all who have known anything of literary life, must instantly acknowledge the correctness. The author's heart never was more completely laid open, with all its hopes, fears, fatigues, and enjoyments, its bitter and its glorious experiences. In the last hours of Walter Maynard, she makes him utter what must, at that period, have been daily more and more her own conviction. "I am far cleverer than I was. I have felt, have thought so much! Talk of the mind exhausting itself! — never! Think of the mass of material which every day accumulates! Then experience, with its calm, clear light, corrects so many youthful fallacies; every day we feel our higher moral responsibility, and our greater power."

They are the convictions of "higher moral responsibility and greater power," which strike us so forcibly in the later writings of L.E.L.

But what shall we say to the preparation of prussic acid, and to its preservation by Lady Marchmont? What of the perpetual creed of L.E.L., that all affection brings wo and death? What of the Improvisatrice in her earliest work, already quoted: —

> "I ever had, from earliest youth,
>   A feeling what my fate would be."

And then the fate itself?

Whether this melancholy belief in the tendency of the great subject of her writings, both in prose and poetry; this irresistible annunciation, like another Cassandra, of wo and desolation; this evolution of scenes and characters in her last work, bearing such dark resemblance to those of her own after-experience; this tendency in all her plots to a tragic catastrophe, and this final tragedy itself, whether these be all mere coincidences or not, they are still but the parts of an unsolved mystery. If they be, they are more than strange, and ought to make us superstitious. But surely, if ever

Coming events cast their shadows before,

they did so in the foreboding tone of this gifted spirit. However these things be, we come from a fresh perusal of her works, since her lamented death, with a higher opinion of her intellectual and moral constitution, and with a livelier sense of the peculiar character of her genius.

Appendix B: Poems Written for and about "L.E.L."

1. [Bernard Barton (1784–1849), nicknamed "The Quaker Poet;" friend of Charles Lamb. "To L.E.L. On his or her Poetic Sketches in the *Literary Gazette*" published in LG for 9 February 1822.]

TO L.E.L.

On his or her* Poetic Sketches in the Literary Gazette.

To me there's more of Minstrel stealth
   In thy brief overflowings
Of fancy, — more of Thought's best wealth, —
   And Feeling's sweetest glowings; —
Than I can find in many a tome,
O'er which, from page to page, I roam.

Such gentle music may pass by
   The cold, or careless hearer;—
To me it's witching melody
   Is, from it's softness, dearer:
Its gushing forth, its dying fall,
Surpass the notes of Nourmahal.

I know not who, or what thou art;
   Nor do I seek to know thee,
While Thou, performing thus thy part,
   Such banquets canst bestow me.
Then be, as long as thou shalt list,
My viewless, nameless Melodist.

BERNARD BARTON.

---

* We have pleasure in saying that the sweet poems under this signature are by a lady, yet in her teens! The admiration with which they have been so generally read, could not delight their fair author more than it has those who in the *Literary Gazette* cherished her infant genius. — *Ed.*

2. ["W.L.R." "To L.E.L." Published in LG for 15 February 1823.]

TO L.E.L.[*]

'Tis sweet, e'en to a wither'd heart,
    To hear the sounds that once were dear;
When bliss and hope alike depart,
    Their echo soothes the lonely ear.

'Tis sweet to listen to the wile
    That cheats us with what ne'er can be;
'Tis sweet to smile when others smile;
    'Tis sweeter far to weep with thee.

Thy song can call back to my mind
    Remembrances too fondly cherish'd,
Thoughts that *will* linger still behind,
    Tho' all my hopes and fears have perish'd.
And when thy strain is o'er, I feel
    As if some 'witching dream had vanish'd,
And long in waking yet to steal
    The gleam of joy that truth has banish'd.

Oh! strike again thy plaintive lyre,
    Awake once more those notes of woe;
My tears have been like streams of fire,
    But sweetly to thy verse they flow.
Long may the sorrows of thy song
    Be to thy guileless heart unknown;
And whilst thou melt thy readers' hearts,
    May ev'ry bliss reign in thine own! — W.L.R.

29 January 1823.

---

[*] It is something like self-praise to admit into our columns any thing complimentary to what has appeared in them; but the many tributes we receive to the genius addressed in these lines will escape this censure, when we acknowledge them as due to a young and a female minstrel, and expressive of feelings very generally excited by her beautiful productions.

3. ["B." "To L.E.L." Published in *The Literary Magnet* 2 (1824).]

STRANGER! whoe'er thou art, thy plaintive lyre
    Hath sooth'd the sorrows of an aching breast;
When Hope's fair dreams in sorrow's dawn expire,
    'Tis thine to lull a care-torn soul to rest.
For thou dost weep the visions that in Fancy's hour
    Rose to the eye, and cheated the young heart.
Delusive dream! which, like a faded flow'r,
    No charm, save recollection, can impart.
Though disappointment oft hath chill'd thy tale,
    And sear'd a heart, to love and sorrow prone,
Yet, as thy soften'd murmurs expire i' th' gale,
    And speak of loves forgot, of joys for ever flown,
    Lady, I mourn thy griefs, forgetful of mine own!

                                                                          B.

4. [Winthrop Mackworth Praed (1802–39), poet. Landon based her character "Mr. Lillian" in *Romance and Reality* on Praed. "A Preface" was first published in 1824. Text from *The Poems of Winthrop Mackworth Praed. With a Memoir by the Rev. Derwent Coleridge.* London: Moxon, 1844.]

A PREFACE.

I have a tale of Love to tell; —
Lend me thy light lute, L.E.L.
Lend me thy lute! what other strings
Should speak of those delicious things,
Which constitute Love's joys and woes
In pretty duodecimos?
Thou knowest every herb and flower,
Of wondrous name, and wondrous power,
Which, gathered where white wood-doves nestle,
And beat up by poetic pestle,
Bind gallant knights in fancied fetters,

And set young ladies writing letters:
Thou singest songs of floods and fountains,
Of mounted lords and lordly mountains,
Of dazzling shields and dazzling glances,
Of piercing frowns and piercing lances,
Of leaping brands and sweeping willows,
Of dreading seas and dreaming billows,
Of sunbeams which are like red wine,
Of odorous lamps of argentine,
Of cheeks that burn, of hearts that freeze,
Of odours that send messages,
Of kingfishers and silver pheasants,
Of gems to which the Sun makes presents,
Of miniver and timeworn walls,
Of clairschachs and of atabals.
Within thy passion-haunted pages
Throng forward girls — and distant ages,
The lifeless learns at once to live,
The dumb grows strangely talkative,
Resemblances begin to strike
In things exceedingly unlike,
All nouns, like statesmen, suit all places,
And verbs, turned lawyers, hunt for cases.

Oh! if it be a crime to languish
Over thy scenes of bliss or anguish,
To float with Raymond o'er the sea,
To sigh with dark-eyed Rosalie,
And sit in reverie luxurious
Till tea grows cold, and aunts grow furious,
I own the soft impeachment true,
And burn the Westminster Review.
Lend me thy lute; I'll be a poet;
All Paternoster Row shall know it!

I'll rail in rhyme at cruel Fate
From Temple Bar to Tyburn Gate;
Old Premium's daughter in the City
Shall feel that love is kin to pity,
Hot ensigns shall be glad to borrow
My notes of rapture and of sorrow,
And I shall hear sweet voices sighing
"So young! — and I am told he's dying!"
Yes! I shall wear a wreath eternal,
For full twelve months, in Post and Journal,
Admired by all the Misses Brown
Who go to school at Kentish Town,
And worshipped by the fair Arachne
Who makes my handkerchiefs at Hackney!

Vain, vain! — take back the lute! I see
Its chords were never meant for me.
For thine own song, for thine own hand,
That lute was strung in Fairy-land;
And, if a stranger's thumb should fling
Its rude touch o'er one golden string, —
Good night to all the music in it!
The string would crack in half a minute.
Take back the lute! I make no claim
To inspiration or to fame;
The hopes and fears that bards should cherish,
I care not when they fade and perish;
I read political economy,
Voltaire and Cobbett, and gastronomy,
And, when I would indite a story
Of woman's faith or warrior's glory,
I always wear a night-cap sable,
And put my elbows on the table,
And hammer out the tedious toil
By dint of Walker, and lamp-oil.
I never feel poetic mania,
I gnaw no laurel with Urania,

I court no critic's tender mercies,
I count the feet in all my verses,
And own myself a screaming gander
Among the shrill swans of Maeander!

5. [Mrs. Cornwall Baron Wilson (*née* Margaret Harries) (1797–1846), poet, author, editor of *New Monthly Belle Assemblée*.]

A. "Impromptu: On Seeing the Portrait of the Fair Author of the 'Improvisatrice,' in the Exhibition." [Published in *La Belle Assemblée* 2 (July 1825).]

—"Her sweetest song was giv'n to *love!*"
Moore.

SAY, lovely songstress, canst thou tell,
What is the cause — the potent spell,
That makes thee sing of LOVE alone,
And scorn all other themes to own?
Why dost thou only wake the lyre
To tears of passion — sighs of fire?
Oh! choose some higher, nobler theme,
Fit for a youthful minstrel's dream!
To purer numbers wake thy lay,
Worthy our best poetic day!
Why not to WAR attune thy powers,
And strew the conqueror's path with flowers?
Or round RELIGION'S sacred shrine
The Muse's holiest wreaths entwine?
And let the full-voiced choir of song
Float, in soft notes, the breeze along!
Oh! there is many a hidden mine
Of feeling, in a soul like thine,
That only wants some hand to throw
Aside the veil that hides its glow,
And shew the world, in colours fair,
How rich the gems that sparkle there!

Say, lovely songstress, canst thou tell,
What is the cause — the potent spell,
That makes thee sing of LOVE alone,
And scorn all other themes to own?

Woburn Place, June 1825.

B. "Elegiac Tribute to the Memory of L.E.L." [Published in NMM 55 (January 1839).]

"Only one doom for the Poet is recorded."*

O N L Y one doom! writ in misfortune's page
For earth's most highly gifted; — does the lyre,
To those who woo it, such a fate presage
To damp the kindling thoughts, that would aspire,
Prometheus-like, to sport with heavenly fire? —
Alas! 'tis even so! — Fame's laurel wreath
Distils its poison on the brow beneath!

Thy grave is made, under a foreign sky,
And in a stranger soil; — thine ashes rest
In a far-distant clime; — no kindred eye
Soften'd thy death-pangs, — saw thy heaving breast
Gasp its last sigh, or caught the fond bequest
Thy murmuring lip had breathed to friends afar; —
Lone was thy setting, Genius' "Polar Star!" —†

There should have knelt around thee, mourning friends,
With anxious hearts, in that all-fearful hour
When weeping Love in silent prayer ascends

---

* "The Death of Camoens," by L.E.L. Vide New Monthly Magazine, June, 1838.

† Vide L.E.L.'s last published poem, in the New Monthly Magazine for January, 1839.

To Heav'n, that it will raise the drooping Flower
(A "broken reed," to save its human power);
And the last murmur of thy parting groan
Should not have pass'd, unheeded and unknown!

Thine should have been a tomb within the aisles
Where "storied urn and animated bust"
Rise to our mighty dead; — where Honour smiles
Above the spot, enshrining Genius' dust!
Where Kingly crowns and Heroes' trophies rust; —
There, among England's gifted, great, and good,
The urn that holds thine ashes should have stood.

This Fate forbids! — but in thy lyric page
Thine epitaph is written; — down the stream
Of gliding years, to many a distant age,
Shall float thy magic numbers; — as a dream,
Haunting the mem'ry with sweet sounds, that seem
Like snatches of some old familiar strain,
Waking fond thoughts of childhood's hours again!

For thou wert Feeling's own impassion'd child!
Her girdling spells were on thee; — and thy heart
Was as a living lyre, whose chords the wild
Soft breezes kiss'd to music; — forth would start,
At NATURE'S touch (for thou disdainedst ART),
The gushing stream of Song; — the kindling flame
Breathed on by thee, in answering numbers came.

But mute is now that lyre! hush'd as the heart
Whose pulses were its echo; — for the strings
Of both, alas! are broken. — As depart
Day's beams, and o'er the dial twilight flings
The dusky shadow of her brooding wings,
So, from the world, thy lyric light hath pass'd,
And Death has hush'd the Swan's sweet notes at last!

Jan. 4, 1839.

6. [John Greenleaf Whittier (1807-92), American poet. "To the Author of The Improvisatrice." Published in LG for 19 June 1830.]

I K N O W thee not, high Spirit! but the sympathy of thought
Hath often to my hour of dreams thy living presence brought;
And I feel that I could love thee with the fondness of a brother,
As the sainted ones of Paradise bear love for one another.

For I know thy spirit hath been poured full freely in thy song,
Where feeling hath been prodigal, and passion hath been strong—
That the secrets of thy bosom are burning on thy lyre,
In the nature of thy worshipping, a ministry of fire.

Young priestess at a holy shrine, I scarce can deem that years
So few and beautiful as thine are registered in tears —
That the gift of thy affections hath gone abroad in vain —
A rose-leaf on the autumn wind — a foam-wreath on the main!

Yet blended with thy beautiful and intellectual lays,
I read a mournful consciousness of cold and evil days;
Of the weariness existence feels when its sunlight has gone down,
And from the autumn of the heart the flowers of Hope are strown;—

Of the coldness of the hollow world, its vanities that pass
Like tinges from the sunset, or night-gems from the grass —
Its mocking and unmeaning praise, the flatterer's fatal art —
Flowers madly to the bosom clasped, with serpents at their heart!

And oh! if things like these have been the chasteners of thy years,
How hath thy woman's spirit known the bitterness of tears!
How have thy girlhood visions — the warm, wild thought of youth,
Folded their sunny pinions, and darkened into truth!

O wearily, most wearily, unto the child of song,
The heavy tide of being rolls, a sunless wave, along —
When the promise of existence fades before the time of noon,

And the evening of the soul comes on, unblest by star or moon!

God help thee in thy weary way! and if the silver tone
Of Fame hath music for an ear so chastened as thine own,
Thou hast it from another clime, where heart and mind are free,
And where the brave and beautiful have bowed themselves to thee.

And one whose home hath been among the mountains of the
      North,
Where the cataract mocks the earthquake, and the giant streams
      come forth —
Where spirits in their robes of flame dance o'er the cold blue sky,
And to the many-voiced storm the eagle makes reply!

A worshipper before the shrine at which thy spirit bendeth,
While on its pure and natural gifts the holy flame descendeth,
Hath poured his tribute on thine ear, as he would praise a star
Whose beams had wandered down to him from their blue home
      and far.

Lady! amidst the clarion-note of well-deserved fame,
It were, perhaps, but vain to hope this feeble lay might claim
A portion of thy fair regard, or win a thought of thine
To linger on a gift so frail and dissonant as mine.

But onward in thy skyward path — a thousand eyes shall turn
To where, like heaven's unwasting stars, thy gifts of spirit burn —
A thousand hearts shall wildly thrill where'er thy lays are known,
And stately manhood blend its praise with woman's gentlest tone.

Farewell! — the hand that traces this may perish ere life's noon,
And the spirit that hath guided it may be forgot as soon —
Forgotten with its lofty hopes — the fevered dreams of mind —
Unnoted, stealing to the dead without a name behind.

But thou upon the human heart, in characters of flame,
And on the heaven of intellect, hast registered thy name;

The gifted ones of fallen earth shall worship at thy shrine,
And sainted spirits joy to hold companionship with thine.

J. GREENLEAF WHITTIER.
Haverhill, Massachusetts,
8th of 1st Month, 1830

7. [Anonymous. "Literary Dialogues No. 1: Neddy Bulwer and Letty Landon." Published in *The Age* **(25 December 1831).]**

N.   Child of Love and Muse of Passion
      Pretty Letty — that is you.

L.E.L.   Ned, in all *you* lead the fashion
      Neddy mine, indeed you do.

N.   Letty, sweet is thy *Romancing*
      Charming thy *Reality.*

L.E.L.   But appear! what eyes are glancing
      Ladies eyes — dear Ned, at thee.

N.   Beauteous *Improvisatrice!*
      Violet of *Golden* hue.

L.E.L.   Spare my blushes, I beseech thee —
      Falkland, Pelham, Devereux.

N.   Poesy's enraptured dwelling!
      Song-born Sappho of our Age.

L.E.L.   Cease, O poet, all excelling
      Senator and peerless sage!
      [*Neddy bows, brays and exits*]

8. [Elizabeth Barrett Browning (1806–61). In a letter to Henry Fothergill Chorley dated 7 January 1845, Browning discussed English women poets, and wrote of Landon: "But you shall not think me exclusive. Of poor L.E.L. for instance, I could write with *more* praiseful appreciation than you can. It appears to me that she had the gift — though in certain respects she dishonoured the art — and her latter lyrics are, many of them, of great beauty and melody, such as, having once touched the ear of a reader, live on in it." (Sir Frederic George Kenyon, *Letters of Elizabeth Barrett Browning*, 2 vols. New York: Macmillan, 1898: 1:232.)]

A. "Stanzas Addressed to Miss Landon, and Suggested by Her 'Stanzas on the Death of Mrs. Hemans.'" [Published (under the pseudonym "B.") in NMM 45 (1835).]

> Thou bay-crown'd living one — who o'er
>   The bay-crown'd dead art bowing,
> And o'er the shadeless, moveless brow
>   Thy human shadow throwing;
> And o'er the sighless, songless lips
>   The wail and music wedding —
> Dropping o'er the tranquil eyes
>   Tears not of *their* shedding:
>
> Go! take thy music from the dead,
>   Whose silentness is sweeter;
> Reserve thy tears for living brows,
>   For whom such tears are meeter;
> And leave the violets in the grass,
>   To brighten where thou treadest,
> No flowers for *her!* Oh! bring no flowers —
>   Albeit "Bring flowers," thou saidest.
>
> But bring not near her solemn corse
>   A type of human seeming;
> Lay only dust's stern verity

Upon her dust undreaming.
And while the calm perpetual stars
    Shall look upon it solely;
Her spherèd soul shall look on *them,*
    With eyes more bright and holy.

Nor mourn, oh living one, because
    Her part in life was mourning:
Would she have lost the poet's flame,
    For anguish of the burning?
The minstrel harp, for the strain'd string?
    The tripod, for th' afflated
Woe? or the vision, for those tears
    Through which it shone dilated?

Perhaps she shudder'd while the world's
    Cold hand her brow was wreathing:
But wrong'd she ne'er that mystic breath
    Which breath'd in all her breathing, —
Which drew from rocky earth and man
    Abstractions high and moving, —
Beauty, if not the beautiful, —
    And love, if not the loving.

Such visionings have paled in sight
    The *Saviour* she descrieth,
And little recks who wreath'd the brow
    That on His bosom lieth.
The whiteness of His innocence
    O'er all her garments flowing,
There learneth she that sweet "new song"
    She will not mourn in knowing.

Be blessed, crown'd and living one:
    And when thy dust decayeth,
May thine own England say for thee
    What now for her it sayeth, —

"Albeit softly in our ears
     Her silver song was ringing,
The footsteps of her parting soul
     Were softer than her singing."

                                        B.

B. "L.E.L.'s Last Question." [The text is of the first publication in *The Athenaeum*, 26 January 1839.]

"Do you think of me as I think of you,
My friends, my friends?" She said it from the sea,
The English minstrel in her minstrelsy —
While under brighter skies than erst she knew,
Her heart grew dark, and gropëd as the blind,
To touch, across the waves, friends left behind —
"Do you think of me as I think of you?"

It seemed not much to ask — *as I of you* —
We all do ask the same — no eyelids cover
Within the meekest eyes that question over —
And little in this world the loving do,
But sit (among the rocks?) and listen for
The echo of their own love evermore —
Do you think of me as I think of you?

Love-learnëd, she had sung of only love —
And as a child asleep (with weary head
Dropped on the fairy-book he lately read),
Whatever household noises round him move,
Hears in his dream some elfin turbulence —
Even so, suggestive to her inward sense,
All sounds of life assumed one tune of love.

And when the glory of her dream withdrew,
When knightly gestes and courtly pageantries
Were broken in her visionary eyes
By tears, the solemn seas attested true —

Forgetting that sweet lute beside her hand,
She asked not "Do you praise me, O my land,"
But, "Think ye of me, friends, as I of you?"

True heart to love, that pourëd many a year
Love's oracles for England, smooth and well, —
Would God, thou hadst an inward oracle
In that lone moment, to confirm thee dear!
For when thy questioned friends in agony
Made passionate response, "We think of thee,"
Thy place was in the dust — too deep to hear!

Could she not wait to catch the answering breath? —
Was she content with that drear ocean's sound,
Dashing his mocking infinite around
The craver of a little love? — beneath
Those stars, content — where last her song had gone?
They, mute and cold in radiant life, as soon
Their singer was to be, in darksome death!

Bring your vain answers — cry, "We think of thee!"
How think ye of her? — in the long ago
Delights! — or crowned by new bays? — not so —
None smile, and none are crowned where lyeth she —
With all her visions unfulfilled, save one,
Her childhood's, of the palm-trees in the sun —
And lo! — their shadow on her sepulchre!

Do you think of me as I think of you? —
O friends, O kindred, O dear brotherhood
Of the whole world — what are we that we should
For covenants of long affection sue? —
Why press so near each other, when the touch
Is barred by graves? Not much, and yet too much,
This, "Think upon me as I think of you."

But, while on mortal lips I shape anew

A sigh to mortal issues, verily
Above th' unshaken stars that see us die,
A vocal pathos rolls — and HE who drew
All life from dust, and *for* all, tasted death,
By death, and life, and love appealing, saith,
Do you think of me as i think of you?

9. [(Samuel) Laman Blanchard (1804-45), poet, editor, biographer of Landon. The publication date of "On First Seeing the Portrait of L.E.L." is uncertain; it was republished in *Life and Literary Remains of L.E.L.* (Philadelphia: Lea & Blanchard, 1841): 1:123-24.]

ON FIRST SEEING THE PORTRAIT OF L.E.L.

———

"Is this the face that fired a thousand ships,
And burned the topless towers of Ilium!
Sweet Helen!" — MARLOWE.

———

Ah no! not Helen, Hel—e—n
Of old — but L.E.L.;
Those letters which the spell-bound pen
Have vainly sought to spell.

Not Helen, who so long ago
Set Paris in a blaze;
But one who laid proud London low,
And lit up later days.

Is *this* your meaning, mystic Three!
Hand-writing on Fame's wall!
Ye thrice fair letters, can ye be
A lady, after all?

How have I wondered what ye meant,
Ye alphabetic Graces!

And so you really represent
    One of dear Nature's faces!

How, how I've guessed! your meaning rare,
    No guessing seemed to touch;
Ye riddles! the weird sisters ne'er
    Bewitch'd me half so much.

One knows the power of D.C.L.;
    The grandeur of K.G.;
And F.R.S. will science spell,
    And valour G.C.B.

The sage, the schoolboy, both can tell
    The worth of L.S.D.;
But, then, the worth of L.E.L.!
    All *letters* told in three!

[handwritten margin note: Pounds Shillings Pence]

In vain I've sought to illustrate
    Each letter with a word;
'Twas only trying to translate
    The language of a bird.

I've read ye, L.E.L., quite bare;
    Thus — Logic, Ethics, Lays;
Lives, Episodes, and Lyrics fair —
    I've guess'd away my days.

One wild young fancy was the sire
    Of fifty following after;
Like these — Love, Eden, and the Lyre,
    Light, Elegance, and Laughter.

I've drawn from all the stars that shine
    Interpretations silly;
From flowers — the Lily, Eglantine,
    And, then, another Lily.

Now fancy's dead; no thought can strike,
    No guess, solution, stricture;
And L.E.L. is — simply like
    This dainty little picture.

Life to her lays! However Fame
    'Mongst brightest names may set hers,
These three initials — nameless name —
    Shall never be *dead letters*!

10. [John A. Heraud (1799-1887), poet, dramatist, drama crit-
ic for *The Athenaeum*. "To L.E.L." was published in *The Eng-
lish Bijou Almanac* for 1838 (an annual edited by Landon).]

Sappho of a polished age!
    Loves and graces sweetly fling
Chastened splendours o'er thy page,
    Like moonlight on a fairy's wing.
Feelings fresh as morning's dews,
    Breathings gentle as the May's,
Verses soft as violet's hues,
    Once sported in thy happy lays.

Sad is now thy plaintive strain,
    Melancholy is thy mood —
Bring us back thy youth again!
    For Cheerfulness befits the good.
Yet, if thou be sad — 'tis well!
    If we weep, — 'tis not in vain!
Sighs, attuned to Sappho's shell,
    Allure us into love with pain!

11. ["Father Prout" (Francis Sylvester Mahoney) (1804-66), Irish humourist, contributor to *Fraser's Magazine* and *Bentley's Miscellany*. The publication date of "The Angel of Poetry," written in imitation of a poem by Pierre Jean de Béranger (1780-1857), is uncertain. The text is from *The Reliques of Father Prout*, ed. Oliver Yorke. London: Bell, 1868.]

Lady! for thee a holier key shall harmonise the chord —
In Heaven's defence Omnipotence drew an avenging sword;
But when the bolt had crush'd revolt, one angel, fair though frail,
Retain'd his lute, fond attribute! to charm that gloomy vale.
The lyre he kept his wild hand swept; the music he'd awaken
Would sweetly thrill from the lonely hill where he sat apart
      forsaken:
There he'd lament his banishment, his thoughts to grief abandon,
And weep his full. 'Twas pitiful to see him weep, fair Landon!

He wept his fault! Hell's gloomy vault grew vocal with his song;
But all throughout derision's shout burst from the guilty throng:
God pitying view'd his fortitude in that unhallow'd den;
Free'd him from hell, but bade him dwell amid the sons of men.
Lady! for us, an exile thus, immortal Poesy
Came upon earth, and lutes gave birth to sweetest minstrelsy;
And poets wrought their spellwords, taught by that angelic mind,
And music lent soft blandishment to fascinate mankind.

Religion rose! man sought repose in the shadow of her wings;
Music for her walked harbinger, and Genius touch'd the strings:
Tears from the tree of Araby cast on her altar burn'd,
But earth and wave most fragrance gave where Poetry sojourn'd.
Vainly, with hate inveterate, hell labour'd in its rage,
To persecute that angel's lute, and cross his pilgrimage;
Unmov'd and calm, his songs pour'd balm on sorrow all the while;
Vice he unmask'd, but virtue bask'd in the radiance of his smile.

O where, among the fair and young, or in what kingly court,
In what gay path where Pleasure hath her favourite resort,

Where hast thou gone, angelic one? Back to thy native skies?
Or dost thou dwell in cloister'd cell, in pensive hermit's guise?
Methinks I ken a denizen of this our island — nay,
Leave me to guess, fair poetess! queen of the matchless lay!
The thrilling line, lady! is thine; the spirit pure and free;
And England views that angel muse, Landon! reveal'd in THEE!

**12. [Anonymous. "Sweet L.E.L. I much admire your verse."
Published in a review of *Flowers of Loveliness* in *The Gentle-
man's Magazine* 8 (December 1837).]**

> Sweet L.E.L. I much admire your verse,
> I never better saw — but have much worse.
> If you continue long to write so well,
> How great your fame will be, I cannot tell.
> But this I think — admire my quaint conceit —
> That you all other poetesses beat;
> And then, all rivals laid upon the shelf, —
> In faith I think that then — *you'll beat yourself.*

**13. [Maria Jane Jewsbury (1800-33). For biographical infor-
mation, see note to "On the Writings of Mrs. Hemans."
Jewsbury published "To L.E.L. — After Meeting Her for the
First Time" in *Fisher's Drawing Room Scrap Book* for 1839 to
accompany an engraving of Jewsbury.]**

TO L.E.L. — AFTER MEETING HER FOR THE FIRST TIME.

> GOOD night! I have no jewels
>   As parting gifts to bring;
> But here's a frank and kind farewell,
>   Thou gay and gifted thing!
>
> In the lonely hours of night,
>   When the face puts off its mask,
> When the fevered day is over,
>   And the heart hath done its task.

When reason mourns the vanities
   That stoop the lofty will,
Till the spirit's rack of worldliness
   Is struck, and yields its rill.

Then, then, I think of thee, friend,
   With sad, soft, earnest thought,
As of a child from fairy land
   Into the desert brought:

Forgetting there the visions
   That make of childhood part;
And singing songs of fairy land,
   Without the fairy heart:

As of a rose at noontide,
   Waving proudly to the view,
Yet wanting, in its crimson depth,
   The early drop of dew:

As of a tree in autumn,
   With its green leaves turned to gold;
But having on the healthy bough
   A faint decaying hold:

As of rills that run in summer
   With bright but hollow glee,
Wilt thou blame me, my too careless friend,
   If thus I think of thee?

I would my home were lovely
   As some which thou hast sung —
I would there were around it
   All lavish beauty flung —

I would bear thee to its bosom,
   Thou shouldst dwell with nature free,

And the dew of early truthfulness
   Would soon come back to thee.

Thou shouldst dwell in some fairy valley,
   Amid the true and kind,
And morn should make to each mountain
   A Memnon to thy mind.

Alas! alas! my dwelling
   Is amid a way-worn world;
And my vision, like a banner,
   But opened to be furled.

And yet my thoughts turn to thee,
   They kind and anxious turn —
I foresee for thee a future
   Which will have too much to learn.

Thy life is false and feverish,
   It is like a masque to thee:
When the task and glare are over,
   And thou grievest — come to me.

                    M.J.J.

14. [Camilla Toulmin (1812–95), later Mrs. Newton Crosland; novelist, essayist. "On the Death of Mrs. Maclean (L.E.L.)" published in *Bentley's Miscellany* 5 (1839).]

And thou art dead! It falls upon the ear,
   And heart, with a most strange, and startling sound;
For there doth seem a halo bright and clear,
   The young, and lov'd, and gifted to surround,
As if to shield them from the tyrant's power;
   And while we build for them high hopes on earth,
We in their future picture not that hour,
   Which quells all hope that has so low a birth.

Thy genius was a mine of Poesy!
    Yet some there were, who, though it gave rich ore,
Still deem'd most precious veins untouch'd did lie,
    (Thyself, perchance, unconscious of such store,)
And fondly thought that in that far-off clime,
    Choosing some lofty and unhackney'd strain
With mind matured by travel, change, and time,
    Thy lyre's rich music oft would wake again!

Life's chequer'd book had but just turn'd for thee
    A new and glowing page of hope and love, —
Alas! the records brief were doom'd to be, —
    Death severs ties nought else could ever move.
And cold the brow where hangs thy wreath of fame,
    Yet not a leaf of it is lost or faded;
And faithfully enshrin'd shall be thy name,
    In hearts that sorrow for thy loss has shaded.

And thou hast only now a foreign grave, —
    Far from all memories of olden time;
Where skies are bright, and palm-trees gently wave
    In the hot air of Afric's sultry clime;
And stars which there keep nightly watch above
    Are strange, and shed no rays on this dear land,
Which yet, methinks, that thou full well didst love,
    And yearn to, even from that distant strand!

15. [Mary Howitt (1799-1888), Landon's friend, appended this tribute, "L'Envoi," to William Howitt's essay on L.E.L. in *Fisher's Drawing Room Scrap Book for 1840.*]

L'ENVOI.

Farewell, farewell! Thy latest word is spoken;
    The lute thou lovedst hath given its latest tone;
Yet not without a lingering, parting token
    Hast thou gone from us, young and gifted one!
And what in love thou gavest, here we treasure,
    Sweet words of song penned in those far-off wilds,
And pure and righteous thoughts, in lofty measure,
    Strong as a patriot's, gentle as a child's.
Here shrine we them, like holy relics keeping,
    That they who loved thee may approach and read;
May know thy latest thoughts; may joy in weeping
    That thou wast worthy to be loved indeed!
Farewell, farewell! And as thy heart could cherish
    For love, a flower, the sere leaf of a tree, —
So from these pages shall not lightly perish
    Thy latest lays — memento flowers of thee!

                                              M.H.

16. [Bartholomew Simmons (1804-50), Irish poet, contributor to *Blackwood's Magazine.* "Lines in an Album to which Letitia Elizabeth Landon Had Been a Contributor" published in *Bentley's Miscellany* 7 (1840).]

As certain pilgrims bound of yore
To far Judea's sacred shore
Were vow'd a rosary to say
At every shrine upon their way,
So it befits the Bard, each time
An Album cheers his road, to rhyme.
Here, then, a wandering minstrel, weary
With life's long journey dim and dreary,

Pauses amid the desert waste
To hail this shelter spread for Taste,
And bless the fair and graceful powers
That gather'd here Wit's scatter'd flowers,
And strew'd these leaves with fancies bright,
    And won sweet poesy to pour
Such freshness o'er them that the wight
    Now scribbling, shrinks from scribbling more.

Yet, ere I part each favour'd leaf,
    Where Genius look'd, and left a spell,
How can this heart repress its grief
While lingering o'er yon record brief
    Of her the lost — the loved so well?
The radiant lady of the lute!
    The fire-lipped Sappho of the Isles!
And, is the Queen of Music mute,
    Who woke our tears and smiles?
Immortal Passion's priestess, wo
    To us to whom thy songs shall be
But springs in bitterness to flow
    Above thy lucid memory:
For, as we point to all thou 'st done,
    Remembrance of thine early fate
Will count what wreaths were left unwon
    Till Grief grows desolate!
Strange fate! fierce Afric's ocean laves,
    Or leaps in thunder by the bed;
And Afric's sultry palm-tree waves
    Above the gentle head
Of HER who deep should take her rest
Far in her own belovèd west, —
In some green nook, — some violet dell,
Beneath the rose she sang so well,
Soothed by the lull of some sweet river,
Sparklingly pure and bright, like her, the Lost for Ever!

17. [Charles Swain (1801-74), poet. "A Vision of Tombs. Addressed to the *Forget Me Not*" first published in the *Forget Me Not for 1840.*]

Forget them not! oh, still forget them not!
  The Bards whose spirit hath inspired thy page;
Be not the memory of the dead forgot,
  Whose genius is thy proudest heritage!
Alas for life! what bosom might presage
  The shadow of the grave was with each name?
Some, gray and lonely at the door of age!
  Some in the golden morning of their fame —
Yet on the path of death all stricken down the same!

A vision of far tombs oppressed my sight;
  I saw Kilmeny wandering down the glen
To seek her SHEPHERD by the hill's lone height,
  Her ETTRICK BARD, she ne'er might find again!
And SCOTT — that Ocean mid the stream of men!
  That Alp, amidst all mental greatness reared!
He, too, bowed down to Death's recording pen:
  And NEELE, GALT, INGLIS, MALCOLM — names endeared —
Passed pale, as one by one their visioned tombs appeared!

The voice of Spring is breathing! where art thou,
  Daughter of Genius, whose exalted mind
From Nature's noblest and sublimest brow
  Snatched Inspiration! thou, whose heart combined
Passions most pure, affections most refined;
  Whose Muse with silver clarion wakes the land,
Thrilling the finer feelings of mankind!
  Thine is the song to *arm* a patriot hand,
Or start a thousand spears midst Freedom's mountain band!

Thine is the song to fill the Mother's heart,
  Whose children bless thee — HEMANS — round her knee!
Thine is the gifted page that can impart

A beauty born of immortality!
The temple — shrine — and trophied urn — to thee
    Where themes enduring! where'er Grief had trod,
Or Hope fled tired from human misery,
    Thou stood'st with Song uplifted to thy God,
Thou soothedst the mourner's tears e'en by the burial sod!

The beauteous spirit of the minstrel dead
    Comes with the harmonies and hues of morn;
Sits with my sorrowing heart when day hath fled,
    And folds her glorious wings — elysian born!
A broken rose and violet dim adorn
    With their expressive grace her silent lyre:
But, oh! the wreath by that immortal worn!
    The inspiration and the seraph fire
Which light those pleading eyes that unto heaven aspire!

Still mourns Erinna — ever by that coast,
    Whose dismal winds shriek to each weeping cloud,
Whose waves sweep solemn as a funeral host,
    Still mourns she Love's own Minstrel, in her shroud;
The Sappho of that isle, in genius proud;
    The IMPROVISATRICE of our land;
The daughter of our soil — our fame-endowed!
    For *her* Erinna seeks the fatal strand,
And lifts to distant shores her woe-prophetic hand!

The blighted one! the breast, whose sister tear
    Sprang to each touch of feeling — heaves no more!
Our LANDON, silent on her funeral bier,
    Far from our heart, sleeps on a foreign shore;
The voice of her — the song-inspired — is o'er;
    Oh, she who wept for others found no tone
To soothe the many parting griefs she bore;
    None had a tear for that sweet spirit lone —
All sorrows found a balm save that far Minstrel's own!

Thou, who received'st her rose-encircled head,
   Our Minstrel in the bloom of her young fame,
Give back our lost and loved! Restore our dead!
   Return once more her first and dearest name!
We *claim* her ashes! 'tis a Nation's claim!
   Her — in her wealth of mind — to thee we gave;
Yet — *plead we for the dust of that dear frame*:
   Oh, bear our world-lamented o'er the wave!
Let England hold at last — 'tis all she asks — *her Grave!*

**18. [Edward Henry Bickersteth (1825-1906), Bishop of Exeter,
hymn writer. "Elegy to L.E.L." published in *Poems and Songs
by E.H.B.* (London: Pickering, 1848.)]**

ELEGY TO L.E.L.

Scarce had the wind, which rocked thine ocean bed,
   Borne thee, oh! Landon, to a far-off strand:
Ere tears are falling o'er the minstrel dead,
   And sounds of woe are wafted o'er the land.

Queen of the tuneful lyre! — those tears are thine —
   Long will thy fatherland thy mem'ry keep;
The laurel which thy minstrel lute did twine,
   Wreathed with the cypress, o'er thy tomb will weep.

Ah! 'tis thy legacy — thou ne'er mayst wake
   Its silvery strings to charm the list'ning throng;
Hushed is the heart which could such music make,
   Shivered the chords, and silent is the song.

Thou wast too full of passion — and the shell,
   Worn by the spirit, all too frail and weak;
The parting hour was as thy funeral knell,
   Thou could'st not bear another home to seek.

To leave thy hearthstone, and thine early friends;
To burst the bonds which nature flings around
Sweet friendship's footsteps, and to life still lends
A hallowing charm, wherewith our hearts are bound.

Alas! to lose thee thus! to hear no more
Th' enchanting echo of thine haunting song;
To know that, resting on a foreign shore,
To stranger hands thine obsequies belong.

Ah! who will honour thine abandoned urn!
Will one fond hand strew roses o'er thy bier?
In vain, bright flowers await thy loved return;
In vain, we weep for one, alas! so dear.

Bright is the sun, with rays of burning light,
The stars with silver radiance gild the sky;
Still, as of yore, the silent queen of night
Sheds a pale lustre from her throne on high.

All — all endure, but where is now our boast?
The poet of all hearts — our pride is dead;
Wake — wake, sweet music o'er that far off coast;
Fling — fling sweet garlands o'er her lowly head.

19. [Christina Rossetti (1830–94). "L.E.L." was first published in *The Victoria Magazine* I (May 1863). The present text is from *The Prince's Progress and Other Poems* (1866).]

L.E.L.

"Whose heart was breaking for a little love."

E.B. BROWNING.

Downstairs I laugh, I sport and jest with all:
    But in my solitary room above
I turn my face in silence to the wall;
    My heart is breaking for a little love.
        Though winter frosts are done,
        And birds pair every one,
And leaves peep out, for springtide is begun.

I feel no spring, while spring is wellnigh blown,
    I find no nest, while nests are in the grove:
Woe's me for mine own heart that dwells alone,
    My heart that breaketh for a little love.
        While golden in the sun
        Rivulets rise and run,
While lilies bud, for springtide is begun.

All love, are loved, save only I; their hearts
    Beat warm with love and joy, beat full thereof:
They cannot guess, who play the pleasant parts,
    My heart is breaking for a little love.
        While beehives wake and whirr,
        And rabbit thins his fur,
In living spring that sets the world astir.

I deck myself with silks and jewelry,
    I plume myself like any mated dove:
They praise my rustling show, and never see
    My heart is breaking for a little love.

While sprouts green lavender
With rosemary and myrrh,
For in quick spring the sap is all astir.

Perhaps some saints in glory guess the truth,
    Perhaps some angels read it as they move,
And cry one to another full of ruth,
    "Her heart is breaking for a little love."
        Though other things have birth,
        And leap and sing for mirth,
When springtime wakes and clothes and feeds the earth.

Yet saith a saint: "Take patience for thy scathe;"
    Yet saith an angel: "Wait, for thou shalt prove
True best is last, true life is born of death,
    O thou, heart-broken for a little love.
        Then love shall fill thy girth,
        And love make fat thy dearth,
When new spring builds new heaven and clean new earth."

20. [Walter Savage Landor (1775-1864). "A Lament for L.E.L." was first published by Richard Robert Madden in *The Literary Life and Correspondence of the Countess of Blessington* (New York: Harper, 1855), 2: 293-94. Madden states that the MS of the poem, discovered among the papers of Lady Blessington, "bear[s] no signature, but [is written] in the hand-writing of W.S. Landor."]

"The sweet singer departed — the summer bird gone from the garden
    of his love — it hath waited for him — will he not come again?"

A dirge for the departed! bend we low
    Around the bed of her unwakening rest
Still be the hoarse voice of discordant woe,
    Still as the heart within her marble breast,
Which stirs not at the cry of those she loved the best.

A dirge — Oh weave it of low murmurings,
  And count the pauses by warm dropping tears.
Sweeter, yet sadder than the woodlark sings,
Amid the shower of April's fitful wings,
Be the faint melody; the name it bears,
  Shall thrill our England's heart, for many linked years.

Our far-off England! oft times would she sit,
  With moist eyes gazing o'er the lustrous deep,
Through distance, change, and time; beholding it
  In its green beauty, while the sea did keep
A whispering noise, to lull her spirit's visioned sleep.

And fondly would she watch the evening breeze
  Steal, crushing the smooth ocean's sultry blue,
As 'twere a message from her own tall trees,
Waving her back to them, and flowers, and bees,
  And loving looks, from which her young heart drew
  Its riches, and all the joys her winged childhood knew.

And smiling in their distant loveliness,
  Like phantoms of the desert — till the tide
Of passionate yearnings burst in wild excess
  Over her gentle heart: the home sick bride
  Whelming both lute and life, and the sweet minstrel died.

Spring shall return to that beloved shore,
  With health of leaves, and buds, and wild wood songs,
But hers the sweetest, with its tearful lore,
  Its womanly fond gushes come no more,
  Breathing the cadenced poesy that throngs
  To pure and fervid lips unstained by cares and wrongs.

Oh! never more shall her benignant spell
  Fan those dim embers in a worldly heart,
Which once were love and sympathy — nor tell
  Of griefs borne patiently with such sweet art

As wins e'en selfish pain from brooding oe'r his smart.

Oh never more! the burden of the strain,
   Be those sad hopeless words! — then make her bed
Near shadowy boughs, that she may dwell again
   Where her own English violets bloom and fade,
The sole sweet records clustered o'er her head
   In this strange land — to tell where our beloved is laid.

Appendix C

["Lezione per L'amore": the first published version of "Song" ("Where, oh, where's the chain to fling.")]

LEZIONE PER L'AMORE.

WHERE, oh, where's the chain to fling,
One that will chain Cupid's wing —
One that will have longer power
Than the April sun or shower?
Form it not of eastern gold —
Golden fetters never hold;
They may chain, but not confine,
Not allure — but only shine.
Neither form it all of bloom —
Never does Love find his tomb
Sudden, soon, as when he meets
Death amid unvarying sweets.
But if you would fling a chain,
And not fling it quite in vain,
Like a fairy, form a spell
Of all that is changeable;
Like the purple tints that deck
The gay peacock's sunny neck;
Or the many hues that play
In the colouring morning's ray.
Never let a hope appear
Without its companion, fear;
Only smile to sigh, and then
Change into a smile again.
Be to-day as sad and pale
As minstrel with his lovelorn tale;
But to-morrow gay as all
Your life had been a festival.
If a woman would secure

All that makes her reign endure —
And, alas! her reign must be
Ever most in fantasy —
Never let a curious eye
Gaze upon the heart too nigh —
Never let the veil be thrown
Quite aside, as all were known,
Of delight and tenderness
In the spirit's last recess;
And one spell — all spells above —
Never let her own her love.

Appendix D: An Index to the Poetry of Letitia Elizabeth Landon (1802-38), by Glenn Dibert-Himes and Cynthia Lawford

In the case of poems belonging to a series or group, the poems are listed alphabetically by their series titles only when the poems lack individual titles. A series title is not listed alphabetically when all the poems contained in that series possess individual titles; instead, the series, or group, is noted parenthetically next to the individual poem title. Those poems which, in any instance of publication, lack both individual titles and series titles are each listed as "[untitled poem]."

Poems published in annuals, or gift books, frequently have erroneous publication dates: these books were published in the autumn or winter preceding the new year for which they were expected to be given as presents. For example, *The Keepsake for 1831* was published in 1830, though the latter date was not printed on the title page; in other cases, the publication date was printed as the same as the year that the annual was "for," despite the fact that it was actually published the preceding autumn. In this bibliography, the publication dates of the annuals have received bracketed corrections.

Those poems with epigraphs that both clearly are or might be lines of poetry are recorded here as "prefixed" lines, including quotes from other poets as well as epigraphs by Landon. In many cases, it has not been ascertained whether the epigraphs are by Landon or someone else, and until traced to another poet, it may be assumed that the epigraphs have been composed by Landon. The quote marks that sometimes appear around poetic epigraphs when first published have not been included here because the practice of using quote marks seems to have been irregular and therefore unreliable: each poetic epigraph needs to be thoroughly investigated to provide assurance that Landon did not write it, as well as to discover who did. Epigraphs that Landon has written in prose or that are undoubtedly from prose sources are excluded from this bibliography. Some poetic epigraphs may also be missing.

Collections of Landon's poetry published between 1821 and 1841 have contributed to the records of this bibliography. Those collections published after 1841 have not contributed, though the vast majority of the titles under which those collections list Landon's poems are referred to here. Periodicals and miscellaneous anthologies published throughout the 1820s, 1830s, and 1840s have also contributed to the records of this bibliography, and, unless specified otherwise, it should be assumed that any periodical in question was published in London. Poems published in various collections and periodicals after the 1840s are not included in this list; however, some of the new titles assigned these reprinted poems are listed here, followed only by the direction to see the entry for the poem under its original title. Because Landon wrote such a profusion of poetry for a wide range of periodicals, many of them extremely scarce today, this bibliography cannot make any claims for completeness. Undoubtedly, there are more Landon poems to be found.

The Abbey, Near Mussooree. The Seat of J. C. Glyn, Esq.

   1st line: "Alone, alone, on the mountain brow,"
   in Landon, Letitia E. *Fisher's Drawing Room Scrap-Book, 1838.* London, Paris, and
   New York: Fisher, Son; Germany: Black and Armstrong, and Asher, 1837. 24.

Absence.

   1st line: "I will not say, I fear your absent one"
   Prefixed lines begin: "And all the fix'd delights of house and home—"
   in Landon, Letitia E. *The Fate of Adelaide, A Swiss Romantic Tale; and Other Poems.*
   London: John Warren, 1821. 75-76.

Absence.

   1st line: "Oh! never can we feel how dear"
   Prefixed line from Thomas Campbell: "Song is but the eloquence of truth."
   in Landon, Letitia E. *The Fate of Adelaide, A Swiss Romantic Tale; and Other Poems.*
   London: John Warren, 1821. 110-12.

The Absent. (No. 1 in series of "Songs").

   1st line: "There is no music on the strings"
   in *The Literary Gazette* 694 (May 8, 1830): 307-08.

[An Act of Parliament]. (Suggested poem title, as poem is the motto for Chapter 24
titled "An Act of Parliament"; poem appears elsewhere as "Love").

   1st line: "Love is a thing of frail and delicate growth;"
   in Landon, Letitia E. *Ethel Churchill: or, The Two Brides.* Vol. 2. London: Henry Col-
   burn, 1837. 183.

Address.

   1st line: "We dream no more that fairies dwell"
   in Landon, Letitia E. *Schloss's English Bijou Almanac for 1837.* London: Albert
   Schloss, [1836]. N. pag. [1 page].

Addressed To —.

   1st line: "The bee, when varying flowers are nigh,"
   in Landon, Letitia E. *The Fate of Adelaide, A Swiss Romantic Tale; and Other Poems.*
   London: John Warren, 1821. 154.

The Adieu.

   1st line: "A fair good-night to thee, love, a fair good-night to thee;"
   Prefixed lines by Thomas Hood begin: "It was not in the winter, our loving lot
   was cast;"
   in *The Literary Souvenir; or, Cabinet of Poetry and Romance [for 1828].* Ed. Alaric A.
   Watts. London: Longman, Rees, Orme, Brown, and Green, 1828 [1827]. 346-348;
   in *The Album Wreath of Music and Literature [for 1835].* London: R. Willoughby,
   [1834?]. 22.

The Adieu.

   1st line: "We'll miss her at the morning hour,"
   in *The Keepsake for 1833.* Ed. Frederic Mansel Reynolds. London: Longman, Rees,
   Orme, Brown, Green, and Longman; Paris: Rittner and Goupill; Frankfirt: Charles
   Jügil, [1832]. 103-104.
   in *The Ladies' Wreath; A Selection from the Female Poetic Writers of England and Ameri-
   ca.* Ed. Mrs. Sarah J. Hale. Boston: Marsh, Capen, and Lyon; New York: D. Apple-
   ton, 1837. 127-28.

Admiral Benbow.

   1st line: "The Admiral stood upon the deck,"
   in Landon, Letitia E. *Fisher's Drawing Room Scrap-Book, 1838.* London, Paris, and

New York: Fisher, Son; Germany: Black and Armstrong, and Asher, 1837. 50-52.

Admiral Collingwood. (Poem appears elsewhere as "Admiral Lord Collingwood").
1st line: "Methinks it is a glorious thing"
in Landon, Letitia E. *The Vow of the Peacock, and Other Poems.* London: Saunders, Otley, 1835. 324-328.

Admiral Lord Collingwood. (This poem appears elsewhere as "Admiral Collingwood").
1st line: "Methinks it is a glorious thing,"
in Landon, Letitia E. *Fisher's Drawing Room Scrap-Book, 1833.* London: H. Fisher, R. Fisher and P. Jackson, 1833 [1832]. 55-56.

Affection. (One of the "Fragments" from *Ethel Churchill* selected by Blanchard; poem appears elsewhere as an "[untitled poem]").
1st line: "There is in life no blessing like affection:"
in Blanchard, Laman. *Life and Literary Remains of L. E. L.* Vol. 2. London: Henry Colburn, 1841. 269.

Affection's Comfort. (Poem appears elsewhere as "[Love]").
1st line: "Oh! yet one smile; though dark may lour"
in *Affection's Gift for 1844.* London: H. G. Clarke, [1843?]. 50-51.

Affection's Timidity. (Poem appears elsewhere as "[Difficulties]" and "Love's Timidity").
1st line: "I do not ask to offer thee"
in *Affection's Gift for 1844.* London: H. G. Clarke, [1843?]. 74.

The African. (Poem appears elsewhere as "The African Prince").
1st line: "It was a king in Africa,"
in Landon, Letitia E. *Fisher's Drawing Room Scrap-Book [for 1832].* London: Fisher, Son, and Jackson, 1832 [1831]. 35-36.

The African Prince. (Poem appears elsewhere as "The African").
1st line: "It was a king in Africa,"
in Landon, Letitia E. *The Zenana and Minor Poems of L.E.L.* London: Fisher, Son; Paris: Quai de L'Ecole, [1839]. 78-82.

Age. (One of the "Fragments" from *Ethel Churchill* selected by Blanchard; poem appears elsewhere as "[A Request Refused]").
1st line: "Age is a dreary thing when left alone"
in Blanchard, Laman. *Life and Literary Remains of L. E. L.* Vol. 2. London: Henry Colburn, 1841. 283.

Age and Youth. (First, a suggested poem title, as poem is motto for Chapter 1 titled "Age and Youth"; then, poem is published under this title as one of the "Fragments" from *Ethel Churchill* in Blanchard).
1st line: "'I tell thee,' said the old man, 'what is life.'"
in Landon, Letitia E. *Ethel Churchill: or, The Two Brides.* Vol. 1. London: Henry Colburn, 1837. 1;
in Blanchard, Laman. *Life and Literary Remains of L. E. L.* Vol. 2. London: Henry Colburn, 1841. 258.

Agnes.
1st line: "It is his hands — it is his words —"
in Landon, Letitia E. *Fisher's Drawing Room Scrap-Book, 1839.* London: Fisher, Son; Paris: Quai de L'Ecole, [1838]. 7-10.

Airey Force.
1st line: "Aye, underneath yon shadowy side"
in Landon, Letitia E. *Fisher's Drawing Room Scrap-Book, 1834.* London: H. Fisher, R. Fisher, and P. Jackson; Paris: Rittner and Goupil; Berlin and St. Petersburg: Asher;

New York: Jackson, 1833. 41.

The Aisle of Tombs.
> 1st line: "The quiet and the chillness"
> in Landon, Letitia E. *Fisher's Drawing Room Scrap-Book, 1836.* London and Paris: Fisher, Son; Berlin: Asher; New York: Jackson, [1835]. 52–53.

Alas, Alas, I cannot choose but love him.
> 1st line: "I have a dream upon my heart,"
> in *The Literary Gazette* 423 (Feb. 26, 1825): 140.

Alexander and Phillip. (One of the "Sketches From History").
> 1st line: "He stood by the river's side"
> in Landon, Letitia E. *The Troubadour; Catalogue of Pictures, and Historical Sketches.* London: Hurst, Robinson; Edinburgh: A. Constable, 1825. 312–16.

Alexander on the Banks of the Hyphasis. (No. II of fourth series of "Subjects for Pictures" in *The New Monthly*; no. XI in "Subjects for Pictures" in *Life and Literary Remains*).
> 1st line: "Lonely by the moonlit waters,"
> Prefixed lines to "Subjects for Pictures" begin: "What seek I here to gather into words?"
> in *The New Monthly Magazine* 50 (1837): 319–21;
> in Blanchard, Laman. *Life and Literary Remains of L. E. L.* Vol. 2. London: Henry Colburn, 1841. 221–24.

Alice Lee.
> 1st line: "Through the dim and lonely forest"
> in *Forget Me Not; A Christmas, New Year's, and Birthday Present, for 1839.* Ed. Frederic Shoberl. London: R. Ackermann, [1838]. 231–234.

All Over the World with Thee, My Love! (Poem appears elsewhere as the fourth untitled poem within a series of "Songs").
> 1st line: "All over the world with thee, my love!"
> in *The Literary Sketch-Book* 1 (Nov. 22, 1823): 232.

[An Allusion to the Past]. (Suggested poem title, as poem is motto to Chapter 7 titled "An Allusion to the Past"; poem appears elsewhere as "Memory").
> 1st line: "Ah! there are memories that will not vanish;"
> in Landon, Letitia E. *Ethel Churchill: or, The Two Brides.* Vol. 2. London: Henry Colburn, 1837. 48.

The Almond Tree.
> 1st line: "Fleeting and falling,"
> in *The Literary Gazette* 440 (June 25, 1825): 413.

[Alteration]. (Suggested poem title, as poem is motto for Chapter 3 titled "Alteration").
> 1st line: "My heart hath turned aside"
> in Landon, Letitia E. *Ethel Churchill: or, The Two Brides.* Vol. 2. London: Henry Colburn, 1837. 19.

The Altered River.
> 1st line: "Thou lovely river, thou art now"
> in *The Keepsake, for 1829.* Ed. Frederic Mansel Reynolds. London: Hurst, Chance, 1829 [1828]. 310–11;
> in Landon, Letitia E. *The Vow of the Peacock, and Other Poems.* London: Saunders and Otley, 1835. 316–18.

Amina.
> 1st line: "Not yet to the dancers — love, leave not thy seat;"

in Landon, Letitia E. *Heath's Book of Beauty. 1836.* Ed. Marguerite Blessington, the Countess of. London: Longman, Rees, Orme, Brown, Green, and Longman; Paris: Rittner and Goupil; Berlin: Asher, [1835]. 258-260.

The Ancestress, A Dramatic Sketch.

1st line: "It is in this we differ; I would seek,"
in Landon, Letitia E. *The Venetian Bracelet, The Lost Pleiad, A History of the Lyre, and Other Poems.* London: Longman, Rees, Orme, Brown, and Green, 1829. 117-72.

Anecdote of Sobieski. (Poem appears elsewhere as "The Soldier's Bride").

1st line: "The white plume was upon his head,"
in *The Literary Gazette* 456 (Oct. 15, 1825): 668.

[Another London Life]. (Suggested poem title, as poem is the motto for Chapter 17 titled "Another London Life"; poem appears elsewhere as "A Comparison").

1st line: "A pretty, rainbow sort of life enough;"
in Landon, Letitia E. *Ethel Churchill: or, The Two Brides.* Vol. 1. London: Henry Colburn, 1837. 167.

Answer.

1st line: "The wreath you gave me, love, is dead,"
in Landon, Letitia E. *The Fate of Adelaide, A Swiss Romantic Tale; and Other Poems.* London: John Warren, 1821. 105-06.

Answer To —.

1st line: "Twine not the cypress round my harp —"
in Landon, Letitia E. *The Fate of Adelaide, A Swiss Romantic Tale; and Other Poems.* London: John Warren, 1821. 121-22.

[Anticipation]. (Suggested poem title, as poem is motto for Chapter 3 titled "Anticipation"; poem appears elsewhere as "Parting").

1st line: "We do not know how much we love,"
in Landon, Letitia E. *Ethel Churchill: or, The Two Brides.* Vol. 1. London: Henry Colburn, 1837. 29.

Antinous.

1st line: "The thick curls cluster round thy graceful head,"
in *The Literary Gazette* 382 (May 15, 1824): 316.

Antioch.

1st line: "When the vulture on the wind"
in Landon, Letitia E. *Fisher's Drawing Room Scrap-Book, 1837.* London, Paris, and New York: Fisher, Son; Germany: Black and Armstrong, and Asher, 1836. 38-39.

Antony and Cleopatra. An Anecdote from Plutarch.

1st line: "Glorious was the marble hall,"
in *The New Monthly Magazine* 14 (1825): 249-50;
in Blanchard, Laman. *Life and Literary Remains of L. E. L.* Vol. 2. London: Henry Colburn, 1841. 302-05.

Apologue: The Thought Suggested By A Spanish Saying, "Air — Fire — Water — Shame." (Dramatic poem with four speakers, Water, Fire, Air, and Shame; Water speaks first; one of the "Fragments").

1st line: "Seek for me in the Arab maid's bower,"
in Landon, Letitia E. *The Improvisatrice; and Other Poems.* London: Hurst, Robinson; Edinburgh: A. Constable, 1824. 315-17.

April.

1st line: "Of all the months that fill the year"
in *The Literary Gazette* 324 (April 5, 1823): 219;

in Landon, Letitia E. *The Vow of the Peacock, and Other Poems*. London: Saunders and Otley, 1835. 238-41.

The Arab Maid.

1st line: "From the dark and sunless caverns,"

Prefixed lines begin: "While sad suspense and chill delay"

in *Finden's Tableaux*. London: Charles Tilt, 1837. 23-26;

in *Finden's Tableaux of National Character, Beauty, and Costume*. London: T.G. March, 1843. 8.

Ariadne Watching the Sea after the Departure of Theseus. (No. II of fifth series of "Subjects for Pictures," mistakenly designated series "No. IV," in *The New Monthly*; no. XIII in "Subjects for Pictures" in *Life and Literary Remains*).

1st line: "Lonely — lonely on the shore — "

Prefixed lines to "Subjects for Pictures" begin: "What seek I here to gather into words?"

in *The New Monthly Magazine* 53 (1838): 79-81;

in Blanchard, Laman. *Life and Literary Remains of L. E. L.* Vol. 2. London: Henry Colburn, 1841. 228-31.

Arion. (Part IV of series, "Fragments in Rhyme" in The Literary Gazette; part of "Fragments" in *The Improvisatrice; and Other Poems*).

1st line: "The winds are high, the clouds are dark,"

in *The Literary Gazette* 305 (Nov. 23, 1822): 745;

as "Arion: A Tale," in Landon, Letitia E. *The Improvisatrice; and Other Poems*. London: Hurst, Robinson; Edinburgh: A. Constable, 1824. 240-49.

Ariosto To His Mistress.

1st line: "I send thee, my beloved one,"

Prefixed lines begin: "He who told of fair Olympia, loved and left of old."

in *The New Monthly Magazine* 46 (1836): 441-42.

[Arrived at Home]. (Suggested poem title, as poem is the motto for Chapter 8 titled "Arrived at Home"; poem appears elsewhere as "A Noble Lady").

1st line: "A pale and stately lady, with a brow"

in Landon, Letitia E. *Ethel Churchill: or, The Two Brides*. Vol. 1. London: Henry Colburn, 1837. 84.

The Artist's Studio.

1st line: "The light came dim, but beautiful, through blinds,"

Prefixed lines begin: "Methinks"

in *The Literary Gazette* 340 (July 26, 1823): 474-75.

[Asking for an Invitation]. (Suggested poem title, as poem is motto for Chapter 4 titled "Asking for an Invitation"; poem appears elsewhere as "Earth Leads to Heaven").

1st line: "This is a weary and a wretched life,"

in Landon, Letitia E. *Ethel Churchill: or, The Two Brides*. Vol. 3. London: Henry Colburn, 1837. 21.

The Aspen Tree.

1st line: "The quiet of the evening hour"

in *The Literary Gazette* 709 (Aug. 21, 1830): 548;

in Landon, Letitia E. *The Vow of the Peacock, and Other Poems*. London: Saunders and Otley, 1835. 280-82.

The Assar Mahal—Ruins Near Agra.

1st line: "Alas, o'er the palace in ruins"

in Landon, Letitia E. *Fisher's Drawing Room Scrap-Book, 1833*. London: H. Fisher, R.

Fisher, and P. Jackson, 1833 [1832]. 26.

[The Assignation]. (Suggested poem title, as poem is the motto of Chapter 32 titled "The Assignation"; poem appears elsewhere as "Unguided Will").

1st line: "God, in thy mercy, keep us with thy hand!"

in Landon, Letitia E. *Ethel Churchill: or, The Two Brides.* Vol. 3. London: Henry Colburn, 1837. 247.

The Astrologer.

1st line: "Alas! for our ancient believings,"

in Landon, Letitia E. *Fisher's Drawing Room Scrap-Book, 1836.* London and Paris: Fisher, Son; Berlin: Asher; New York: Jackson, [1835]. 14.

Atalanta, represented as a Huntress with her bow. (Part of series, "Medallion Wafers").

1st line: "A Huntress with her silver bow,"

in *The Literary Gazette* 314 (Jan. 25, 1823): 60.

[An Audience]. (Suggested poem title, as poem is motto for Chapter 32 titled "An Audience").

1st line: "Not with the world to teach us, may we learn"

in Landon, Letitia E. *Ethel Churchill: or, The Two Brides.* Vol. 2. London: Henry Colburn, 1837. 252.

[The Author and the Actress]. (Suggested poem title, as poem is motto for Chapter 14 titled "The Author and the Actress"; poem appears elsewhere as "Pleasure Becomes Pain" and is an altered version of the epigraph for "Moralising").

1st line: "I cannot count the changes of my heart,"

in Landon, Letitia E. *Ethel Churchill: or, The Two Brides.* Vol. 3. London: Henry Colburn, 1837. 98.

The Awakening of Endymion. (No. I in the Third Series of "Subjects For Pictures" in *The New Monthly Magazine*; no. VII in "Subjects for Pictures" in *Life and Literary Remains*).

1st line: "Lone upon a mountain, the pine-trees wailing round him,"

Prefixed lines to "Subjects for Pictures" begin: "What seek I here to gather into words?"

in *The New Monthly Magazine* 49 (1837): 73-74;

in Blanchard, Laman. *Life and Literary Remains of L. E. L.* Vol. 2. London: Henry Colburn, 1841. 213-15.

Bacchus and Ariadne. (Part of "Classical Sketches"; it appears elsewhere as an untitled poem designated Scene II in a series of "Dramatic Scenes").

1st line: "'Tis finished now: look on my picture, Love!"

in Landon, Letitia E. *The Vow of the Peacock, and Other Poems.* London: Saunders and Otley, 1835. 121-30.

Ballad.

1st line: "He raised the golden cup from the board,"

in Landon, Letitia E. *The Troubadour; Catalogue of Pictures, and Historical Sketches.* London: Hurst, Robinson, 1825. 28.

Ballad.

1st line: "My ship is weighing from the land,"

in *The Literary Souvenir; or, Cabinet of Poetry and Romance [for 1828].* Ed. Alaric A. Watts. London: Longman, Rees, Orme, Brown, and Green, 1828 [1827]. 136-37.

Ballad.

1st line: "'O go not forth to night, my child,'"

in *The Literary Gazette* 557 (Sept. 22, 1827): 621;

in *The Beauties of the Magazines* 1 (Sept. 29, 1827): 61.
Ballad.
   1st line: "Over the land, and over the sea,"
   in *The Literary Gazette* 407 (Nov. 6, 1824): 712.
   in *Friendship's Offering, or, the Annual Remembrancer: A Christmas Present, or New Year's Gift, for 1825.* London: Lupton Relfe, 1825 [1824]. 237-38.
Ballad of Crescentius. (Poem appears elsewhere as "Crescentius" and "Execution of Crescentius")
   1st line: "I look'd upon his brow, — no sign"
   in *The New York Literary Gazette* 1 (Dec. 24, 1825): 248.
The Banner of Five Byzants.
   1st line: "St. George for merrie England!"
   in *Friendship's Offering. A Literary Album and Christmas and New Year's Present for 1828.* Ed. Charles Knight. London: Smith, Elder, 1828 [1827]. 13-14.
The Banquet of Aspasia and Pericles. (No. II in first series of "Subjects For Pictures" in *The New Monthly*; no. II. in "Subjects for Pictures" in *Life and Literary Remains*).
   1st line: "Waken'd by the small white fingers,"
   Prefixed lines to "Subjects for Pictures" begin: "What seek I here to gather into words?"
   in *The New Monthly Magazine* 47 (1836): 176-78;
   in Blanchard, Laman. *Life and Literary Remains of L. E. L.* Vol. 2. London: Henry Colburn, 1841. 199-202.
Baptismal Font.
   1st line: "Princes and kings upreared the mighty fane,"
   in Landon, Letitia E. *Fisher's Drawing Room Scrap-Book, 1841.* London: Fisher, Son; Paris: Quai de L'Ecole, [1840]. 6.
The Basque Girl and Henri Quatre. (Sixth sketch in Third Series of "Poetical Sketches"; "Poetical" should be corrected to "Poetic" to agree with other series in *The Literary Gazette*).
   1st line: "'Twas one of those sweet spots which seem just made"
   Prefixed lines begin: "Love! summer flower, how soon thou art decay'd!"
   in *The Literary Gazette* 299 (Oct. 12, 1822): 648-49;
   in Landon, Letitia E. *The Improvisatrice; and Other Poems.* London: Hurst, Robinson; Edinburgh: A. Constable, 1824. 212-18.
The Battle Field.
   1st line: "He sleeps — the night wind o'er the battle field"
   Prefixed lines begin: "It was a battle field, and the cold moon"
   in Landon, Letitia E. *The Venetian Bracelet, The Lost Pleiad, A History of the Lyre, and Other Poems.* London: Longman, Rees, Orme, Brown, and Green, 1829. 275-77.
The Bayadere: An Indian Tale. (Only Part II is in *Ladies Pocket Magazine*).
   1st line: "There were seventy pillars around the hall,"
   [Part] I., in *The Literary Gazette* 345 (Aug. 30, 1823): 556;
   1st line: "The loorie brought to his cinnamon nest"
   Part II., in *The Literary Gazette* 346 (Sept. 6, 1823): 571;
   1st line: "The moonlight is on a little bower,"
   Part III., in *The Literary Gazette* 347 (Sept. 13, 1823): 585;
   whole poem in Landon, Letitia E. *The Improvisatrice; and Other Poems.* London: Hurst, Robinson; Edinburgh: A. Constable, 1824. 155-78;
   in *The Ladies' Pocket Magazine* 2 (1837): 183-92.

Beethoven.
> 1st line: "A stately and a solemn song,"
> in Landon, Letitia E. *Schloss's English Bijou Almanac for 1839.* London: Albert Schloss, [1838]. N. pag. [3 pages].

Belinda; or, The Loveletter.
> 1st line: "Another soft and scented page,"
> in Landon, Letitia E. *Heath's Book of Beauty. 1833.* London: Longman, Rees, Orme, Brown, Green, and Longman; Paris: Rittner and Goupil; Frankfort: C. Jügel, [1832]. 149-150;
> in *Ladies' Penny Gazette* 1 (Dec. 29, 1832): 76.

Bells.
> 1st line: "How sweet on the breeze of the evening swells"
> in *The Literary Gazette* 244 (Sept. 22, 1821): 601-02.

The Beloved Always Near. (Translation; poem in First Series of "Versions from the German").
> 1st line: "I see thee when the sunshine lies golden on the sea —"
> in *The Literary Gazette* 937 (Jan. 3, 1835): 11.

Belvoir Castle, — Seat of the Duke of Rutland. ("Inscribed to Lady Emmeline Stuart Wortley").
> 1st line: "'Tis an old and stately castle,"
> in Landon, Letitia E. *Fisher's Drawing Room Scrap-Book, 1837.* London, Paris, and New York: Fisher, Son; Germany: Black and Armstrong, Asher, 1836. 45-46.

Benares.
> 1st line: "City of idol temples, and of shrines,"
> in Landon, Letitia E. *Fisher's Drawing Room Scrap-Book [for 1832].* London: Fisher, Son, and Jackson, 1832 [1831]. 34.

Beverley Minster.
> 1st line: "Built in far other times, those sculptured walls"
> in Landon, Letitia E. *Fisher's Drawing Room Scrap-Book, 1836.* London: Fisher, Son; Berlin: Asher; New York: Jackson, [1835]. 29.

The Billet-Doux.
> 1st line: "Yes! sweet letter, I will keep thee"
> in *The Literary Souvenir, and Cabinet of Modern Art [for 1835].* Ed. Alaric A. Watts. London: Whittaker, 1835 [1834]. 85-87.

The Bird.
> 1st line: "Take that singing bird away!"
> in *The Literary Gazette* 355 (Nov. 8, 1823): 715.

Birthday in Spring.
> 1st line: "The sights and the sounds of loveliness"
> in *The Literary Gazette* 528 (March 3, 1827): 139.

A Birthday Tribute Addressed to Her Royal Highness The Princess Alexandrina Victoria on Attaining her Eighteenth Year. (Published separately under poem title).
> 1st line: "When has the day the loveliest of its hours"
> London: Fisher, Son, 1837. 7-19.

Bitter Experience. (One of the "Fragments" from *Ethel Churchill* selected by Blanchard; poem appears elsewhere as "[Prudence in Politics]").
> 1st line: "How often, in this cold and bitter world,"
> in Blanchard, Laman. *Life and Literary Remains of L. E. L.* Vol. 2. London: Henry Colburn, 1841. 288.

The Black Hunt of Litzou. (Translation; poem in First Series of "Versions from the German").

1st line: "What is the light from yon deep wood flashing —"
in *The Literary Gazette* 937 (Jan. 3, 1835): 11.

Black Linn of Linklater.

1st line: "But of Himself, Him only speak these hills!"
Prefixed line from Victor Hugo: "Tonjours lui — lui partout."
in Landon, Letitia E. *Fisher's Drawing Room Scrap-Book, 1837.* London, Paris, New York: Fisher, Son; Germany: Black and Armstrong, and Asher, 1836. 53.

The Black Seal.

1st line: "Far, far across the sunny sea,"
in *Friendship's Offering; and Winter's Wreath: A Christmas and New Year's Present, for 1836.* London: Smith, Elder, 1836 [1835]. 361-64.

The Black-Rock Fort and Light-House.

1st line: "Thank God, thank God — the beacon light"
in Landon, Letitia E. *Fisher's Drawing Room Scrap-Book [for 1832].* London: Fisher, Son, and Jackson, 1832 [1831]. 19.

Bona, the Pirate's Song.

1st line: "To the mast nail our flag, it is dark as the grave,"
in Landon, Letitia E. *Fisher's Drawing Room Scrap-Book, 1837.* London, Paris, and New York: Fisher, Son; Germany: Black and Armstrong, and Asher, 1836. 29.

The Boon.

1st line: "Come tell me, love, if I had power"
in *Friendship's Offering; and Winter's Wreath: A Christmas and New Year's Present, for 1836.* London: Smith, Elder, 1836 [1835]. 37-38.

Borro Boedoor.

1st line: "An ancient temple of an ancient faith,"
in Landon, Letitia E. *Fisher's Drawing Room Scrap Book, 1836.* London and Paris: Fisher, Son; Berlin: Asher; New York: Jackson, [1835]. 39-41.

Boscastle Waterfall and Quarry.

1st line: "Oh, gloomy quarry! thou dost hide in thee"
in Landon, Letitia E. *Fisher's Drawing Room Scrap-Book, 1833.* London: H. Fisher, R. Fisher and P. Jackson, 1833 [1832]. 22.

The Bridal Day.

1st line: "She leans beside her mirror, in her old accustomed place,"
in *Friendship's Offering; and Winter's Wreath: A Christmas and New Year's Present, for 1837.* London: Smith, Elder, 1837 [1836]. 181-82;
in *Blackwood's Lady's Magazine* 2 (1837): 72.

Bridal Flowers. (One of the "Fragments" from *Ethel Churchill* selected by Blanchard; poem appears elsewhere as "[The Marriage]").

1st line: "Bind the white orange-flowers in her hair"
in Blanchard, Laman. *Life and Literary Remains of L. E. L.* Vol. 2. London: Henry Colburn, 1841. 285.

The Bridal Morning.

1st line: "Thy bridal morning! They are now"
in *Forget Me Not; A Christmas and New Year's Present for 1828.* Ed. Frederic Shoberl. London: R. Ackermann, [1827]. 103-05.

British Residency at Hyderabad. The Nizam's Daughter. (See "The Nizam's Daughter").

The Broken Heart

1st line: "My heart is like the failing hearth"

as "Song," in Landon, Letitia E. *The Golden Violet with its Tales of Romance and Chivalry: And Other Poems* London: Longman, Rees, Orme, Brown, and Green, 1827

in *The Lady's Magazine* 7 (1827): 95-96.

Broken Vows.

1st line: "And this is all I have left now,"

in *The Literary Gazette* 552 (Aug. 18, 1827): 539.

Burns and his Highland Mary (Vignette). (See also "Robert Burns and his Highland Mary").

1st line: "Summer, sweet summer, calls from the earth"

in [Collier, J. and Letitia E. Landon]. *The Pictorial Album; or, Cabinet of Paintings. For the Year 1837.* Illus. George Baxter. London: Chapman and Hall, 1837. 1-4.

Byron.

1st line: "Thy lute upon the Grecian ground"

in Landon, Letitia E. *The English Bijou Almanac for 1836.* London: Albert Schloss, [1835]. N. pag. [3 pages].

The Cadet[s]. An Indian Sketch.

1st line: "The ship rode o'er the waters gallantly,"

Lines prefixed as "New words to the Air of 'The Campbells are coming'" begin: "The banners are flashing, hurrah, hurrah!"

in *The Literary Gazette* 315 (Feb. 1, 1823): 74-75.

Cafes in Damascus.

1st line: "Languidly the night wind bloweth"

in Landon, Letitia E. *Fisher's Drawing Room Scrap-Book, 1837.* London, Paris, and New York: Fisher, Son; Germany: Black and Armstrong, and Asher, 1836. 9;

as "Cafés in Damascus" in *The Zenana and Minor Poems of L. E. L.* London: Fisher, Son; Paris: Quai de L'Ecole, [1839]. 212-14.

Caldron Snout. — Westmorland. (Poem appears elsewhere as "Long Years Have Past Since Last I Stood").

1st line: "Long years have past since last I stood"

Prefixed lines begin: "A place of rugged rocks, adown whose sides"

in Landon, Letitia E. *Fisher's Drawing Room Scrap-Book, 1835.* London: H. Fisher, R. Fisher, and P. Jackson, 1835 [1834]. 44-45.

Calypso Watching the Ocean. (No. I in second series of "Subjects For Pictures" in *The New Monthly*; no. IV in "Subjects for Pictures" in *Life and Literary Remains*).

1st line: "Years, years, have passed away,"

Prefixed lines to "Subjects for Pictures" begin: "What seek I here to gather into words?"

in *The New Monthly Magazine* 48 (1836): 20-21;

in Blanchard, Laman. *Life and Literary Remains of L. E. L.* Vol. 2. London: Henry Colburn, 1841. 204-07.

Can You Forget Me?

1st line: "Can you forget me? — I who have so cherished,"

in Landon, Letitia E. *Fisher's Drawing Room Scrap-Book, 1838.* London, Paris, and New York: Fisher, Son; Germany: Black and Armstrong, and Asher, 1837. 36-37.

The Canterbury Bell.
　1st line: "'I see it grow beneath my hand,'"
　in Landon, Letitia E. *Flowers of Loveliness; Twelve Groups of Female Figures, Emblematic of Flowers*. London: Ackermann, 1838. N. pag. [2 pages].
Captain Cook. (Poem appears elsewhere as "To My Brother").
　1st line: "Do you recall the fancies of many years ago,"
　in Landon, Letitia E. *Fisher's Drawing Room Scrap-Book, 1838*. London, Paris, and New York: Fisher, Son; Germany: Black and Armstrong, and Asher, 1837. 23.
The Carclaze Tin-Mine, Cornwall.
　1st line: "Those stately galleys cut the seas,"
　in Landon, Letitia E. *Fisher's Drawing Room Scrap-Book [for 1832]*. London: Fisher, Son, and Jackson, 1832 [1831]. 39.
Carrick-a-Rede, Ireland.
　1st line: "He dwelt amid the gloomy rocks,"
　in Landon, Letitia E. *Fisher's Drawing Room Scrap-Book [for 1832]*. London: Fisher, Son, and Jackson, 1832 [1831]. 9.
The Carrier Pigeon.
　1st line: "Ah, gentle bird, that, on my heart now lying,"
　in [Collier, J. and Letitia E. Landon]. *The Pictorial Album; or, Cabinet of Paintings. For the Year 1837*. Illus. George Baxter. London: Chapman and Hall, 1837. 16-18.
The Carrier-Pigeon Returned. (No. I in fourth series of "Subjects for Pictures" in *The New Monthly*; no. X in "Subjects for Pictures" in *Life and Literary Remains*).
　1st line: "Sunset has flung its glory o'er the floods,"
　Prefixed lines to "Subjects for Pictures" begin: "What seek I here to gather into words?"
　in *The New Monthly Magazine* 50 (1837): 318-19;
　in Blanchard, Laman. *Life and Literary Remains of L. E. L.* Vol. 2. London: Henry Colburn, 1841. 218-21.
Carthage.
　1st line: "Low it lieth — earth to earth —"
　in Landon, Letitia E. *Fisher's Drawing Room Scrap-Book, 1837*. London, Paris, and New York: Fisher, Son; Germany: Black and Armstrong, and Asher, 1836. 27.
The Castilian Nuptials. (Fourth sketch in Third Series of "Poetical Sketches" in *The Literary Gazette*, which should be corrected to "Poetic Sketches"; poem is part of "A Series of Tales" in *The Vow of the Peacock, and Other Poems*).
　1st line: "Fair is the form that in yon orange bower,"
　Prefixed lines begin: "And days fled by,"
　in *The Literary Gazette* 297 (Sept. 28, 1822): 616-17;
　in Landon, Letitia E. *The Vow of the Peacock, and Other Poems*. London: Saunders and Otley, 1835. 162-74.
Castle Building.
　1st line: "You may smile at the fanciful structures I rear,"
　in Landon, Letitia E. *The Fate of Adelaide, A Swiss Romantic Tale; and Other Poems*. London: John Warren, 1821. 123-24.
The Castle of Chillon.
　1st line: "Fair lake, thy lovely and thy haunted shore"
　in Landon, Letitia E. *Fisher's Drawing Room Scrap-Book, 1838*. London, Paris, and New York: Fisher, Son; Germany: Black and Armstrong, and Asher, 1837. 49.

Castruccio Castrucani; or, The Triumph of Lucca. A Tragedy. (A five-act drama in poetry; the first line is spoken by the First Citizen).

    1st line: "How was he taken? for he would have fought"

    in Blanchard, Laman. *Life and Literary Remains of L. E. L.* Vol. 2. London: Henry Colburn, 1841. 1-78.

The Caves of Elephanta.

    1st line: "What know we of them? Nothing — there they stand,"

    in Landon, Letitia E. *Fisher's Drawing Room Scrap-Book, 1835.* London: H. Fisher, R. Fisher, and P. Jackson, 1835 [1834]. 55.

The Cedars of Lebanon.

    1st line: "Ye ancients of the earth, beneath whose shade"

    in Landon, Letitia E. *Fisher's Drawing Room Scrap-Book, 1838.* London, Paris, and New York: Fisher, Son; Germany: Black and Armstrong, and Asher, 1837. 29;

    in *The Zenana and Minor Poems of L. E. L.* London: Fisher, Son; Paris: Quai de L'Ecole, [1839]. 267-69.

Cemetery of the Smolensko Church.

    1st line: "They gather, with the summer in their hands,"

    in Landon, Letitia E. *Fisher's Drawing Room Scrap-Book, 1837.* London, Paris, and New York: Fisher, Son; Germany: Black and Armstrong, and Asher, 1836. 16;

    in *The Zenana and Minor Poems of L. E. L.* London: Fisher, Son; Paris: Quai de L'Ecole, [1839]. 220-21.

[The Challenge]. (Suggested poem title, as poem is the motto for Chapter 30 titled "The Challenge"; poem appears elsewhere as "The Power of Words").

    1st line: "'Tis a strange mystery, the power of words!"

    in Landon, Letitia E. *Ethel Churchill: or, The Two Brides.* Vol. 3. London: Henry Colburn, 1837. 231.

[The Chamber of Death]. (Suggested poem title, as poem is motto for Chapter 33 titled "The Chamber of Death"; poem appears elsewhere as "The Ruined Mind").

    1st line: "Ah! sad it is to see the deck"

    in Landon, Letitia E. *Ethel Churchill: or, The Two Brides.* Vol. 3. London: Henry Colburn, 1837. 263.

Change. (Part III of series of "Fragments" in *The Literary Gazette*; one of the "Fragments" in *The Improvisatrice; and Other Poems*)

    1st line: "And this is what is left of youth! —"

    in *The Literary Gazette.* 344 (Aug. 23, 1823): 540;

    in Landon, Letitia E. *The Improvisatrice; and Other Poems.* London: Hurst, Robinson; Edinburgh: A. Constable, 1824. 286-88;

    in *The Ladies' Wreath; A Selection from the Female Poetic Writers of England and America.* Ed. Mrs. Sarah J. Hale. Boston: Marsh, Capen, and Lyon; New York: D. Appleton, 1837. 130-31.

Change. (One of the "Fragments" from *Ethel Churchill* selected by Blanchard; poem appears elsewhere as "[Meeting of Old Friends]").

    1st line: "How much of change lies in a little space!"

    in Blanchard, Laman. *Life and Literary Remains of L. E. L.* Vol. 2. London: Henry Colburn, 1841. 280.

Change.

    1st line: "I only asked, oh! let me hear"

    in *The Casket, A Miscellany, Consisting of Unpublished Poems.* Ed. Mrs. Blencowe. London: John Murray, 1829. 185-86.

The Change.

　1st line: "Thy features do not wear the light"

　in *The Literary Gazette* 578 (Feb. 16, 1828): 107;

　in Landon, Letitia E. *The Vow of the Peacock, and Other Poems.* London: Saunders and Otley, 1835. 277-79.

Change.

　1st line: "When those eyes have forgotten the smile they wear now,"

　Prefixed lines begin: "I would not care, at least so much, sweet Spring,"

　in *The Literary Gazette* 624 (Jan. 3, 1829): 12;

　in Landon, Letitia E. *The Vow of the Peacock, and Other Poems.* London: Saunders and Otley, 1835. 296-98.

Change.

　1st line: "Where are the flowers, the beautiful flowers,"

　Prefixed lines begin: "We say that people and that things are changed;"

　in *The Literary Gazette* 642 (May 9, 1829): 308-09.

Change.

　1st line: "The wind is sweeping o'er the hill,"

　in *The Amulet, a Christian and Literary Remembrancer [for 1829].* Ed. S. C. Hall. London: Frederick Westley and A. H. Davis; Wightman, 1829 [1828]. 309-310.

Changes.

　1st line: "Leaves grow green to fall,"

　in *The Literary Gazette* 508 (Oct. 14, 1826): 652.

Changes in London. (First, a suggested poem title, as poem serves as motto for Chapter 29 titled "Changes in London"; then is published under this title as one of "Fragments" from *Ethel Churchill* in Blanchard).

　1st line: "The presence of perpetual change"

　in Landon, Letitia E. *Ethel Churchill: or, The Two Brides.* Vol. 2. London: Henry Colburn, 1837. 226;

　in Blanchard, Laman. *Life and Literary Remains of L. E. L.* Vol. 2. London: Henry Colburn, 1841. 282.

Chant of Corinne at the Capitol. (Translation of "poetic effusion" from the French of Madame de Staël in Book 2, Chapter 3).

　1st line: "Cradle of Letters! Mistress of the World!"

　in Staël-Holstein, Anne Louise Germaine de. *Corinne; or Italy.* Trans. Isabel Hill ["with metrical versions of the odes by L. E. Landon"]. Standard Novels. 24. London: Richard Bentley; Dublin: Cumming; Edinburgh: Bell and Bradfute; Paris: Galignani, 1833. 25-31.

Chapter-House, Furness Abbey.

　1st line: "'Young friend, if, after struggles, toils, and many a passion past,'"

　in Landon, Letitia E. *Fisher's Drawing Room Scrap-Book, 1835.* London: H. Fisher, R. Fisher, and P. Jackson, 1835 [1834]. 49.

The Charm Gone. (One of the "Fragments" from *Ethel Churchill* selected by Blanchard; poem appears elsewhere as "[Ranelagh]").

　1st line: "I did not wish to see his face,"

　in Blanchard, Laman. *Life and Literary Remains of L. E. L.* Vol. 2. London: Henry Colburn, 1841. 300.

The Charmed Fountain.

　1st line: "O'er the stream a willow tree"

　in *The New Monthly Magazine* 14 (1825): 528.

The Chase, or the Fate of the Stag. (Poem appears elsewhere as "The Stag").
   1st line: "It is morning, and the sky,"
   in *The Lady's Magazine* 6 (Nov. 1826): 597-98.
A Child Screening a Dove from a Hawk. By Stewardson. (One of the "Poetical Sketches of Modern Pictures").
   1st line: "Ay, screen thy favourite dove, fair child,"
   in Landon, Letitia E. *The Troubadour; Catalogue of Pictures, and Historical Sketches.* London: Hurst, Robinson; Edinburgh: A. Constable, 1825. 278-79.
The Chinese Pagoda.
   1st line: "Whene'er a person is a poet,"
   in Landon, Letitia E. *Fisher's Drawing Room Scrap-Book, 1833.* London: H. Fisher, R. Fisher and P. Jackson, 1833 [1832]. 49-50.
The Choice.
   1st line: "Now take thy choice, thou maiden fair,"
   in *Forget Me Not; A Christmas and New Year's Present for 1826.* Ed. Frederic Shoberl. London: R. Ackermann, [1825]. 18.
The Choice.
   1st line: "The Spanish lady sat alone within her evening bower,"
   in Landon, Letitia E. *Heath's Book of Beauty. 1833.* London: Longman, Rees, Orme, Brown, Green, and Longman; Paris: Rittner and Goupil; Frankfort: C. Jügel, [1832]. 111-113.
Christ Blessing the Bread.
   1st line: "Bow thee to earth, and from thee cast"
   in Landon, Letitia E. *The Easter Gift, A Religious Offering.* London: Fisher, Son, 1832. 10-11.
Christ Blessing Little Children.
   1st line: "If ever in the human heart"
   in Landon, Letitia E. *The Easter Gift, A Religious Offering.* London: Fisher, Son, 1832. 45-47;
   in *The Literary Gazette* 791 (Mar. 17, 1832): 171.
Christ Crowned With Thorns.
   1st line: "Too little do we think of thee,"
   in Landon, Letitia E. *The Easter Gift, A Religious Offering.* London: Fisher, Son, 1832. 7-9.
Christine.
   1st line: "I cannot, cannot change my tone,"
   Prefixed lines by Barry Cornwall begin: "Oh! Love can take"
   in *The Literary Souvenir, or, Cabinet of Poetry and Romance [for 1825].* Ed. Alaric Watts. London: Hurst, Robinson; Edinburgh: A. Constable, 1825 [1824]. 65-73.
Christmas.
   1st line: "Now out upon you, Christmas!"
   in *The Literary Gazette* 782 (Jan. 14, 1832): 27-28.
Christmas Carol.
   1st line: "The rose, it is the love of June,"
   Prefixed lines begin: "Ivy, holly, and mistletoe,"
   in *The Literary Gazette* 728 (Jan. 1, 1831): 11.
Christmas in the Olden Time, 1650.
   1st line: "You must come back, my brother,"
   in Landon, Letitia E. *Fisher's Drawing Room Scrap-Book, 1836.* London and Paris:

Fisher, Son; Berlin: Asher; New York: Jackson, [1835]. 47-48.

[The Church]. (Suggested poem title, as poem is motto for Chapter 16, "The Church"; poem appears elsewhere as "The Marriage Vow").
1st line: "The altar, 'tis of death! for there are laid"
in Landon, Letitia. *Ethel Churchill: or, The Two Brides.* Vol. 2. London: Henry Colburn, 1837. 117.

The Church at Polignac.
1st line: "Kneel down in yon chapel, but only one prayer"
in Landon, Letitia E. *Fisher's Drawing Room Scrap-Book, 1837.* London, Paris, and New York: Fisher, Son; Germany: Black and Armstrong, and Asher, 1836. 30;
in *The Zenana and Minor Poems of L. E. L.* London: Fisher, Son; Paris: Quai de L'Ecole, [1839]. 230-32.

Church of the Carmelite Friary.
1st line: "Long years have fled away since last"
in Landon, Letitia E. *Fisher's Drawing Room Scrap-Book, 1833.* London: H. Fisher, R. Fisher and P. Jackson, 1833 [1832]. 51.

The Church of St. John, and the Ruins of Lahneck Castle, Formerly Belonging to the Templars. (Poem appears elsewhere as "A Ruined Castle on the Rhine").
1st line: "On the dark heights that overlook the Rhine,"
in Landon, Letitia E. *Fisher's Drawing Room Scrap-Book, 1838.* London, Paris, and New York: Fisher, Son; Germany: Black and Armstrong, and Asher, 1837. 25.

The Churchyard.
1st line: "The willow shade is on the ground,"
Prefixed lines begin: "The shadow of the church falls o'er the ground,"
in *The Literary Gazette* 624 (Jan. 3, 1829): 11-12;
in Landon, Letitia E. *The Vow of the Peacock, and Other Poems.* London: Saunders and Otley, 1835. 291-95.

Ci-Devant!
1st line: "O no, my heart can never be"
Prefixed lines begin: "I cannot, if I would, call back again"
in *The New Monthly Magazine* 17 (1826): 31-32;
in Blanchard, Laman. *Life and Literary Remains of L. E. L.* Vol. 2. London: Henry Colburn, 1841. 313-15.

The City Church-yard. (Part of series, "Scenes in London," in both publications; no. IV in *The Zenana and Minor Poems*).
1st line: "I pray thee lay me not to rest"
in Landon, Letitia E. *Fisher's Drawing Room Scrap-Book, 1836.* London and Paris: Fisher, Son; Berlin: Asher; New York: Jackson, [1835]. 36-37;
as "The City Churchyard" in *The Zenana and Minor Poems of L. E. L.* London: Fisher, Son; Paris: Quai de L'Ecole, [1839]. 191-94.

The City of the Dead.
1st line: "Laurel! oh fling thy green boughs on the air,"
Prefixed lines begin: "'Twas dark with cypresses and yews which cast"
in *The Bijou; or Annual of Literature and the Arts [for 1828].* London: William Pickering, 1828 [1827]. 13-15;
in Landon, Letitia E. *The Vow of the Peacock, and Other Poems.* London: Saunders and Otley, 1835. 319-23.

The City of Delhi.
1st line: "Thou glorious City of the East, of old enchanted times,"

in Landon, Letitia E. *Fisher's Drawing Room Scrap-Book [for 1832]*. London: Fisher, Son, and Jackson, 1832 [1831]. 44.

Claverhouse at the Battle of Bothwell Brig.
1st line: "He leads them on, the chief, the knight;"
in Landon, Letitia E. *Fisher's Drawing Room Scrap-Book, 1837*. London, Paris, and New York: Fisher, Son; Germany: Black and Armstrong, and Asher, 1836. 37.

Clematis.
1st line: "Around the cross the flower is winding,"
in Landon, Letitia E. *Flowers of Loveliness; Twelve Groups of Female Figures, Emblematic of Flowers*. London: Ackermann, 1838. N. pag. [2 pages].

Cleopatra.
1st line: "On the couch the Queen is lying,"
in [Collier, J. and Letitia E. Landon]. *The Pictorial Album; or, Cabinet of Paintings. For the Year 1837*. Illus. George Baxter. London: Chapman and Hall, 1837. 28-32.

The Coleraine Salmon Leap.
1st line: "I was dreaming that I went"
in Landon, Letitia E. *Fisher's Drawing Room Scrap-Book, 1836*. London and Paris: Fisher, Son; Berlin: Asher; New York: Jackson, [1835]. 46.

Coleridge.
1st line: "He told the lay of Christabelle;"
in Landon, Letitia E. *The English Bijou Almanac for 1837*. London: Albert Schloss, [1836]. N. pag. [3 pages].

Colgong on the Ganges.
1st line: "A lonely tomb — and who within it sleepeth"
in Landon, Letitia E. *Fisher's Drawing Room Scrap-Book 1839*. London: Fisher, Son; Paris: Quai de L'Ecole. 17.

Collegiate Church, Manchester. (Poem appears elsewhere as "The Minster").
1st line: "Dim, thro' the sculptured aisles the sun-beam falls"
in Landon, Letitia E. *Fisher's Drawing Room Scrap-Book, 1833*. London: H. Fisher, R. Fisher and P. Jackson, 1833 [1832]. 7.

The Combat. By Etty. (One of the "Poetical Sketches of Modern Pictures").
1st line: "They fled, — for there was for the brave"
in Landon, Letitia E. *The Troubadour; Catalogue of Pictures, and Historical Sketches*. London: Hurst, Robinson; Edinburgh: A. Constable, 1825. 265-68.

The Coming of Spring. — Schiller. (Translation; poem is in Second Series of "Versions from the German").
1st line: "In a valley sweet with singing"
in *The Literary Gazette* 938 (Jan. 10, 1835): 28.

The Companions. (No. 2 in a series of "Songs").
1st line: "With thy step in the stirrup, one cup of bright wine,"
in *The Literary Gazette* 694 (May 8, 1830): 308.

A Comparison. (One of the "Fragments" from *Ethel Churchill* chosen by Blanchard; poem appears elsewhere as "[Another London Life]").
1st line: "A pretty, rainbow sort of life enough;"
in Blanchard, Laman. *Life and Literary Remains of L. E. L.* Vol. 2. London: Henry Colburn, 1841. 263.

Conclusion. (Part of series, "Medallion Wafers").
1st line: "All, all forgotten! Oh, false Love!"
in *The Literary Gazette* 319 (March 1, 1823): 140.

The Confession. Verses for Music. (An editorial note states that poem is reprinted from *The Shropshire and North Wales Standard*).
   1st line: "Forgive, forgive those gushing tears,"
   The Ladies' Pocket Magazine 2 (1839): 55-56.
The Confession.
   1st line: "I pray thee, father, do not turn"
   in *Forget Me Not; A Christmas and New Year's Present for 1836.* Ed. Frederic Shoberl.
   London: R. Ackermann, [1835]. 195-97.
[The Confession]. (Suggested poem title, as poem is motto for Chapter 14, "The Confession"; poem appears elsewhere as "Secrets").
   1st line: "Life has dark secrets; and the hearts are few"
   in Landon, Letitia E. *Ethel Churchill: or, The Two Brides.* Vol. 1. London: Henry Colburn, 1837. 136.
Confidence. (First, a suggested poem title, as poem serves as motto for Chapter 24 titled "Confidence"; then, poem is given that title as part of Blanchard's selection of "Fragments" from *Ethel Churchill*).
   1st line: "Fear not to trust her destiny with me:"
   in Landon, Letitia E. *Ethel Churchill: or, The Two Brides.* Vol. 1. London: Henry Colburn, 1837. 223;
   in Blanchard, Laman. *Life and Literary Remains of L. E. L.* Vol. 2. London: Henry Colburn, 1841. 270.
[Confidence]. (Suggested poem title, as poem is motto for Chapter 34 titled "Confidence"; poem appears elsewhere as "Faith Ill Requited").
   1st line: "I feel the presence of my own despair;"
   in Landon, Letitia E. *Ethel Churchill: or, The Two Brides.* Vol. 1. London: Henry Colburn, 1837. 293.
[Confidence]. (Suggested poem title, as poem is motto for Chapter 13 titled "Confidence"; poem appears elsewhere as "Music of Laughter").
   1st line: "She had that charming laugh which, like a song,"
   in Landon, Letitia E. *Ethel Churchill: or, The Two Brides.* Vol. 2. London: Henry Colburn, 1837. 97.
The Coniston Curse: A Yorkshire Legend.
   1st line: "They knelt upon the altar steps, but other looks were there"
   in Landon, Letitia E. *The Golden Violet with its Tales of Romance and Chivalry: and Other Poems.* London: Longman, Rees, Orme, Brown, and Green, 1827. 271-82.
Coniston Water.
   1st line: "Thou lone and lovely water, would I were"
   in Landon, Letitia E. *Fisher's Drawing Room Scrap-Book, 1834.* London: H.Fisher, R. Fisher, and P. Jackson; Paris: Rittner and Goupil; Berlin and St. Petersburg: Asher; New York: Jackson, 1833. 54.
[The Consent]. (Suggested poem title, as poem is the motto of Chapter 15 titled "The Consent"; poem appears elsewhere as "Experience Too Late").
   1st line: "It is the past that maketh my despair;"
   in Landon, Letitia E. *Ethel Churchill: or, The Two Brides.* Vol. 1. London: Henry Colburn, 1837. 152.
Constancy.
   1st line: "Aye, let us look on all around,"

Prefixed lines begin: "Can the heart change"
in *The Literary Gazette* 409 (Nov. 20, 1824): 748.

Constancy. (First, a suggested poem title, as poem is the second in a group of six poems described as "Six Songs of Love, Constancy, Romance, Inconstancy, Truth, and Marriage"; then, poem is given that title in *The Lyre*).

1st line: "Oh! say not love was never made"
in *The Literary Gazette* 251 (Nov. 10, 1821): 716;
in *The Lyre. Fugitive Poetry of the Ninteenth Century*. London: Tilt and Bogue, 1841. 321-22.

Constancy. A Song.
1st line: "Forget thee — or forget"
in *The Literary Gazette* 395 (Aug. 14, 1824): 524.

The Contrast. (Second sketch in Second Series of "Poetic Sketches").
1st line: "There were two Portraits: one was of a Girl"
Prefixed lines begin: "And this love:"
in *The Literary Gazette* 277 (May 11, 1822): 297.

[Conversation After Breakfast]. (Suggested poem title, as poem is motto for Chapter 11 titled "Conversation After Breakfast"; poem appears elsewhere as "Cureless Wounds").
1st line: "False look, false hope, and falsest love,"
in Landon, Letitia E. *Ethel Churchill: or, The Two Brides.* Vol. 3. London: Henry Colburn, 1837. 75.

The Convict.
1st line: "The light of two or three pale stars"
Prefixed lines begin: "These are words that we should read like warnings,"
in *The New Monthly Magazine* 32 (1831): 33-36.

Cooper.
1st line: "He was the first who ever told"
in Landon, Letitia E. *The English Bijou Almanac for 1837*. London: Albert Schloss, [1836]. N. pag. [3 pages].

The Cootub Minar, Delhi.
1st line: "'I have forgotten,' 'tis a common phrase"
in Landon, Letitia E. *Fisher's Drawing Room Scrap-Book, 1833*. London: H. Fisher, R. Fisher and P. Jackson, 1833 [1832]. 32.

The Coquette.
1st line: "She danced upon the waters,"
in Landon, Letitia E. *Fisher's Drawing Room Scrap-Book, 1835*. London: H. Fisher, R. Fisher, and P. Jackson, 1835 [1834]. 19-21.

Corfu.
1st line: "Now, doth not summer's sunny smile"
in Landon, Letitia E. *Fisher's Drawing Room Scrap-Book, 1835*. London: H. Fisher, R. Fisher, and P. Jackson, 1835 [1834]. 31-32.

Corfu.
1st line: "Oh, lovely isle! that, like a child,"
in Landon, Letitia E. *Fisher's Drawing Room Scrap-Book, 1838*. London, Paris, and New York: Fisher, Son; Germany: Black and Armstrong, and Asher, 1837. 48-49.

Corinna.

1st line: "She stood alone; but on her every eye"

in Landon, Letitia E. *The Fate of Adelaide, A Swiss Romantic Tale; and Other Poems.* London: John Warren, 1821. 97-98.

Corinna at the Cape of Misena.

1st line: "How much of mind is in this little scroll,"

in *The Amulet; A Christian and Literary Remembrancer [for 1832].* Ed. S. C. Hall. London: Frederick Westley and A. H. Davis, 1832 [1831]. 251-55.

Corinne's Chant in the Vicinity of Naples. (Translation of "poetic effusion" from the French of Madame de Staël in Book 8, Chapter 4).

1st line: "Ay, Nature, History, and Poesie,"

in Staël-Holstein, Anne Louise Germaine de. *Corinne; or Italy.* Trans. Isabel Hill ["with metrical versions of the odes by L. E. Landon"]. Standard Novels. 24. London: Richard Bentley; Dublin: Cumming; Edinburgh: Bell and Bradfute; Paris: Galignani, 1833. 224-29 [break on 227].

The Coronation. (First, poem's title is suggested, as poem is motto for Chapter 1 titled "The Coronation"; then, poem appears under that title as part of Blanchard's selection of "Fragments" from *Ethel Churchill*).

1st line: "What memories haunt the venerable pile!"

in Landon, Letitia E. *Ethel Churchill: or, The Two Brides.* Vol. 2. London: Henry Colburn, 1837. 1;

in Blanchard, Laman. *Life and Literary Remains of L. E. L.* Vol. 2. London: Henry Colburn, 1841. 272.

Cottage Courtship.

1st line: "Now, out upon this smiling,"

in Landon, Letitia E. *Fisher's Drawing Room Scrap-Book, 1835.* London: H. Fisher, R. Fisher, and P. Jackson, 1835 [1834]. 40.

Count Egmont. A Tragedy. — Goethe. (Translation; poem is in Fifth Series of "Versions from the German").

1st line: "Children, ye are too sad! Once this dull room"

Scene I in *The Literary Gazette* 942 (Feb. 7, 1835): 91-92.

1st line: "So true a lover have I never known!"

Scene II in *The Literary Gazette* 945 (Feb. 28, 1835): 138-39.

1st line: "Evening has darken'd o'er the market-place:"

[Scene III] in *The Literary Gazette* 946 (March 7, 1835): 154-55.

1st line: "Old friend and true companion! soothing Sleep,"

[Scene IV] in *The Literary Gazette* 949 (March 28, 1835): 202-3.

The Country Retreat. (Poem appears elsewhere as "Linmouth").

1st line: "Oh lone and lovely solitude,"

in *The Zenana and Minor Poems of L. E. L.* London: Fisher, Son; Paris: Quai de L'Ecole, [1839]. 94-99.

Court of a Turkish Villa, Near Damascus.

1st line: "In the midst a fountain"

in Landon, Letitia E. *Fisher's Drawing Room Scrap-Book, 1839.* London: Fisher, Son; Paris: Quai de L'Ecole, [1838]. 22-23.

[*Courtiers*]. (Suggested poem title, as poem is the motto for Chapter 29 titled "Courtiers"; it is printed beneath heading for letter from "Lady Marchmont to Sir Jasper Meredith"; poem appears elsewhere as "Life Surveyed").

    1st line: "Not in a close and bounded atmosphere"

    in Landon, Letitia E. *Ethel Churchill: or, The Two Brides.* Vol. 1. London: Henry Colburn. 1837. 255.

The Covenanters. (Sketch II in Fourth Series of "Poetic Sketches").

    1st line: "Never! I will not know another home."

    Prefixed lines begin: "Mine home is but a blackened heap"

    in *The Literary Gazette* 357 (Nov. 22, 1823): 747-48;

    in Landon, Letitia E. *The Improvisatrice; and Other Poems.* London: Hurst, Robinson; Edinburgh: A. Constable, 1824. 227-34.

Crescentius. (Poem appears elsewhere as "Ballad of Crescentius" and "Execution of Crescentius").

    1st line: "I looked upon his brow, — no sign"

    in Landon, Letitia E. *The Improvisatrice; and Other Poems.* London: Hurst, Robinson; Edinburgh: A. Constable, 1824. 291-94;

    in *The Cabinet; or the Selected Beauties of Literature.* Second Series. Edinburgh: John Aitken, 1825. 264.

The Criminal.

    1st line: "'Tis silence in that cell, and dim the light"

    1st prefixed lines begin: "His hand is red with blood, and life, aye, life"

    2nd prefixed lines begin: "Ah! woman's love is a night-scented flower,"

    in *The Literary Souvenir, or, Cabinet of Poetry and Romance [for 1825].* Ed. Alaric Watts. London: Hurst, Robinson; Edinburgh: A. Constable, 1825 [1824]. 375-78.

Crossing the Choor Mountains.

    1st line: "He was the first that ever crossed"

    in Landon, Letitia E. *Fisher's Drawing Room Scrap-Book, 1839.* London: Fisher, Son; Paris: Quai de L'Ecole, [1838]. 35-36.

Crossing the River Tonse by a Jhoola.

    1st line: "Light is the bridge across the dark blue river,"

    in Landon, Letitia E. *Fisher's Drawing Room Scrap-Book, 1839.* London: Fisher, Son; Paris: Quai de L'Ecole, [1838]. 41.

The Crusader. (First published as Part III of series of "Ballads").

    1st line: "He is come from the land of the sword and shrine,"

    in *The Literary Gazette* 317 (Feb. 15, 1823): 107;

    in Landon, Letitia E. *The Improvisatrice; and Other Poems.* Hurst, Robinson; Edinburgh: A. Constable, 1824. 305-09;

    in *The Cabinet; or the Selected Beauties of Literature.* Second Series. Edinburgh: John Aitken, 1825. 116-17.

The Cup of Circe. (Poem is third sketch in series, "Sketches from Designs [ed. correction: 'Drawings'] by Mr. Dagley).

    1st line: "She sat a crowned Queen — the ruby's light"

    Prefixed line: "All have drank of the cup of the enchantress."

    in *The Literary Gazette* 290 (Aug. 10, 1822): 504.

Cupid and Psyche.

    1st line: "Love, — oh do not name his name!"

in *The Literary Souvenir; or, Cabinet of Poetry and Romance [for 1827].* Ed. Alaric A. Watts. London: Longman, Rees, Orme, Brown and Green; and John Andrews, 1827 [1826]. 337-39.

Cupid and Swallows Flying From Winter. By Dagley. (One of the "Poetical Sketckes of Modern Pictures").
1st line: "Away, away, o'er land and sea,"
Prefixed line: "We fly from the cold."
in Landon, Letitia E. *The Troubadour; Catalogue of Pictures, and Historical Sketches.* London: Hurst, Robinson; Edinburgh: A. Constable, 1825. 284-88.

Cupid Riding a Peacock. (Part of series, "Medallion Wafers").
1st line: "All the colours glistening"
in *The Literary Gazette* 314 (Jan. 25, 1823): 60.

Cureless Wounds. (One of the "Fragments" selected by Blanchard from *Ethel Churchill*; poem appears elsewhere as "[Conversation After Breakfast]").
1st line: "False look, false hope, and falsest love,"
in Blanchard, Laman. *Life and Literary Remains of L. E. L.* Vol. 2. London: Henry Colburn, 1841. 292.

Curraghmore, A Seat of the Marquis of Waterford.
1st line: "Summer, shining summer,"
in Landon, Letitia E. *Fisher's Drawing Room Scrap-Book [for 1832].* London: Fisher, Son, and Jackson, 1832 [1831]. 37-38.

Curtius.
1st line: "There is a multitude, in number like"
in Landon, Letitia E. *The Fate of Adelaide, A Swiss Romantic Tale; and Other Poems.* London: John Warren, 1821. 77-80;
in *The Lyre. Fugitive Poetry of the Nineteenth Century.* London: Tilt and Bogue, 1841. 18-19.

Custom and Indifference. (Poem is part of Blanchard's selection of "Fragments" from *Ethel Churchill*; it appears elsewhere as "[A Declaration]").
1st line: "I cannot choose, but marvel at the way"
in Blanchard, Laman. *Life and Literary Remains of L. E. L.* Vol. 2. London: Henry Colburn, 1841. 298.

The Cypress.
1st line: "Thou graceful tree,"
in *The Amulet; or, Christian and Literary Remembrancer [for 1826]* . London: William Baynes, Son; Edinburgh: H. S. Baynes, 1826 [1825]. 46-47;
in *The Pledge of Friendship. 1829.* London: W. Marshall, 1829 [1828]. 46-47;
in *The Lyre. Fugitive Poetry of the Nineteenth Century.* London: Tilt and Bogue, 1841. 244.

The Dancing Girl.
1st line: "A light and joyous figure, one that seems"
in Landon, Letitia E. *Fisher's Drawing Room Scrap-Book, 1834.* London: H.Fisher, R. Fisher, and P.Jackson; Paris: Rittner and Goupil; Berlin and St. Petersburg: Asher; New York: Jackson, 1833. 37.

Dangers Faced. (One of the "Fragments" from *Ethel Churchill* selected by Blanchard; poem appears elsewhere as "[The Marriage Morning]" and resembles the 3rd poem in a series of "Songs").
1st line: "My heart is filled with bitter thought,"
in Blanchard, Laman. *Life and Literary Remains of L. E. L.* Vol. 2. London: Henry

Colburn, 1841. 271.

The Danish Warrior's Death Song.
   1st line: "Away, away! your care is vain;"
   in Landon, Letitia E. *The Vow of the Peacock, and Other Poems*. London: Saunders and Otley, 1835. 274-76.

Dartmouth Castle. (Poem appears elsewhere as "The Sea-shore").
   1st line: "I should like to dwell where the deep blue sea"
   in Landon, Letitia E. *Fisher's Drawing Room Scrap-Book, 1833*. London: H. Fisher, R. Fisher and P. Jackson, 1833 [1832]. 53.

Dartmouth Church.
   1st line: "Just where the evening sunbeams rest, there hangs"
   in Landon, Letitia E. *Fisher's Drawing Room Scrap-Book, 1833*. London: H. Fisher, R. Fisher and P. Jackson, 1833 [1832]. 31.

The Dead.
   1st line: "A spirit doth arise"
   in *Fraser's Magazine* 1 (June 1830): 643.

The Dead Robin.
   1st line: "It is dead! — it is dead! — it will wake no more"
   in *The Juvenile Forget Me Not. A Christmas and New Year's Gift, or Birthday Present*. 1832. Ed. Mrs. S. C. [Anna Maria] Hall. London: Frederick Westley and A. H. Davis, [1831]. 21-22;
   in Landon, Letitia E. *Traits and Trials of Early Life*. London: Henry Colburn, 1836. 145-46.

The Deaf Schoolmaster.
   1st line: "He cannot hear the skylark sing,"
   in Landon, Letitia E. *Fisher's Drawing Room Scrap-Book [for 1832]*. London: Fisher, Son, and Jackson, 1832 [1831]. 13.

Dear Gifts. (One of the "Fragments" selected by Blanchard from *Ethel Churchill*; poem appears elsewhere as an "[untitled poem]").
   1st line: "Life's best gifts are bought dearly. Wealth is won"
   in Blanchard, Laman. *Life and Literary Remains of L. E. L.* Vol. 2. London: Henry Colburn, 1841. 265.

Death and the Youth.
   1st line: "'Not yet — the flowers are in my path,'"
   in *The Literary Gazette* 797 (April 28, 1832): 266.

Death in the Flower. (Part of Blanchard's selection of "Fragments" from *Ethel Churchill*; poem appears elsewhere as "[The Laboratory]").
   1st line: "'Tis a fair tree, the almond-tree: there Spring,"
   in Blanchard, Laman. *Life and Literary Remains of L. E. L.* Vol. 2. London: Henry Colburn, 1841. 281.

The Death of Camoens. (Part II of "The Two Deaths" in both publications; within the sixth series of "Subjects for Pictures," incorrectly numbered "V," in *The New Monthly*; no. XIV in "Subjects for Pictures" in *Life and Literary Remains*).
   1st line: "Pale comes the moonlight thro' the lattice gleaming,"
   Prefixed lines to "Subjects for Pictures" begin: "What seek I here to gather into words?"
   in *The New Monthly Magazine* 53 (1838): 179-80;
   in Blanchard, Laman. *Life and Literary Remains of L.E.L.* Vol. 2. London: Henry

Colburn, 1841. 235-38.

Death of the Chevalier Bayard.
   1st line: "His plume was the meteor that led the band,"
   in *The Literary Gazette* 457 (Oct. 22, 1825): 684.

The Death of Heber.
   1st line: "He left a calm and pleasant home,"
   in Landon, Letitia E. *Fisher's Drawing Room Scrap-Book, 1839.* London: Fisher, Son;
   Paris: Quai de L'Ecole, [1838]. 58.

Death of the Lion Among the Ruins of Sbeitlah.
   1st line: "Hurriedly, disturbing night"
   in Landon, Letitia E. *Fisher's Drawing Room Scrap-Book, 1838.* London, Paris, New
   York: Fisher, Son; Germany: Black and Armstrong, and Asher, 1837. 27.

Death of Louis of Bourbon, Bishop of Liege.
   1st line: "How actual, through the lapse of years,"
   in Landon, Letitia E. *Fisher's Drawing Room Scrap-Book, 1838.* London, Paris, and
   New York: Fisher, Son; Germany: Black and Armstrong, and Asher, 1837. 50.

The Death of Margaret Audeley.
   1st line: "The shadow of the yew-trees has left an open space;"
   in *La Belle Assemblée* 15 (Jan. 1832): 21.

The Death of the Sea King. (No. II in Third Series of "Subjects For Pictures" in *The
   New Monthly*; no. VIII in "Subjects for Pictures" in *Life and Literary Remains*).
   1st line: "Dark, how dark the morning"
   Prefixed lines to "Subjects for Pictures" begin: "What seek I here to gather into
   words?"
   in *The New Monthly Magazine* 49 (1837): 74-75;
   in Blanchard, Laman. *Life and Literary Remains of L. E. L.* Vol. 2. London: Henry
   Colburn, 1841. 215-17.

The Death of Sigurd, the Earl of Northumberland. (Part I of "The Two Deaths" in both
   publications; within the sixth series of "Subjects for Pictures", incorrectly num-
   bered "V," in The New Monthly; no. XIV in "Subjects of Pictures" in *Life and Lit-
   erary Remains*).
   1st line: "The Earl lay on his purple bed,"
   Prefixed lines to "Subjects for Pictures" begin: "What seek I here to gather into
   words?"
   in *The New Monthly Magazine* 53 (1838): 177-78;
   in Blanchard, Laman. *Life and Literary Remains of L.E.L.* Vol. 2. London : Henry
   Colburn, 1841. 232-35.

The Death Song.
   1st line: "Are the roses all faded, that thus you should wear"
   in *The Keepsake for 1831.* Ed. Frederic Mansel Reynolds. London: Hurst, Chance;
   Jennings and Chaplin [1830]. 148-49.

Death-bed of Alexander the Great.
   1st line: "On his bed the king was lying —"
   in *The New Monthly Magazine* 45 (1835): 302-04;
   in Blanchard, Laman. *Life and Literary Remains of L.E.L.* Vol. 2. London: Henry
   Colburn, 1841. 242-44.

The Decision of the Flower.
   1st line: "There is a flower, a purple flower"
   Prefixed lines from Southey's *Thalaba* begin: ". . . Tis a history"

in *The Literary Gazette* 408 (Nov. 13, 1824): 721;

in *The Literary Souvenir; or, Cabinet of Poetry and Romance [for 1825]*. Ed. Alaric A. Watts. London: Hurst, Robinson; Edinburgh: A. Constable, 1825 [1824]. 1-2.

[A Declaration]. (Suggested title, as poem is motto for Chapter 13, "A Declaration"; poem appears elsewhere as "Custom and Indifference").

1st line: "I cannot choose, but marvel at the way"

in Landon, Letitia E. *Ethel Churchill: or, The Two Brides.* Vol. 3. London: Henry Colburn, 1837. 89.

The Delectable Mountains. (Poem appears elsewhere as "On Reading a Description of The Delectable Mountains in Bunyan's Pilgrim's Progress").

1st line: "Oh, far away ye are, ye lovely hills,"

in Landon, Letitia E. *Fisher's Drawing Room Scrap-Book, 1837*. London, Paris, and New York: Fisher and Son; Germany: Black and Armstrong, and Asher, 1836. 13.

The Departed. (No. 4 in a series of "Songs").

1st line: "Set thy spur to thy steed, thy sail to the wind,"

in *The Literary Gazette* 694 (May 8, 1830): 308.

The Departed. (Poem appears elsewhere as "Gone").

1st line: "Where's the snow — the summer snow —"

in *The Amulet; or, Christian and Literary Remembrancer [for 1828]*. London: William Baynes, Son; Wightman and Cramp, 1828 [1827]. 325-27.

Derwent Water.

1st line: "I knew her — though she used to make"

in Landon, Letitia E. *Fisher's Drawing Room Scrap-Book, 1837*. London, Paris, and New York: Fisher, Son; Germany: Black and Armstrong, and Asher, 1836. 33.

The Deserter. (Sixth sketch of Second Series of "Poetic Sketches" in *The Literary Gazette*).

1st line: "'Twas a sweet summer morn — the lark had just"

Prefixed lines begin: "Alas, for the bright promise of our youth!"

in *The Literary Gazette*. 281 (June 18, 1822): 362-63;

in Landon, Letitia E. *The Improvisatrice; and Other Poems*. London: Hurst, Robinson; Edinburgh: A. Constable, 1824. 185-92.

Despairing Love. (Seems to be first publication from ms. held by Jerdan).

1st line: "In sooth 'twas foolishness to dream"

in Jerdan, William. "Memoir of L. E. L." *Romance and Reality*. By Letitia E. Landon. Standard Novels. 111. London: Richard Bentley; Edinburgh: Bell and Bradfute, 1848. xix-xxi.

Despondency. (Part of Blanchard's selection of "Fragments" from *Ethel Churchill*; poem appears elsewhere as "[Reminiscences]").

1st line: "Ah, tell me not that memory"

in Blanchard, Laman. *Life and Literary Remains of L. E. L.* Vol. 2. London: Henry Colburn, 1841. 286.

The Devotee.

1st line: "Prayer on her lips — yet, while the maiden prayeth,"

in Landon, Letitia E. *Fisher's Drawing Room Scrap-Book, 1838*. London, Paris, and New York: Fisher, Son; Germany: Black and Armstrong, and Asher, 1837. 5-6.

[*Different Opinions*]. (Suggested poem title, as poem is motto for Chapter 32 titled "Different Opinions"; poem appears elsewhere as "The Disturbing Spirit").

1st line: "Doubt, despairing, crime, and craft,")
in Landon, Letitia E. *Ethel Churchill: or, The Two Brides*. Vol. 1. London: Henry Colburn, 1837. 279.

Different Thoughts. Suggested by a Picture by G. S. Newton, No. 16, in the British Gallery, and representing a Girl looking at her Lover's Miniature. (In series, "Poetical Catalogue of Pictures").

1st line: "Just one look before I sleep,"
Prefixed line: "Which is the truest reading of thy look?"
in *The Literary Gazette* 322 (March 22, 1823): 189.

[*Different Views of Life*]. (Suggested poem title, as poem is the motto for Chapter 15 titled "Different Views of Life"; poem appears elsewhere as "Illusion" and is an altered version of "Moralising").

1st line: "And thus it is with all that made life fair,"
in Landon, Letitia E. *Ethel Churchill: or, The Two Brides*. Vol. 3. London: Henry Colburn, 1837. 107.

[*Different Views of Youth and Age*]. (Suggested poem title, as poem is motto for Chapter 9 titled "Different Views of Youth and Age"; poem appears elsewhere as "The World Within").

1st line: "There was a shadow on his face, that spake"
in Landon, Letitia E. *Ethel Churchill: or, The Two Brides*. Vol. 1. London: Henry Colburn, 1837. 93.

[*Difficulties*]. (Suggested poem title, as poem is motto for Chapter 12 titled "Difficulties"; poem appears elsewhere as "Affection's Timidity" and as "Love's Timidity").

1st line: "I do not ask to offer thee"
in Landon, Letitia E. *Ethel Churchill: or, The Two Brides*. Vol. 1. London: Henry Colburn, 1837. 118.

Dirge.

1st line: "Lay her in the gentle earth,"
in Landon, Letitia E. *Fisher's Drawing Room Scrap-Book, 1837*. London, Paris, and New York: Fisher, Son; Germany: Black and Armstrong, and Asher, 1836. 35.

Dirge.

1st line: "Oh, calm be thy slumbers!"
in Landon, Letitia E. *The Fate of Adelaide, A Swiss Romantic Tale; and Other Poems.* London: John Warren, 1821. 107-08.

[*The Disclosure*]. (Suggested poem title, as poem is motto for Chapter 37 titled "The Disclosure"; poem appears elsewhere as "Youth and Love").

1st line; "Young, loving, and beloved — these are brief words;"
in Landon, Letitia E. *Ethel Churchill: or, The Two Brides*. Vol. 3. London: Henry Colburn, 1837. 303.

The Disconsolate.

1st line: "Down from her hand it fell, the scroll"
in *Forget Me Not; A Christmas, New Year's, and Birth-day Present for 1831*. Ed. Frederic Shoberl. London: R. Ackermann, [1830]. 215-17.

[*A Discovery*]. (Suggested poem title, as poem is motto for Chapter 27 titled "A Discovery"; poem appears elsewhere as "The Fearful Trust").

1st line: "It is a fearful trust, the trust of love."

in Landon, Letitia E. *Ethel Churchill: or, The Two Brides.* Vol. 3. London: Henry Colburn, 1837. 204.

[Discovery]. (Suggested poem title, as poem is motto for Chapter 22 titled "Discovery"; poem appears elsewhere as "False Appearances").

1st line: "Who, that had looked on her that morn,"
in Landon, Letitia E. *Ethel Churchill: or, The Two Brides.* Vol. 3. London: Henry Colburn, 1837. 163.

Disenchantment.

1st line: "Do not ask me why I loved him,"
in Landon, Letitia E. *Fisher's Drawing Room Scrap-Book, 1838.* London, Paris, and New York: Fisher, Son; Germany: Black and Armstrong, and Asher, 1837. 53-54.

The Distant Grave.

1st line: "They tell me that his grave is made"
in *The New Monthly Magazine* 29 (1830): 428.

The Disturbing Spirit. (One of the "Fragments" from *Ethel Churchill* selected by Blanchard; poem appears elsewhere as "[Different Opinions]").

1st line: "Doubt, despairing, crime, and craft,"
in Blanchard, Laman. *Life and Literary Remains of L. E. L.* Vol. 2. London: Henry Colburn, 1841. 267.

Djouni, the Residence of Lady Hester Stanhope.

1st line: "Oh ladye, wherefore to the desert flying,"
in Landon, Letitia E. *Fisher's Drawing Room Scrap-Book, 1838.* London, Paris, and New York: Fisher, Son; Germany: Black and Armstrong, and Asher, 1837. 19.

Do You Remember It?

1st line: "Do you remember that purple twilight's falling,"
in *The Keepsake for 1832.* Ed. Frederic Mansel Reynolds. London: Longman, Rees, Orme, Brown, and Green, [1831]. 239-40.

Dr. Adam Clarke and the Two Priests of Budha.

1st line: "They heard it in the rushing wind,"
in Landon, Letitia E. *Fisher's Drawing Room Scrap-Book, 1836.* London and Paris: Fisher, Son; Berlin: Asher; New York: Jackson, [1835]. 42-44.

Dr. Morrison and his Chinese Attendants.

1st line: "They bend above the page with anxious eyes,"
in Landon, Letitia E. *Fisher's Drawing Room Scrap-Book, 1838.* London, Paris, and New York: Fisher, Son; Germany: Black and Armstrong, and Asher, 1837. 37.

Doubt. (One of the "Fragments" selected by Blanchard from *Ethel Churchill*; poem appears elsewhere as "[The End of Doubt]").

1st line: "I tell thee death were far more merciful"
in Blanchard, Laman. *Life and Literary Remains of L. E. L.* Vol. 2. London: Henry Colburn, 1841. 269.

[Doubts]. (Suggested poem title, as poem is motto for Chapter 8 titled "Doubts"; poem is an excerpt, with some revisions, from "The Future").

1st line: "Ask me not, love, what may be in my heart"
in Landon, Letitia E. *Ethel Churchill: or, The Two Brides.* Vol. 2. London: Henry Colburn, 1837. 56.

Dramatic Scene. Ianthe — Guido — Manfred.

1st line: "I can but weep your welcome, oh my own"
in *The Literary Gazette* 325 (April 12, 1823): 235-36.

Dramatic Scenes [series of two untitled poems]. (Poems are individually designated as "I" and "II"; their dramatic speakers are, respectively, Agnes and Julian; Leonardi and Alvine; Scene II appears elsewhere as "Bacchus and Ariadne").

    I., 1st line: "Oh, never, never!"

    Prefixed line: "The very life of love is confidence."

    in *The Literary Gazette* 301 (Oct. 26, 1822): 681-82;

    II., 1st line: "'Tis finished now: look on my picture, Love!"

    in *The Literary Gazette* 302 (Nov. 2, 1822): 697-98.

The Dream. (Part of Second Series of "Fragments by L. E. L.").

    1st line: "Farewell! and yet how may I teach"

    Prefixed lines to series begin: "Gleamings of poetry, — if I may give"

    in *The Literary Gazette* 364 (Jan. 10, 1824): 27-28.

A Dream.

    1st line: "I was wand'ring in my sleep —"

    in *The Literary Gazette* 474 (Feb. 18, 1826): 108.

The Dream.

    1st line: "Of thee, love, I was dreaming"

    Prefixed lines begin: "Sleep hath its own world,"

    in *The New Monthly Magazine* 44 (1835): 468.

The Dream in the Temple of Serapis.

    1st line: "The heavy night is falling,"

    in *The New Monthly Magazine* 46 (1836): 30-31;

    in Blanchard, Laman. *Life and Literary Remains of L. E. L.* Vol. 2. London: Henry Colburn, 1841. 239-41.

Dry Feet.

    1st line: "You do not like the streamlet,"

    in *The Juvenile Forget-Me-Not: A Christmas and New-Year's Gift, or Birth-day Present. 1837.* Ed. Mrs. S. C. [Anna Maria] Hall. London: Frederick Westley and A. H. Davis, [1836]. 219-20.

The Duchess of Kent.

    1st line: "A widow with an only child,"

    in Landon, Letitia E. *Schloss's English Bijou Almanac for 1839.* London: Albert Schloss, [1838]. N. pag. [3 pages].

[The Duel]. (Suggested poem title, as poem is motto for Chapter 31 titled "The Duel"; poem appears elsewhere as "Moonlight").

    1st line: "The moonlight falleth lovely over earth;"

    in Landon, Letitia E. *Ethel Churchill: or, The Two Brides.* Vol. 3. London: Henry Colburn, 1837. 239.

Dunold Mill-Hole. In the village of Kellet, about five miles from Lancaster.

    1st line: "I fly from the face of my foe in his might,"

    in Landon, Letitia E. *Fisher's Drawing Room Scrap-Book, 1836.* London and Paris: Fisher, Son; Berlin: Asher; New York: Jackson, [1835]. 32.

Dunstanburgh Castle.

    1st line: "There was no flag upon the mast,"

    in Landon, Letitia E. *Fisher's Drawing Room Scrap-Book, 1839.* London: Fisher, Son; Paris: Quai de L'Ecole, [1838]. 61-62.

Durham Cathedral.
　　1st line: "Those dark and silent aisles are fill'd with night,"
　　in Landon, Letitia E. *Fisher's Drawing Room Scrap-Book. 1835.* London: H. Fisher, R.
　　Fisher, and P. Jackson. 1835 [1834]. 39.
A Dutch Interior.
　　1st line: "They were poor, and by their cabin,"
　　in Landon, Letitia E. *Fisher's Drawing Room Scrap-Book, 1837.* London, Paris, and
　　New York: Fisher, Son; Germany: Black and Armstrong, and Asher, 1836. 23.
The Dying Child.
　　1st line: "Her cheek is flush'd with fever red;"
　　Prefixed lines begin: "My God! and is the daily page of life"
　　in Landon, Letitia E. *The Venetian Bracelet, The Lost Pleiad, A History of the Lyre, and
　　Other Poems.* London: Longman, Rees, Orme, Brown, and Green, 1829. 244-48.
The Dying Child. Paraphrased from the German.
　　1st line: "Oh mother, what brings music here?"
　　in *The Literary Gazette* 797 (Apr. 28, 1832): 266.
The Dying Spaniard's Charge. From the Mountains overlooking Granada."
　　1st line: "My gasping breath, I feel thee fail:"
　　in *The Literary Gazette* 588 (Apr. 26, 1828): 267.
The Earl of Sandwich.
　　1st line: "They called the Islands by his name,"
　　in Landon, Letitia E. *Fisher's Drawing Room Scrap-Book, 1837.* London, Paris, and
　　New York: Fisher, Son; Germany: Black and Armstrong, and Asher, 1836. 50;
　　in *The Zenana and Minor Poems of L. E. L.* London: Fisher, Son; Paris: Quai de
　　L'Ecole, [1839]. 244-45.
The Early Dream. (One of the "Fragments" from *Ethel Churchill* selected by Blanchard;
　　poem appears elsewhere as "[Return to Courtenaye Hall]" and, with "ah" instead
　　of "oh" in the first line, is an altered version of "Song" and an "[untitled poem]").
　　1st line: "Ah! never another dream can be"
　　in Blanchard, Laman. *Life and Literary Remains of L. E. L.* Vol. 2. London: Henry
　　Colburn, 1841. 29.
An Early Passage in Sir John Perrot's Life.
　　1st line: "The evening tide is on the turn; so calm the waters flow,"
　　in *The Keepsake for 1832.* Ed Frederic Mansel Reynolds. London: Longman, Rees,
　　Orme, Brown, and Green, [1831]. 179-83.
Earth Leads to Heaven. (One of the "Fragments" from *Ethel Churchill* selected by Blan-
　　chard; poem appears elsewhere as "[Asking for an Invitation]").
　　1st line: "This is a weary and a wretched life,"
　　in Blanchard, Laman. *Life and Literary Remains of L. E. L.* Vol. 2. London: Henry
　　Colburn, 1841. 292.
The Earth's Division. (Translation; poem in Second Series of "Versions from the Ger-
　　man").
　　1st line: "The fair earth, it shall be for all,"
　　in *The Literary Gazette* 938 (Jan. 10, 1835): 28.
Edith.
　　1st line: "Weep not, weep not, that in the spring"
　　in *The Keepsake for 1832.* Ed Frederic Mansel Reynolds. London: Longman, Rees,
　　Orme, Brown, and Green, [1831]. 94-95;
　　in Landon, Letitia E. *The Vow of the Peacock, and Other Poems.* London: Saunders

and Otley, 1835. 306-08.

Egeria's Grotto.
    1st line: "A silver Fountain with a changeful shade"
    in *The New Monthly Magazine* 16 (1826): 167-68;
    in Blanchard, Laman. *Life and Literary Remains of L. E. L.* Vol. 2. London: Henry
    Colburn, 1841. 305-06.

El Wuish.
    1st line: "Leila, the flowers are withered now,"
    in Landon, Letitia E. *Fisher's Drawing Room Scrap-Book [for 1832].* London: Fisher,
    Son, and Jackson, 1832 [1831]. 40.

Elise.
    1st line: "O let me love her! she has past"
    in *The Literary Gazette* 558 (Sept. 29, 1827): 636.

Ellen. A Fragment.
    1st line: "Is she not beautiful, although so pale?"
    in *The Lyre. Fugitive Poetry of the Nineteeth Century.* London: Tilt and Bogue, 1841.
    315-17.

The Emerald Ring. A Superstition. (One of the "Fragments").
    1st line: "It is a gem which hath the power to show"
    in Landon, Letitia E. *The Improvisatrice; and Other Poems.* London: Hurst, Robinson;
    Edinburgh: A. Constable, 1824. 300-01.

The Emigrants.
    1st line: "They dwelt amid the woods, where they had built"
    in *The Friendship's Offering. A Literary Album [for 1826].* Ed. Thomas K. Hervey. Lon-
    don: Lupton Relfe, 1826 [1825]. 185-90.

Empire of Woman. — Schiller. (Translation; in Fourth Series of "Versions from the Ger-
    man").
    1st line: "Her might is gentleness — she winneth sway"
    in *The Literary Gazette* 940 (Jan. 24, 1835): 59.

The Enchanted Island. By Danby. (One of the "Poetical Sketches of Modern Pictures").
    1st line: "And there the island lay, the waves around"
    in Landon, Letitia E. *The Troubadour; Catalogue of Pictures, and Historical Sketches.*
    London: Hurst, Robinson; Edinburgh: A. Constable, 1825. 280-83.

[The End]. (Suggested poem title, as poem is motto for Chapter 40 titled "The End";
    poem appears elsewhere as "The Farewell").
    1st line: "Farewell!"
    in Landon, Letitia E. *Ethel Churchill: or, The Two Brides.* Vol. 3. London: Henry Col-
    burn, 1837. 323.

[The End of Doubt]. (Suggested poem title, as poem is motto for Chapter 33 titled
    "The End of Doubt"; poem appears elsewhere as "Doubt").
    1st line: "I tell thee death were far more merciful"
    in Landon, Letitia E. *Ethel Churchill: or, The Two Brides.* Vol. 1. London: Henry Col-
    burn, 1837. 287.

Epigram on a Miser.
    1st line: "His heart is like a maggot-eaten nut:"
    in *The Literary Gazette* 767 (Oct. 1, 1831): 635.

Erinna.
    1st line: "My hand is on the lyre, which never more"
    Prefixed lines begin: "Was she of spirit race, or was she one"

in Landon, Letitia E. *The Golden Violet with its Tales of Romance and Chivalry: and Other Poems*. London: Longman, Rees, Orme, Brown, and Green, 1827. 241-68.

Eskdale, Cumberland.

1st line: "Oh! no: I do not wish to see"

in Landon, Letitia E. *Fisher's Drawing Room Scrap-Book, 1836*. London and Paris: Fisher, Son; Berlin: Asher; New York: Jackson, [1835]. 37.

Etty's Rover.

1st line: "Thou lovely and thou happy child,"

in Landon, Letitia E. *Fisher's Drawing Room Scrap-Book . 1835*. London: H. Fisher, R. Fisher, and P. Jackson. 1835 [1834]. 5-6.

Eucles Announcing the Victory of Marathon.

1st line: "He cometh from the purple hills,"

in Landon, Letitia E. *Fisher's Drawing Room Scrap-Book, 1837*. London, Paris, and New York: Fisher, Son; Germany: Black and Armstrong, and Asher, 1836. 25.

Euthanasia.

1st line: "Death came like a friend to restore thee"

in *The Literary Gazette* 552 (Aug. 18, 1827): 540.

The Eve of St. John. (No. X in the series, "Fragments in Rhyme," in *The Literary Gazette*).

1st line: "There is a flower, a magical flower,"

in *The Literary Gazette* 310 (Dec. 28, 1822): 825;

in *The Ladies' Wreath; A Selection from the Female Poetic Writers of England and America*. Ed. Mrs. Sarah J. Hale. Boston: Marsh, Capen, and Lyon; New York: D. Appleton, 1837. 129-30.

[An Evening Alone]. (Suggested poem title, as poem is motto for Chapter 35 titled "An Evening Alone"; poem appears elsewhere as "Fate").

1st line: "The steps of Fate are dark and terrible;"

in Landon, Letitia E. *Ethel Churchill: or, The Two Brides*. Vol. 1. London: Henry Colburn, 1837. 302.

The Evening Prayer.

1st line: "Alone, alone! — no other face"

in *The Juvenile Forget Me Not. A Christmas and New Year's Gift, or Birthday Present. 1832*. Ed. Mrs. S. C. [Anna Maria] Hall. London: Frederick Westley and A. H. Davis, [1831]. 65-66.

The Evening Star.

1st line: "Ah! loveliest! that through my casement gleaning,"

in Landon, Letitia E. *Fisher's Drawing Room Scrap-Book, 1837*. London, Paris, and New York: Fisher, Son; Germany: Black and Armstrong, and Asher, 1836. 54.

The Evening Star.

1st line: "How beautiful the twilight sky,"

in *The Amulet. A Christian and Literary Remembrancer [for 1833]*. Ed. S.C. Hall. London: Frederick Westley and A. H. Davis, 1833 [1832]. 215-216.

The Evening Star.

1st line: "I come from the caves of the silent sea,"

in *The Amulet [for 1836]*. Ed. S. C. Hall. London: Frederick Westley and A. H. Davis, 1836 [1835]. 199-200.

Execution of Crescentius. (Poem appears elsewhere as "Ballad of Crescentius" and "Crescentius").

1st line: "I looked upon his brow, — no sign"

in *The Literary Gazette* 339 (July 19, 1823): 459.

The Exile. (Translation of "Les Derniers Paroles" by l'Abbé de la Mennais).
1st line: "I wandered through the nations, and I gazed"
in *The Literary Gazette* 927 (Oct. 25, 1834): 723.

Expectation.
1st line: "She looked from out the window"
in Landon, Letitia E. *Fisher's Drawing Room Scrap-Book, 1837.* London, Paris, and New York: Fisher, Son: Germany: Black and Armstrong, and Asher, 1836. 20;
in *The Zenana and Minor Poems of L. E. L.* London: Fisher, Son; Paris: Quai de L'Ecole, [1839]. 222-24.

Experience.
1st line: "My very heart is filled with tears! I seem"
in *The New Monthly Magazine* 46 (1836): 467;
in Blanchard, Laman. *Life and Literary Remains of L. E. L.* Vol. 2. London: Henry Colburn, 1841. 256-58.

Experience Too Late. (One of the "Fragments" from Ethel Churchill selected by Blanchard; poem appears elsewhere as "[The Consent]").
1st line: "It is the past that maketh my despair;"
in Blanchard, Laman. *Life and Literary Remains of L. E. L.* Vol. 2. London: Henry Colburn, 1841. 284.

Fable. (Described as "Imitated from the French of La Motte.").
1st line: "Four souls, that on earth had just yielded their breath,"
in Landon, Letitia E. *The Fate of Adelaide, A Swiss Romantic Tale; and Other Poems.* London: John Warren, 1821. 125-28.

The Factory.
1st line: "There rests a shade above yon town,"
Prefixed line: "'Tis an accursed thing! —"
in Landon, Letitia E. *The Vow of the Peacock, and Other Poems.* London: Saunders and Otley, 1835. 231-37;
in *The Christian Lady's Magazine* 10 (1838): 219-22.

Faded Flowers.
1st line: "Lingers yet a perfum'd breath"
in *The Literary Gazette* 414 (Dec. 25, 1824): 825.

The Fair Maid of Perth.
1st line: "A fair, pale beauty — with a shadow lustre"
in Landon, Letitia E. *Fisher's Drawing Room Scrap-Book, 1839.* London: Fisher, Son; Paris: Quai de L'Ecole, [1838]. 42.

Fairies. (First appears as prefixed lines to "Stanzas").
1st line: "Race of the rainbow wing, the deep blue eye,"
in *Literary Gems* [of New York] 1 (1833): 82.

Fairies on the Sea Shore. By Howard. (Dramatic poem, whose speakers are the First, Second, and Third Fairies, Fourth Spirit, and Chorus of Fairies; First Fairy speaks first lines; poem is one of the "Poetical Sketches of Modern Pictures").
1st line: "My home and haunt are in every leaf,"
in Landon, Letitia E. *The Troubadour; Catalogue of Pictures, and Historical Sketches.* London: Hurst, Robinson: Edinburgh: A. Constable, 1825. 292-96.

Fairy Land.
   1st line: "It came, as Aladdin uprose at thy call,"
   in *The Casket, A Miscellany, Consisting of Unpublished Poems.* Ed. Mrs. Blencowe.
   London: John Murray, 1829. 216-217.
The Fairy of the Fountains.
   1st line: "Why did she love her mother so?"
   in Landon, Letitia E. *Fisher's Drawing Room Scrap-Book. 1835.* London: H. Fisher, R.
   Fisher, and P. Jackson. 1835 [1834]. 57-64;
   in *The Zenana and Minor Poems of L. E. L.* London: Fisher, Son; Paris: Quai de
   L'Ecole, [1839]. 141-74.
The Fairy Queen Sleeping. By Stothard. (One of the "Poetical Sketches of Modern Pic-
tures").
   1st line: "We have been o'er land and sea,"
   Prefixed lines begin: "She lay upon a bank, the favourite haunt"
   in Landon, Letitia E. *The Troubadour; Catalogue of Pictures, and Historical Sketches.*
   London: Hurst, Robinson; Edinburgh: A. Constable, 1825. 269-72.
Faith Destroyed. (One of the "Fragments" from *Ethel Churchill* selected by Blanchard;
   poem appears elsewhere as "[A Late Breakfast]").
   1st line: "Why did I love him? I looked up to him"
   in Blanchard, Laman. *Life and Literary Remains of L. E. L.* Vol. 2. London: Henry
   Colburn, 1841. 291.
Faith Ill Requited. (One of the "Fragments" from *Ethel Churchill* selected by Blanchard;
   poem appears elsewhere as "[Confidence]").
   1st line: "I feel the presence of my own despair;"
   in Blanchard, Laman. *Life and Literary Remains of L. E. L.* Vol. 2. London: Henry
   Colburn, 1841. 269.
The Falcon-Messenger. (Part of series, "Imitations of Servian Poetry").
   1st line: "The warrior loosed the silken string"
   in *The Literary Gazette* 538 (May 12, 1827): 300.
False Appearances. (One of the "Fragments" from *Ethel Churchill* selected by Blanchard;
   poem appears elsewhere as "[Discovery]").
   1st line: "Who, that had looked on her that morn,"
   in Blanchard, Laman. *Life and Literary Remains of L. E. L.* Vol. 2. London:
   Henry Colburn, 1841. 294.
The False One. (Sketch III in Fourth Series of "Poetic Sketches").
   1st line: "Ride on, ride with thy bridal company,"
   Prefixed line: "And what most women suffer, thus betrayed?"
   in *The Literary Gazette* 358 (Nov. 29, 1823): 763.
Fame: An Apologue. The Three Brothers. (Poem appears elsewhere as "The Three Broth-
ers").
   1st line: "They dwelt in a valley of sunshine, those Brothers;"
   in *The Literary Gazette* 648 (June 20, 1829): 412.
Fantasies Inscribed to T. Crofton Croker, Esq.
   1st line: "I'm weary, I'm weary, — this cold world of ours;"
   in Landon, Letitia E. *The Venetian Bracelet, The Lost Pleiad, A History of the Lyre, and
   Other Poems.* London: Longman, Rees, Orme, Brown, and Green, 1829. 229-31.
The Farewell. (One of the "Fragments" from *Ethel Churchill* selected by Blanchard;
   poem appears elsewhere as "[The End]").
   1st line: "Farewell!"

in Blanchard, Laman. *Life and Literary Remains of L. E. L.* Vol. 2. London: Henry Colburn, 1841. 300.

The Farewell.

1st line: "Farewell! companion of my solitude!"

in Landon, Letitia E. *The Fate of Adelaide, A Swiss Romantic Tale; and Other Poems.* London: John Warren, 1821. 69-70.

The Farewell.

1st line: "I dare not look upon that face,"

in Landon, Letitia E. *Fisher's Drawing Room Scrap-Book, 1839.* London: Fisher, Son; Paris: Quai de L'Ecole, [1838]. 5-6;

in *Blackwood's Lady's Magazine* 6 (March 1839): 148-49.

Farewell.

1st line: "My little Fairy Chronicle,"

in Landon, Letitia E. *Schloss's English Bijou Almanac for 1839.* London: Albert Schloss. N. pag. [2 pages].

Farewell.

1st line: "One word, altho' that word must pass"

in *The Literary Gazette* 438 (June 11, 1825): 379.

The Farewell.

1st line: "Yes, I am changed; yes, much much changed"

in *The Literary Gazette* 375 (March 27, 1824): 203.

Farewell! and Never Think of Me. (Set to music by Miss Wesley of Bath, printed here; poem appears elsewhere as part of "On a Star," called "Song," and as "Think of Me").

1st line: "Farewell! and never think of me"

in *The Harmonicon* 6[?] (1829): 186-187.

Farewell! Oh My Brother! (Poem appears elsewhere as "Warkworth Castle, Northumberland").

1st line: "Come, up with the banner, and on with the sword,"

in *The Zenana and Minor Poems of L. E. L.* London: Fisher, Son; Paris: Quai de L'Ecole, [1839]. 281-83.

Fate. (One of the "Fragments" of *Ethel Churchill* selected by Blanchard; poem appears elsewhere as "[An Evening Alone]").

1st line: "The steps of fate are dark and terrible"

in Blanchard, Laman. *Life and Literary Remains of L. E. L.* Vol. 2. London: Henry Colburn, 1841. 268.

The Fate of Adelaide, A Swiss Romantic Tale.

1st line: "Romantic Switzerland! thy scenes are traced"

in Landon, Letitia E. *The Fate of Adelaide, A Swiss Romantic Tale; and Other Poems.* London: John Warren, 1821. 1-66.

The Father's Love. (One of the "Fragments" from *Ethel Churchill* selected by Blanchard; poem appears elsewhere as "[Return Home]").

1st line: "'Tis not my home — he made it home"

in Blanchard, Laman. *Life and Literary Remains of L. E. L.* Vol. 2. London: Henry Colburn, 1841. 288-89.

The Fearful Trust. (One of the "Fragments" from *Ethel Churchill* selected by Blanchard; poem appears elsewhere as "[A Discovery]").

1st line: "It is a fearful trust, the trust of love."

in Blanchard, Laman. *Life and Literary Remains of L. E. L.* Vol. 2. London: Henry

Colburn, 1841. 298.

The Feast of Life. (Poem appears elsewhere as "Lines. The Feast of Life").
1st line: "I bid thee to my mystic Feast,"
in Landon, Letitia E. *The Vow of the Peacock, and Other Poems.* London: Saunders and Otley, 1835. 334-35.

Felicia. (See "Disenchantment").

Felicia Hemans.
1st line: "No more, no more — oh, never more returning,"
in Landon, Letitia E. *Fisher's Drawing Room Scrap-Book, 1838.* London, Paris, and New York: Fisher, Son; Germany: Germany: Black and Armstrong, and Asher, 1837. 10-11;
in *The Zenana and Minor Poems of L. E. L.* London: Fisher, Son; Paris: Quai de L'Ecole, [1839]. 246-51.

The Female Convict. (Part IX of the series, "Fragments in Rhyme," in *The Literary Gazette*; one of the "Fragments" in *The Improvisatrice; and Other Poems*).
1st line: "She shrank from all, and her silent mood"
in *The Literary Gazette* 309 (Dec. 21, 1822): 808;
in Landon, Letitia E. *The Improvisatrice; and Other Poems.* London: Hurst, Robinson; Edinburgh: A. Constable, 1824. 256-60.

Female Faith.
1st line: "She loved you when the sunny light"
in *The Ladies' Wreath; A Selection from the Female Poetic Writers of England and America.* Ed. Mrs. Sarah J. Hale. Boston: Marsh, Capen, and Lyon; New York: D. Appleton, 1837. 123.

Female Head on the left of "the Hours." (Printed under the series title, "Poetical Catalogue of Paintings": but to agree with the rest of the series, for "Paintings," read "Pictures"; poem is described in brackets as "Sketched from Sir John Leicester's Gallery," a description it shares with the poem, "The Hours, by Howard").
1st line: "A dream of saddest beauty: one pale smile"
in *The Literary Gazette* 328 (May 3, 1823): 287.

Fenella's Escape.
1st line: "Within the stately palace,"
in *The Keepsake for 1836.* Ed. The Hon. Mrs. Caroline Norton. London: Longman, Rees, Orme, Brown, Green, and Longman, 1836 [1835]. 215-16.

The Festa of Madonna dei Fiori.
1st line: "They gathered in that holy place,"
in *The Amulet. A Christian and Literary Remembrancer [for 1835].* Ed. S. C. Hall. London: Frederick Westley and A. H. Davis, 1835 [1834]. 9-11.

The Festival.
1st line: "It is a festal meeting,"
in *Friendship's Offering and Winter's Wreath: A Christmas and New Year's Present, for 1836.* London: Smith, Elder, 1836 [1835]. 73-76.

The Festival.
1st line; "The young and the lovely are gathered:"
in *The Literary Gazette* 697 (May 29, 1830): 354;
in Landon, Letitia E. *The Vow of the Peacock, and Other Poems.* London: Saunders and Otley, 1835. 341-47.

[The Fête]. (Suggested poem title, as poem is the motto for Chapter 4 titled "The Fête"; poem appears elsewhere as "A Portrait").

1st line: "Many were lovely there; but, of that many,"

in Landon, Letitia E. *Ethel Churchill: or, The Two Brides.* Vol. 2. London: Henry Colburn, 1837. 27.

[The Fête]. (Suggested poem title, as poem is the motto for Chapter 8 titled "The Fête").

1st line: "Not to the present is our hour confined,"

in Landon, Letitia E. *Ethel Churchill: or, The Two Brides.* Vol. 3. London: Henry Colburn, 1837. 54.

The Fete. (First, a suggested poem title, as poem is the motto for Chapter 18 titled "The Fête"; then, poem is included in Blanchard's selection of "Fragments" from *Ethel Churchill*).

1st line: "There was a feast that night,"

in Landon, Letitia E. *Ethel Churchill: or, The Two Brides.* Vol. 2. London: Henry Colburn, 1837. 132-33;

in Blanchard, Laman. *Life and Literary Remains of L. E. L.* Vol. 2. London: Henry Colburn, 1841. 278.

[The Fête at Sir Robert Walpole's]. (Suggested poem title, as poem is the motto for Chapter 5 titled "The Fête at Sir Robert Walpole's"; poem appears elsewhere as "The Poor").

1st line: "Few, save the poor, feel for the poor:"

in Landon, Letitia E. *Ethel Churchill: or, The Two Brides.* Vol. 3. London: Henry Colburn, 1837. 31.

[The Fête at Sir Robert Walpole's Continued]. (Suggested poem title, as poem is the motto for Chapter 6 titled "The Fête at Sir Robert Walpole's Continued"; poem appears elsewhere as "A Lady's Beauty").

1st line: "Ladye, thy white brow is fair,"

in Landon, Letitia E. *Ethel Churchill: or, The Two Brides.* Vol. 3. London: Henry Colburn, 1837. 38.

Fidelity. (First sketch in Fifth Series of "Poetic Sketches").

1st line: "There is a low sweet sound of voice and lute"

Prefixed lines begin: "There is"

in *The Literary Gazette* 391 (July 17, 1824): 460-61.

The First Ball.

1st line: "Ay, wreathe the tresses o'er thy brow,"

in *Friendship's Offering, A Literary Album and Christmas and New Year's Present for 1828.* Ed. Charles Knight. London: Smith, Elder, 1828 [1827]. 273-76.

[A First Disappointment]. (Suggested poem title, as poem is the motto for Chapter 30 titled "A First Disappointment").

1st line: "The deep, the long, the dreaming hours,"

in Landon, Letitia E. *Ethel Churchill: or, The Two Brides.* Vol. 1. London: Henry Colburn, 1837. 265.

The First Doubt. (First, a suggested poem title, as poem is motto for Chapter 5 titled "The First Doubt"; then, poem is titled thus when included in Blanchard's selection of "Fragments" from *Ethel Churchill*).

1st line: "Youth, love, and rank, and wealth — all these combined,"

in Landon, Letitia E. *Ethel Churchill: or, The Two Brides.* Vol. 2. London: Henry Colburn. 1837. 35;

in Blanchard, Laman. *Life and Literary Remains of L. E. L.* Vol. 2. London: Henry Colburn, 1841. 273.

The First Grave.

1st line: "A single grave! — the only one"

in *The Literary Gazette* 658 (Aug. 29, 1829): 571;

in Landon, Letitia E. *The Vow of the Peacock, and Other Poems.* London: Saunders and Otley, 1835. 329-33; as *The First Grave, in the New Churchyard at Brompton,* in *The Modern Poets and Artists of Great Britain.* Ed. S. C. Hall. London: Whittaker, 1838. Vol. 3 of *The Book of Gems.* 3 vols. 1836-38. 181-83.

[A First Night]. (Suggested poem title, as poem is motto for Chapter 9 titled "A First Night"; poem appears elsewhere as "The Poet's First Essay").

1st line: "It is a fearful stake the poet casts,"

in Landon, Letitia E. *Ethel Churchill: or, The Two Brides.* Vol. 2. London: Henry Colburn, 1837. 64.

Fishing Boats in the Monsoon.

1st line: "Born yet awhile, my wasting lamp,"

in Landon, Letitia E. *Fisher's Drawing Room Scrap-Book, 1836.* London and Paris: Fisher, Son; Berlin: Asher; New York: Jackson, [1835]. 25-26.

The Flight Into Egypt.

1st line: "A glorious landscape — clear as faith the sky,"

in Landon, Letitia E. *The Easter Gift, A Religious Offering.* London: Fisher, Son, 1832. 12-13.

The Floating Beacon. (Part I in series of "Fragments").

1st line: "Why art thou thus, thou lovely bark,"

in *The Literary Gazette* 344 (Aug. 23, 1823): 540.

Flowers Love's Language.

1st line: "Beautiful language! Love's peculiar own,"

in *The Album of Love.* The Mirror Library. 3. New York: n.p., 1844. 15.

Follow Me!

1st line: "Follow me! — 'tis to the battle-field —"

Prefixed lines begin: "A summer morning, with its calm, glad light,"

in *The Literary Gazette* 709 (Aug. 21, 1830): 548;

in Landon, Letitia E. *The Vow of the Peacock, and Other Poems.* London: Saunders and Otley, 1835. 336-37.

For Music. (No. 3 in a series of "Songs").

1st line: "Thou art looking on the face of night, my love!"

in *The Literary Gazette* 284 (June 29, 1822): 410.

The Forgotten One.

1st line: "I have no early flowers to fling"

in *The Keepsake for 1831.* Ed Frederic Mansel Reynolds. London: Hurst, Chance; Jennings, Chaplin, [1830]. 205-08.

The Forgotten One.

1st line: "No shadow rests upon the place"

in Landon, Letitia E. *The Vow of the Peacock, and Other Poems..* London: Saunders, Otley, 1835. 309-15.

The Forgotten One.

1st line: "Thou art forgotten! thou, whose feet"

in *Selections From Female Poets. A Present for Ladies.* Boston: Samuel Coleman, 1837. 56.

The Forsaken.

1st line: "I have caught the last wave of his snow-white plume, —"

Prefixed lines begin: "I dreamed a dream, that I had flung a chain"

in *The Literary Souvenir; or, Cabinet of Poetry and Romance [for 1826]*. London: Hurst, Robinson; Edinburgh: A. Constable, 1826 [1825]. 159-61.

The Forsaken. (Third Series of "Fragments by L. E. L.").

1st line: "Oh cast that shadow from thy brow"

Prefixed lines to series begin: "Gleamings of poetry, — if I may give"

in *The Literary Gazette* 365 (Jan. 17, 1824): 41.

The Fountain. A Ballad.

1st line: "Why startest thou back from that fount of sweet water?"

in *The Casket, A Miscellany, Consisting of Unpublished Poems*. Ed. Mrs. Blencowe. London: John Murray, 1829. 183-84.

Fountain's Abbey.

1st line: "Alas, alas! those ancient towers,"

in Landon, Letitia E. *Fisher's Drawing Room Scrap-Book, 1836*. London and Paris: Fisher, Son; Berlin: Asher; New York: Jackson, [1835]. 41.

Fountain's Abbey.

1st line: "Never more, when the day is o'er,"

in Landon, Letitia E. *Fisher's Drawing Room Scrap-Book. 1833*. London: H. Fisher, R. Fisher and P. Jackson, 1833 [1832]. 48;

in *The Zenana and Minor Poems of L. E. L.* London: Fisher, Son; Paris: Quai de L'Ecole, [1839]. 106-07.

Fowey Harbour, and Polruan Castle, &c.

1st line: "The ladye sat in her lonely tower,"

in Landon, Letitia E. *Fisher's Drawing Room Scrap-Book [for 1832]*. London: Fisher, Son, and Jackson, 1832 [1831]. 31.

A Fragment. (Poem appears elsewhere as the 5th poem in a group of "Fragments").

1st line: "Do any thing but love; or if thou lovest"

in *Ladies' Penny Gazette* 1 (Feb. 2, 1833): 116;

in *The Argus* 2 (Oct. 13, 1832): 16.

Fragment.

1st line: "I know but little of her history,"

in *The Literary Gazette* 559 (Oct. 6, 1827): 651.

Fragment. (Poem appears elsewhere as 1st poem in group of "Fragments").

1st line: "I look'd upon the twilight star,"

in *The Album Wreath of Music and Literature [for 1835]*. London: R. Willoughby, [1834?]. 31.

Fragment.

1st line: "I saw her amid pleasure's gayest haunts —"

in Landon, Letitia E. *The Fate of Adelaide, A Swiss Romantic Tale; and Other Poems*. London: John Warren, 1821. 137-38.

Fragment.

1st line: "Is not this grove"

in *The Literary Gazette* 188 (Aug. 26, 1820): 556-57;

in Landon, Letitia E. *The Fate of Adelaide, A Swiss Romantic Tale; and Other Poems*. London: John Warren, 1821. 149-53.

Fragment.
   1st line: "It is not spring, but still the new-come year"
   in Landon, Letitia E. *The Fate of Adelaide, A Swiss Romantic Tale; and Other Poems.*
   London: John Warren, 1821. 91-92.
Fragment.
   1st line: "Love thee! yes, yes! the storms that rend aside"
   in Landon, Letitia E. *The Fate of Adelaide, A Swiss Romantic Tale; and Other Poems.*
   London: John Warren, 1821. 73-74.
Fragment.
   1st line: "Oh it is veriest vanity to love! —"
   in *The Literary Gazette* 343 (Aug. 16, 1823): 524.
Fragment.
   1st line: "A solitude"
   in *The Literary Gazette* 352 (Oct. 18, 1823): 667.
Fragments [series of five untitled poems]. (1st poem appears elsewhere as "Fragment"; 2nd
   poem appears elsewhere as "The Oak"; 5th poem shares the first line with "Love's
   Lament").
   1st poem, 1st line: "I looked upon the twilight Star,"
   2nd poem, 1st line: "... It is the last survivor of a race"
   3rd poem, 1st line: "I should have prized thy heart, if none"
   4th poem, 1st line: "There is a curse laid on the human heart"
   5th poem, 1st line: "Nay, pray thee, let me weep, for tears"
   in *The Literary Gazette* 326 (April 19, 1823): 251.
Fragments [series of five untitled poems]. (5th poem appears elsewhere as "A Fragment").
   1st poem, 1st line: "The lights are fair in my father's hall,"
   2nd poem, 1st line: "Love once dwelt in a palmy isle,"
   3rd poem, 1st line: "A blue Italian sky, — yet scarce more blue"
   4th poem, 1st line: "Then fare thee well, love, for a little while!"
   5th poem, 1st line: "Do any thing but love; or if thou lovest"
   Prefixed line to group: "Just two or three faint chords."
   in *The Literary Gazette* 327 (April 26, 1823): 268-69.
Fragments [contains two untitled poems]. (Poems individually designated by "I" and "II").
   I., 1st line: "There are ten thousand visions of delight"
   II., 1st line: "No more, no more, why should I dream"
   in *The Literary Gazette* 498 (Aug. 5, 1826): 492.
Fragments by L. E. L. Fourth Series [contains one untitled poem]. (Poem appears elsewhere
   as "The Thessalian Fountain"; the Fourth Series contains one other poem, titled
   "Song" and printed beneath the untitled poem).
   1st line: "A small clear fountain, with green willow trees"
   Prefixed lines to series begin: "Gleamings of poetry, — if I may give"
   in *The Literary Gazette* 366 (Jan. 24, 1824): 58.
Fragments. Fifth Series [contains four untitled poems]. (To accord with the other series of
   "Fragments by L. E. L.," "by L. E. L." should be added to this series's title and the
   series should be numbered "Seventh" rather than "Fifth").
   1st poem, 1st line: "My heart is as a grave,"
   2nd poem, 1st line: "Now for the gay, the cold, the free,"
   3rd poem, 1st line: "Oh, no, my heart is given"
   4th poem, 1st line: "Forget thee — I may not forget,"

Prefixed lines to group begin: "Gleamings of poetry, if I may give"
in *The Literary Gazette* 439 (June 18, 1825): 396.

[A Friend at Court]. (Suggested poem title, as poem is motto for Chapter 33 titled "A Friend at Court"; poem appears elsewhere as "The Lost").
    1st line: "I did not know till she was lost,"
    in Landon, Letitia E. *Ethel Churchill: or, The Two Brides.* Vol. 2. London: Henry Colburn, 1837. 259.

The Frozen Ship.
    1st line: "The fair ship cut the billows,"
    in Landon, Letitia E. *The Vow of the Peacock, and Other Poems.* London: Saunders, Otley, 1835. 256–60.

The Funeral. (Poem appears elsewhere as "Windleshaw Abbey").
    1st line: "Mark you not yon sad procession;"
    in *The Zenana and Minor Poems of L. E. L.* London: Fisher, Son; Paris: Quai de L'Ecole, [1839]. 135–37.

The Funeral Bride. An Italian Legend.
    1st line: "It is but daybreak — yet Count Leon's halls"
    in *The New Monthly Magazine* 16 (1826): 284–86.

Furness Abbey, in the Vale of Nightshade, Lancashire.
    1st line: "I wish for the days of the olden time,"
    in Landon, Letitia E. *Fisher's Drawing Room Scrap-Book [for 1832].* London: Fisher, Son, and Jackson, 1832 [1831]. 33;
    in *The Zenana and Minor Poems of L. E. L.* London: Fisher, Son; Paris: Quai de L'Ecole, [1839]. 75–77.

Futtypore Sicri. The Favorite Residence of the Emperor Ackbar.
    1st line: "The summer palace of the king,"
    in Landon, Letitia E. *Fisher's Drawing Room Scrap-Book. 1833.* London: H. Fisher, R. Fisher and P. Jackson. 1833 [1832]. 52.

The Future. (An excerpt of poem appears elsewhere as "[Doubts]").
    1st line: "Ask me not, love, what can be in my heart;"
    in *The New Monthly Magazine* 40 (1834): 303–04;
    in Blanchard, Laman. *Life and Literary Remains of L. E. L.* Vol. 2. London: Henry Colburn, 1841. 252–54.

[Gaieties and Absurdities]. (Suggested poem title, as poem is motto for Chapter 6 titled "Gaieties and Absurdities"; poem is printed beneath heading for letter from "Lady Marchmont to Sir Jasper Meredith"; poem appears elsewhere as "Self-Blindness").
    1st line: "What Shakspeare said of lovers, might apply"
    in Landon, Letitia E. *Ethel Churchill: or, The Two Brides.* Vol. 2. London: Henry Colburn. 1837. 42.

The Ganges.
    1st line: "On sweeps the mighty river — calmly flowing,"
    in Landon, Letitia E. *Fisher's Drawing Room Scrap-Book, 1838.* London, Paris, and New York: Fisher, Son; Germany: Black and Armstrong, and Asher, 1837. 33–34;
    in *The Zenana and Minor Poems of L. E. L.* London: Fisher, Son; Paris: Quai de L'Ecole, [1839]. 277–80.

The Gathering. — Koerner. (Translation; part of First Series of "Versions from the German").
    1st line: "The people are risen — the storm is unbound —"
    in *The Literary Gazette* 937 (Jan. 3, 1835): 11–12.

The Gathering of the Chieftains at Beteddein, the Palace of the Prince of the Druses.
   1st line: "They come from the mountains, in thousands they come —"
   in Landon, Letitia E. *Fisher's Drawing Room Scrap-Book, 1839.* London: Fisher, Son;
   Paris: Quai de L'Ecole, [1838]. 13.
Genius. (One of the "Fragments" from *Ethel Churchill* selected by Blanchard; poem
   appears elsewhere as "[A Secretaryship]").
   1st line: "Alas! and must this be the fate"
   in Blanchard, Laman. *Life and Literary Remains of L. E. L.* Vol. 2. London: Henry
   Colburn, 1841. 294.
*Genius. Lines suggested by a View of the Sculpture designed by Mr. Lough, and described in
   last week's Literary Gazette.*
   1st line: "Glory of earth, and light from heaven,"
   in *The Literary Gazette* 539 (May 19, 1827): 317-18.
The Gentle Student. (Poem appears elsewhere as "The Student").
   1st line: "Bend, gentle student, o'er the page,"
   in *The Amulet. A Christian and Literary Remembrancer [for 1833].* Ed. S.C. Hall. Lon-
   don: Frederick Westley and A. H. Davis, 1833 [1832]. 33-34.
Gentleness Pictured. (One of the "Fragments" from *Ethel Churchill* selected by Blan-
   chard; poem appears elsewhere as "[The Jewels Given]").
   1st line: "A gentle creature was that girl,"
   in Blanchard, Laman. *Life and Literary Remains of L. E. L.* Vol. 2. London: Henry
   Colburn, 1841. 266.
Geraldine.
   1st line: "Lonely and deep as the fountain when springing"
   in Landon, Letitia E. *Heath's Book of Beauty. 1833.* London: Longman, Rees, Orme,
   Brown, Green, and Longman; Paris: Rittner and Goupil; Frankfort: C. Jügel,
   [1832]. 180-81.
The Giant's Causeway.
   1st line: "They met beside the stormy sea, those giant kings of old,"
   in Landon, Letitia E. *Fisher's Drawing Room Scrap-Book [for 1832].* London: Fisher,
   Son, and Jackson, 1832 [1831]. 43.
Gibralter. From the Queen of Spain's Chair.
   1st line: "High on the rock that fronts the sea"
   in Landon, Letitia E. *Fisher's Drawing Room Scrap-Book, 1838.* London, Paris, and
   New York: Fisher, Son; Germany: Black and Armstrong, and Asher, 1837. 45.
Gibralter — From the Sea.
   1st line: "Down 'mid the waves, accursed bark,"
   in Landon, Letitia E. *Fisher's Drawing Room Scrap-Book, 1838.* London, Paris, and
   New York: Fisher, Son; Germany: Black and Armstrong, and Asher, 1837. 20-21.
Gibraltar. Scene During the Plague. (Poem appears elsewhere as "Scene During the
   Plague at Gibraltar").
   1st line: "At first, I only buried one,"
   in Landon, Letitia E. *Fisher's Drawing Room Scrap-Book, 1837.* London, Paris, and
   New York: Fisher, Son; Germany: Black and Armstrong, and Asher, 1836. 51.
Gifts For the Past.
   1st line: "The past — now what shall we give the past?"
   in *The Edinburgh Literary Journal* 163 (Dec. 24, 1831): 359-360.

Gifts Misused. (One of the "Fragments" from *Ethel Churchill* selected by Blanchard; poem appears elsewhere as an "[untitled poem]").
　　1st line: "Oh, what a waste of feeling and of thought"
　　in Blanchard, Laman. *Life and Literary Remains of L. E. L.* Vol. 2. London: Henry Colburn, 1841. 277.

The Gipsy's Prophecy.
　　1st line: "Ladye, throw back thy raven hair,"
　　Prefixed by lines from *Duke of Mantua* beginning: "A turban girds her brow, white as the sea-foam"; followed by the line: "This was the Sybil."
　　in *The Literary Gazette* 351 (Oct. 11, 1823): 650.

A Girl At Her Devotions. By Newton. (One of the "Poetical Works on Modern Pictures").
　　1st line: "She was just risen from her bended knee,"
　　in Landon, Letitia E. *The Troubadour; Catalogue of Pictures, and Historical Sketches.* London: Hurst, Robinson; Edinburgh: A. Constable, 1825. 297-300.

Giulia Grisi.
　　1st line: "I heard her; and the air was filled"
　　in Landon, Letitia E. *The English Bijou Almanac for 1838.* London: Albert Schloss, [1837]. N. pag. [3 pages].

Gladesmuir. (Second sketch in Third Series of "Poetical Sketches"; "Poetical" should be corrected to "Poetic" to agree with other series in *The Literary Gazette*).
　　1st line: "There is not"
　　in *The Literary Gazette* 295 (Sept. 14, 1822): 583-84;
　　in Landon, Letitia E. *The Improvisatrice; and Other Poems.* London: Hurst, Robinson; Edinburgh: A. Constable, 1824. 193-203.

The Glen. (Part of group of "Landscapes").
　　1st line: "It was a little glen — a solitude —"
　　Prefixed lines begin: "And must"
　　in *The Literary Gazette* 402 (Oct. 2, 1824): 636.

Glencoe.
　　1st line: "Lay by the harp, sing not that song,"
　　in *The Literary Gazette* 338 (July 12, 1823): 443;
　　in Landon, Letitia E. *The Vow of the Peacock, and Other Poems.* London: Saunders and Otley, 1835. 242-48.

Glengariffe.
　　1st line: "Oh lovely Picture, thou art one to haunt"
　　in Landon, Letitia E. *Fisher's Drawing Room Scrap-Book. 1833.* London: H. Fisher, R. Fisher, and P. Jackson, 1833 [1832]. 33.

Goethe.
　　1st line: "A proud and mighty monument"
　　in Landon, Letitia E. *The English Bijou Almanac for 1837.* London: Albert Schloss, [1836]. N. pag. [3 pages].

The Golden Violet.
　　1st line: "To-morrow, to-morrow, thou loveliest May,"
　　in Landon, Letitia E. *The Golden Violet with its Tales of Romance and Chivalry: and Other Poems.* London: Longman, Rees, Orme, Brown, and Green, 1827. 1-239.

Gone. (Poem appears elsewhere as "The Departed").

1st line: "Where's the snow — the summer snow —"

in *The Album Wreath of Music and Literature [for 1835].* London: R. Willoughby, [1834?]. 30.

Good Angels. (Dramatic monologue spoken by the Angel of Earth).

1st line: "Triumph, for my task is done —"

in *The Keepsake for 1832.* Ed. Frederic Mansel Reynolds. London: Longman, Rees, Orme, Brown, and Green, [1831]. 129-30.

"Good Night!"

1st line: "Good night! — what a sudden shadow"

in *The New Monthly Magazine* 31 (1831): 484.

Gossipping. (First, a suggested poem title, as poem is motto for Chapter 12 titled "Gossipping"; then poem is given this title when included in Blanchard's selection of "Fragments" from *Ethel Churchill*).

1st line: "These are the spiders of society;"

in Landon, Letitia E. *Ethel Churchill: or, The Two Brides.* Vol. 2. London: Henry Colburn, 1837. 91;

in Blanchard, Laman. *Life and Literary Remains of L. E. L.* Vol. 2. London: Henry Colburn, 1841. 276.

The Grandmother.

1st line: "What care they that the winter-wind"

in *The Juvenile Forget-Me-Not: A Christmas and New-Year's Gift, or Birth-day Present. 1833.* Ed. Mrs. S. C. [Anna Maria] Hall. London: R. Ackermann, 1833 [1832]. 65-66.

The Grass-rope Bridge, at Teree, in the Province of Gurwall.

1st line: "We had to watch the fading"

in Landon, Letitia E. *Fisher's Drawing Room Scrap-Book.* London: Fisher, Son, and Jackson 1832 [1831]. 25.

The Grecian Garden.

1st line: "'Tis lonely as my own sad heart,"

in *The Literary Souvenir, and Cabinet of Modern Art [for 1835].* Ed. Alaric A. Watts. London: Whittaker, 1835 [1834]. 174-176.

Greece; or, the Slighted Clytie. (Appears elsewhere as "Mr. Martin's Picture of Clytie").

1st line: "It was a beautiful embodied thought,"

in *Ladies' Penny Gazette* 1 (Jan. 19, 1833): 99-100;

in *Ladies' Penny Gazette* 2 (July 26, 1834): 299.

The Greek Girl.

1st line: "Oh! not as I could once have sung, not as I once could sing —"

in *The Amulet; A Christian and Literary Remembrancer [for 1832].* Ed. S. C. Hall. London: Frederick Westley and A. H. Davis, 1832 [1831]. 87-90.

Greek Song.

1st line: "Well, fill the goblet, till the wave"

in *The Literary Gazette* 477 (March 11, 1826): 155.

The Grey Cross. (One of the "Fragments").

1st line: "A grey Cross stands beneath yon old beech tree;"

in Landon, Letitia E. *The Improvisatrice; and Other Poems.* London: Hurst, Robinson; Edinburgh: A. Constable, 1824. 289-90.

The Guerilla Chief.
> 1st line: "It stood beneath a large old chesnut-tree,"
> Prefixed lines begin: "But the war-storm came on the mountain gale,"
> in Landon, Letitia E. *The Improvisatrice; and Other Poems.* London: Hurst, Robinson; Edinburgh: A. Constable, 1824. 143-54.

Gulnare.
> 1st line: "Oh, never more the flowers will stoop"
> in Landon, Letitia E. *Heath's Book of Beauty. 1833.* London: Longman, Rees, Orme, Brown, Green, and Longman; Paris: Rittner and Goupil; Frankfort: C. Jügel, [1832]. 151-154

The Gypsy's Prophecy.
> 1st line: "Ladye, throw back thy raven hair,"
> in *The Literary Gazette* 351 (Oct. 11, 1824): 650.

Hagar and Ishmael.
> 1st line: "They sank amid the wilderness,"
> in Landon, Letitia E. *The Easter Gift, A Religious Offering.* London: Fisher, Son, 1832. 17-19.

Hall i' th' Wood.
> 1st line: "Change, change, wondrous change,"
> in Landon, Letitia E. *Fisher's Drawing Room Scrap-Book. 1833.* London: H. Fisher, R. Fisher, and P. Jackson, 1833 [1832]. 41.

The Hall of Glennaquoich.
> 1st line: "No more the voice of feasting is heard amid those halls,"
> in Landon, Letitia E. *Fisher's Drawing Room Scrap-Book, 1837.* London, Paris, and New York: Fisher, Son; Germany: Black and Armstrong, and Asher, 1836. 43.

The Hall of Statues.
> 1st line: "Rich the crimson curtains fell,"
> in *The Literary Gazette* 753 (June 25, 1831): 411-12.

Hannibal's Oath. (One of the "Sketches from History").
> 1st line: "And the night was dark and calm,"
> in Landon, Letitia E. *The Troubadour; Catalogue of Pictures, and Historical Sketches.* London: Hurst, Robinson; Edinburgh: A. Constable, 1825. 309-11.

Happiness Within. (One of the "Fragments" from *Ethel Churchill* selected by Blanchard; poem appears elsewhere as "[The Season]").
> 1st line: "And yet it is a wasted heart:"
> in Blanchard, Laman. *Life and Literary Remains of L. E. L.* Vol. 2. London: Henry Colburn, 1841. 290.

Happy Hours. (First publication of ms. dated May 31, 1836).
> 1st line: "Where are they — those happy hours,"
> in Blanchard, Laman. *Life and Literary Remains of L. E. L.* Vol. 1. London: Henry Colburn, 1841. 154-55.

The Happy Isle. (Part V of series, "Fragments in Rhyme").
> 1st line: "There was a light upon the stream,"
> in *The Literary Gazette* 306 (Nov. 30, 1822): 761.

Head of Ariadne. (Part of the series, "Medallion Wafers" in *The Literary Gazette*; one of the "Classical Sketches" in *The Vow of the Peacock, and Other Poems*).
> 1st line: "Oh, why should Woman ever love,"

in *The Literary Gazette* 319 (March 1, 1823): 139-40;

in Landon, Letitia E. *The Vow of the Peacock, and Other Poems.* London: Saunders and Otley, 1835. 143-45.

Head of Tyrtëus. (Part of the series, "Medallion Wafers").

1st line: "Glorious Bard! whose lyre was heard"

in *The Literary Gazette* 316 (Feb. 8, 1823): 91.

The Heart's Omens. (One of the "Fragments" from *Ethel Churchill* selected by Blanchard; poem appears elsewhere as "[The Truth of Presentiments]").

1st line: "I felt my sorrow ere it came,"

in Blanchard, Laman. *Life and Literary Remains of L. E. L.* Vol. 2. London: Henry Colburn, 1841. 284.

The Heath.

1st line: "Ah, gentle flower! on which the wind"

in Landon, Letitia E. *Flowers of Loveliness; Twelve Groups of Female Figures, Emblematic of Flowers.* London: R. Ackermann, 1838. N. pag. [2 pages].

Hebe.

1st line: "Youth! thou art a lovely time,"

in Landon, Letitia E. *Fisher's Drawing Room Scrap-Book, 1834.* London: H. Fisher, R. Fisher, and P. Jackson; Paris: Rittner and Goupil; New York: Jackson; Berlin and St. Petersburg: Asher, 1833. 48;

in *The Zenana and Minor Poems of L. E. L.* London: Fisher, Son; Paris: Quai de L'Ecole, [1839]. 117-18.

Hemans.

1st line: "Where the purple violet groweth"

in Landon, Letitia E. *The English Bijou Almanac for 1836.* London: Albert Schloss, [1835]. N. pag. [3 pages].

Henry IV. to the Fair Gabrielle.

1st line: "Nay, fling back that veil, — 'tis a shame to the sky"

in *The Literary Souvenir, and Cabinet of Modern Art [for 1835].* Ed. Alaric A. Watts. London: Whittaker, 1835 [1834]. 75-76.

Hercules and Iole. (Part of series, "Medallion Wafers").

1st line: "She held the cup; and he the while"

in *The Literary Gazette* 316 (Feb. 8, 1823): 91.

The Hermit's Grave.

1st line: "The days are gone when pilgrims knelt"

in *The Literary Gazette* 766 (Sept. 24, 1831): 620;

in *The Amulet [for 1836].* Ed. S. C. Hall. London: Frederick Westley and A. H. Davis, 1836 [1835]. 38-41.

Hindoo and Mahommedan Buildings.

1st line: "History hath but few pages — soon is told"

in Landon, Letitia E. *Fisher's Drawing Room Scrap-Book. 1835.* London: H. Fisher, R. Fisher, and P. Jackson. 1835 [1834]. 9-10.

The Hindoo Girl's Song.

1st line: "Float on — float on — my haunted bark,"

in Landon, Letitia E. *Fisher's Drawing Room Scrap-Book, 1836.* London and Paris: Fisher, Son; Berlin: Asher; New York: Jackson, [1835]. 16;

in *The Zenana and Minor Poems of L. E. L.* London: Fisher, Son; Paris: Quai de L'Ecole, [1839]. 195-96.

The Hindoo Mother. (Described as a "Vignette").

   1st line: "She leaves it to the sacred stream,"

   in Landon, Letitia E. *Fisher's Drawing Room Scrap-Book, 1836.* London and Paris: Fisher, Son; Berlin: Asher; New York: Jackson, [1835]. 5–6.

Hindoo Temples and Palace at Madura. (Poem appears elsewhere as "On an Engraving of Hindoo Temples").

   1st line: "Little the present careth for the past,"

   in Landon, Letitia E. *Fisher's Drawing Room Scrap-Book, 1836.* London and Paris: Fisher, Son; Berlin: Asher; New York: Jackson, [1835]. 50–51.

Hindoo Temples at Benares.

   1st line: "And day by day, and hour by hour,"

   in Landon, Letitia E. *Fisher's Drawing Room Scrap-Book. 1833.* London: H. Fisher, R. Fisher and P. Jackson, 1833 [1832]. 23.

Hindoo Temples on the Mountain-Lake of Aboo.

   1st line: "From the hills they descend, as wild as the river"

   in Landon, Letitia E. *Fisher's Drawing Room Scrap-Book, 1839.* London: Fisher, Son; Paris: Quai de L'Ecole, [1838]. 21.

The History of the Lily.

   1st line: "It grew within a lonely dell,"

   in *The Literary Gazette* 907 (June 7, 1834): 401–02.

A History of the Lyre.

   1st line: "'Tis strange how much is mark'd on memory,"

   Prefixed lines begin: "Sketches indeed, from that most passionate page,"

   in Landon, Letitia E. *The Venetian Bracelet, The Lost Pleiad, A History of the Lyre, and Other Poems.* London: Longman, Rees, Orme, Brown, and Green, 1829. 85–115.

Home.

   1st line: "Aye, here, dear love, is just a home,"

   in *Friendship's Offering, or, the Annual Remembrancer: A Christmas Present, or New Year's Gift, for 1825.* London: Lupton Relfe, 1825 [1824]. 200–02.

Home. (Part of "Fragments").

   1st line: "I left my home; — 'twas in a little vale,"

   in Landon, Letitia E. *The Improvisatrice; and Other Poems.* London: Hurst, Robinson; Edinburgh: A. Constable, 1824. 297–99.

Homes of Splendour.

   1st line: "When I see Homes, of Beauty and of Splendour,"

   in Norton, The Hon. Mrs. Caroline. *Fisher's Drawing Room Scrap-Book. 1849.* London: Peter Jackson, Late Fisher, Son, [1848]. 59–60.

Honister Crag. — Cumberland.

   1st line: "Not where the green grass hides"

   in Landon, Letitia E. *Fisher's Drawing Room Scrap-Book. 1835.* London: H. Fisher, R. Fisher, and P. Jackson, 1835 [1834]. 11.

Hope. (One of the "Fragments" from *Ethel Churchill* selected by Blanchard; poem appears elsewhere as "[A Poet's Midnight]").

   1st line: "Is not the lark companion of the spring?"

   in Blanchard, Laman. *Life and Literary Remains of L. E. L.* Vol. 2. London: Henry Colburn, 1841. 261.

Hope and Love. (One of the "Fragments from *Ethel Churchill* selected by Blanchard; poem appears elsewhere as "[A Project]" and as an untitled poem within a series of "Songs").

1st line: "The sun was setting o'er the sea,"
in Blanchard, Laman. *Life and Literary Remains of L. E. L.* Vol. 2. London: Henry Colburn, 1841. 284.

Hope, from a design by a Lady. (Part of the series, "Poetical Catalogue of Pictures").

1st line: "Radiant Spirit! first of all"
Prefixed lines begin: "She leant upon an Anchor, and a smile,"
in *The Literary Gazette* 321 (Mar. 15, 1823): 171.

Horse-shoe Fall, Niagara. The Indian Girl. (Poem appears elsewhere as "She Sat Alone Beside Her Hearth").

1st line: "She sat alone beside her hearth —"
in Landon, Letitia E. *Fisher's Drawing Room Scrap-Book, 1836.* London and Paris: Fisher, Son; Berlin: Asher; New York: Jackson, [1835]. 19-22.

The Hours, by Howard. (Printed under the series title, "Poetical Catalogue of Paintings": but to agree with the rest of the series, for "Paintings," read "Pictures"; poem is described in brackets as "Sketched from Sir John Leicester's Gallery," a description it shares with the poem, "The Female Head on the left of 'the Hours'").

1st line: "Wouldst thou know what life should be,"
in *The Literary Gazette* 328 (May 3, 1823): 286.

The House in which Roscoe was Born.

1st line: "A lowly roof, an English farm-house roof —"
in Landon, Letitia E. *Fisher's Drawing Room Scrap-Book [for 1832].* London: Fisher, Son, and Jackson, 1832 [1831]. 41.

Howth Light-house.

1st line: "Look from the lattice, look forth, my child —"
in Landon, Letitia E. *Fisher's Drawing Room Scrap-Book. 1835.* London: H. Fisher, R. Fisher, and P. Jackson, 1835 [1834]. 33.

Humanity Angelic. (One of the "Fragments" from *Ethel Churchill* selected by Blanchard; poem appears elsewhere as "[The Sick Room]").

1st line: "If ever angels walked on weary earth"
in Blanchard, Laman. *Life and Literary Remains of L. E. L.* Vol. 2. London: Henry Colburn, 1841. 275.

Hurdwar — The Gate of Vishnoo.

1st line: "Fling wide the sacred city gates"
in Landon, Letitia E. *Fisher's Drawing Room Scrap-Book, 1838.* London, Paris, and New York: Fisher, Son; Germany: Black and Armstrong, and Asher, 1837. 42.

Hurdwar, a Place of Hindoo Pilgrimage.

1st line: "I love the feeling which, in former days,"
in Landon, Letitia E. *Fisher's Drawing Room Scrap Book.* London: Fisher, Son, and Jackson, 1832 [1831]. 18.

The Huron's Child. — Herder. (Translation; poem is part of Fourth Series of "Versions from the German").

1st line: "The only child within the tent"
in *The Literary Gazette* 940 (Jan. 24, 1835): 59.

The Hyacinth.
　　1st line: "Where is the bee its sweetest music bringing, —"
　　in Landon, Letitia E. *Flowers of Loveliness; Twelve Groups of Female Figures, Emblematic of Flowers.* London: R. Ackermann, 1838. N. pag. [2 pages].
I knew I loved in vain. (Part of series of "Songs").
　　1st line: "I knew I lov'd in vain;"
　　in *The Literary Gazette* 429 (Apr. 9, 1825): 236.
Ideal Likenesses.
　　1st line: "A sweet but happy looking face, the mouth"
　　in *The New Monthly Magazine* 14 (1825): 485-86.
Illusion. (One of the "Fragments" from *Ethel Churchill* selected by Blanchard; poem appears elsewhere as "[Different Views of Life]"; poem is an altered version of "Moralising").
　　1st line: "And thus it is with all that made life fair,"
　　in Blanchard, Laman. *Life and Literary Remains of L. E. L.* Vol. 2. London: Henry Colburn, 1841. 293.
Imitations of Servian Poetry [contains one untitled poem]. (This series also contains, on the same page, poems titled "Song," "The Falcon-Messenger," and "Song").
　　1st line: "The maiden turned her head away —"
　　in *The Literary Gazette* 538 (May 12, 1827): 300.
Immolation of a Hindoo Widow. (Poem appears elsewhere as "A Suttee").
　　1st line: "Gather her raven hair in one rich cluster,"
　　in Landon, Letitia E. *Fisher's Drawing Room Scrap-Book, 1836.* London and Paris: Fisher, Son; Berlin: Asher; New York: Jackson, [1835]. 7.
Immortality. (One of the "Fragments" from Ethel Churchill selected by Blanchard; poem appears elsewhere as "[The Last Letter]").
　　1st line: "Strong as the death it masters, is the hope"
　　in Blanchard, Laman. *Life and Literary Remains of L. E. L.* Vol. 2. London: Henry Colburn, 1841. 287.
The Improvisatrice.
　　1st line: "I am a daughter of that land,"
　　in Landon, Letitia E. *The Improvisatrice; and Other Poems.* London: Hurst, Robinson; Edinburgh: A. Constable, 1824. 1-105.
Inconstancy. (First, a suggested poem title, as poem is the fourth in a group of six poems described as "Six Songs of Love, Constancy, Romance, Inconstancy, Truth, and Marriage"; then poem is given that title in *The Lyre*).
　　1st line: "How vain to cast my love away"
　　in *The Literary Gazette* 251 (Nov. 10, 1821): 716;
　　in *The Lyre. Fugitive Poetry of the Nineteenth Century.* London: Tilt and Bogue, 1841. 323-24.
The Inconstant.
　　1st line: "And deem'st thou that my heart could be"
　　in *The Literary Souvenir; or, Cabinet of Poetry and Romance [for 1827].* Ed. Alaric A. Watts. London: Longman, Rees, Orme, Brown, and Green; and John Andrews, 1827 [1826]. 248-49.
The Incredulity of St. Thomas.
　　1st line: "Still doth that spirit linger upon earth;"
　　in Landon, Letitia E. *The Easter Gift, A Religious Offering.* London: Fisher, Son, 1832. 37-40.

The Indian Girl. (See "Horse-shoe Fall, Niagara. The Indian Girl").

Indian Song. Founded on a romantic species of Divination practised by Indian Maidens. (Part of the Third Series of "Fragments by L. E. L.").

　1st line: "To the moonlit waters of the lake"

　Prefixed lines to series begin: "Gleamings of poetry, — if I may give"

　in *The Literary Gazette* 365 (Jan. 17, 1824): 41.

Inez. (One of the "Fragments" in *The Improvisatrice; and Other Poems*).

　1st line: "The lips that breathed this song were fair"

　Prefixed lines begin: "Alas, that clouds should ever steal"

　in *The Literary Gazette* 331 (May 24, 1823): 332-33;

　in Landon, Letitia E. *The Improvisatrice; and Other Poems.* London: Hurst, Robinson; Edinburgh: A. Constable, 1824. 271-81.

The Infant Christ With Flowers.

　1st line: "Sweet Lord, as in those infant hands"

　in Landon, Letitia E. *The Easter Gift, A Religious Offering.* London: Fisher, Son, 1832. 34.

The Infant St. John.

　1st line: "Lo, on the midnight winds a young child's voice"

　in Landon, Letitia E. *The Easter Gift, A Religious Offering.* London: Fisher, Son, 1832. 41-44.

Infanticide in Madagascar.

　1st line: "A luxury of summer green"

　in Landon, Letitia E. *Fisher's Drawing Room Scrap-Book, 1838.* London, Paris, and New York: Fisher, Son; Germany: Black and Armstrong, and Asher, 1837. 40-41.

Infidelity. (Sketch the Second in the Fifth Series of "Poetic Sketches").

　1st line: "There were three lovely pictures. In the first"

　Prefixed lines begin: "And in that Castle was a pictured hall,"

　in *The Literary Gazette* 392 (July 24, 1824): 475.

The Influence of the Dead. (First, a suggested poem title, as poem is the motto for Chapter 34 titled "The Influence of the Dead"; poem then is given this title when included in Blanchard's selection of "Fragments" from *Ethel Churchill*).

　1st line: "Who are the spirits watching by the dead?"

　in Landon, Letitia E. *Ethel Churchill: or, The Two Brides.* Vol. 2. London: Henry Colburn, 1837. 267;

　in Blanchard, Laman. *Life and Literary Remains of L. E. L.* Vol. 2. London: Henry Colburn, 1841. 280.

[The Influence of an Invitation]. (Suggested poem title, as poem is the motto for Chapter 3 titled "The Influence of an Invitation"; poem appears elsewhere as "The Littleness of Life").

　1st line: "Life is so little in its vanities,"

　in Landon, Letitia E. *Ethel Churchill: or, The Two Brides.* Vol. 3. London: Henry Colburn, 1837. 13.

Influence of Poetry. (One of the "Fragments" from *Ethel Churchill* selected by Blanchard; poem appears elsewhere as "[Sir Robert Walpole and House]").

　1st line: "This is the charm of poetry: it comes"

　in Blanchard, Laman. *Life and Literary Remains of L. E. L.* Vol. 2. London: Henry Colburn, 1841. 282.

Interior of a Moorish Palace.

　1st line: "Hamooda holds a feast to-night —"

in Howitt, Mary and Letitia E. Landon. *Fisher's Drawing Room Scrap-Book. 1840.* London: Fisher, Son; Paris: Quai de L'Ecole, [1839]. 9.

Interior of the Warwick Chapel.
1st line: "Low before the cross she weepeth,"
in [Collier, J. and Letitia E. Landon]. *The Pictorial Album; or, Cabinet of Paintings. For the Year 1837.* Illus. George Baxter. London: Chapman and Hall, 1837. 43-45.

[An Interview]. (Suggested poem title, as poem is the motto for Chapter 27 titled "An Interview"; poem appears elsewhere as "Pride in Trifles").
1st line: "Why, life must mock itself to mark how small"
in Landon, Letitia E. *Ethel Churchill: or, The Two Brides.* Vol. 2. London: Henry Colburn, 1837. 208.

Introduction.
1st line: "And has my heart enough of song"
in Landon, Letitia E. *Fisher's Drawing Room Scrap-Book. 1835.* London: H. Fisher, R. Fisher, and P. Jackson, 1835 [1834]. 1-3.

Introduction.
1st line: "Another year — again our page"
in Landon, Letitia E. *Fisher's Drawing Room Scrap-Book, 1837.* London, Paris, and New York: Fisher, Son; Germany: Black and Armstrong, and Asher, 1836. 3-5.

Introduction. (Part of the series, "Medallion Wafers").
1st line: "I do so prize the slightest thing"
in *The Literary Gazette* 314 (Jan. 25, 1823): 60.

[Introduction]. (Suggested poem title, as poem is the motto for Chapter 18 titled "Introduction"; poem appears elsewhere as "Necessity").
1st line: "In the ancestral presence of the dead"
in Landon, Letitia E. *Ethel Churchill: or, The Two Brides.* Vol. 3. London: Henry Colburn, 1837. 133.

The Ionian Captive. ("Her" changed to "the" in first line in *The Zenana and Minor Poems*).
1st line: "Sadly the captive o'er her flowers is bending,"
in Landon, Letitia E. *Fisher's Drawing Room Scrap-Book, 1838.* London, Paris, and New York: Fisher, Son; Germany: Black and Armstrong, and Asher, 1837. 28;
in *The Zenana and Minor Poems of L. E. L.* London: Fisher, Son; Paris: Quai de L'Ecole, [1839]. 264-66.

The Iris.
1st line: "It boots not keeping back the scroll,"
in Landon, Letitia E. *Flowers of Loveliness; Twelve Groups of Female Figures, Emblematic of Flowers.* London: R. Ackermann, 1838. N. pag. [2 pages].

The Island. (Sketch V in Fourth Series of "Poetic Sketches").
1st line: "A summer isle, one over which the wind"
Prefixed lines begin: "Adieu, adieu, thou faithless world,"
in *The Literary Gazette* 360 (Dec. 13, 1823): 793-94.

Ismael Fitzadam. (See "On the Death of Ismael Fitzadam" and "Lines Suggested by the Death of Ismael Fitzadam").

Ithaca. (Poem appears elsewhere as "Town and Harbour of Ithaca").
1st line: "By another light surrounded"
in *The Zenana and Minor Poems of L. E. L.* London: Fisher, Son; Paris: Quai de L'Ecole, [1839]. 238-40.

Ivy Bridge, Devonshire. (Poem set to music by Henry Russell, printed on pages 29-30).
1st line: "O, recall not the past, though this valley be filled"
in Landon, Letitia E. *Fisher's Drawing Room Scrap-Book. 1835*. London: H. Fisher, R. Fisher, and P. Jackson, 1835 [1834]. 28.

Jacob Blessing Ephraim and Manasseh.
1st line: "The old man's head is white with age,"
in Landon, Letitia E. *Fisher's Drawing Room Scrap-Book, 1839*. London: Fisher, Son; Paris: Quai de L'Ecole, [1838]. 15;
in *The Wesleyan-Methodist Magazine* 17 (1838): 880.

Jahara Baug, Agra. The History of Shah Dara's Flight and Death.
1st line: "It was the lovely twilight-time went down o'er Agra's towers,"
in Landon, Letitia E. *Fisher's Drawing Room Scrap Book . 1835*. London: H. Fisher, R. Fisher, and P. Jackson, 1835 [1834]. 24-25.

Jesuits in Procession — Valetta, Malta.
1st line: "Whence rose the sect that 'neath yon azure dome,"
in Landon, Letitia E. *Fisher's Drawing Room Scrap-Book, 1838*. London, Paris, and New York: Fisher, Son; Germany: Black and Armstrong, and Asher, 1837. 6.

[The Jewels Given]. (Suggested poem title, as poem is the motto for Chapter 22 titled "The Jewels Given"; poem appears elsewhere as "Gentleness Pictured").
1st line: "A gentle creature was that girl,"
in Landon, Letitia E. *Ethel Churchill: or, The Two Brides.* Vol. 1. London: Henry Colburn, 1837. 212.

John Kemble.
1st line: "Oh! glorious triumph, thus to sway at will"
in Landon, Letitia E. *Fisher's Drawing Room Scrap-Book, 1834*. London: H.Fisher, R. Fisher, and P. Jackson; Paris: Rittner and Goupil; Berlin and St. Petersburg: Asher; New York: Jackson, 1833. 34.

Judas Returning the Thirty Pieces.
1st line: "The thirty pieces down he flung, for which his Lord he sold,"
in Landon, Letitia E. *The Easter Gift, A Religious Offering*. London: Fisher, Son, 1832 [1831]. 25-26.

Juliet After the Masquerade. By Thompson. (One of the "Poetical Sketches of Modern Pictures"; poem appears in a variant form as "Juliet After the Masquerade. From a Picture by Thom[p]son").
1st line: "She left the festival, for it seem'd dim"
in Landon, Letitia E. *The Troubadour; Catalogue of Pictures, and Historical Sketches.* London: Hurst, Robinson; Edinburgh: A. Constable, 1825. 260-64.

Juliet After The Masquerade. From a Picture, by Henry Thom[p]son, Esq., R.A.. (Poem is a variant of "Juliet After the Masquerade. By Thompson").
1st line: "She has left the lighted hall,"
Prefixed lines begin: "Those fond, vague dreams, that make love's happiness;"
in *The Literary Souvenir; or, Cabinet of Poetry and Romance [for 1828]*. Ed. Alaric A. Watts. London: Longman, Rees, Orme, Brown, and Green, 1828 [1827]. 57-61.

The Jumma Musjid. — The Principal Mosque at Agra.
1st line: "Yon mosque alone remains to tell,"
in Landon, Letitia E. *Fisher's Drawing Room Scrap-Book [for 1832]*. London: Fisher, Son, and Jackson, 1832 [1831]. 42.

Kalendria. A Port in Cilicia.
1st line: "Do you see yon vessel riding,"

in Landon, Letitia E. *Fisher's Drawing Room Scrap-Book, 1838*. London, Paris, and New York: Fisher, Son; Germany: Black and Armstrong, and Asher, 1837. 38-39.

"Kate is Craz'd."
> 1st line: "How wonderful! how beautiful! these words"
> Prefixed lines by Cowper begin: "There often wanders one, whom better days"
> in Howitt, Mary and Letitia E. Landon. *Fisher's Drawing Room Scrap-Book. 1840*. London: Fisher, Son, [1839]. 10.

Kate Kearney. (Poem appears elsewhere as "The Upper Lake of Killarney").
> 1st line: "Why doth the maiden turn away"
> in *The Zenana and Minor Poems of L.E.L.* London: Fisher, Son; Paris: Quai de L'Ecole, [1839]. 72-74.

The Keepsake.
> 1st line: "Oh! do not take the picture,"
> in Landon, Letitia. *Fisher's Drawing Room Scrap-Book*. London: Fisher, Son; Paris: Quai de L'Ecole, [1838]. 30;
> in *Blackwood's Lady's Magazine* 6 (March 1839): 147-48.

The Kings of Golconda. (Poem appears elsewhere as "The Tombs of the Kings of Golconda").
> 1st line: "Morning is round the shining palace,"
> in *The Zenana and Minor Poems of L. E. L.* London: Fisher, Son; Paris: Quai de L'Ecole, [1839]. 252-57.

The Knight.
> 1st line: "Farewell to thee, dearest! my banner is playing"
> in *The Literary Gazette* 377 (April 10, 1824): 236.

The Knight's Tale. (Third sketch in Fifth Series of "Poetic Sketches" in *The Literary Gazette*; one of "A Series of Tales" in *The Vow of the Peacock, and Other Poems*).
> 1st line: "And there are bitter tears in Arnold's hall —"
> Prefixed lines begin: "Oh, there are evil moments in our life,"
> in *The Literary Gazette* 393 (July 31, 1824): 492-93;
> in Landon, Letitia E. *The Vow of the Peacock, and Other Poems*. London: Saunders and Otley, 1835. 216-227.

Körner's Grave. — Anon. (Translation; poem is part of Third Series of "Versions from the German").
> 1st line: "Where is my soldier's grave — where have you laid him?"
> in *The Literary Gazette* 939 (Jan. 17, 1835): 44.

The Kylas, Caves of Ellora.
> 1st line: "The East, it is thy birth-place, thou bright sun;"
> in Landon, Letitia E. *Fisher's Drawing Room Scrap-Book. 1833*. London: H. Fisher, R. Fisher, and P. Jackson, 1833 [1832]. 47.

[The Laboratory]. (Suggested poem title, as poem is the motto for Chapter 41 titled "The Laboratory"; poem appears elsewhere as "Death in the Flower").
> 1st line: "'Tis a fair tree, the almond-tree: there Spring"
> in Landon, Letitia E. *Ethel Churchill: or, The Two Brides*. Vol. 2. London: Henry Colburn, 1837. 324.

Lady Blessington.
> 1st line: "Yet on the haunted canvas dwells"
> in Landon, Letitia E. *Schloss's English Bijou Almanac for 1839*. London: Albert Schloss, [1838]. N. pag. [3 pages].

Lady Caroline Maxsé.
    1st line: "Lady, lovely lady mine,"
    in *Heath's Book of Beauty. 1836.* Ed. Marguerite Blessington, the Countess of. London: Longman, Rees, Orme, Brown, Green, and Longman; Paris: Rittner and Goupil; Berlin: A. Asher, [1835]. 62-63.

The Lady Egerton.
    1st line: "I know not of thy history —"
    in *Heath's Book of Beauty. 1836.* Ed. Marguerite Blessington, the Countess of. London: Longman, Rees, Orme, Brown, Green, and Longman; Paris: Rittner and Goupil; Berlin: A. Asher, [1835]. 191-92.

[Lady Marchmont's Journal]. (Suggested poem title, as poem is the motto for Chapter 18 titled "Lady Marchmont's Journal"; poem appears elsewhere as "Self-Reproach").
    1st line: "Deep in the heart is an avenging power,"
    in Landon, Letitia E. *Ethel Churchill: or, The Two Brides.* Vol. 3. London: Henry Colburn, 1837. 118.

[Lady Marchmont's Journal]. (Suggested poem title, as poem is the motto for Chapter 12 titled "Lady Marchmont's Journal"; poem appears elsewhere as "The Mask of Gaiety").
    1st line: "'Tis strange to think, if we could fling aside"
    in Landon, Letitia E. *Ethel Churchill: or, The Two Brides.* Vol. 3. London: Henry Colburn, 1837. 82.

[Lady Marchmont's Journal]. (Suggested poem title, as poem is the motto for Chapter 21 titled "Lady Marchmont's Journal"; poem consists of a few stanzas from "We Might Have Been").
    1st line: "We might have been! — these are but common words,"
    in Landon, Letitia E. *Ethel Churchill: or, The Two Brides.* Vol. 3. London: Henry Colburn, 1837. 158.

The Lady Marian.
    1st line: "Her silken cloak around her thrown,"
    in Landon, Letitia E. *Traits and Trials of Early Life.* London: Henry Colburn, 1836. 115-18.

A Lady's Beauty. (One of the "Fragments" from *Ethel Churchill* selected by Blanchard; poem appears elsewhere as "[The Fête at Sir Walpole's Continued]").
    1st line: "Ladye, thy white brow is fair,"
    in Blanchard, Laman. *Life and Literary Remains of L. E. L.* Vol. 2. London: Henry Colburn, 1841. 291.

The Lake. (Part of the series, "Landscapes").
    1st line: "The last pale light was on the sky,"
    in *The Literary Gazette* 402 (Oct. 2, 1824): 636.

The Lake of Como.
    1st line: "Again I am beside the lake,"
    in Landon, Letitia E. *Fisher's Drawing Room Scrap-Book, 1837.* London, Paris, and New York: Fisher, Son; Germany: Black and Armstrong, and Asher, 1836. 21.

Lament for the Past Year. (Poem in First Series of "Fragments by L. E. L.").
    1st line: "Farewell, thou shadowy Year, farewell!"
    Prefixed lines to First Series begin: "Gleamings of poetry, — if I may give"
    in *The Literary Gazette* 363 (Jan. 3, 1824): 10.

L'Amore Dominatore. (Part of "Classical Sketches" in *The Vow of the Peacock, and Other Poems*).

1st line: "They built a temple for the God,"
in *The Literary Souvenir; or, Cabinet of Poetry and Romance [for 1826]*. Ed. Alaric A. Watts. London: Hurst, Robinson; Edinburgh: A. Constable, 1826 [1825]. 247-51;
in Landon, Letitia E. *The Vow of the Peacock, and Other Poems*. London: Saunders and Otley, 1835. 154-61.

The Lamp. (Part of Sixth Series of "Fragments by L. E. L.").

1st line: "Brightly the stars shed their light,"
Prefixed lines to series begin: "Gleamings of poetry, — if I may give"
in *The Literary Gazette* 368 (Feb. 7, 1824): 91.

Lancaster.

1st line: "Oh, pleasant on a winter night,"
in Landon, Letitia E. *Fisher's Drawing Room Scrap-Book. 1833*. London: H. Fisher, R. Fisher, and P. Jackson, 1833 [1832]. 28-30.

Lancaster Castle.

1st line: "Dark with age these towers look down"
in Landon, Letitia E. *Fisher's Drawing Room Scrap-Book, 1837*. London, Paris, and New York: Fisher, Son; Germany: Black and Armstrong, and Asher, 1836. 41.

Langdale Pikes.

1st line: "Rise up, rise up, the cheerful sun"
in Landon, Letitia E. *Fisher's Drawing Room Scrap-Book,. 1833*. London: H. Fisher, R. Fisher, and P. Jackson, 1833 [1832]. 27.

[The Last Letter]. (Suggested poem title, as poem is the motto for Chapter 35 titled "The Last Letter"; poem appears elsewhere as "Immortality").

1st line: "Strong as the death it masters, is the hope"
in Landon, Letitia E. *Ethel Churchill: or, The Two Brides*. Vol. 2. London: Henry Colburn, 1837. 282.

The Last Look.

1st line: "The shade of the willow fell dark on the tide,"
in *The New Monthly Magazine* 31 (1831): 71;
in Blanchard, Laman. *Life and Literary Remains of L. E. L.* Vol. 2. London: Henry Colburn, 1841. 301-02.

The Last Night with the Dead. (First, a suggested poem title, as poem is the motto for Chapter 39 titled "The Last Night with the Dead"; poem then is given this title when included in Blanchard's selection of "Fragments" from *Ethel Churchill*).

1st line: "How awful is the presence of the dead!"
in Landon, Letitia E. *Ethel Churchill: or, The Two Brides*. Vol. 2. London: Henry Colburn, 1837. 313;
in Blanchard, Laman. *Life and Literary Remains of L. E. L.* Vol. 2. London: Henry Colburn, 1841. 282.

The Last of the St. Aubyns.

1st line: "And here they met: — where should Love's meeting be —"
in Landon, Letitia E. *Heath's Book of Beauty. 1833*. London: Longman, Rees, Orme, Brown, Green, and Longman; Paris: Rittner, Goupil; Frankfort: C. Jügel, [1832]. 259-64.

The Last Request.

1st line: "Sinking on his couch he lies —"
in Landon, Letitia E. *Fisher's Drawing Room Scrap-Book, 1839*. London: Fisher, Son;

Paris: Quai de L'Ecole, [1838]. 39.

The Last Song of Corinne. (Translation of a French ode by Madame de Staël in Book 20, Chapter 5).

1st line: "Take ye my solemn farewell! O my friends"

in Staël-Holstein, Anne Louise Germaine de. *Corinne; or Italy.* Trans. Isabel Hill ["with metrical versions of the odes by L. E. Landon"]. Standard Novels. 24. London: Richard Bentley; Dublin: Cumming; Edinburgh: Bell and Bradfute; Paris: Galignani, 1833. 385-88.

[A Late Breakfast]. (Suggested poem title, as poem is motto for Chapter 10 titled "A Late Breakfast"; poem appears elsewhere as "Faith Destroyed").

1st line: "Why did I love him? I looked up to him"

in Landon, Letitia E. *Ethel Churchill: or, The Two Brides.* Vol. 3. London: Henry Colburn, 1837. 68.

The Laurel.

1st line: "Not to the silent bitterness of tears"

Prefixed lines begin: "Fling down the Laurel from her golden hair;"

in Landon, Letitia E. *Flowers of Loveliness; Twelve Groups of Female Figures, Emblematic of Flowers.* London: Ackermann, 1838. N. pag. [2 pages].

Le Chapeau Noir.

1st line: "A courtly beauty — one whose life"

in *The Amulet [for 1836].* Ed. S. C. Hall. London: Frederick Westley and A. H. Davis, 1836 [1835]. 226-28.

Leander And Hero. (Part of "Classical Sketches" in *The Vow of the Peacock, and Other Poems*).

1st line: "It is a tale that many songs have told,"

in *The Literary Gazette* 318 (Feb. 22, 1823): 124;

in Landon, Letitia E. *The Vow of the Peacock, and Other Poems.*. London: Saunders and Otley, 1835. 133-42.

The Legacy.

1st line: "The same, yet not the same — her face"

in *The Amulet; A Christian and Literary Remembrancer [for 1831].* Ed. S. C. Hall. London: Frederick Westley and A. H. Davis, 1831 [1830]. 277-79.

The Legacy of the Lute.

1st line: "Come, take the lute — the lute I loved,"

in *The Literary Gazette* 578 (Feb. 16, 1828): 107;

in Landon, Letitia E. *The Vow of the Peacock, and Other Poems.* London: Saunders and Otley, 1835. 338-40.

The Legacy of the Roses.

1st line: "Oh! plant them above me, the soft, the bright,"

in *The Literary Gazette* 709 (Aug. 21, 1830): 548.

A Legend of Teignmouth.

1st line: "Some few brief hours, my gallant bark,"

Prefixed lines begin: "A story of the olden time, when hearts"

in Landon, Letitia E. *Fisher's Drawing Room Scrap-Book, 1834.* London: H.Fisher, R. Fisher, and P.Jackson; Paris: Rittner, Goupil; Berlin and St. Petersburg: Asher; New York: Jackson, 1833. 38-40.

A Legend of Tintagel Castle.

1st line: "Alone in the forest, Sir Lancelot rode"

in Landon, Letitia E. *Fisher's Drawing Room Scrap-Book. 1833.* London: H. Fisher, R.

Fisher, and P. Jackson, 1833 [1832]. 8-9;
in *The Zenana and Minor Poems of L.E.L.* London: Fisher, Son; Paris: Quai de
L'Ecole, [1839]. 85-89.

Legendary Fragments.
1st line: "'And we meet thus again?' he said;"
Prefixed lines begin: "The lady turn'd her weary from a world;"
in *The Keepsake for 1831.* Ed Frederic Mansel Reynolds. London: Hurst, Chance;
Jennings, Chaplin, [1830]. 172-75.

Leonora. (Poem appears in an altered version elsewhere as "Unavailing Regret").
1st line: "Farewell! and when the charm of change"
Prefixed lines begin: "She was the loveliest lady of our line,"
in Landon, Letitia E. *Heath's Book of Beauty. 1833.* London: Longman, Rees, Orme,
Brown, Green, and Longman; Paris: Rittner, Goupil; Frankfort: C. Jügel, [1832]. 54.

The Lesson.
1st line: "Come, dearest, to your lesson,"
in *The Juvenile Forget-Me-Not: A Christmas and New-Year's Gift, or Birth-day
Present. 1836.* Ed. Mrs. S. C. [Anna Maria] Hall. London: Frederick Westley and A.
H. Davis, 1836 [1835]. 150-51.

[The Letters]. (Suggested poem title, as poem is the motto for Chapter 26 titled "The
Letters").
1st line: "It is a weary and a bitter hour"
in Landon, Letitia E. *Ethel Churchill: or, The Two Brides.* Vol. 3. London: Henry Col-
burn, 1837. 194.

[The Letters Restored]. (Suggested poem title, as poem is the motto for Chapter 28
titled "The Letters Restored"; poem appears elsewhere as "Remorse").
1st line: "Alas! he brings me back my early years,"
in Landon, Letitia E. *Ethel Churchill: or, The Two Brides.* Vol. 3. London: Henry Col-
burn, 1837. 215.

Lezione per L'Amore.
1st line: "Where, oh, where's the chain to fling,"
in *The Literary Gazette* 469 (Jan. 14, 1826): 26.
as "Song" in *The Golden Violet, with its Tales of Romance and Chivalry: and Other
Poems.* London: Longman, Rees, Orme, Brown, and Green, 1827

Life.
1st line: "It is in vain —"
in *The Literary Gazette* 487 (May 20, 1826): 316.

Life's Mask. (One of the "Fragments" from *Ethel Churchill* selected by Blanchard; poem
appears elsewhere as an "[untitled poem]").
1st line: "Which was the true philosopher? — the sage"
in Blanchard, Laman. *Life and Literary Remains of L.E.L.* Vol. 2. London: Henry
Colburn, 1841. 261.

Life Surveyed. (One of the "Fragments" from *Ethel Churchill* selected by Blanchard;
poem appears elsewhere as "[Courtiers]").
1st line: "Not in a close and bounded atmosphere"
in Blanchard, Laman. *Life and Literary Remains of L. E. L.* Vol. 2. London: Henry
Colburn, 1841. 267.

Lights and Shadows. (Part of Fifth Series of "Fragments by L. E. L.").
1st line: "It spread beneath the summer sky,"
Prefixed lines to series begin: "Gleamings of poetry, — if I may give"

in *The Literary Gazette* 367 (Jan. 31, 1824): 74.

The Lily of the Valley.
> 1st line: "It is the last token of love and of thee!"
> Prefixed lines begin: "A fair young face — yet mournful in its youth —"
> in Landon, Letitia E. *Fisher's Drawing Room Scrap-Book, 1836.* London and Paris: Fisher, Son; Berlin: Asher; New York: Jackson, [1835]. 9-10.

Lincoln Cathedral.
> 1st line: "'Twas the deep forest bodied forth that fane,"
> in Landon, Letitia. *Fisher's Drawing Room Scrap-Book, 1837.* London, Paris, and New York: Fisher, Son; Germany: Black and Armstrong, and Asher, 1836. 15.

Lines.
> 1st line: "She kneels by the grave where her lover sleeps;"
> in Landon, Letitia E. *The Fate of Adelaide, A Swiss Romantic Tale; and Other Poems.* London: John Warren, 1821. 139-40.

Lines.
> 1st line: "There is no smile to answer thine,"
> Prefixed lines begin: "Dear Child, we now are left alone on earth,"
> in *The Literary Gazette* 343 (Aug. 16, 1823): 524.

Lines Addressed to Alaric A. Watts, Esq. on receiving a Copy of his Poetical Fragments and Sketches. (Poem appears elsewhere as "To Alaric A. Watts, Esq." and as "To the Author of 'Poetical Sketches'").
> 1st line: "There is a dear and a lovely power"
> in *The Literary Gazette* 355 (Nov. 8, 1823): 715.

Lines Addressed to Colonel H———, on his Return from Waterloo.
> 1st line: "Who envies not the glory of the brave!"
> in Landon, Letitia E. *The Fate of Adelaide, A Swiss Romantic Tale; and Other Poems.* London: John Warren, 1821. 101-02.

Lines Addressed To Miss Bisset.
> 1st line: "Came it not like enchantment on the soul,"
> in Landon, Letitia E. *The Fate of Adelaide, A Swiss Romantic Tale; and Other Poems.* London: John Warren, 1821. 135-36.

Lines. The Feast of Life. (Poem appears elsewhere as "The Feast of Life").
> 1st line: "I bid thee to my mystic Feast,"
> in *The Bijou; or Annual of Literature and the Arts [for 1829].* London: William Pickering, 1829 [1828]. 118.

Lines of Life.
> 1st line: "Well, read my cheek, and watch my eye, —"
> Prefixed lines begin: "Orphan in my first years, I early learnt"
> in Landon, Letitia E. *The Venetian Bracelet, The Lost Pleiad, A History of the Lyre, and Other Poems.* London: Longman, Rees, Orme, Brown, and Green, 1829. 265-74;
> in *The Ladies' Wreath; A Selection from the Female Poetic Writers of England and America.* Ed. Mrs. Sarah J. Hale. Boston: Marsh, Capen, and Lyon; New York: D. Appleton, 1837. 119-22.

Lines on ——.
> 1st line: "I saw thy cheek when 'twas fresh as spring,"
> in Landon, Letitia E. *The Fate of Adelaide, A Swiss Romantic Tale; and Other Poems.* London: John Warren, 1821. 88-90.

Lines on the Bust of a Lady.
> 1st line: "A face of perfect beauty, such as haunts"

in *The Amulet. A Christian and Literary Remembrancer [for 1833]*. Ed. S. C. Hall. London: Frederick Westley and A. H. Davis, 1833 [1832]. 214.

Lines on Curran's Picture.
    1st line: "Oh! is it not a gallant sight to mark"
    in Landon, Letitia E. *Fisher's Drawing Room Scrap-Book [for 1832]*. London: Fisher, Son, and Jackson, 1832 [1831]. 29-30.

Lines on the Mausoleum of the Princess Charotte at Clarement.
    1st line: "Alas! how many storm-clouds hang"
    in *The Gentlemen's Magazine* 94 (Jan. 1824): 71-72.

Lines on May Day. From a Picture by Leslie. (See "On May-Day, by Leslie").

Lines on Newton's Picture of the Disconsolate.
    1st line: "The room was hung with pictures, and the tints"
    Prefixed lines begin: "The present is the painter's — never words"
    in *The Literary Gazette* 630 (Feb. 14, 1829): 113.

Lines on the Portrait of Mrs. Maberly.
    1st line: "What may be the music"
    in *Heath's Book of Beauty. 1839*. Ed. Marguerite Blessington, Countess of. London: Longman, Rees, Orme, Brown, Green, and Longman, 1839 [1838]. 179.

Lines. Suggested by a Drawing of W. Daniel's, Esq. A.R.A., representing the Hindoo Girls floating their Tributary Offerings down the Ganges.
    1st line: "They bend above the moonlit stream,"
    in *The Literary Gazette* 1034 (Nov. 12, 1836): 730.

Lines Suggested by the Death of Ismael Fitzadam. (Part of article, "Neglected Genius. No. 1. Ismael Fitzadam"; poem is an altered version of "On the Death of Ismael Fitzadam").
    1st line: "It was a harp just fit to pour"
    in *The Literary Magnet* 2 (1826): 203-04.

Lines Suggested on Visiting Newstead Abbey.
    1st line: "What makes the poet? — Nothing but to feel"
    in Landon, Letitia E. *Fisher's Drawing Room Scrap-Book, 1839*. London: Fisher, Son; Paris: Quai de L'Ecole, [1838]. 44-45.

Lines. Supposed to be the prayer of the Supplicating Nymph in Mr. Lawrence Macdonald's Exhibition of Sculpture.
    1st line: "The myrtle wreath that I have laid"
    in *The Literary Gazette* 741 (April 2, 1831): 220.

Lines to —.
    1st line: "No, no! thou hast broken the spell that entwin'd me —"
    in Landon, Letitia E. *The Fate of Adelaide, A Swiss Romantic Tale; and Other Poems*. London: John Warren, 1821. 133-34.

Lines to —.
    1st line: "Think of me, and I'll tell thee when"
    in Landon, Letitia. *The Fate of Adelaide, A Swiss Romantic Tale; and Other Poems*. London: John Warren, 1821. 71-72.

Lines to the Author after Reading the Sorrows of Rosalie. (Poem appears elsewhere as "To the Author of the Sorrows of Rosalie").
    1st line: "They tell me, lady, that thy face"
    Prefixed lines begin: "One of those gifted ones that walk the earth,"
    in *The Literary Gazette* 628 (Jan. 31, 1829): 76.

Lines written under a Picture of a Girl burning a Love-letter. (Part II in series, "Fragments in Rhyme" in *The Literary Gazette*; one of the "Fragments" in *The Improvisatrice; and Other Poems*).

    1st line: "I took the scroll: I could not brook"
    Prefixed lines begin: "The lines were filled with many a tender thing,"
    in *The Literary Gazette* 304 (Nov. 16, 1822): 729;
        in Landon, Letitia E. *The Improvisatrice: and Other Poems*. London: Hurst, Robinson; Edinburgh: Archibald Constable, 1824. 238-39.

Linmouth. (Poem appears elsewhere as "The Country Retreat").

    1st line: "Oh lone and lovely solitude,"
    in Landon, Letitia E. *Fisher's Drawing Room Scrap-Book. 1833*. London: H. Fisher, R. Fisher, and P. Jackson, 1833 [1832]. 39-40.

The Little Boy's Bed-Time. (Translation from a work by Madame Desborde Valmore).

    1st line: "Sleep, little Paul, what, crying, hush! the night is very dark;"
    Prefixed lines from Victor Hugo begin: "Hush! no more fire, no noise — all round is still."
    in Landon, Letitia E. *Traits and Trials of Early Life*. London: H. Colburn, 1836. 111-12.

The Little Gleaner. (No. III in Third Series of "Subjects For Pictures" in *The New Monthly*; no. IX in "Subjects for Pictures" in *Life and Literary Remains*).

    1st line: "Very fair the child was, with hair of darkest auburn, —"
    Prefixed lines to "Subjects for Pictures" begin: "What seek I here to gather into words?"
    in *The New Monthly Magazine* 49 (1837): 76;
    in Blanchard, Laman. *Life and Literary Remains of L. E. L.* Vol. 2. London: Henry Colburn, 1841. 218.

The Little Mountaineer.

    1st line: "Her naked feet are nothing loath"
    in *The Juvenile Forget-Me-Not: A Christmas and New-Year's Gift, or Birth-day Present. 1836*. Ed. Mrs. S. C. [Anna Maria] Hall. London: R. Ackermann; Frederick Westley and A. H. Davis, 1836 [1835]. 31-32.

Little Red Riding Hood.

    1st line: "Come back, come back together,"
    in *The Modern Poets and Artists of Great Britain*. Ed. S. C. Hall. London: Whittaker, 1838. Vol. 3 of *The Book of Gems*. 3 vols. 1836-38. 179-81.

The Little Shroud..

    1st line: "She put him on a snow-white shroud,"
    in *The Literary Gazette* 797 (April 28, 1832): 266;
    in Landon, Letitia E. *The Vow of the Peacock, and Other Poems*. London: Saunders and Otley, 1835. 287-90.

The Littleness of Life. (One of the "Fragments" from *Ethel Churchill* selected by Blanchard; poem appears elsewhere as "[The Influence of an Invitation]").

    1st line: "Life is so little in its vanities,"
    in Blanchard, Laman. *Life and Literary Remains of L. E. L.* Vol. 2. London: Henry Colburn, 1841. 291.

Liverpool.

    1st line: "Where are they bound, those gallant ships,"
    in Landon, Letitia E. *Fisher's Drawing Room Scrap-Book. 1833*. London: H. Fisher, R. Fisher, and P. Jackson, 1833 [1832]. 13-15.

London.
   1st line: "Terrible City! London — thou"
   in *The Album Wreath of Music and Literature [for 1835].* London: R. Willoughby, [1834?]. 82.
[A London Life]. (Suggested poem title, as poem is the motto for Chapter 16 titled "A London Life"; poem appears elsewhere as "The Poet's Lot").
   1st line: "The poet's lovely faith creates"
   in Landon, Letitia E. *Ethel Churchill: or, The Two Brides.* Vol. 1. London: Henry Colburn, 1837. 158.
Long Lonkin.
   1st line: "The lord said to his ladie,"
   in Landon, Letitia E. *Fisher's Drawing Room Scrap-Book. 1835.* London: H. Fisher, R. Fisher, and P. Jackson, 1835 [1834]. 11-12.
A Long While Ago.
   1st line: "Still hangeth down the old accustom'd willow,"
   in *The New Monthly Magazine* 52 (1838): 372-73;
   in Blanchard, Laman. *Life and Literary Remains of L. E. L.* Vol. 2. London: Henry Colburn, 1841. 254-56.
Long Years Have Past Since Last I Stood. (Poem appears elsewhere as "Caldron Snout. — Westmorland").
   1st line: "Long years have past since last I stood"
   Prefixed lines begin: "A place of rugged rocks, adown whose sides"
   in *The Zenana and Minor Poems of L.E.L.* London: Fisher, Son; Paris: Quai de L'Ecole, [1839]. 131-34.
Lord And Lady Derby.
   1st line: "The times are peaceful, and we know"
   in Landon, Letitia E. *Fisher's Drawing Room Scrap-Book. 1833.* London: H. Fisher, R. Fisher, and P. Jackson, 1833 [1832]. 3-5.
[Lord Marchmont's Jealousy]. (Suggested poem title, as poem is motto for Chapter 25 titled "Lord Marchmont's Jealousy").
   1st line: "You never loved me! never cared for me!"
   in Landon, Letitia E. *Ethel Churchill: or, The Two Brides.* Vol. 3. London: Henry Colburn, 1837. 187.
Lord Melbourne.
   1st line: "It is a glorious task to guide"
   in Landon, Letitia E. *Fisher's Drawing Room Scrap-Book, 1837.* London, Paris, and New York: Fisher, Son; Germany: Black and Armstrong, and Asher, 1836. 28.
The Lost. (One of the "Fragments" from *Ethel Churchill* selected by Blanchard; poem appears elsewhere as "[A Friend at Court]").
   1st line: "I did not know till she was lost,"
   in Blanchard, Laman. *Life and Literary Remains of L. E. L.* Vol. 2. London: Henry Colburn, 1841. 286.
The Lost Pleiad.
   1st line: "He was weary of flinging the feather'd reed,"
   Prefixed lines begin: "A story from the stars; or rather one"
   in Landon, Letitia E. *The Venetian Bracelet, The Lost Pleiad, A History of the Lyre, and Other Poems.* London: Longman, Rees, Orme, Brown, and Green, 1829. 51-83.
The Lost Ship.
   1st line: "Deep in the silent waters,"

in *The Literary Gazette* 834 (Jan. 12, 1833): 27.

The Lost Star.

1st line: "A light is gone from yonder sky,"

in *The Literary Souvenir; or, Cabinet of Poetry and Romance [for 1828].* Ed. Alaric A. Watts. London: Longman, Rees, Orme, Brown, and Green. 1828 [1827]. 20-21;

in Landon, Letitia E. *The Vow of the Peacock, and Other Poems.* London: Saunders and Otley, 1835. 271-73.

Louise, Duchess of La Valliere.

1st line: "Alone — again alone — ah! let me kneel"

in Landon, Letitia E. *Fisher's Drawing Room Scrap-Book. 1839.* London: Fisher, Son; Paris: Quai de L'Ecole, [1838]. 18-20;

in *Blackwood's Lady's Magazine* 6 (1839): 154-55.

Love. (One of the "Fragments" from *Ethel Churchill* selected by Blanchard; poem appears elsewhere as "[An Act of Parliament]").

1st line: "Love is a thing of frail and delicate growth;"

in Blanchard, Laman. *Life and Literary Remains of L. E. L.* Vol. 2. London: Henry Colburn, 1841. 278.

Love. (Poem appears elsewhere as "Love, Hope, and Beauty").

1st line: "Love may be increased by fears,"

in *The Album Wreath of Music and Literature [for 1835].* London: R. Willoughby, [1834?]. 53.

Love.

1st line: "Love, unrequited love! — the heart"

in *The Album Wreath and Bijou Littéraire [for 1834].* Ed. John Francis. London: De la Rue, James, and Rudd, 1834 [1833?]. N. pag. [1 page].

Love.

1st line: "A mystery thou art, thou mighty one!"

in *The Album of Love.* The Mirror Library. 3. New York: n.p., 1844. 14.

Love. (First, a suggested poem title, as poem is the first in a group of six poems titled "Six Songs of Love, Constancy, Romance, Inconstancy, Truth, and Marriage"; then poem is given that title when it appears in a slightly altered version in *The Lyre*; poem appears elsewhere as "Affection's Comfort").

1st line: "Oh! yet one smile, tho' dark may lower"

in *The Literary Gazette* 251 (Nov. 10, 1821): 716;

in *The Lyre. Fugitive Poetry of the Nineteenth Century.* London: Tilt and Bogue, 1841. 321.

Love. (One of the "Fragments").

1st line: "She prest her slight hand to her brow, or pain"

in Landon, Letitia E. *The Improvisatrice; and Other Poems.* London: Hurst, Robinson; Edinburgh: Archibald Constable, 1824. 302-03.

Love, Hope, and Beauty. (Poem appears elsewhere as "Love").

1st line: "Love may be increased by fears,"

in Landon, Letitia E. *The Improvisatrice; and Other Poems.* London: Hurst, Robinson; Edinburgh: A. Constable, 1824. 304.

Love in Absence.

1st line: "Oh, tell me not that this is life,"

in *The Literary Gazette* 377 (Apr. 10, 1824): 236.

The Love Letter.

1st line: "'Pray thee, maiden, heed him not,"

in Landon, Letitia E. *Fisher's Drawing Room Scrap-Book. 1833*. London: H. Fisher, R. Fisher, and P. Jackson, 1833 [1832]. 25.

Love a Mystery. (One of the "Fragments" from *Ethel Churchill* selected by Blanchard; poem appears elsewhere as an "[untitled poem]").
  1st line: "It matters not its history — Love has wings,"
  in Blanchard, Laman. *Life and Literary Remains of L. E. L.* Vol. 2. London: Henry Colburn, 1841. 289.

Love Nursed by Solitude.
  1st line: "Young Love, thou art belied: they speak of thee,"
  in *The Album of Love.* The Mirror Library. 3. New York: n.p., 1844. 7.

Love Nursed by Solitude. By W. I. Thomson, Edinburgh. (One of the "Poetical Sketches of Modern Pictures").
  1st line: "Ay, surely it is here that Love should come,"
  in Landon, Letitia E. *The Troubadour; Catalogue of Pictures, and Historical Sketches.* London: Hurst, Robinson; Edinburgh: A. Constable, 1825. 289-91.

Love sleeping beneath a Palm-Tree. (Part of the series, "Medallion Wafers").
  1st line: "Ah, this is ours! that gentle Love"
  in *The Literary Gazette* 316 (Feb. 8, 1823): 91.

A Love Song. (Poem appears elsewhere as "Song").
  1st line: "Are other eyes beguiling, Love?"
  in *Affection's Gift for 1844.* London: H. G. Clarke, [1843?]. 32-33.

Love Tormenting the Soul.
  1st line: "Young tyrant, and young torturer!"
  in *The Literary Souvenir; or, Cabinet of Poetry and Romance [for 1828]*. Ed. Alaric A. Watts. London: Longman, Rees, Orme, Brown, and Green, 1828 [1827]. 402-04.

Love touching the Horns of a Snail, which is shrinking from his hand. (Second sketch in series, "Sketches from Designs by Mr. Dagley"; "Designs" should be corrected to "Drawings").
  1st line: "Oh, you have wronged me! — but, or e'er I tell"
  Prefixed lines begin: "Love's feeling is more soft, and sensible,"
  in *The Literary Gazette* 289 (Aug. 3, 1822): 487.

The Lovely little Flower. — Goethe. (Translation; part of the First Series of "Versions from the German").
  1st line: "I know a lovely little flower, a flower for which I pine —"
  in *The Literary Gazette* 937 (Jan. 3, 1835): 11.

A Lover's Dream.
  1st line: "It was a dream, as bright as e'er"
  in Landon, Letitia E. *The Fate of Adelaide, A Swiss Romantic Tale; and Other Poems.* London: John Warren, 1821. 113-14.

The Lover's Rock. (Part of Third Series of "Poetical Sketches"; "Poetical" should be corrected to "Poetic" to agree with other series in *The Literary Gazette*; one of "A Series of Tales" in *The Vow of the Peacock, and Other Poems*).
  1st line: "Most beautiful, most happy! must there be"
  Prefixed lines from Robert Burns begin: "Oh why should Fate such pleasure have,"
  in *The Literary Gazette* 298 (Oct. 5, 1822): 633-34;
  in Landon, Letitia E. *The Vow of the Peacock, and Other Poems.* London: Saunders and Otley, 1835. 175-83.

Love's Auguries. (See also "Love's Happiness").

    1st line: "There are a thousand fanciful things"

    in *The Album of Love.* The Mirror Library. 3. New York: n.p., 1844. 18.

Love's Choice. (Described as "From the same": that is, like "The Phoenix and the Dove" on page 115, "the Hint [for "Love's Choice" has been] taken from the French of Millevoix").

    1st line: "Too long the daring power of love"

    in Landon, Letitia E. *The Fate of Adelaide, A Swiss Romantic Tale; and Other Poems.* London: John Warren, 1821. 116.

Love's Ending. (One of the "Fragments" from *Ethel Churchill* selected by Blanchard; poem appears elsewhere as "[The Result]").

    1st line: "And this, then, is love's ending. It is like"

    in Blanchard, Laman. *Life and Literary Remains of L. E. L.* Vol. 2. London: Henry Colburn, 1841. 268.

Love's Followers. (One of the "Fragments" from *Ethel Churchill* selected by Blanchard; poem appears elsewhere as "[The Morality of Diamonds]").

    1st line: "There was an evil in Pandora's box"

    in Blanchard, Laman. *Life and Literary Remains of L. E. L.* Vol. 2. London: Henry Colburn, 1841. 262.

Love's Happiness. (See also "Love's Auguries").

    1st line: "There are a thousand fanciful things"

    in *The Pledge of Friendship.* London: W. Marshall. 1827 [1826]. 25-28.

Love's Lament. (Poem shares 1st line with 5th poem of "Fragments" in *The Literary Gazette* of April 19, 1823).

    1st line: "Nay, pray thee, let me weep, for tears"

    in *The Literary Gazette* 381 (May 8, 1824): 299.

Love's Last Lesson.

    1st line: "Teach it me, if you can, — forgetfulness!"

    in Landon, Letitia. *The Golden Violet with its Tales of Romance and Chivalry: and Other Poems.* London: Longman, Rees, Orme, Brown, and Green, 1827. 298-306.

Love's Last Words. (No. 2 in a series of "Songs").

    1st line: "Light be around thee, hope be thy guide;"

    in *The Literary Gazette* 284 (June 29, 1822): 410.

Love's Motto.

    1st line: "Is it that natural impulse of the heart,"

    in *Forget Me Not; A Christmas and New Year's Present for 1827.* Ed. Frederic Shoberl. London: R. Ackermann, [1826]. 1-2.

Love's Parting Wreath.

    1st line: "I give thee, love, a blooming braid;"

    in Landon, Letitia E. *The Fate of Adelaide, A Swiss Romantic Tale; and Other Poems.* London: John Warren, 1821. 103-04.

Love's Reproaches.

    1st line: "I deeply feel what Love"

    in *The Literary Gazette* 427 (Mar. 26, 1825): 203.

Love's Signal Flower.

    1st line: "She flung her on his breast,"

    Prefixed lines begin: "How much there is of the heart's eloquence"

    in *Forget Me Not; A Christmas, New Year's, Birthday Present, for 1844.* Ed. Frederic Shoberl. London: Ackermann, [1843]. 9-14.

Love's Slaves. (One of the "Fragments" from *Ethel Churchill* selected by Blanchard; poem appears elsewhere as "[Midnight]").

   1st line: "Where is the heart that has not bowed"
   in Blanchard, Laman. *Life and Literary Remains of L. E. L.* Vol. 2. London: Henry Colburn, 1841. 293.

Love's Timidity. (One of the "Fragments" from *Ethel Churchill*; poem appears elsewhere as "[Difficulties]" and as "Affection's Timidity").

   1st line: "I do not ask to offer thee"
   in Blanchard, Laman. *Life and Literary Remains of L. E. L.* Vol. 2. London: Henry Colburn, 1841. 264.

Love's Wreath. (Poem in First Series of "Fragments by L. E. L.").

   1st line: "It is an April's wreath: blue violets,"
   Prefixed lines to series begin: "Gleamings of poetry, — if I may give"
   in *The Literary Gazette* 363 (Jan. 3, 1824): 10.

The Lute.

   1st line: "Oh! sing again that mournful song,"
   in *The Amulet. A Christian and Literary Remembrancer.* Ed. S.C. Hall. London: Frederick Westley, A. H. Davis, 1833 [1832]. 311-12;
   in *Literary Inquirer* [of Buffalo, New York] 1 (Feb. 12, 1833): 32.

The Lute.

   1st line: "Wake not again, thou sweet-voiced lute!"
   in *Forget Me Not, A Christmas and New Year's Present for 1825.* Ed. Frederic Shoberl. London: Ackermann, [1824]. 72.

The Lyrist.

   1st line: "The laurel-wreath is round thine hair,"
   in *The Friendship's Offering. A Literary Album [for 1827].* Ed. Thomas K. Hervey. London: Lupton Relfe, 1827 [1826]. 181-83.

Macao.

   1st line: "Good Heaven! whatever shall I do?"
   in Landon, Letitia E. *Fisher's Drawing Room Scrap-Book. 1833.* London: H. Fisher, R. Fisher, and P. Jackson, 1833 [1832]. 42.

Madeira.

   1st line: "On the deep and quiet sea"
   in *Forget Me Not, A Christmas, New Year's, and Birthday Present, for 1835.* Ed. Frederic Shoberl. London: Ackermann, [1834]. 65-68.

Madeline.

   1st line: "I pray thee leave me not; my heart"
   in Landon, Letitia E. *Heath's Book of Beauty. 1833.* London: Longman, Rees, Orme, Brown, Green, and Longman; Paris: Rittner, Goupil; Frankfort: C. Jügel, [1832]. 114-16.

The Madonna and Child.

   1st line: "Thrice blessed and thrice beautiful;"
   Prefixed line: "Blessed art Thou among Women"
   in Landon, Letitia. *The Easter Gift, A Religious Offering.* London: Fisher, Son, 1832. 14-16.

The Magdalen.

   1st line: "The plaining murmur of the midnight wind,"
   in Landon, Letitia E. *The Easter Gift, A Religious Offering.* London: Fisher, Son, 1832. 27-33.

The Maiden Astrologer.
　　1st line: "Over the terrace the bright stars shine,"
　　Prefixed lines begin: "Her thoughts were not like girlhood's; bird nor flower"
　　in *The Literary Souvenir [for 1831]*. Ed. Alaric A. Watts. London: Longman, Rees,
　　Orme, Brown, and Green, 1831 [1830]. 146-148.
Malibran. (Appears next to four pages of music: "'Rondo' in Balfe's Opera of the maid
　　of Artois").
　　1st line: "Mournfully ah! mournfully"
　　in Landon, Letitia E. *The English Bijou Almanac for 1837*. London: Albert Schloss,
　　[1836]. N. pag. [3 pages].
Manchester.
　　1st line: "Go back a century on the town,"
　　in Landon, Letitia E. *Fisher's Drawing Room Scrap-Book. 1835*. London: H. Fisher, R.
　　Fisher, and P. Jackson, 1835 [1834]. 35-36;
　　in *The Casket and Penny Novelist* 9 (1835): 6.
A Maniac visited by his Family in Confinement: by Davis. (In series, "Poetical Catalogue
　　of Pictures").
　　1st line: "His arms are bound with iron, though they look"
　　in *The Literary Gazette* 324 (Apr. 5, 1823): 219.
Manmadin, the Indian Cupid, floating down the Ganges. (Part of series, "Fragments in
　　Rhyme," in *The Literary Gazette*; one of the "Fragments" in *The Improvisatrice; and
　　Other Poems*).
　　1st line: "There is darkness on the sky,"
　　in *The Literary Gazette* 308 (Dec. 14, 1822): 793-94;
　　in Landon, Letitia E. *The Improvisatrice; and Other Poems*. London: Hurst, Robinson;
　　Edinburgh: Archibald Constable, 1824. 250-55.
Mardale Head. (An altered version of the poem appears elsewhere as "The Past").
　　1st line: "Weep for the love that fate forbids,"
　　Prefixed lines begin: "Why should I seek these scenes again, the past"
　　in Landon, Letitia E. *Fisher's Drawing Room Scrap-Book. 1835*. London: H. Fisher, R.
　　Fisher, and P. Jackson, 1835 [1834]. 52.
The Mariner's Child to his Mother.
　　1st line: "Oh, weep no more, sweet mother,"
　　in *The Juvenile Keepsake 1830*. Ed. Thomas Roscoe. London: Hurst, Chance, 1830
　　[1829]. 101-02.
Marius at the Ruins of Carthage.
　　1st line: "He turn'd him from the setting sun,"
　　in *The Keepsake for 1833*. Ed. Frederic Mansel Reynolds. London: Longman, Rees,
　　Orme, Brown, Green, and Longman; Paris: Rittner and Goupill; Frankfirt: Charles
　　Jügil, [1832]. 65-66.
[The Marriage]. (Suggested poem title, as poem is the motto for Chapter 23 titled
　　"The Marriage"; poem appears elsewhere as "Bridal Flowers").
　　1st line: "Bind the white orange-flowers in her hair,"
　　in Landon, Letitia E. *Ethel Churchill: or, The Two Brides*. Vol. 1. London: Henry Col-
　　burn, 1837. 218.
Marriage. (Poem appears elsewhere as "Matrimonial Creed").
　　1st line: "He must be rich whom I could love,"
　　in *The Lyre. Fugitive Poetry of the Nineteenth Century*. London: Tilt and Bogue, 1841.
　　325.

[The Marriage Morning]. (Suggested poem title, as poem is motto for Chapter 20 titled "The Marriage Morning"; poem appears elsewhere as "Dangers Faced" and resembles the 3rd poem in a series of "Songs").

  1st line: "My heart is filled with bitter thought,"
  in Landon, Letitia E. *Ethel Churchill: or, The Two Brides.* Vol. 1. London: Henry Colburn, 1837. 200.

The Marriage Vow. (One of the "Fragments" from *Ethel Churchill* selected by Blanchard; poem appears elsewhere as "[The Church]").

  1st line: "The altar, 'tis of death! for there are laid"
  in Blanchard, Laman. *Life and Literary Remains of L. E. L.* Vol. 2. London: Henry Colburn, 1841. 277.

Martin.

  1st line: "Mighty painter, thou hast bowed"
  in Landon, Letitia E. *The English Bijou Almanac for 1836.* London: Albert Schloss, [1835]. N. pag. [3 pages].

The Marvel of Peru.

  1st line: "A radiant beauty of the lovely south,"
  in Landon, Letitia E. *Flowers of Loveliness; Twelve Groups of Female Figures, Emblematic of Flowers.* London: Ackermann, 1838. N. pag. [2 pages].

The Mask.

  1st line: "Unveil'd, unmask'd! not so, not so!"
  in Landon, Letitia E. *Heath's Book of Beauty. 1833.* London: Longman, Rees, Orme, Brown, Green, and Longman; Paris: Rittner, Goupil; Frankfort: C. Jügel, [1832]. 51-53.

Mask of Gaiety. (One of the "Fragments" from *Ethel Churchill* selected by Blanchard; poem appears elsewhere as "[Lady Marchmont's Journal]").

  1st line: "'Tis strange to think, if we could fling aside"
  in Blanchard, Laman. *Life and Literary Remains of L. E. L.* Vol. 2. London: Henry Colburn, 1841. 296.

[The Masked Ball]. (Suggested poem title, as poem is motto for Chapter 23 titled "The Masked Ball"; poem appears elsewhere as "Stern Truth").

  1st line: "Life is made up of vanities — so small,"
  in Landon, Letitia. *Ethel Churchill: or, The Two Brides.* Vol. 3. London: Henry Colburn, 1837. 172.

Matrimonial Creed. (The sixth poem and the only poem with a definite title in a group of six poems called, "Six Songs of Love, Constancy, Romance, Inconstancy, Truth, and Marriage"; poem appears elsewhere as "Marriage").

  1st line: "He must be rich whom I could love,"
  in *The Literary Gazette* 251 (Nov. 10, 1821): 716.

[A Matrimonial Tête-à-tête]. (Suggested poem title, as poem is motto for Chapter 22 titled "A Matrimonial Tête-à-tête"; poem appears elsewhere as "Want of Sympathy").

  1st line: "These are the things that fret away the heart —"
  in Landon, Letitia E. *Ethel Churchill: or, The Two Brides.* Vol. 2. London: Henry Colburn, 1837. 167.

Matlock. To the Memory of a Favourite Child (the Daughter of a Friend) who Died There. (Poem appears elsewhere as "To the Memory of a Favorite Child, the Daughter of a Friend").

  1st line: "Her voice is on the haunted air,"

in Landon, Letitia E. *Fisher's Drawing Room Scrap-Book, 1839*. London: Fisher, Son; Paris: Quai de L'Ecole, [1838]. 49-51.

May Morning.

1st line: "Up with the morning, and up with the sun,"

in *The Amulet [for 1836]*. Ed. S. C. Hall. London: Frederick Westley and A. H. Davis, 1836 [1835]. 84-85.

Meditation.

1st line: "How quietly has Night come down,"

Prefixed lines begin: "A sweet and melancholy face, that seems"

in *Heath's Book of Beauty. 1833*. London: Longman, Rees, Orme, Brown, Green, and Longman; Paris: Rittner, Goupil; Frankfort: C. Jügel, [1832]. 176-79.

[Meeting]. (Suggested poem title, as poem is motto for Chapter 38 titled "Meeting"; poem appears elsewhere as "Peace Wrought by Pain").

1st line: "Over that pallid face were wrought"

in Landon, Letitia E. *Ethel Churchill: or, The Two Brides.* Vol. 3. London: Henry Colburn, 1837. 313.

[Meeting of Old Friends]. (Suggested poem title, as poem is motto for Chapter 25 titled "Meeting of Old Friends"; poem appears elsewhere as "Change").

1st line: "How much of change lies in a little space!"

in Landon, Letitia E. *Ethel Churchill: or, The Two Brides.* Vol. 2. London: Henry Colburn, 1837. 194.

Memory. (One of the "Fragments" from *Ethel Churchill* selected by Blanchard; poem appears elsewhere as "[An Allusion to the Past]").

1st line: "Ah! there are memories that will not vanish;"

in Blanchard, Laman. *Life and Literary Remains of L.E.L.* Vol. 2. London: Henry Colburn, 1841. 272.

Memory. (Part of the series, "Three Extracts from the Diary of a Week" in both publications, no. III in *Life and Literary Remains*; poem appears elsewhere as "[A Scene at the Masquerade]").

1st line: "I do not say bequeath unto my soul"

Prefixed lines to series: "A record of the inward world, whose facts"

in *The New Monthly Magazine* 49 (1837): 481;

in Blanchard, Laman. *Life and Literary Remains of L. E. L.* Vol. 2. London: Henry Colburn, 1841. 251-52.

Memory.

1st line: "It is fading around me, that shadowy splendour"

in *The Literary Gazette* 888 (Jan. 25, 1834): 63.

Memory. (No. 3 in a series of "Songs").

1st line: "A voice of gentle singing"

in *The Literary Gazette* 694 (May 8, 1830): 308.

The Message. — Anon. (Translation; part of Fourth Series of "Versions from the German").

1st line: "A moment, ladye nightingale!"

in *The Literary Gazette* 940 (Jan. 24, 1835): 59.

The Michaelmas Daisy.

1st line: "Last smile of the departing year,"

in *The Literary Gazette* 165 (Mar. 18, 1820): 190.

The Middle Temple Gardens. (Poem appears elsewhere as an "[untitled poem]" and as "The Temple Garden").
1st line: "The fountain's low singing is heard on the wind,"
in Landon, Letitia E. *The Vow of the Peacock and Other Poems.*. London: Saunders and Otley, 1835. 348-52.

[Midnight]. (Suggested poem title, as poem is the motto for Chapter 29 titled "Midnight"; poem appears elsewhere as "Love's Slaves").
1st line: "Where is the heart that has not bowed"
in Landon, Letitia E. *Ethel Churchill: or, The Two Brides.* Vol. 3. London: Henry Colburn, 1837. 224.

Mignonette.
1st line: "Thou fairy flower! how lovely"
in Landon, Letitia E. *Flowers of Loveliness; Twelve Groups of Female Figures, Emblematic of Flowers.* London: Ackermann, 1838. N. pag. [2 pages].

Miller's Dale, Derbyshire.
1st line: "Do you remember, Love, the lake"
in Landon, Letitia E. *Fisher's Drawing Room Scrap-Book, 1838.* London, Paris, and New York: Fisher, Son; Germany: Black and Armstrong, and Asher, 1837. 22.

The Mind's Unrest. (One of the "Fragments" from *Ethel Churchill* selected by Blanchard; poem appears elsewhere as an "[untitled poem]").
1st line: "Mind, dangerous and glorious gift!"
in Blanchard, Laman. *Life and Literary Remains of L. E. L.* Vol. 2. London: Henry Colburn, 1841. 287.

The Mine. (First sketch in Third Series of "Poetical Sketches"; "Poetical" should be corrected to "Poetic" to agree with the other series).
1st line: "They were two lovers. — Oh how much is said"
Prefixed lines begin: "Alas, the strange varieties of life!"
in *The Literary Gazette* 294 (Sept. 7, 1822): 569.

The Minster. (Poem appears elsewhere as "Collegiate Church, Manchester").
1st line: "Dim thro' the sculptured aisles the sunbeam falls"
in *The Zenana and Minor Poems of L. E. L.* London: Fisher, Son; Paris: Quai de L'Ecole, [1839]. 83-84.

The Minstrel of Portugal. (Third sketch of Third Series of "Poetical Sketches"; "Poetical" should be corrected to "Poetic" to agree with the rest of the series in *The Literary Gazette*).
1st line: "Come, love, we'll rest us from our wanderings:"
Prefixed lines begin: "Their path had been a troubled one, each step"
in *The Literary Gazette* 296 (Sept. 21, 1822): 601;
in Landon, Letitia E. *The Improvisatrice; and Other Poems.* London: Hurst, Robinson; Edinburgh: A. Constable, 1824. 204-11;
in *Blackwood's Lady's Magazine* 6 (1839): 163-65.

The Minstrel's Monitor.
1st line: "Silent and dark as the source of yon river,"
in *The Literary Souvenir; or, Cabinet of Poetry and Romance [for 1827].* Ed. Alaric A. Watts. London: Longman, Rees, Orme, Brown, and Green; and John Andrews. 1827 [1826]. 103-104;
in *The Lady's Magazine* 7 (Dec. 1826): 652-53;
in Landon, Letitia E. *The Vow of the Peacock, and Other Poems.* London: Saunders and Otley, 1835. 261-63.

The Missionary.
　1st line: "It is a glorious task to seek,"
　in Landon, Letitia E. *Fisher's Drawing Room Scrap-Book, 1834.* London: H. Fisher, R. Fisher, and P. .Jackson; Paris: Rittner, Goupil; Berlin and St. Petersburg: Asher; New York: Jackson, 1833. 52-53.

The Missionary's Wife.
　1st line: "Not through the quiet shadows of our vale"
　in Howitt, Mary. *Fisher's Drawing Room Scrap-Book. 1841.* London: Fisher, Son; Paris: Quai de L'Ecole, [1840]. 54.

Mr. Martin's Picture of Clytie. (Fifth sketch in Second Series of "Poetic Sketches"; regarding prefixed lines, see editorial note in *The Literary Gazette* 281 (June 8, 1822): 363; poem appears elsewhere as "Greece; or, the Slighted Clytie").
　1st line: "It was a beautiful embodied thought,"
　Prefixed lines begin: "Greece,";
　in *The Literary Gazette* 280 (June 1, 1822): 346-47.

Mrs. Somerville.
　1st line: "She has brought down beside the hearth"
　in Landon, Letitia E. *The English Bijou Almanac for 1837.* London: Albert Schloss, [1836]. N. pag. [3 pages].

Mrs. Wombwell.
　1st line: "Ah, Beauty! what a charm hast thou!"
　in *Heath's Book of Beauty. 1838.* Ed. Marguerite Blessington, Countess of. London: Longman, Rees, Orme, Brown, Green, and Longmans, [1837]. 33-34.

Mont Blanc. (A variant of "Mont Blanc" in *The Bijou*).
　1st line: "Thou monarch of the open air,"
　in *The Ladies' Wreath; A Selection from the Female Poetic Writers of England and America.* Ed. Mrs. Sarah J. Hale. Boston: Marsh, Capen, and Lyon; New York: D. Appleton, 1837. 134-35.

Mont Blanc. (A variant of the poem appears as "Mont Blanc" in *The Ladies' Wreath*).
　1st line: "Thou monarch of the upper air,"
　in *The Bijou; or Annual of Literature and the Arts [for 1829].* London: William Pickering, 1829 [1828]. 225-27.

The Montmorency Waterfall and Cone.
　1st line: "We do not ask for the leaves and flowers"
　in Landon, Letitia E. *Fisher's Drawing Room Scrap-Book, 1836.* London and Paris: Fisher, Son; Berlin: Asher; New York: Jackson, [1835]. 27.

Moon.
　1st line: "The Moon is sailing o'er the sky,"
　in *The Literary Gazette* 479 (Mar. 25, 1826): 186;
　in Landon, Letitia E. *The Vow of the Peacock, and Other Poems.* London: Saunders and Otley, 1835. 254-55;
　as *The Moon,* in *The Modern Poets and Artists of Great Britain.* Ed. S. C. Hall. London: Whittaker, 1838. Vol. 3 of *The Book of Gems.* 3 vols. 1836-38. 183.

Moonlight. (One of the "Fragments" from *Ethel Churchill* selected by Blanchard; poem appears elsewhere as "[The Duel]").
　1st line: "The moonlight falleth lovely over the earth;"
　in Blanchard, Laman. *Life and Literary Remains of L. E. L.* Vol. 2. London: Henry Colburn, 1841. 296.

Moonlight.
    1st line: "There are no stars: thou lovely moon,"
    in *The Amulet; A Christian and Literary Remembrancer [for 1832]*. Ed. S. C. Hall. London: Frederick Westley, A. H. Davis, 1832 [1831]. 317-18.
Moonlight. T. C. Hofland. (Appears to be a response to a painting by Hofland, which may be called "Moonlight," exhibited at the British Gallery along with Brockedon's "Raphael Showing his Mistress her Portrait"; Landon's poetic response to the latter is placed directly above "Moonlight" on the page).
    1st line: "A luxury of deep repose! the heart"
    in *The Literary Gazette* 379 (Apr. 24, 1824): 268.
The Moorish Maiden's Vigil. (No. III. in the second series of "Subjects for Pictures" in *The New Monthly*; no. VI in "Subjects for Pictures" in *Life and Literary Remains*).
    1st line: "Does she watch him, fondly watch him,"
    Prefixed lines to "Subjects for Pictures" begin: "What seek I here to gather into words?"
    in *The New Monthly Magazine* 48 (1836): 24-25;
    in Blanchard, Laman. *Life and Literary Remains of L. E. L.* Vol. 2. London: Henry Colburn, 1841. 210-13.
Moralising. (An altered version of the poem appears elsewhere as both "Illusion" and "[Different Views of Life]"; an altered version of the epigraph appears elsewhere as both "[The Author and the Actress]" and "Pleasure Becomes Pain").
    1st line: "And thus it is with all that made life fair: —"
    Prefixed lines begin: "I cannot count the changes of my heart,"
    in *The Literary Gazette* 493 (July 1, 1826): 412.
[The Morality of Diamonds]. (Suggested poem title, as poem is motto for Chapter 2 titled "The Morality of Diamonds"; poem appears elsewhere as "Love's Followers").
    1st line: "There was an evil in Pandora's box"
    in Landon, Letitia E. *Ethel Churchill: or, The Two Brides.* Vol. 1. London: Henry Colburn, 1837. 16.
The Mosque at Cordova.
    1st line: "Round the purple shadow"
    in Howitt, Mary and Letitia E. Landon. *Fisher's Drawing Room Scrap-Book. 1840.* London: Fisher, Son; Paris: Quai de L'Ecole, [1839]. 17-19.
The Mother's Warning.
    1st line: "Pray thee, dear one, heed him not,"
    in *The Amulet [for 1836]*. Ed. S. C. Hall. London: Frederick Westley and A. H. Davis, 1836 [1835]. 166-168;
    in *The Fly* 27 (July 6, 1839): 108.
The Mountain Grave.
    1st line: "She sate beside the rock from which arose"
    in Landon, Letitia E. *The Venetian Bracelet, The Lost Pleiad, A History of the Lyre, and Other Poems.* London: Longman, Rees, Orme, Brown, and Green, 1829. 295-307.
Mozart.
    1st line: "It lingereth on the ear at night,"
    in Landon, Letitia E. *The English Bijou Almanac for 1838.* London: Albert Schloss, [1837]. N. pag. [3 pages].

Much Change in a Little Time. (First, a suggested poem title, as poem is motto for Chapter 6 titled "Much Change in a Little Time"; then given that title when selected by Blanchard as one of the "Fragments" from *Ethel Churchill*).

  1st line: "And she too — that beloved child, was gone —"

  in Landon, Letitia E. *Ethel Churchill: or, The Two Brides.* Vol. 1. London: Henry Colburn, 1837. 59;

  in Blanchard, Laman. *Life and Literary Remains of L. E. L.* Vol. 2. London: Henry Colburn, 1841. 258.

Music of Laughter. (One of the "Fragments" from *Ethel Churchill* selected by Blanchard; poem appears elsewhere as "[Confidence]").

  1st line: "She had that charming laugh which, like a song,"

  in Blanchard, Laman. *Life and Literary Remains of L. E. L.* Vol. 2. London: Henry Colburn, 1841. 274.

Musings.

  1st line: "Methinks we must have known some former state"

  in *The Ladies' Wreath; A Selection from the Female Poetic Writers of England and America.* Ed. Mrs. Sarah J. Hale. Boston: Marsh, Capen, and Lyon; New York: D. Appleton, 1837. 124-26.

My Harp! (Part of series, "Extracts from my Pocket Book").

  1st line: "Come, gentle harp, and let me hold"

  in *The Literary Gazette* 349 (Sept. 27, 1823): 619.

A Name.

  1st line: "They named him —ah! yet"

  in *The New Monthly Magazine* 49 (1837): 172-73.

The Nameless Grave.

  1st line: "A nameless grave, — there is no stone"

  in Landon, Letitia E. *The Venetian Bracelet, The Lost Pleiad, A History of the Lyre, and Other Poems.* London: Longman, Rees, Orme, Brown, and Green, 1829. 225-28.

Nathan and David.

  1st line: "The monarch knelt, and, in the dust,"

  in Landon, Letitia E. *The Easter Gift, A Religious Offering.* London: Fisher, Son, 1832. 35-36.

The Nativity.

  1st line: "Far in the desert east it shone,"

  in Landon, Letitia E. *The Easter Gift, A Religious Offering.* London: Fisher, Son, 1832. 22-24.

Necessity. (Part of series, "Three Extracts from the Diary of a Week" in both publications, no. II in *Life and Literary Remains*; poem appears elsewhere as "Introduction").

  1st line: "In the ancestral presence of the dead"

  Prefixed lines to series: "A record of the inward world, whose facts"

  in *The New Monthly Magazine* 49 (1837): 480;

  in Blanchard, Laman. *Life and Literary Remains of L. E. L.* Vol. 2. London: Henry Colburn, 1841. 250-51.

Neftah, in the Jereed.

  1st line: "It is a little azure bird,"

  in Howitt, Mary. *Fisher's Drawing Room Scrap-Book. 1841.* London: Fisher, Son; Paris: Quai de L'Ecole, [1840]. 13.

The Neglected.
   1st line: "My mother! she was laid to rest"
   in *The Album Wreath of Music and Literature [for 1835]*. London: R. Willoughby,
   [1834?]. 80.
The Neglected One.
   1st line: "And there is silence in that lonely hall,"
   in Landon, Letitia E. *The Venetian Bracelet, The Lost Pleiad, A History of the Lyre, and
   Other Poems*. London: Longman, Rees, Orme, Brown, and Green. 1829. 201-08.
A Nereid Floating on a Shell. (Part of series, "Medallion Wafers," in *The Literary Gazette*;
   one of the "Classical Sketches" in *The Vow of the Peacock, and Other Poems*).
   1st line: "Thy dwelling is the coral cave,"
   in *The Literary Gazette* 319 (Mar. 1, 1823): 140;
   in Landon, Letitia E. *The Vow of the Peacock, and Other Poems*. London: Saunders
   and Otley, 1835. 146-48.
The New Year.
   1st line: "Let the black clouds sweep o'er the sky,"
   in *The Literary Gazette* 885 (Jan. 4, 1834): 11.
New Year's Eve.
   1st line: "There is no change upon the air,"
   in Landon, Letitia E. *The Venetian Bracelet, The Lost Pleiad, A History of the Lyre, and
   Other Poems*. London: Longman, Rees, Orme, Brown, and Green, 1829. 278-83.
Night.
   1st line: "'Tis night, but such delicious time"
   in *Frost's New Town and Country Ladies' Memorandum Book* (1835): 39-40.
Night at Sea. (Ms. dated August 15, 1838).
   1st line: "The lovely purple of the noon's bestowing"
   in *The New Monthly Magazine* 55 (1839): 30-32;
   in Blanchard, Laman. *Life and Literary Remains of L. E. L.* Vol. 1. London: Henry
   Colburn, 1841. 191-95.
A Night in May.
   1st line: "Light and glad through the rooms the gay music is waking,"
   Prefixed lines begin: "A night not sacred to Spring's opening leaves,"
   in Landon, Letitia E. *The Venetian Bracelet, The Lost Pleiad, A History of the Lyre, and
   Other Poems*. London: Longman, Rees, Orme, Brown, and Green, 1829. 209-17.
The Night-Blowing Convolvulus.
   1st line: "Not to the sunny hours"
   in Landon, Letitia E. *Flowers of Loveliness; Twelve Groups of Female Figures, Emblemat-
   ic of Flowers*. London: Ackermann, 1838. N. pag. [2 pages].
The Nizam's Daughter. (First line missing "as" in *The Zenana and Minor Poems of L. E. L.*).
   1st line: "She is as yet a child in years,"
   in Landon, Letitia E. *Fisher's Drawing Room Scrap-Book. 1835*. London: H. Fisher, R.
   Fisher, and P. Jackson. 1835 [1834]. 37-38;
   in *The Zenana and Minor Poems of L. E. L.* London: Fisher, Son; Paris: Quai de
   L'Ecole, [1839]. 127-30.
A Noble Lady. (One of the "Fragments" from Ethel Churchill selected by Blanchard;
   poem appears elsewhere as "[Arrived at Home]").
   1st line: "A pale and stately lady, with a brow"
   in Blanchard, Laman. *Life and Literary Remains of L. E. L.* Vol. 2. London: Henry
   Colburn, 1841. 284.

Nymph and Zephyr: A Statuary Group, by Westmacott. (One of the "Poetical Sketches of Modern Pictures").

1st line: "And the summer sun shone in the sky,"

in Landon, Letitia E. *The Troubadour; Catalogue of Pictures, and Historical Sketches.* London: Hurst, Robinson; Edinburgh: A. Constable, 1825. 301-02.

The Oak. (Part of "Fragments"; poem appears elsewhere as the 2nd poem in a series of five untitled poems titled "Fragments" in *The Literary Gazette* of Apr. 19, 1823, p. 251).

1st line: ". . . It is the last survivor of a race"

in Landon, Letitia E. *The Improvisatrice; and Other Poems.* London: Hurst, Robinson; Edinburgh: A. Constable, 1824. 282-83.

Ode to Retirement.

1st line: "Pale maiden, that dost sit with downcast eye,"

Prefixed lines begin: "Nor those alone prefer a life recluse,"

in Landon, Letitia E. *Fisher's Drawing Room Scrap-Book, 1839.* London: Fisher, Son; Paris: Quai de L'Ecole, [1838]. 28.

The Offering.

1st line: "I see them fading round me,"

in *The Amulet; A Christian and Literary Remembrancer [for 1831].* Ed. S. C. Hall. London: Frederick Westley, A. H. Davis, 1831 [1830]. 146-48.

An Old Man Over the Body of his Son. (One of the "Classical Sketches").

1st line: "I am too proud by far to weep,"

in Landon, Letitia E. *The Vow of the Peacock, and Other Poems.* London: Saunders and Otley, 1835. 152-53.

An old Man standing by the dead body of a Youth. (Part of the series, "Medallion Wafers"; poem appears elsewhere as "An Old Man Over the Body of his Son").

1st line: "I am too proud by far to weep,"

in *The Literary Gazette* 319 (Mar. 1, 1823): 140.

[An Old Man's View of Life]. (Suggested poem title, as poem is motto for Chapter 31 titled "An Old Man's View of Life").

1st line: "We tremble even in our happiness;"

in Landon, Letitia E. *Ethel Churchill: or, The Two Brides.* Vol. 1. London: Henry Colburn, 1837. 271.

The Old Times.

1st line: "Do you recall what now is living only"

in *The New Monthly Magazine* 51 (1837): 346;

in *The Casket of Literature, Science, and Entertainment* 50 (Dec. 16, 1837): 798;

in Blanchard, Laman. *Life and Literary Remains of L. E. L.* Vol. 2. London: Henry Colburn, 1841. 311-12.

Olinthus Gregory, LLD., F.R.A.S., &c. (Poem appears elsewhere as "To Olinthus Gregory").

1st line: "Is there a spot where Pity's foot,"

in Landon, Letitia E. *Fisher's Drawing Room Scrap-Book. 1835.* London: H. Fisher, R. Fisher, and P. Jackson, 1835 [1834]. 27-28.

The Omen.

1st line: "Oh! how we miss the young and bright,"

in Landon, Letitia E. *The Golden Violet with its Tales of Romance and Chivalry: and Other Poems.* London: Longman, Rees, Orme, Brown, and Green, 1827. 283-90.

On the Death of Ismael Fitzadam. (A note states that poem is reprinted from *The Literary Gazette*, but this printing of the poem has not been located; poem appears elsewhere in an altered version as "Lines Suggested by the Death of Ismael Fitzadam").

  1st line: "His was a harp just fit to pour"
  in *The Gentleman's Magazine* 93 (Sept. 1823): 263-64;
  in *The Lyre. Fugitive Poetry of the Nineteenth Century.* London: Tilt and Bogue, 1841. 38-40.

On an Engraving of Hindoo Temples. (Poem appears elsewhere as "Hindoo Temples and Palace at Madura").

  1st line: "Little the present careth for the past,"
  in *The Zenana and Minor Poems of L. E. L.* London: Fisher, Son; Paris: Quai de L'Ecole, [1839]. 207-11.

On May-Day, by Leslie. (Printed under the series title, "Poetical Catalogue of Paintings": but to agree with the rest of the series, for "Paintings," read "Pictures").

  1st line: "Beautiful and radiant May,"
  in *The Literary Gazette* 328 (May 3, 1823): 286.

On the Picture of a Young Girl.

  1st line: "A beautiful and laughing thing,"
  in *The Literary Gazette* 330 (May 17, 1823): 316.

On the Portrait of Miss Cockayne.

  1st line: "A dark-eyed beauty, one on whom the south"
  in *Heath's Book of Beauty. 1839.* Ed. Marguerite Blessington, Countess of. London: Longman, Rees, Orme, Brown, Green, and Longman, 1839 [1838]. 275-76.

On the Portrait of Sir Robert Peel. (Poem appears elsewhere as "Sir Robert Peel").

  1st line: "Dim through the curtains came the purple twilight slowly,"
  in *The Zenana and Minor Poems of L. E. L.* London: Fisher, Son; Paris: Quai de L'Ecole, [1839]. 215-17.

On Reading a Description of The Delectable Mountains in Bunyan's Pilgrim's Progress. (Poem appears elsewhere as "The Delectable Mountains").

  1st line: "Oh far away ye are, ye lovely hills,"
  in *The Zenana and Minor Poems of L. E. L.* London: Fisher, Son; Paris: Quai de L'Ecole, [1839]. 218-19.

On a Star. (One of the "Fragments"; part of poem appears elsewhere as "Farewell! and Never Think of Me" and "Think of Me").

  1st line: "Beautiful Star that art wandering through"
  in Landon, Letitia E. *The Improvisatrice; and Other Poems.* London: Hurst, Robinson; Edinburgh: A. Constable, 1824. 295-96.

On Wordsworth's Cottage, Near Grasmere Lake. (Poem appears elsewhere as "Rydal Water and Grasmere Lake, the Residence of Wordsworth").

  1st line: "Not for the glory on their heads"
  in *The Zenana and Minor Poems of L. E. L.* London: Fisher, Son; Paris: Quai de L'Ecole, [1839]. 270-76.

One Day.

  1st line: "The sunshine of the morning"
  Prefixed line: "And this the change from morning to midnight."
  in Landon, Letitia E. *The Golden Violet with its Tales of Romance and Chivalry: and Other Poems.* London: Longman, Rees, Orme, Brown, and Green, 1827. 291-97.

Opinions. (First, a suggested poem title, as poem is motto for Chapter 11 of *Ethel Churchill* titled "Opinions"; then poem is given that title when included in Blanchard's selection of "Fragments" from *Ethel Churchill*).

1st line: "He scorned them from the centre of his heart,"

in Landon, Letitia E. *Ethel Churchill: or, The Two Brides.* Vol. 1. London: Henry Colburn, 1837. 109;

in Blanchard, Laman. *Life and Literary Remains of L. E. L.* Vol. 2. London: Henry Colburn, 1841. 233.

The Oriental Nosegay. By Pickersgill. (One of the "Poetical Sketches of Modern Pictures").

1st line: "Through the light curtains came the perfumed air,"

in Landon, Letitia E. *The Troubadour; Catalogue of Pictures, and Historical Sketches.* London: Hurst, Robinson; Edinburgh: A. Constable, 1825. 273-77.

Ornaments. (One of the "Fragments" from *Ethel Churchill* selected by Blanchard; poem appears elsewhere as "[The Toilets]").

1st line: "Bring from the east, bring from the west,"

in Blanchard, Laman. *Life and Literary Remains of L. E. L.* Vol. 2. London: Henry Colburn, 1841. 266.

The Orphan Ballad Singers. (Poem is set to music by Henry Russell, printed on two pages directly before the poem).

1st line: "Oh, weary, weary are our feet,"

in Landon, Letitia E. *Fisher's Drawing Room Scrap-Book. 1835.* London: H. Fisher, R. Fisher, and P. Jackson, 1835 [1834]. 15.

Othman.

1st line: "Morning, bright morning, thou art on the wave,"

in *The Pledge of Friendship; A Christmas Present, and New Year's Gift [for 1828].* London: W. Marshall, 1828 [1827]. 289-92.

Our Present May.

1st line: "'The month of flowers,' May,"

Prefixed line from Southwell: "May is full of flowers."

in *The Literary Gazette* 799 (May 12, 1832): 300.

Outlines for a Portrait. (No. III in series, "Fragments in Rhyme").

1st line: "'Tis a dark and flashing eye,"

in *The Literary Gazette* 304 (Nov. 16, 1822): 729.

Oxford Street. (Part of series, "Scenes in London," in both publications; no. II in *The Zenana and Minor Poems of L. E. L.*).

1st line: "Life in its many shapes was there,"

in Landon, Letitia E. *Fisher's Drawing Room Scrap-Book, 1836.* London and Paris: Fisher, Son; Berlin: Asher; New York: Jackson, [1835]. 57-58;

in *The Zenana and Minor Poems of L. E. L.* London: Fisher, Son; Paris: Quai de L'Ecole, [1839]. 183-86.

The Painter. (Sketch I in Fouth Series of "Poetic Sketches" in *The Literary Gazette*; one of "A Series of Tales" in *The Vow of the Peacock, and Other Poems*).

1st line: "He was a lonely and neglected child:"

Prefixed lines begin: "I know not which is the most fatal gift,"

in *The Literary Gazette* 356 (Nov. 15, 1823): 730-31;

in Landon, Letitia E. *The Vow of the Peacock, and Other Poems.* London: Saunders and Otley, 1835. 184-93.

The Painter's Love. (No. VI in series, "Fragments in Rhyme," in *The Literary Gazette*; one of the "Fragments" in *The Improvisatrice; and Other Poems*).
    1st line: "Your skies are blue, your sun is bright;"
    in *The Literary Gazette* 307 (Dec. 7, 1822): 776-77;
    in Landon, Letitia E. *The Improvisatrice; and Other Poems.* London: Hurst, Robinson; Edinburgh: Archibald Constable, 1824. 261-70.
The Palace Called Beautiful.
    1st line: "He wandered on a weary way,"
    in Landon, Letitia E. *Fisher's Drawing Room Scrap-Book, 1836.* London and Paris: Fisher, Son; Berlin: Asher; New York: Jackson, [1835]. 54.
The Palace of the Seven Stories.
    1st line: "The past it is a fearful thing,"
    in Landon, Letitia E. *Fisher's Drawing Room Scrap-Book [for 1832].* London: Fisher, Son, and Jackson, 1832 [1831]. 10.
The Pansy.
    1st line: "His name is on the haunted flower,"
    Prefixed lines from Shakespeare begin: "A little purple flower,"
    in Landon, Letitia E. *Flowers of Loveliness; Twelve Groups of Female Figures, Emblematic of Flowers.* London: Ackermann, 1838. N. pag. [2 pages].
[Parting]. (Suggested poem title, as poem is motto for Chapter 39 titled "Parting").
    1st line: "That is love"
    in Landon, Letitia E. *Ethel Churchill: or, The Two Brides.* Vol. 3. London: Henry Colburn, 1837. 318.
Parting. (One of the "Fragments" from *Ethel Churchill* selected by Blanchard; poem appears elsewhere as "[Anticipation]").
    1st line: "We do not know how much we love,"
    in Blanchard, Laman. *Life and Literary Remains of L. E. L.* Vol. 2. London: Henry Colburn, 1841. 289.
The Parting Charge.
    1st line: "I see the white sails of thy ship,"
    in *Forget Me Not, A Christmas and New Year's Present for 1825.* Ed. Frederic Shoberl. London: R. Ackermann, [1824]. 55-56.
The Parting Word.
    1st line: "I leant within the window"
    in *The New Monthly Magazine* 45 (1835): 155.
    Parting Words. (Poem appears elsewhere as an untitled poem, no. II, within a series of "Songs" and no. II within series, "Song by L. E. L.").
    1st line: "May morning light fall o'er thee,"
    in *Friendship's Offering; and Winter's Wreath: A Christmas and New Year's Present for 1837.* London: Smith, Elder, 1837 [1836]. 71-72.
The Past. (First, a suggested poem title, as poem is motto for Chapter 11 titled "The Past"; then, poem is given this title when included in Blanchard's selection of "Fragments" from *Ethel Churchill*; poem is an altered version of "Mardale Head").
    1st line: "Weep for the love that fate forbids;"
    in Landon, Letitia E. *Ethel Churchill: or, The Two Brides.* Vol. 2. London: Henry Colburn, 1837. 82;
    in Blanchard, Laman. *Life and Literary Remains of L. E. L.* Vol. 2. London: Henry Colburn, 1841. 273.

Past Hours.

    1st line: "Ah, surely there are moments when thy heart"

    in *The New Monthly Magazine* 51 (1837): 345.

Pasta.

    1st line: "I see thee, with thy night black hair"

    in Landon, Letitia E. *Schloss's English Bijou Almanac for 1839.* London: Albert Schloss, [1838]. N. pag. [3 pages].

Pauline's Price. — Goethe. (Translation; part of Second Series of "Versions from the German").

    1st line: "Sweet Pauline, could I buy thee"

    in *The Literary Gazette* 938 (Jan. 10, 1835): 28.

Peace Wrought by Pain. (One of the "Fragments" from *Ethel Churchill* selected by Blanchard; poem appears elsewhere as "[Meeting]").

    1st line: "Over that pallid face were wrought"

    in Blanchard, Laman. *Life and Literary Remains of L. E. L.* Vol. 2. London: Henry Colburn, 1841. 298.

The Peri. (No. VIII in the series, "Fragments in Rhyme").

    1st line: "It was a bower of roses, linked by wreaths"

    in *The Literary Gazette* 308 (Dec. 14, 1822): 794.

Petrarch's Dream. (No. I in the first series of "Subjects For Pictures" in The New Monthly; no. I in "Subjects for Pictures" in *Life and Literary Remains*).

    1st line: "Rosy as a waking bride"

    Prefixed lines to "Subjects for Pictures" begin: "What seek I here to gather into words?"

    in *The New Monthly Magazine* 47 (1836): 175-76;

    in Blanchard, Laman. *Life and Literary Remains of L. E. L.* Vol. 2. London: Henry Colburn, 1841. 197-99.

The Phantom.

    1st line: "I come from my home in the depth of the sea,"

    in Landon, Letitia E. *Fisher's Drawing Room Scrap-Book, 1836.* London and Paris: Fisher, Son; Berlin: Asher; New York: Jackson, [1835]. 40-41.

The Phantom Bride.

    1st line: "And over hill and over plain"

    in *The Literary Gazette* 400 (Sept. 18, 1824): 604-5.

The Phoenix and the Dove.. (Poem's source noted thus: "The Hint taken from the French of Millevoix"; "Love's Choice" is "From the same").

    1st line: "My wings are bright with the rainbow's dyes,"

    in Landon, Letitia E. *The Fate of Adelaide, A Swiss Romantic Tale; and Other Poems.* London: John Warren, 1821. 115.

Piccadilly. (Part of the series, "Scenes in London" in both publications; no. I in *The Zenana and Minor Poems of L. E. L.*).

    1st line: "The sun is on the crowded street,"

    in Landon, Letitia E. *Fisher's Drawing Room Scrap-Book, 1836.* London and Paris: Fisher, Son; Berlin: Asher; New York: Jackson, [1835]. 11-12;

    in *The Zenana and Minor Poems of L. E. L.* London: Fisher, Son; Paris: Quai de L'Ecole, [1839]. 178-82.

Pile of Fouldrey Castle, Lancashire.

    1st line: "No memory of its former state,"

    in Landon, Letitia E. *Fisher's Drawing Room Scrap-Book [for 1832]* London: Fisher,

Son, and Jackson, 1832 [1831]. 7-8.

The Pilgrim
 1st line: "And Palmer, grey Palmer, by Galilee's wave,
 in *Death's Doings; Consisting of Numerous Original Compositions in Prose and Verse.*
 Illus. Richard Dagley. 1st ed. London: J. Andrews; W. Cole, 1826. 31-33.

The Pilgrim.
 1st line: "Vain folly of another age, —"
 in *Emmanuel: A Christian Tribute of Affection and Duty; for the Year of our Lord 1830.*
 Ed. The Rev. William Shepherd. London: Saumel Maunder, 1830 [1829]. 102-04.

The Pirate's Song. (See "Bona. The Pirate's Song").

The Pirate's Song off the Tiger Island.
 1st line: "Our prize is won, our chase is o'er,"
 in Landon, Letitia E. *Fisher's Drawing Room Scrap-Book [for 1832].* London: Fisher,
 Son, and Jackson, 1832 [1831]. 15-16.

Pleasure Becomes Pain. (One of the "Fragments" from *Ethel Churchill* selected by Blan-
 chard; poem appears elsewhere as "[The Author and the Actress]" and is an altered
 version of the epigraph for "Moralising").
 1st line: "I cannot count the changes of my heart,"
 in Blanchard, Laman. *Life and Literary Remains of L. E. L.* Vol. 2. London: Henry
 Colburn, 1841. 292.

The Pledge.
 1st line: "Come, let your cup flash sunshine-like"
 in *The Literary Gazette* 597 (June 28, 1828): 412.

The Poet.
 1st line: "Oh say not that truth does not dwell with the lyre,"
 in *The Literary Gazette* 275 (Apr. 27, 1822): 264.

Poetic Fragments [contains three untitled poems]. (Numbered Fifth Series: to agree with
 the other series, "Poetic Fragments" should be changed to "Poetic Sketches" and
 numbered instead Sixth Series; poems are individually designated as "First," "Sec-
 ond," and "Third"; prefixed lines are, unusually, signed "L. E. L.").
 First (p. 812), 1st line: "'Twas Spring, the tree stood by the stream,"
 Second (p. 812), 1st line: "There was a paleness on his brow that spoke"
 Third (pp. 812-13), 1st line: "Last night the midnight wind,"
 Lines prefixed to this series begin: "I have a gush"
 in *The Literary Gazette* 465 (Dec. 17, 1825): 812-13.

Poetic Sketches [contains six untitled poems]. (First series only; poems individually desig-
 nated by "Sketch the First," "Sketch Second," etc.).
 Sketch the First, 1st line: "There are dark yew-trees gathered round, beneath"
 Prefixed lines begin: "Who shall bring healing to thy heart's despair,"
 in *The Literary Gazette* 260 (Jan. 12, 1822): 27-28;
 Sketch Second, 1st line: "It lay mid trees, a little quiet nest"
 Prefixed lines begin: "Oh, Power of love! so fearful, yet so fair"
 in *The Literary Gazette* 261 (Jan. 19, 1822): 44-45;
 Sketch Third, 1st line: "'Tis hidden from the sun by the tall elms,"
 Prefixed lines begin: "You must make"
 in *The Literary Gazette* 262 (Jan. 26, 1822): 59;
 Sketch Fourth, 1st line: "The shore was reefed with rocks, whose rugged sides"
 Prefixed lines begin: "I do love"

in *The Literary Gazette* 263 (Feb. 2, 1822): 71;

Sketch Fifth, 1st line: "The palms flung down their shadow, and the air"
1st set of prefixed lines begin: "Glad meetings, tender partings, which upstay"
2nd set of prefixed lines begin: "May never was the month of love,"
in *The Literary Gazette* 264 (Feb. 9, 1822): 89;

Sketch Sixth, 1st line: "Down swept the gathered waters over rocks"
1st set of prefixed lines begin: "She had no thought from him apart,"
2nd set of prefixed lines begin: "Alas, life is a weary voyage, made"
in *The Literary Gazette* 265 (Feb. 16, 1822): 105.

Poetical Portraits [contains six untitled poems]. (Poems are individually designated "No. I.,"
"No. II.," etc.).

No. I. (pp. 175-78), 1st line: "O no, sweet lady, not to thee"
No. II. (pp. 179-81), 1st line: "Ah! little do those features wear"
No. III. (pp. 182-88), 1st line: "His hand is on the snowy sail,"
No. IV. (pp. 188-90), 1st line: "His brow is pale with high and passionate thoughts,"
No. V. (pp. 190-95), 1st line: "Thy beauty! not a fault is there;"
No. VI. (pp. 196-98), 1st line: "The light is kindling in his eye,"
in Landon, Letitia E. *The Venetian Bracelet, The Lost Pleiad, A History of the Lyre, and
Other Poems.* London: Longman, Rees, Orme, Brown, and Green, 1829. 175-98.

The Poet's First Essay. (One of the "Fragments" from *Ethel Churchill* selected by Blan-
chard; poem appears elsewhere as "[A First Night]").
1st line: "It is a fearful stake the poet casts,"
in Blanchard, Laman. *Life and Literary Remains of L. E. L.* Vol. 2. London: Henry
Colburn, 1841. 276.

The Poet's Grave.
1st line: "'Tis his tomb — and trails around it"
in Landon, Letitia E. *Fisher's Drawing Room Scrap-Book, 1839.* London: Fisher, Son;
Paris: Quai de L'Ecole, [1838]. 47-48.

The Poet's Lot. (One of the "Fragments" from *Ethel Churchill* selected by Blanchard;
poem appears elsewhere as "[A London Life]").
1st line: "The poet's lovely faith creates"
in Blanchard, Laman. *Life and Literary Remains of L. E. L.* Vol. 2. London: Henry
Colburn, 1841. 261.

A Poet's Love. (One of the "Fragments" from *Ethel Churchill* selected by Blanchard;
poem appears elsewhere as an "[untitled poem]").
1st line: "Faint and more faint amid the world of dreams,"
in Blanchard, Laman. *Life and Literary Remains of L. E. L.* Vol. 2. London: Henry
Colburn, 1841. 279.

[A Poet's Midnight]. (Suggested poem title, as poem is motto for Chapter 5 titled "A
Poet's Midnight"; poem appears elsewhere as "Hope").
1st line: "Is not the lark companion of the spring?"
in Landon, Letitia E. *Ethel Churchill: or, The Two Brides.* Vol. 1. London: Henry Col-
burn, 1837. 52.

The Poet's Past. (One of the "Fragments" from *Ethel Churchill* selected by Blanchard;
poem appears elsewhere as "[The Usual Destiny of the Imagination]").
1st line: "Remembrance makes the poet: 'tis the past"
in Blanchard, Laman. *Life and Literary Remains of L. E. L.* Vol. 2. London: Henry
Colburn, 1841. 295.

The Poet's Power.
   1st line: "Oh, never had the poet's lute a hope,"
   in *The Ladies' Wreath; A Selection from the Female Poetic Writers of England and America.* Ed. Mrs. Sarah J. Hale. Boston: Marsh, Capen, and Lyon; New York: D. Appleton, 1837. 126-27.
The Poet's Retreat.
   1st line: "Oh! not in stately halls, or gilded rooms,"
   in *The Literary Gazette* 381 (May 8, 1824): 299.
The Poisoned Arrow. (Tale II in series of "Metrical Tales").
   1st line: "'Tis an old tale of love and truth"
   Prefixed line: "Love lives on Hope and Memory."
   in *The Literary Gazette* 372 (Mar. 6, 1824): 154-55.
The Polar Star.
   1st line: "A star has left the kindling sky —,"
   in *The New Monthly Magazine* 55 (1839): 28-29;
   in *The Fly* 6 (Feb. 9, 1839): 24;
   in Blanchard, Laman. *Life and Literary Remains of L. E. L.* Vol. 1. London: Henry Colburn, 1841. 190-91.
The Poor. (One of the "Fragments" from *Ethel Churchill* selected by Blanchard; poem appears elsewhere as "[The Fête at Sir Robert Walpole's]").
   1st line: "Few, save the poor, feel for the poor:"
   in Blanchard, Laman. *Life and Literary Remains of L. E. L.* Vol. 2. London: Henry Colburn, 1841. 290.
[Pope's Villa]. (Suggested poem title, as poem is motto for Chapter 18 titled "Pope's Villa"; poem appears elsewhere as "Weakness Ends With Love").
   1st line: "I say not, regret me; you will not regret;"
   in Landon, Letitia E. *Ethel Churchill: or, The Two Brides.* Vol. 1. London: Henry Colburn, 1837. 185.
The Poppy.
   1st line: "Pale are her enchanted slumbers;"
   in Landon, Letitia E. *Flowers of Loveliness; Twelve Groups of Female Figures, Emblematic of Flowers.* London: Ackermann, 1838. N. pag. [2 pages].
The Portrait. (Numbered "5" in a series of "Songs").
   1st line: "Ah! let me look upon thy face,"
   in *The Literary Gazette* 694 (May 8, 1830): 308.
Portrait.
   1st line: "I gaz'd admiringly upon his face;"
   in Landon, Letitia E. *The Fate of Adelaide, A Swiss Romantic Tale; and Other Poems.* London: John Warren, 1821. 93-94.
A Portrait. (One of the "Fragments" from *Ethel Churchill* selected by Blanchard; poem appears elsewhere as "[The Fête]").
   1st line: "Many were lovely there; but, of that many,"
   in Blanchard, Laman. *Life and Literary Remains of L. E. L.* Vol. 2. London: Henry Colburn, 1841. 271.
Portrait of a Girl, in the British Gallery, by T. Stewardson. (Part of the series, "Poetical Catalogue of Pictures").
   1st line: "In truth, dear Love, 'twas a fitting gift"
   Prefixed lines begin: "I do but give faint utterance to the thoughts"
   in *The Literary Gazette* 321 (Mar. 15, 1823): 171.

Portrait of a Lady. By Sir Thomas Lawrence. (One of the "Poetical Sketches of Modern Pictures").

1st line: "Lady, thy lofty brow is fair,"

in Landon, Letitia E. *The Troubadour; Catalogue of Pictures, and Historical Sketches.* London: Hurst, Robinson; Edinburgh: A. Constable, 1825. 257-59.

The Portrait of Lord Byron, at Newstead Abbey. (Poem is "Inscribed to Lord Byron's Sister, Mrs. George Leigh").

1st line: "It is the face of youth — and yet not young;"

in Howitt, Mary and Letitia E. Landon. *Fisher's Drawing Room Scrap-Book. 1840.* London: Fisher, Son; Paris: Quai de L'Ecole, [1839]. 11-14.

Portrait of Sappho.

1st line: "Her head was bending down"

in *The Lady's Cabinet Album.* New York: E. Sands, 1837. 158-159.

Portrait Painting. (Poem appears elsewhere as "Sir Thomas Lawrence," but with epigraph part of poem's main body).

1st line: "The softness of Ionian night"

Prefixed lines begin: "Divinest art, the stars above"

in *The Ladies' Wreath; A Selection from the Female Poetic Writers of England and America.* Ed. Mrs. Sarah J. Hale. Boston: Marsh, Capen, and Lyon; New York: D. Appleton, 1837. 136-37.

Portraits [contains two untitled poems]. (Poems numbered "1" and "2").

1., 1st line: "She leant her head bowed down upon her hand,"

2., 1st line: "His brow was like the marble, which the sun"

in *The Literary Gazette* 437 (June 4, 1825): 363.

[Poverty]. (Suggested poem title, as poem is motto for Chapter 34 titled "Poverty"; poem appears elsewhere as "Sorrows and Pleasures").

1st line: "It is an awful thing how we forget"

in Landon, Letitia E. *Ethel Churchill: or, The Two Brides.* Vol. 3. London: Henry Colburn, 1837. 272.

The Power of Words. (One of the "Fragments" from *Ethel Churchill* selected by Blanchard; poem appears elsewhere as "[The Challenge]").

1st line: "'Tis a strange mystery, the power of words!"

in Blanchard, Laman. *Life and Literary Remains of L. E. L.* Vol. 2. London: Henry Colburn, 1841. 295.

Presentiment. (First, a suggested poem title, as poem is motto for Chapter 17 titled "Presentiment"; then, poem is given this title when included in Blanchard's selection of "Fragments" from *Ethel Churchill*).

1st line: "I feel the shadow on my brow,"

in Landon, Letitia E. *Ethel Churchill: or, The Two Brides.* Vol. 2. London: Henry Colburn, 1837. 123;

in Blanchard, Laman. *Life and Literary Remains of L. E. L.* Vol. 2. London: Henry Colburn, 1841. 283.

Preston.

1st line: "Lo! the banquet is over, — but one, only one,"

in Landon, Letitia E. *Fisher's Drawing Room Scrap-Book, 1834.* London: H. Fisher, R. Fisher, and P. Jackson; Paris: Rittner and Goupil; Berlin and St. Petersburg: Asher; New York: Jackson, 1833. 50-51.

Pride in Trifles. (One of the "Fragments" from *Ethel Churchill* selected by Blanchard; poem appears elsewhere as "[An Interview]").

  1st line: "Why, life, must mock itself, to mark how small"
  in Blanchard, Laman. *Life and Literary Remains of L. E. L.* Vol. 2. London: Henry Colburn, 1841. 281.

The Pride of Love.

  1st line: "'Tis strange with how much power and pride"
  in *The Album of Love.* The Mirror Library. 3. New York: n.p., 1844. 6[?].

Prince Ahmed and the Fairy. A Sketch from the Arabian Nights.

  1st line: "On he past"
  in *Forget Me Not, A Christmas and New Year's Present for 1826.* Ed. Frederic Shoberl. London: R. Ackermann, [1825]. 347-48.

Prince Charles Edward.

  1st line: "Dark the wave, and dark the cloud,"
  in Landon, Letitia E. *Fisher's Drawing Room Scrap-Book, 1839.* London: Fisher, Son; Paris: Quai de L'Ecole, [1838]. 29.

The Princess Charlotte.

  1st line: "The tears of a nation were shed for her doom,"
  in Landon, Letitia E. *Fisher's Drawing Room Scrap-Book. 1833.* London: H. Fisher, R. Fisher, and P. Jackson, 1833 [1832]. 24.

The Princess Victoria.

  1st line: "And art thou a Princess? — in sooth, we may well"
  in Landon, Letitia E. *Fisher's Drawing Room Scrap-Book [for 1832].* London: Fisher, Son, and Jackson, 1832 [1831]. 5-6.

The Princess Victoria.

  1st line: "A fair young face o'er which is only cast"
  in Landon, Letitia E. *Fisher's Drawing Room Scrap-Book, 1837.* London, Paris, and New York: Fisher, Son; Germany: Black and Armstrong, and Asher, 1836. 22.

The Prisoner.

  1st line: "'Now come and see the linnet that I have caught to-day,"
  in Landon, Letitia E. *Traits and Trials of Early Life.* London: Henry Colburn, 1836. 119-20.

[A Project]. (A suggested poem title, as poem is motto for Chapter 28 titled "A Project"; poem appears elsewhere as "Hope and Love" and as an untitled poem within a series of "Songs").

  1st line: "The sun was setting o'er the sea,"
  in Landon, Letitia E. *Ethel Churchill: or, The Two Brides.* Vol. 2. London: Henry Colburn, 1837. 219.

The Prophetess.

  1st line: "In the deep silence of the midnight hours,"
  in Landon, Letitia E. *Fisher's Drawing Room Scrap Book, 1838.* London, Paris, and New York: Fisher, Son; Germany: Black and Armstrong, and Asher, 1837. 43-44;
  in *The Zenana and Minor Poems of L. E. L.* London: Fisher, Son; Paris: Quai de L'Ecole, [1839]. 284-88.

The Proposal.

  1st line: "The summer sun looks laughing through the bough"
  in *The Amulet. A Christian and Literary Remembrancer [for 1835].* Ed. S. C. Hall. London: Frederick Westley and A. H. Davis, 1835 [1834]. 95-96.

[A Proposal of Marriage]. (A suggested poem title, as poem is motto for Chapter 13 titled "A Proposal of Marriage"; poem appears elsewhere as "Resolves").

    1st line: "What mockeries are our most firm resolves!"

    in Landon, Letitia E. *Ethel Churchill: or, The Two Brides.* Vol. 1. London: Henry Colburn, 1837. 125.

[Prudence in Politics]. (Suggested poem title, as poem is motto for Chapter 23 titled "Prudence in Politics"; poem appears elsewhere as "Bitter Experience").

    1st line: "How often, in this cold and bitter world,"

    in Landon, Letitia E. *Ethel Churchill: or, The Two Brides.* Vol. 2. London: Henry Colburn, 1837. 175.

[Publishing]. (Suggested poem title, as poem is motto for Chapter 2 titled "Publishing"; poem appears elsewhere as "Small Miseries").

    1st line: "Life's smallest miseries are, perhaps, its worst:"

    in Landon, Letitia E. *Ethel Churchill: or, The Two Brides.* Vol. 2. London: Henry Colburn, 1837. 9.

Pulo Penang.

    1st line: "Never — that fairy isle can be"

    in Landon, Letitia E. *Fisher's Drawing Room Scrap-Book, 1836.* London and Paris: Fisher, Son; Berlin: Asher; New York: Jackson, [1835]. 56.

The Queen.

    1st line: "And has that young & graceful hand"

    in Landon, Letitia E. *The English Bijou Almanac for 1838.* London: Albert Schloss, [1837]. N. pag. [3 pages].

Queen Elizabeth's Entrance into Kenilworth.

    1st line: "Lonely sits the lovely lady,"

    in Landon, Letitia E. *Fisher's Drawing Room Scrap-Book, 1839.* London: Fisher, Son; Paris: Quai de L'Ecole, [1838]. 31-34.

The Queen of Portugal.

    1st line: "Young daughter of a race of kings,"

    in Landon, Letitia E. *Fisher's Drawing Room Scrap-Book. 1833.* London: H. Fisher, R. Fisher, and P. Jackson, 1833 [1832]. 6.

Queen's Room, Sizergh Hall, Westmoreland.

    1st line: "Ay, regal the chamber, and stately the gloom"

    in Landon, Letitia E. *Fisher's Drawing Room Scrap-Book, 1836.* London and Paris: Fisher, Son; Berlin: Asher; New York: Jackson, [1835]. 49.

Raffaelle.

    1st line: "Oh, born beneath those summer hours,"

    in Landon, Letitia E. *The English Bijou Almanac for 1836.* London: Albert Schloss, [1835]. N. pag. [3 pages].

[Ranelagh]. (Suggested poem title, as poem is motto for Chapter 2 titled "Ranelagh"; poem appears elsewhere as "The Charm Gone").

    1st line: "I did not wish to see his face,"

    in Landon, Letitia E. *Ethel Churchill: or, The Two Brides.* Vol. 3. London: Henry Colburn, 1837. 7.

Raphael Sanzio. (First half of poem is enclosed in brackets).

    1st line: "[Ah! not for him the dull and measured eye"

    in Landon, Letitia E. *Fisher's Drawing Room Scrap-Book. 1835.* London: H. Fisher, R. Fisher, and P. Jackson, 1835 [1834]. 50-52.

Raphael Showing His Mistress Her Portrait. By Mr. Brockedon. (British Gallery). (A poetic
response to a painting by Brockedon exhibited in the British Gallery).
    1st line: "I've thought upon thy brow when Night"
    Prefixed lines begin: "Surely he imaged this from his own heart?"
    in *The Literary Gazette* 379 (Apr. 24, 1824): 268.
Raphael's Death-Bed.
    1st line: "'Twas a twilight of Italy and spring,"
    in *The Friendship's Offering. A Literary Album [for 1826].* Ed. Thomas K. Hervey. Lon-
    don: Lupton Relfe, 1826 [1825]. 73-75.
Realities.
    1st line: "I made myself a little boat"
    in *The Literary Gazette* 432 (Apr. 30, 1825): 284.
Rebecca.
    1st line: "She looketh on the glittering scene"
    in Landon, Letitia E. *Fisher's Drawing Room Scrap-Book, 1837.* London, Paris, and
    New York: Fisher, Son; Germany: Black and Armstrong, and Asher, 1836. 11-12.
The Record. (One of the "Sketches From History").
    1st line: "He sleeps, his head upon his sword,"
    in Landon, Letitia E. *The Troubadour; Catalogue of Pictures, and Historical Sketches.*
    London: Hurst, Robinson; Edinburgh: A. Constable, 1825. 317-20.
Regatta, — Windermere Lake.
    1st line: "With sunshine on their canvass,"
    in Landon, Letitia E. *Fisher's Drawing Room Scrap-Book, 1837.* London, Paris, and
    New York: Fisher, Son; Germany: Black and Armstrong, and Asher, 1836. 49.
Remembrance.
    1st line: "Love taketh many colours, and weareth many shapes,"
    Prefixed line: "What doth it here at such an hour?"
    in *The Keepsake for 1837.* Ed. Lady Emmeline Stuart Wortley. London: Longman,
    Rees, Orme, Brown, Green, and Longman; Paris: Delloy, [1836]. 28-30.
Remembrance. (One of the "Fragments" from *Ethel Churchill* selected by Blanchard;
    poem appears elsewhere as "[The Remembrance of the Dead]").
    1st line: "Pale Memory sits lone, brooding o'er the past,"
    in Blanchard, Laman. *Life and Literary Remains of L. E. L.* Vol. 2. London: Henry
    Colburn, 1841. 281.
Remembrance. (Part of the Fifth Series of "Fragments by L. E. L.").
    1st line: "That Portrait! aye, it was a lovely face."
    Prefixed lines to series begin: "Gleamings of poetry, — if I may give"
    in *The Literary Gazette* 367 (Jan. 31, 1824): 74.
[The Remembrance of the Dead]. (Suggested poem title, as poem is motto for Chapter
    40 titled "The Remembrance of the Dead"; poem appears elsewhere as "Remem-
    brance").
    1st line: "Pale Memory sits lone, brooding o'er the past,"
    in Landon, Letitia E. *Ethel Churchill: or, The Two Brides.* Vol. 2. London: Henry Col-
    burn, 1837. 318.
[Reminiscences]. (Suggested poem title, as poem is motto for Chapter 26 titled "Remi-
    niscences"; poem appears elsewhere as "Despondency").
    1st line: "Ah, tell me not that memory"
    in Landon, Letitia E. *Ethel Churchill: or, The Two Brides.* Vol. 2. London: Henry Col-
    burn, 1837. 201.

Remorse. (One of the "Fragments" from *Ethel Churchill* selected by Blanchard; poem appears elsewhere as "[The Letters Restored]").

    1st line: "Alas! he brings me back my early years,"

    in Blanchard, Laman. *Life and Literary Remains of L. E. L.* Vol. 2. London: Henry Colburn, 1841. 294.

The Reply of the Fountain.

    1st line: "How deep within each human heart,"

    in Landon, Letitia E. *Fisher's Drawing Room Scrap-Book, 1834*. London: H. Fisher, R. Fisher, and P. Jackson; Paris: Rittner and Goupil; Berlin and St. Petersburg: Asher; New York: Jackson, 1833. 42–44;

    in *The Zenana and Minor Poems of L. E. L.* London: Fisher, Son; Paris: Quai de L'Ecole, [1839]. 111–16.

[A Request]. (Suggested poem title, as poem is motto for Chapter 36 titled "A Request"; poem appears elsewhere as "The Young Poet's Fate").

    1st line: "Trace the young poet's fate"

    in Landon, Letitia E. *Ethel Churchill: or, The Two Brides*. Vol. 3. London: Henry Colburn, 1837. 292.

[A Request Refused]. (Suggested poem title, as poem is motto for Chapter 36 titled "A Request Refused"; poem appears elsewhere as "Age").

    1st line: "Age is a dreary thing when left alone:"

    in Landon, Letitia E. *Ethel Churchill: or, The Two Brides*. Vol. 2. London: Henry Colburn, 1837. 292.

Requiem.

    1st line: "Oh! cold are thy slumbers, and low is thy grave,"

    in *The Literary Gazette* 253 (Nov. 24, 1821): 749.

Resolves.

    1st line: "Glide thou gentle river on,"

    in *The Amulet; or, Christian and Literary Remembrancer [for 1827]*. London: W. Baynes and Son, and Wightman and Cramp, 1827 [1826]. 304.

Resolves. (One of the "Fragments" from *Ethel Churchill* selected by Blanchard; poem appears elsewhere as "[A Proposal of Marriage]").

    1st line: "What mockeries are our most firm resolves;"

    in Blanchard, Laman. *Life and Literary Remains of L. E. L.* Vol. 2. London: Henry Colburn, 1841. 265.

Restormel Castle.

    1st line: "It was the last Chief of Restormel,"

    in Landon, Letitia E. *Fisher's Drawing Room Scrap-Book [for 1832]*. London: Fisher, Son, and Jackson, 1832 [1831]. 26.

[The Result]. (Suggested poem title, as poem is motto for Chapter 25 titled "The Result"; poem appears elsewhere as "Love's Ending").

    1st line: "And this, then, is love's ending. It is like"

    in Landon, Letitia E. *Ethel Churchill: or, The Two Brides*. Vol. 1. London: Henry Colburn, 1837. 231.

Retirement. A Picture in the British Gallery, by Leaky.

    1st line: "It was a stream in Thessaly, the banks"

    in *The Literary Souvenir; or, Cabinet of Poetry and Romance [for 1826]*. Ed. Alaric A. Watts. London: Hurst, Robinson; Edinburgh: A. Constable, 1826 [1825]. 385–86.

The Return.

    1st line: "'Drop down your oars, the waters trace'"

in *The Keepsake for 1831*. Ed. Frederic Mansel Reynolds. London: Hurst, Chance; Jennings and Chapline, [1830]. 273-74.

[Return Home]. (Suggested poem title, as poem is motto for Chapter 38 titled "Return Home"; poem appears elsewhere as "The Father's Love").
    1st line: "'Tis not my home — he made it home"
    in Landon, Letitia E. *Ethel Churchill: or, The Two Brides*. Vol. 2. London: Henry Colburn, 1837. 308.

[Return To Courtenaye Hall]. (Suggested poem title, as poem is motto for Chapter 19 titled "Return to Courtenaye"; poem appears elsewhere as "The Early Dream" and, with "ah" instead of "oh" in the first line, is an altered version of "Song" and an "[untitled poem]").
    1st line: "Ah! never another dream can be"
    in Landon, Letitia E. *Ethel Churchill: or, The Two Brides*. Vol. 3. London: Henry Colburn, 1837. 145.

Retzsch.
    1st line: "Close it not yet — that graceful page,"
    in Landon, Letitia E. *The English Bijou Almanac for 1836*. London: Albert Schloss, [1835]. N. pag. [3 pages].

Revenge.
    1st line: "Ay, gaze upon her rose-wreathed hair,"
    in Landon, Letitia E. *The Venetian Bracelet, The Lost Pleiad, A History of the Lyre, and Other Poems*. London: Longman, Rees, Orme, Brown, and Green, 1829. 232-35.

The Reverse.
    1st line: "Farewell, farewell, thou heartless one!"
    in *The Literary Gazette* 377 (Apr. 10, 1824): 236.

Rienzi showing Nina the Tomb of his Brother. (No. III in first series of "Subjects For Pictures" in *The New Monthly*; no. III in "Subjects for Pictures" in *Life and Literary Remains*).
    1st line: "It was hidden in a wild wood"
    Prefixed lines to "Subjects for Pictures" begin: "What seek I here to gather into words?"
    in *The New Monthly Magazine* 47 (1836): 178-79;
    in Blanchard, Laman. *Life and Literary Remains of L. E. L.* Vol. 2. London: Henry Colburn, 1841. 202-04.

The Right Honourable Lord Durham, Now on an Embassy at the Court of Russia.
    1st line: "What are the glories, which on history's page"
    in Landon, Letitia E. *Fisher's Drawing Room Scrap-Book. 1833*. London: H. Fisher, R. Fisher, and P. Jackson, 1833 [1832]. 34-35.

The River of the Water of Life. (Pilgrim's Progress).
    1st line: "Oh, glittering river, — doth the willow stoop"
    in Landon, Letitia E. *Fisher's Drawing Room Scrap-Book. 1835*. London: H. Fisher, R. Fisher, and P. Jackson, 1835 [1834]. 19.

The River Wear.
    1st line: "Come back, come back, my childhood,"
    in Landon, Letitia E. *Fisher's Drawing Room Scrap-Book, 1838*. London, Paris, and New York: Fisher, Son; Germany: Black and Armstrong, and Asher, 1837. 46-47.

Robert Blake, Admiral and General of the Parliamentary Forces.
    1st line: "What! will they sweep the channels,"
    in Landon, Letitia E. *Fisher's Drawing Room Scrap-Book, 1837*. London, Paris, and

New York: Fisher, Son; Germany: Black and Armstrong, and Asher, 1836. 14-15.

Robert Burns and his Highland Mary. (See also "Burns and his Highland Mary").
1st line: "A Highland girl, a peasant he,"
in *The Literary Souvenir [for 1831]*. Ed. Alaric A. Watts. London: Longman, Rees, Orme, Brown, and Green, 1831 [1830]. 177-180.

Roland's Tower. A Legend of the Rhine.
1st line: "Where, like a courser starting from the spur,"
Prefixed line: "Oh, Heaven! the deep fidelity of love!"
in Landon, Letitia E. *The Improvisatrice; and Other Poems*. London: Hurst, Robinson; Edinburgh: Archibald Constable, 1824. 129-42.

Romance. (Part of Sixth Series of "Fragments by L. E. L.").
1st line: "Maiden, listen! thy hunter's horn —"
Prefixed lines to series: "Gleamings of poetry, — if I may give"
in *The Literary Gazette* 368 (Feb. 7, 1824): 91.

Romance. (First, a suggested poem title, as poem is third in series of six poems titled "Six Songs of Love, Constancy, Romance, Inconstancy, Truth, and Marriage"; then, poem is given that title in *The Lyre*).
1st line: "Oh! come to my slumber"
in *The Literary Gazette* 251 (Nov. 10, 1821): 716;
in *The Lyre. Fugitive Poetry of the Nineteenth Century*. London: Tilt and Bogue, 1841. 322-23.

Rome.
1st line: "Oh! how thou art changed, thou proud daughter of fame,"
in *The Literary Gazette* 164 (Mar. 11, 1820): 173.

Rosalie.
1st line: "'Tis a wild tale — and sad, too, as the sigh"
in Landon, Letitia E. *The Improvisatrice; and Other Poems*. London: Hurst, Robinson; Edinburgh: A. Constable, 1824. 109-28.
as *Rosalie. A Tale*, in *The Ladies' Pocket Magazine* 2 (1837): 6-13.

Rosalie. (Sketch the Third in the Second Series of "Poetic Sketches").
1st line: "We met in secret: mystery is to love"
Prefixed line: "The green grass, with a cypress tree above,"
in *The Literary Gazette* 278 (May 18, 1822): 314.

The Rose. (One of the "Fragments" from *Ethel Churchill* selected by Blanchard; poem appears elsewhere as an "[untitled poem]").
1st line: "Why, what a history is on the rose!"
in Blanchard, Laman. *Life and Literary Remains of L. E. L.* Vol. 2. London: Henry Colburn, 1841. 274.

The Rose and Laurel Leaf.
1st line: "On thy path of music whither"
in *Forget Me Not, A Christmas and New Year's Present for 1830*. Ed. Frederic Shoberl. London: R. Ackermann, [1829]. 380.

The Rose of Eden-Dale and her Hothouse Flowers.
1st line: "They were so beautiful this morn —"
in *The Juvenile Forget-Me-Not: A Christmas and New-Year's Gift, or Birth-day Present. 1833*. Ed. Mrs. S. C. [Anna Maria] Hall. London: R. Ackermann; Westley and Davis, 1833 [1832]. 223-24.

A Ruined Castle on the Rhine, Formerly Belonging to the Templars. (Poem appears elsewhere as "The Church of St. John, and the Ruins of Lahneck Castle").
1st line: "On the dark heights that overlook the Rhine,"
in *The Zenana and Minor Poems of L.E.L.* London: Fisher, Son; Paris: Quai de L'Ecole, [1839]. 261-63.

The Ruined Cottage.
1st line: "None will dwell in that cottage, for they say"
Prefixed lines begin: "Oh there is"
in *Forget Me Not, A Christmas and New Year's Present for 1825.* Ed. Frederic Shoberl. London: R. Ackermann, [1824]. 120-23.

The Ruined Mind. (One of the "Fragments" from *Ethel Churchill* selected by Blanchard; poem appears elsewhere as "[The Chamber of Death]").
1st line: "Ah! sad it is to see the deck"
in Blanchard, Laman. *Life and Literary Remains of L. E. L.* Vol. 2. London: Henry Colburn, 1841. 297.

Ruins about the Taj Mahal.
1st line: "Mournfully they pass away,"
in Landon, Letitia E. *Fisher's Drawing Room Scrap-Book, 1836.* London and Paris: Fisher, Son; Berlin: Asher; New York: Jackson, [1835]. 35.

Ruins at Balbec.
1st line: "The crowned monarch sat on his throne,"
in Landon, Letitia E. *Fisher's Drawing Room Scrap-Book, 1839.* London: Fisher, Son; Paris: Quai de L'Ecole, [1838]. 57.

Runjeet-Singh, and his Suwarree of Seiks.
1st line: "The hunters were up in the light of the morn,"
in Landon, Letitia E. *Fisher's Drawing Room Scrap-Book, 1838.* London, Paris, and New York: Fisher, Son; Germany: Black and Armstrong, and Asher, 1837. 7.

The Rush-Bearing at Ambleside.
1st line: "Summer is come, with her leaves and her flowers —"
in Landon, Letitia E. *Fisher's Drawing Room Scrap-Book, 1836.* London and Paris: Fisher, Son; Berlin: Asher; New York: Jackson, [1835]. 23;
in *The Zenana and Minor Poems of L. E. L.* London: Fisher, Son; Paris: Quai de L'Ecole, [1839]. 204-06.

Rydal Water and Grasmere Lake, the Residence of Wordsworth. (Poem appears elsewhere as "On Wordsworth's Cottage, Near Grasmere Lake").
1st line: "Not for the glory on their heads"
in Landon, Letitia E. *Fisher's Drawing Room Scrap-Book, 1838.* London, Paris, and New York: Fisher, Son; Germany: Black and Armstrong, and Asher, 1837. 30-32.

St. George's Hospital, Hyde-Park Corner. (Sketch the Fourth in Second Series of "Poetic Sketches" in *The Literary Gazette*).
1st line: "I left the crowded street and the fresh day,"
Prefixed lines begin: "These are familiar things, and yet how few"
in *The Literary Gazette* 279 (May 25, 1822): 331;
in Landon, Letitia E. *The Improvisatrice; and Other Poems.* London: Hurst, Robinson; Edinburgh: A. Constable, 1824. 179-84;
in *Ladies' Penny Gazette* 2 (Aug. 9, 1834): 317.

St. John in the Wilderness.
1st line: "Afar, he took a gloomy cave,"
in Landon, Letitia E. *The Easter Gift, A Religious Offering.* London: Fisher, Son,

1832. 20-21.

St. Knighton's Kieve.
1st line: "Silent and still was the haunted stream,"
in Landon, Letitia E. *Fisher's Drawing Room Scrap-Book. 1835.* London: H. Fisher, R.
Fisher, and P. Jackson, 1835 [1834]. 47-48.

St. Mawgan Church & Lanhern Nunnery, Cornwall.
1st line: "It stands amid the sheltering boughs,"
in Landon, Letitia E. *Fisher's Drawing Room Scrap-Book. 1835.* London: H. Fisher, R.
Fisher, and P. Jackson, 1835 [1834]. 16-17.

St. Valerie. (Poem appears elsewhere as "Sta Valerie").
1st line: "Raised on the rocky barriers of the sea"
in *The Pledge of Friendship. 1826.* London: W. Marshall, [1825]. 107-08.

Sta Valerie. (Part of series, "Fragments in Rhyme"; numbered incorrectly "XII"; should
be regarded as "XI"; poem appears elsewhere as "St. Valerie").
1st line: "Raised on the rocky barriers of the sea,"
in *The Literary Gazette* 311 (Jan. 4, 1823): 12.

The Sacred Shrines of Dwarka.
1st line: "Such was the faith of old — obscure and vast,"
in Landon, Letitia E. *Fisher's Drawing Room Scrap-Book, 1837.* London, Paris, and
New York: Fisher, Son; Germany: Black and Armstrong, and Asher, 1836. 17.

The Sailor. (Sketch VI in Fourth Series of "Poetic Sketches" in *The Literary Gazette*).
1st line: "An aged Widow with one only child,"
Prefixed lines begin: "Oh gloriously upon the deep"
in *The Literary Gazette* 361 (Dec. 20, 1823): 811;
in Landon, Letitia E. *The Improvisatrice; and Other Poems.* London: Hurst, Robinson;
Edinburgh: A. Constable, 1824. 219-26.

The Sailor.
1st line: "Now tell me of my brother,"
in Landon, Letitia E. *Traits and Trials of Early Life.* London: Henry Colburn, 1836.
113-14.

The Sailor's Bride; or, The Bonaventure.
1st line: "The day is yet rosy with wakening from sleep,"
in Landon, Letitia E. *Fisher's Drawing Room Scrap-Book, 1839.* London: Fisher, Son;
Paris: Quai de L'Ecole, [1838]. 37-38;
in *Blackwood's Lady's Magazine* 6 (March 1839): 134-35.

Sans Souci.
1st line: "Come ye forth to our revel by moonlight,"
in *The Bijou; or Annual of Literature and the Arts [for 1828].* London: William Picker-
ing, 1828 [1827]. 77-80.

Sappho. (Sketch the First in Second Series of "Poetic Sketches" in *The Literary Gazette*;
one of the "Classical Sketches" in *The Vow of the Peacock, and Other Poems*).
1st line: "She leant upon her harp, and thousands looked"
Prefixed lines begin: "She was one"
in *The Literary Gazette* 276 (May 4, 1822): 282;
in Landon, Letitia E. *The Vow of the Peacock, and Other Poems.* London: Saunders
and Otley, 1835. 115-20;
in *The Lyre. Fugitive Poetry of the Nineteenth Century.* London: Tilt and Bogue, 1841.
114-16.

Sarnat, A Boodh Monument.
   1st line: "Dim faith of other times, when earth was young,"
   in Landon, Letitia E. *Fisher's Drawing Room Scrap-Book. 1833.* London: H. Fisher, R.
   Fisher, and P. Jackson, 1833 [1832]. 16-17.
Sassoor, in the Deccan. (Poem appears elsewhere as "Thoughts on Christmas-day in
   India").
   1st line: "It is Christmas, and the sunshine"
   in Landon, Letitia E. *Fisher's Drawing Room Scrap-Book. 1835.* London: H. Fisher, R.
   Fisher, and P. Jackson, 1835 [1834]. 7-8.
The Savoyard in Grosvenor Square. (Part of series, "Scenes in London," in both publica-
   tion; no. III in *The Zenana and Minor Poems of L. E. L.*).
   1st line: "He stands within the silent square,"
   in Landon, Letitia E. *Fisher's Drawing Room Scrap-Book, 1836.* London and Paris:
   Fisher, Son; Berlin: Asher; New York: Jackson, [1835]. 28-29;
   in *The Zenana and Minor Poems of L. E. L.* London: Fisher, Son; Paris: Quai de
   L'Ecole, [1839]. 187-90.
Scale Force, Cumberland.
   1st line: "It sweeps, as sweeps an army,"
   in Landon, Letitia E. *Fisher's Drawing Room Scrap Book, 1837.* London, Paris, and
   New York: Fisher, Son; Germany: Black and Armstrong, and Asher, 1836. 52.
[A Scene at the Masquerade]. (Suggested poem title, as poem is motto for Chapter 24
   titled "A Scene at the Masquerade"; poem appears elsewhere as "Memory").
   1st line: "I do not say, bequeath unto my soul"
   in Landon, Letitia E. *Ethel Churchill: or, The Two Brides.* Vol. 3. London: Henry Col-
   burn, 1837. 181.
[A Scene by Moonlight]. (Suggested poem title, as poem is motto for Chapter 9 titled
   "A Scene by Moonlight").
   1st line: "Thou canst not restore me"
   in Landon, Letitia E. *Ethel Churchill: or, The Two Brides.* Vol. 3. London: Henry Col-
   burn, 1837. 61.
Scene During the Plague at Gibraltar. (Poem appears elsewhere as "Gibraltar. Scene Dur-
   ing the Plague").
   1st line: "At first, I only buried one,"
   in *The Zenana and Minor Poems of L. E. L.* London: Fisher, Son; Paris: Quai de
   L'Ecole, [1839]. 241-43.
Scene in Bundelkhund.
   1st line: "She sat beneath the palm-tree, as the night"
   in Landon, Letitia E. *Fisher's Drawing Room Scrap-Book. 1835.* London: H. Fisher, R.
   Fisher, and P. Jackson, 1835 [1834]. 46.
Scene in Kattiawar.
   1st line: "I have a steed, to leave behind"
   in Landon, Letitia E. *Fisher's Drawing Room Scrap-Book. 1835.* London: H. Fisher, R.
   Fisher, and P. Jackson, 1835 [1834]. 22-23.
Scene in Lebanon. "The Prettiest and One of the Boldest Passes in Lebanon."
   1st line: "Ye mountains, gloomy with the past,"
   in Howitt, Mary and Letitia E. Landon. *Fisher's Drawing Room Scrap-Book. 1840.*
   London: Fisher, Son; Paris: Quai de L'Ecole, [1839]. 23.
Schiller.
   1st line: "Oh, many are the lovely shapes"

in Landon, Letitia E. *The English Bijou Almanac for 1836*. London: Albert Schloss, [1835]. N. pag. [3 pages].

The Scroll.
1st line: "The maiden's cheek blush'd ruby bright,"
in *Death's Doings; Consisting of Numerous Original Compositions in Prose and Verse.* Illus. Richard Dagley. 1st ed. London: J. Andrews; W. Cole, 1826. 33-34.

The Sea of Love. (Translation; part of "Third Series" of "Versions from the German").
1st line: "Whither would ye draw me, fair and faithless eyes, —"
in *The Literary Gazette* 939 (Jan. 17, 1835): 44.

The Sea-shore. (Poem appears elsewhere as "Dartmouth Castle").
1st line: "I should like to dwell where the deep blue sea"
in *The Zenana and Minor Poems of L. E. L.* London: Fisher, Son; Paris: Quai de L'Ecole, [1839]. 108-110.

[The Season]. (Suggested poem title, as poem is motto for Chapter 1 titled "The Season"; poem appears elsewhere as "Happiness Within").
1st line: "And yet it is a wasted heart:"
in Landon, Letitia E. *Ethel Churchill: or, The Two Brides.* Vol. 3. London: Henry Colburn, 1837. 1.

Second Fitte. (Seems to be first publication from ms. held by Jerdan).
1st line: "Oh pray thee do not name his name!"
in Jerdan, William. "Memoir of L. E. L." *Romance and Reality.* By Letitia E. Landon. Standard Novels. 111. London: Richard Bentley; Edinburgh: Bell and Bradfute, 1848. xxi-xxii.

Second Sight. A Dramatic Scene. (Dramatic speakers: Ronald and Ellen).
1st line: "Oh! I will chide thee, truant! Look how fair,"
in *Forget Me Not, A Christmas and New Year's Present for 1825.* Ed. Frederic Shoberl. London: R. Ackermann, [1824]. 22-28.

The Secret Discovered.
1st line: "Of all the things that angels see,"
in *Friendship's Offering; and Winter's Wreath: A Christmas and New Year's Present, for 1837.* London: Smith, Elder, 1837 [1836]. 320-24;
in *Blackwood's Lady's Magazine* 1 (Dec. 1836): 277.

[A Secretaryship]. (Suggested poem title, as poem is motto for Chapter 17 titled "A Secretaryship"; poem appears elsewhere as "Genius").
1st line: "Alas! and must this be the fate"
in Landon, Letitia E. *Ethel Churchill: or, The Two Brides.* Vol. 3. London: Henry Colburn, 1837. 125.

Secrets. (One of the "Fragments" from *Ethel Churchill* selected by Blanchard; poem appears elsewhere as "[The Confession]").
1st line: "Life has dark secrets; and the hearts are few"
in Blanchard, Laman. *Life and Literary Remains of L. E. L.* Vol. 2. London: Henry Colburn, 1841. 263.

Self-Blindness. (One of the "Fragments" from *Ethel Churchill* selected by Blanchard; poem appears elsewhere as "[Gaieties and Absurdities]").
1st line: "What Shakespeare said of lovers, might apply"
in Blanchard, Laman. *Life and Literary Remains of L. E. L.* Vol. 2. London: Henry Colburn, 1841. 274.

Self-Reproach. (One of the "Fragments" from *Ethel Churchill* selected by Blanchard; poem appears elsewhere as "[Lady Marchmont's Journal]").

　　1st line: "Deep in the heart is an avenging power,"
　　in Blanchard, Laman. *Life and Literary Remains of L. E. L.* Vol. 2. London: Henry Colburn, 1841. 293.

Separation.

　　1st line: "Aye, think of me in after years,"
　　in *The Pledge of Friendship; A Christmas Present, and New Year's Gift [for 1828].* London: W. Marshall, 1828 [1827]. 111-113.

The Serenade.

　　1st line: "'Tis midnight, and there is a world of stars"
　　in *Death's Doings; Consisting of Numerous Original Compositions in Prose and Verse.* Illus. Richard Dagley. 1st ed. London: J. Andrews; W. Cole, 1826. 69-72.

The Shadow.

　　1st line: "I hung o'er the side of the vessel while cleaving"
　　in *The Literary Gazette* 504 (Sept. 16, 1826): 588;
　　in *The Casket* 3 (Feb. 24, 1827): 24.

The Shamrock.

　　1st line: "Hope, mirth, and love, these are the bonds"
　　in *The Juvenile Forget-Me-Not: A Christmas and New-Year's Gift, or Birth-day Present. 1833.* London: R. Ackermann; Westley and Davis, 1833 [1832]. 25-27.

She Sat Alone Beside Her Hearth. (Poem appears elsewhere as "Horse-shoe Fall, Niagara. The Indian Girl").

　　1st line: "She sat alone beside her hearth —"
　　in *The Zenana and Minor Poems of L. E. L.* London: Fisher, Son; Paris: Quai de L'Ecole, [1839]. 197-203.

The Shepherd Boy.

　　1st line: "Like some vision olden"
　　in Landon, Letitia E. *Fisher's Drawing Room Scrap-Book. 1835.* London: H. Fisher, R. Fisher, and P. Jackson, 1835 [1834]. 54;
　　in *The Zenana and Minor Poems of L. E. L.* London: Fisher, Son; Paris: Quai de L'Ecole, [1839]. 138-40.

The Shrine and Grotto of Santa Rosalia.

　　1st line: "Had she not birth — that gives its place"
　　in Howitt, Mary and Letitia E. Landon. *Fisher's Drawing Room Scrap Book. 1840.* London : Fisher, Son; Paris: Quai de L'Ecole, [1839]. 15-16.

Shuhur, Jeypore.

　　1st line: "A lonely grave, far from all kindred ties;"
　　in Landon, Letitia E. *Fisher's Drawing Room Scrap-Book, 1834.* London: H.Fisher, R. Fisher, and P. Jackson; Paris: Rittner and Goupil; Berlin and St. Petersburg: Asher; New York: Jackson, 1833. 49.

The Sicilian Girl to the Madonna.

　　1st line: "Madonna, I have gathered flowers,"
　　in *The Literary Gazette* 710 (Aug. 28, 1830): 565.

[The Sick Room]. (Suggested poem title, as poem is motto for Chapter 19 titled "The Sick Room"; poem appears elsewhere as "Humanity Angelic").

　　1st line: "If ever angels walked on weary earth"
　　in Landon, Letitia E. *Ethel Churchill: or, The Two Brides.* Vol. 2. London: Henry Colburn, 1837. 139.

The Sick Room. (First, a suggested poem title, as poem is motto for Chapter 20 titled "The Sick-room"; then poem is given this title when included in Blanchard's selection of "Fragments" from *Ethel Churchill*).

    1st line: "'Tis midnight, and a starry shower"

    in Landon, Letitia E. *Ethel Churchill: or, The Two Brides.* Vol. 3. London: Henry Colburn, 1837. 153;

    in Blanchard, Laman. *Life and Literary Remains of L. E. L.* Vol. 2. London: Henry Colburn, 1841. 299.

Sir Adalbert: Ballad.

    1st line: "Sir Adalbert, Sir Adalbert, why dost thou pass the wine?"

    in *The Literary Gazette* 598 (July 5, 1828): 427.

Sir Guilbert.

    1st line: "Why is thy bark upon the sea —"

    in *The New Monthly Magazine* 16 (1826): 417-18.

Sir Robert Peel. (Poem appears elsewhere as "On the Portrait of Sir Robert Peel").

    1st line: "Dim through the curtains came the purple twilight slowly,"

    in Landon, Letitia E. *Fisher's Drawing Room Scrap-Book, 1837.* London, Paris, and New York: Fisher, Son; Germany: Black and Armstrong, and Asher, 1836. 10.

[Sir Robert Walpole and House]. (Suggested poem title, as poem is motto for Chapter 30 titled "Sir Robert Walpole and House"; poem appears elsewhere as "Influence of Poetry").

    1st line: "This is the charm of poetry: it comes"

    in Landon, Letitia E. *Ethel Churchill: or, The Two Brides.* Vol. 2. London: Henry Colburn, 1837. 236.

Sir T. Lawrence.

    1st line: "Thy hand is cold! thy colours weave"

    in Landon, Letitia E. *Schloss's English Bijou Almanac for 1839.* London: Albert Schloss, [1838]. N. pag. [3 pages].

Sir Thomas Hardy, Governor of Greenwich Hospital.

    1st line: "Silence is now upon the seas,"

    in Landon, Letitia E. *Fisher's Drawing Room Scrap-Book, 1836.* London and Paris: Fisher, Son; Berlin: Asher; New York: Jackson, [1835]. 38.

Sir Thomas Lawrence. (Poem appears elsewhere as "Portrait Painting," with first four lines as an epigraph).

    1st line: "Divinest art, the stars above"

    in Landon, Letitia E. *Fisher's Drawing Room Scrap-Book. 1833.* London: H. Fisher, R. Fisher, and P. Jackson, 1833 [1832]. 11-12;

    in *The Zenana and Minor Poems of L. E. L.* London: Fisher, Son; Paris: Quai de L'Ecole, [1839]. 90-93.

Sir Thomas Tyldesley.

    1st line: "The dew on the forest is steaming and white,"

    in Landon, Letitia E. *Fisher's Drawing Room Scrap-Book, 1839.* London: Fisher, Son; Paris: Quai de L'Ecole, [1838]. 40.

Sir Walter Scott.

    1st line: "Dead! — it was like a thunderbolt"

    in Landon, Letitia E. *Fisher's Drawing Room Scrap-Book. 1833.* London: H. Fisher, R. Fisher, and P. Jackson, 1833 [1832]. 44-46;

    in *The Zenana and Minor Poems of L. E. L.* London: Fisher, Son; Paris: Quai de L'Ecole, [1839]. 100-05.

Sir Walter Scott.

    1st line: "Now honour to the glorious head"

    in Landon, Letitia E. *The English Bijou Almanac for 1838.* London: Albert Schloss, [1837]. N. pag. [3 pages].

Sir William Stanley.

    1st line: "King Henry sat amid his court, and of the nobles there"

    Prefixed lines begin: "The man was old, his hair was grey —"

    in Landon, Letitia E. *Fisher's Drawing Room Scrap-Book, 1837.* London, Paris, and New York: Fisher, Son; Germany: Black and Armstrong, and Asher, 1836. 42.

The Sisters.

    1st line: "The morning light is in their hair,"

    in Landon, Letitia E. *Fisher's Drawing Room Scrap-Book, 1839.* London: Fisher, Son; Paris: Quai de L'Ecole, [1838]. 16.

The Sisters. (Tale III in series of "Metrical Tales" in *The Literary Gazette*; one of "A Series of Tales" in *The Vow of the Peacock, and Other Poems*).

    1st line: "Now, Maiden, wilt thou come with me,"

    in *The Literary Gazette* 373 (Mar. 13, 1824): 170-71;

    in Landon, Letitia E. *The Vow of the Peacock, and Other Poems.* London: Saunders and Otley, 1835. 208-15.

A Sister's Love.

    1st line: "My little sister! — whom I less"

    in [Collier, J. and Letitia E. Landon]. *The Pictorial Album; or, Cabinet of Paintings. For the Year 1837.* Illus. George Baxter. London: Chapman and Hall, 1837. 69-71.

Site of the Castle of Ulysses. Song of the Sirens. (Imitation of Homer).

    1st line: "Hither, famed Ulysses, steer,"

    in Landon, Letitia E. *Fisher's Drawing Room Scrap-Book, 1837.* London, Paris, and New York: Fisher, Son; Germany: Black and Armstrong, and Asher, 1836. 18-19.

Skeleton Group in the Rameswur, Caves of Ellora. Supposed to Represent the Nuptials of Siva and Parvati.

    1st line: "He comes from Kilas, earth and sky,"

    in Landon, Letitia E. *Fisher's Drawing Room Scrap-Book [for 1832].* London: Fisher, Son, and Jackson, 1832 [1831]. 32.

A Sketch.

    1st line: "'They're passing now adown our vale;'"

    in *The Literary Gazette* 636 (Mar. 28, 1829): 212.

Sketch. (Poem appears elsewhere as "The Warrior. A Sketch").

    1st line: "The warrior went forth in the morning light, —"

    in *The Literary Gazette* 353 (Oct. 25, 1823): 682.

Sketch of a Painting of Santa Malvidera, escaped miraculously from Shipwreck.

    1st line: "She knelt upon the rock; her graceful arms"

    in Landon, Letitia E. *The Fate of Adelaide, A Swiss Romantic Tale; and Other Poems.* London: John Warren, 1821. 81-82.

Sketch of Scenery.

    1st line: "It was a little glen, which, like a thing"

    in Landon, Letitia E. *The Fate of Adelaide, A Swiss Romantic Tale; and Other Poems.* London: John Warren, 1821. 129-32.

The Sleeping Beauty.

    1st line: "Sleep with honey-dews hath bound her,"

    in *Forget Me Not; A Christmas, New Years, and Birthday Present for 1837.* Ed. Frederic

Shoberl. London: Ackermann, 1837. 263-65.

Sleeping Child.

    1st line: "How innocent, how beautiful thy sleep!"

    in Landon, Letitia E. *The Fate of Adelaide, A Swiss Romantic Tale; and Other Poems.* London: John Warren, 1821. 99-100.

Small Miseries. (One of the "Fragments" from *Ethel Churchill* selected by Blanchard; poem appears elsewhere as as "[Publishing]").

    1st line: "Life's smallest miseries are, perhaps, its worst:"

    in Blanchard, Laman. *Life and Literary Remains of L. E. L.* Vol. 2. London: Henry Colburn, 1841. 272.

The Snowdrop.

    1st line: "Thou beautiful new-comer,"

    in Landon, Letitia E. *Fisher's Drawing Room Scrap-Book, 1836.* London and Paris: Fisher, Son; Berlin: Asher; New York: Jackson, [1835]. 15.

A Society of Antiquaries.

    1st line: "How many are the fancies"

    in Landon, Letitia E. *Fisher's Drawing Room Scrap-Book, 1839.* London: Fisher, Son; Paris: Quai de L'Ecole, [1838]. 43.

The Soldier's Bride. (Poem appears elsewhere as "Anecdote of Sobieski").

    1st line: "The white plume was upon his head,"

    in *Friendship's Offering of Sentiment and Mirth [for 1844].* London: Smith, Elder, 1844 [1843]. N. pag.

The Soldier's Funeral. (No. I in series, "Fragment in Rhyme" in *The Literary Gazette*; one of the "Fragments" in *The Improvisatrice; and Other Poems*).

    1st line: "And the muffled drum rolled on the air,"

    in *The Literary Gazette* 304 (Nov. 16, 1822): 728;

    in Landon, Letitia E. *The Improvisatrice; and Other Poems.* London: Hurst, Robinson; Edinburgh: A. Constable, 1824. 235-37.

The Soldier's Grave. (No. I in series of "Ballads" in *The Literary Gazette*; one of the "Ballads" in *The Improvisatrice; and Other Poems*).

    1st line: "There's a white stone placed upon yonder tomb,"

    in *The Literary Gazette* 317 (Feb. 15, 1823): 107;

    in Landon, Letitia E. *The Improvisatrice: and Other Poems.* London: Hurst, Robinson; Edinburgh: A. Constable, 1824. 318-21.

The Soldier's Home.

    1st line: "Thus spoke the aged wanderer,"

    in Landon, Letitia E. *Traits and Trials of Early Life.* London: Henry Colburn, 1836. 147-50.

Song. (Poem appears elsewhere as "A Love Song").

    1st line: "Are other eyes beguiling, Love?"

    in *The Literary Gazette* 259 (Jan. 5, 1822): 12;

    in *The Lyre. Fugitive Poetry of the Nineteenth Century.* London: Tilt and Bogue, 1841. 96-97.

Song. (Part of series, "Imitations of Servian Poetry").

    1st line: "The desert hath a dreary waste"

    in *The Literary Gazette* 538 (May 12, 1827): 300.

Song.

    1st line: "Dream, dream, let me dream,"

    in *The Casket, A Miscellany, Consisting of Unpublished Poems.* Ed. Mrs. Blencowe.

London: John Murray, 1829. 181-82.

Song.
    1st line: "Fair gifts are flung around thee,"
    in *The Album Wreath and Bijou Littéraire [for 1834]*. Ed. John Francis. London: De la
    Rue, James, and Rudd, 1834 [1833?]. N. pag. [1 page].

Song.
    1st line: "False as thou art, yet still farewell!"
    in *The Literary Gazette* 375 (Mar. 27, 1824): 203.

Song. (Poem appears elsewhere as an untitled poem within a series of "Songs").
    1st line: "Farewell! and soon between us both"
    in *The Fly* 34 (Aug. 24, 1839): 134.

Song.
    1st line: "Farewell to all! I shall not gaze"
    in *The Literary Gazette* 405 (Oct. 23, 1824): 684.

Song.
    1st line: "Farewell! — we shall not meet again"
    in *The Ladies' Wreath; A Selection from the Female Poetic Writers of England and America*. Ed. Mrs. Sarah J. Hale. Boston: Marsh, Capen, and Lyon; New York: D. Appleton, 1837. 133.

Song.
    1st line: "Float, float, down the stream,"
    in *The Literary Gazette* 484 (Apr. 29, 1826): 267.

Song.
    1st line: "Full well I know my heart"
    in *The Fly* 34 (Aug. 24, 1839): 134-35.

Song.
    1st line: "I cannot bear to look on thee,"
    in *The Literary Gazette* 379 (Apr. 24, 1824): 268.

Song.
    1st line: "I gave thee, love, a snow white wreath"
    in *Forget Me Not; A Christmas and New Year's Present for 1828*. Ed. Frederic Shoberl. London: R. Ackermann, [1827]. 216.

Song.
    1st line: "I have a summer gift,"
    in *The Literary Gazette* 434 (May 14, 1825): 316.

Song. (Poem appears elsewhere as an untitled poem, no. I, within a series of "Songs by
L. E. L.").
    1st line: "I loved her! and her azure eyes"
    in *The Casket of Literature, Science and Entertainment* 25 (June 18, 1836): 200.

Song.
    1st line: "I pray thee let me weep to-night,"
    in Landon, Letitia E. *The Venetian Bracelet, The Lost Pleiad, A History of the Lyre, and Other Poems*. London: Longman, Rees, Orme, Brown, and Green, 1829. 284-86.

Song.
    1st line: "I vow'd a vow of faith to thee,"
    in *The New Monthly Magazine* 14 (1825): 593.

Song.
    1st line: "I wrote my name upon the sand;"
    in *The Friendship's Offering. A Literary Album [for 1827]*. Ed. Thomas K. Hervey. Lon-

don: Lupton Relfe, 1827 [1826]. 180.

Song.
    1st line: "Listen to the tale"
    in *The Literary Gazette* 268 (Mar. 9, 1822): 152.

Song.
    1st line: "My own love, my dear love,"
    in *The Literary Gazette* 437 (June 4, 1825): 363.

Song.
    1st line: "Oh breathe not of love,"
    in *The New Monthly Magazine* 14 (1825): 443;
    in Blanchard, Laman. *Life and Literary Remains of L. E. L.* Vol. 2. London: Henry
    Colburn, 1841. 312-13.

Song. (Part of series, "Extracts from my Pocket Book").
    1st line: "Oh do not talk to me of love,"
    in *The Literary Gazette* 349 (Sept. 27, 1823): 619.

Song.
    1st line: "Oh, it is not for the laurel's sake"
    in *The Literary Gazette* 449 (Aug. 27, 1825): 557.

Song. (No. II in a series of "Fragments").
    1st line: "Oh leal I'll be to thee, my love,"
    in *The Literary Gazette* 344 (Aug. 23, 1823): 540.

Song. (Part of First Series of "Fragments by L. E. L.").
    1st line: "Oh meet me once, but once again,"
    Prefixed lines to series begin: "Gleamings of poetry, — if I may give"
    in *The Literary Gazette* 363 (Jan. 3, 1824): 10.

Song. (Poem appears elsewhere as an "[untitled poem]" and, in an altered version, as
    "[Return to Courtenaye Hall]" and "The Early Dream").
    1st line: "Oh never another dream can be"
    in Landon, Letitia E. *The Venetian Bracelet, The Lost Pleiad, A History of the Lyre, and
    Other Poems.* London: Longman, Rees, Orme, Brown, and Green, 1829. 242-43.

Song.
    1st line: "Oh say not that my heart is dead,"
    in *The New Monthly Magazine* 14 (1825): 508.

Song. (Part of Second Series of "Fragments by L. E. L.").
    1st line: "Oh speak not of love"
    Prefixed lines to series begin: "Gleamings of poetry, — if I may give"
    in *The Literary Gazette* 364 (Jan. 10, 1824): 27.

Song.
    1st line: "Oh, you cannot prove false to me, my love,"
    in *The Literary Gazette* 253 (Nov. 24, 1821): 749.

Song.
    1st line: "Our early years — our early years,"
    in Landon, Letitia E. *Heath's Book of Beauty. 1833.* London: Longman, Rees, Orme,
    Brown, Green, and Longman; Paris: Rittner and Goupil; Frankfort: C. Jügel,
    [1832]. 246.

Song. (Part of series, "Imitations of Servian Poetry").
    1st line: "She took a flower, and plucked the leaves,"
    in *The Literary Gazette* 538 (May 12, 1827): 300.

Song.
    1st line: "There were sweet sounds waked from my harp;"
    in *The Literary Gazette* 262 (Jan. 26, 1822): 60.
Song.
    1st line: "There's a shade upon that fountain;"
    in *The Literary Gazette* 467 (Dec. 31, 1825): 843.
Song.
    1st line: "This is enough! this broken heart"
    in *The Literary Gazette* 388 (June 26, 1824): 411.
Song. (Described as "Original").
    1st line: "Think no more of that sweet time,"
    in *The Album Wreath of Music and Literature [for 1835]*. London: R. Willoughby, [1834?]. 102.
Song.
    1st line: "Thou shalt think of me when the stars are weeping"
    in *The Pledge of Friendship; A Christmas Present, and New Year's Gift [for 1828]*. London: W. Marshall, 1828 [1827]. 378-79.
Song.
    1st line: "When last we parted, we stood beneath"
    in *The Literary Gazette* 336 (June 28, 1823): 411.
Song. (Part of Fifth Series of "Fragments by L. E. L.")
    1st line: "The wreath of green leaves that was bound"
    Prefixed lines to series begin: "Gleamings of poetry, — if I may give"
    in *The Literary Gazette* 367 (Jan. 31, 1824): 74.
Song. (Part of series, "Extracts from my Pocket Book").
    1st line: "Yes, still truly thine! Ah, they never Love knew"
    in *The Literary Gazette* 349 (Sept. 27, 1823): 619.
Song by L. E. L. [contains two untitled poems]. (Two poems appear elsewhere as untitled poems in series, "Songs"; 2nd poem appears elsewhere as "Parting Words").
    I., 1st line: "Farewell, and when to-morrow"
    II., 1st line: "May morning light fall o'er thee,"
    in *The Casket of Literature, Science and Entertainment* 5 (Feb. 4, 1837): 71.
Song. My heart is wholly changed.
    1st line: "My heart is wholly changed"
    in *The Literary Gazette* 431 (Apr. 23, 1825): 268.
Song of the Hunter's Bride. (No. II in series of "Ballads" in *The Literary Gazette*; one of the "Ballads" in *The Improvisatrice; and Other Poems*).
    1st line: "Another day — another day,"
    in *The Literary Gazette* 317 (Feb. 15, 1823): 107;
    in Landon, Letitia E. *The Improvisatrice: and Other Poems*. London: Hurst, Robinson; Edinburgh: A. Constable, 1824. 322-25.
Song of the Sirens. (See "Site of the Castle of Ulysses").
Songs [contains one untitled poem]. (No. 1 in series; also in series are "Love's Last Words" and "For Music").
    1st line: "Ah, look upon those withered flowers,"
    in *The Literary Gazette* 284 (June 29, 1822): 410.
Songs [contains two untitled poems].
    1st poem, 1st line: "Beautiful are the hues that lie"
    2nd poem, 1st line: "Last night, a fairy bark, for Hope,"

in *The Literary Gazette* 351 (Oct. 11, 1823): 650.

Songs [contains four untitled poems].

    1st poem, 1st line: "Do you recall one autumn night"

    2nd poem, 1st line: "Young Beauty once dwelt in a bower,"

    3rd poem, 1st line: "They say, that when the oyster shell —"

    4th poem, 1st line: "Do any thing but doubt me, Love!"

    in *The Literary Gazette* 376 (Apr. 3, 1824): 219.

Songs [contains three untitled poems]. (1st poem appears elsewhere as "Song"; 2nd poem appears elsewhere as "Hope and Love" and as "[A Project]"; 3rd poem resembles the "[The Marriage Morning]" and "Dangers Faced").

    1st poem (pp. 825-26), 1st line: "Farewell! and soon between us both"

    2nd poem (p. 826), 1st line: "The sun was setting o'er the sea,"

    3rd poem (p. 826), 1st line: "My heart is filled with bitter thoughts,"

    in *The Literary Gazette* 414 (Dec. 25, 1824): 825-26.

Songs [contains two untitled poems]. (Nos. I and II in series of "Songs"; 2nd poem appears elsewhere as "Parting Words"; two poems appear elsewhere as untitled poems under heading, "Song by L. E. L.").

    I., 1st line: "Farewell, and when to-morrow"

    II., 1st line: "May morning light fall o'er thee,"

    in *The New Monthly Magazine* 49 (1837): 173.

Songs [contains six untitled poems]. (4th poem appears elsewhere as "All Over the World with Thee, My Love!"; 6th poem appears elsewhere as "What was Our Parting?").

    1st poem (p. 203), 1st line: "I'll meet thee at the midnight hour,"

    2nd poem (p. 204), 1st line: "By those eyes of dark beauty,"

    3rd poem (p. 204), 1st line: "Pledge not that sparkling bowl"

    4th poem (p. 204), 1st line: "All over the world with thee, my love!"

    5th poem (p. 204), 1st line: "The dream on the pillow"

    6th poem (p. 204), 1st line: "What was our parting? — one wild kiss,"

    in *The Literary Gazette* 323 (Mar. 29, 1823): 203-04.

Songs [contains two untitled poems].

    1st poem, 1st line: "It is not for your eagle eye,"

    2nd poem, 1st line: "Oh! no, no, this love is not love for me;"

    in *The Literary Gazette* 398 (Sept. 4, 1824): 572.

Songs [three untitled poems].

    1st poem, 1st line: "Oh never throw thy love away"

    2nd poem, 1st line: "Yes, it was here, 'neath midnight skies,"

    3rd poem, 1st line: "I envy thee, thou careless wind!"

    in *The Literary Gazette* 341 (Aug. 2, 1823): 490.

Songs [two untitled poems].

    1st poem (pp. 697-98), 1st line: "The ring you gave, the kiss you gave,"

    2nd poem (p. 698), 1st line: "I will swear to thee by that bright star,"

    in *The Literary Gazette* 354 (Nov. 1, 1823): 697-98.

Songs [contains two untitled poems].

    1st poem, 1st line: "When do I think of thee? —"

    2nd poem, 1st line: "These are the words, the burning words,"

    in *The Literary Gazette* 833 (Jan. 5, 1833): 12.

Songs [contains two untitled poems].

    1st poem, 1st line: "When Love first came to me,"

    2nd poem, 1st line: "I would that I could cease"

in *The Literary Gazette* 470 (Jan. 21, 1826): 43.
Songs by L. E. L. [contains four untitled poems]. (A variation of series, "Songs of Love").
    I., "Farewell, farewell! Of this be sure,"
    II., "Farewell to my first dream of love,"
    III., "My heart is not light as when first, love,"
    IV., "'Twas sweet to look upon thine eyes,"
    in *The Ladies' Penny Gazette* 2 (Dec. 7, 1833): 38.
Songs by L. E. L. [contains four untitled poems]. (No. I appears elsewhere as "Song").
    I. (p. 29), 1st line: "I loved her! and her azure eyes"
    II. (p. 30), 1st line: "A mouth that is itself a rose,"
    III. (p. 30), 1st line: "I send back thy letters:"
    IV. (p. 30), 1st line: "As steals the dew along the flower,"
    in *The New Monthly Magazine* 47 (1836): 29-30.
Songs of Love [contains four untitled poems]. (Part of larger series, "Extracts from my Pocket Book"; 2nd poem is set to "Air, — Here's a health to ane I loo dear"; 3rd poem is set to "Air, — Tam Glen"; three of the poems and epigraph appear elsewhere as four untitled poems within the series, "Songs by L. E. L.").
    1st poem, 1st line: "Oh never may I feel again"
    2nd poem, 1st line: "Farewell to my first dream of love,"
    3rd poem, 1st line: "My heart is not light as when first, love,"
    4th poem, 1st line: "'Twas sweet to look upon thine eyes,"
    Lines prefixed to "Songs of Love": "Farewell, farewell! Of this be sure,"
    in *The Literary Gazette* 350 (Oct. 4, 1823): 635.
Songs on Absence [contains three untitled poems].
    1st poem, 1st line: "My heart is with thee, Love! though now"
    2nd poem, 1st line: "Not when pleasure's chain has bound thee,"
    3rd poem, 1st line: "Dearest! wander where you will,"
    in *The Literary Gazette* 300 (Oct. 19, 1822): 664.
Sonnet.
    1st line: "Green willow! over whom the perilous blast"
    in Landon, Letitia E. *The Fate of Adelaide, A Swiss Romantic Tale; and Other Poems.* London: John Warren, 1821. 83.
Sonnet.
    1st line: "I envy not the traveller's delight,"
    in Landon, Letitia E. *The Fate of Adelaide, A Swiss Romantic Tale; and Other Poems.* London: John Warren, 1821. 109.
Sonnet.
    1st line: "It is not in the day of revelry,"
    in Landon, Letitia E. *The Fate of Adelaide, A Swiss Romantic Tale; and Other Poems.* London: John Warren, 1821. 84.
Sorrows and Pleasures. (One of the "Fragments" from *Ethel Churchill* selected by Blanchard; poem appears elsewhere as "[Poverty]").
    1st line: "It is an awful thing how we forget"
    in Blanchard, Laman. *Life and Literary Remains of L. E. L.* Vol. 2. London: Henry Colburn, 1841. 297.
The Spanish Page, or, the City's Ransom.
    1st line: "She was a chieftain's daughter, and he a captive boy,"
    in Landon, Letitia E. *Fisher's Drawing Room Scrap-Book, 1837.* London, Paris, and New York: Fisher, Son; Germany: Black and Armstrong, and Asher, 1836. 34-35;

in *The Zenana and Minor Poems of L. E. L.* London: Fisher, Son; Paris: Quai de L'Ecole, [1839]. 233-37.

Speke Hall.

1st line: "Oh, fair old House — how Time doth honour thee,"
in Landon, Letitia E. *Fisher's Drawing Room Scrap-Book. 1835.* London: H. Fisher, R. Fisher, and P. Jackson. 1835 [1834]. 23.

The Spirit and the Angel of Death. (Dramatic dialogue between Spirit and Angel of Death).

1st line: "I have been over the joyous earth,"
in *The Friendship's Offering. A Literary Album [for 1827].* London: Ed. Thomas K. Hervey. London: Lupton Relfe, 1827 [1826]. 1-4;
in Landon, Letitia E. *The Vow of the Peacock, and Other Poems.* London: Saunders and Otley, 1835. 264-70.

The Spirit of Dreams.

1st line: "Spirit of the midnight dream,"
in *The Literary Gazette* 532 (Mar. 31, 1827): 204.

The Stag. (Poem appears elsewhere as "The Chase, or the Fate of the Stag").

1st line: "It is morning, and the sky,"
in *Forget Me Not, A Christmas and New Year's Present for 1827.* Ed. Frederic Shoberl. London: R. Ackermann, [1826]. 127-29.

Stanzas. (Prefixed lines appear elsewhere as "Fairies").

1st line: "Alas! alas! the times are fled"
Prefixed lines begin: "Race of the rainbow wing, the deep blue eye"
in *The Literary Gazette* 386 (June 12, 1824): 378-79.

Stanzas.

1st line: "Farewell, farewell! then both are free, —"
in *The Literary Gazette* 332 (May 31, 1823): 349.

Stanzas.

1st line: "I do not weep that thou art laid"
in Landon, Letitia E. *The Fate of Adelaide, A Swiss Romantic Tale; and Other Poems.* London: John Warren, 1821. 85.

Stanzas.

1st line: "I know it is not made to last,"
in *The New Monthly Magazine* 39 (1833): 487-88;
in Blanchard, Laman. *Life and Literary Remains of L. E. L.* Vol. 2. London: Henry Colburn, 1841. 308-11.

Stanzas. (Poem appears elsewhere as "The Visionary").

1st line: "I pray thee, do not speak to me"
Prefixed lines begin: "Oh, never did the sky,"
in *The Edinburgh Literary Journal* 111 (Dec. 25, 1830): 391.

Stanzas.

1st line: "I turn'd into the olive grove"
Prefixed lines begin: "And art thou gone! Ah! life was never made"
in *The Literary Gazette* 420 (Feb. 5, 1825): 92.

Stanzas [contains two untitled poems].

1st poem (pp. 395-96), 1st line: "Is this the harp you used to wake,"
2nd poem (p. 396), 1st line: "Have the dreams of thy youth departed,"
in *The Literary Gazette* 387 (June 19, 1824): 395-96.

Stanzas
   1st line: "The moon is shining o'er the lake"
   Prefixed lines by Alaric A. Watts begin: "I too am changed, I scarce know why,"
   in *The Literary Gazette* 385 (June 5, 1824): 363.
Stanzas.
   1st line: "My heart hath turned way"
   Prefixed lines begin: "Oh life, what wouldst thou be, but that thine end"
   in *The Amulet; or, Christian and Literary Remembrancer [for 1826]*. London: William
   Baynes, Son; Edinburgh: H. S. Baynes, 1826 [1825]. 268-69;
   in *The Pledge of Friendship. 1829*. London: W. Marshall, 1829 [1828]. 268-69.
Stanzas.
   1st line: "Oh, tell me not I shall forget"
   in *The Literary Gazette* 454 (Oct. 1, 1825): 636 [630].
Stanzas.
   1st line: "Twine not those red roses for me, —"
   in *The Literary Gazette* 332 (May 31, 1823): 349.
Stanzas.
   1st line: "We shall not meet again, love,"
   in *The Literary Gazette* 355 (Nov. 8, 1823): 715.
Stanzas.
   1st line: "Well, indeed, may you deem,"
   Prefixed lines begin: "Is this your Creed of Love? It is enough"
   in *The Literary Gazette* 425 (Mar. 12, 1825): 173.
Stanzas. (Poem appear elsewhere as "When Should Lovers Breathe their Vows?").
   1st line: "When should lovers breathe their vows?"
   Prefixed lines from *The Literary Gazette* begin: "And while the moon reigns cold
   above,"
   in *The Literary Gazette* 253 (Nov. 24, 1821): 749.
Stanzas, Adapted to Music by —-.
   1st line: "My heart is as light as the gossamer veil,"
   in Landon, Letitia E. *The Fate of Adelaide, A Swiss Romantic Tale; and Other Poems.*
   London: John Warren, 1821. 119-20.
Stanzas. Is it not so? (Part of Second Series of "Fragments by L. E. L.").
   1st line: "It is a green and sunny place"
   Prefixed lines to series begin: "Gleamings of poetry, — if I may give"
   in *The Literary Gazette* 364 (Jan. 10, 1824): 27.
Stanzas On the Death of Miss Campbell.
   1st line: "Rose of our love, how soon thou art faded,"
   in *The Literary Gazette* 244 (Sept. 22, 1821): 602.
Stanzas on the Death of Mrs. Hemans.
   1st line: "Bring flowers to crown the cup and lute, —"
   Prefixed line from Hemans's *Lays of Many Lands*: "The rose — the glorious rose is
   gone."
   in *The New Monthly Magazine* 44 (May-Aug. 1835): 286-88;
   in *The Ladies' Wreath; A Selection from the Female Poetic Writers of England and Ameri-
   ca*. Ed. Mrs. Sarah J. Hale. Boston: Marsh, Capen, and Lyon; New York: D. Apple-
   ton, 1837. 138-41;
   in Blanchard, Laman. *Life and Literary Remains of L. E. L.* Vol. 2. London: Henry
   Colburn, 1841. 245-48.

Stanzas on the New Year.
　　1st line: "I stood between the meeting Years,"
　　in *The New Monthly Magazine* 16 (1826): 80;
　　in Blanchard, Laman. *Life and Literary Remains of L. E. L.* Vol. 2. London: Henry
　　　Colburn, 1841. 307-08.
Stanzas to the Author of "Mont Blanc," "Ada," &c.
　　1st line: "Thy hands are fill'd with early flowers,"
　　in Landon, Letitia E. *The Venetian Bracelet, The Lost Pleiad, A History of the Lyre, and
　　　Other Poems.* London: Longman, Rees, Orme, Brown, and Green, 1829. 287-94.
Stanzas. Written beneath the Portrait of Lord Byron, painted by Mr. West.
　　1st line: "'Tis with strange feelings that I gaze"
　　in *The Literary Souvenir; or, Cabinet of Poetry and Romance [for 1827].* Ed. Alaric A.
　　　Watts. London: Longman, Rees, Orme, Brown and Green; and John Andrews.
　　　1827 [1826]. 33-36.
The Star.
　　1st line: "Oh! would I might share thy wild car,"
　　in Landon, Letitia E. *The Fate of Adelaide, A Swiss Romantic Tale; and Other Poems.*
　　　London: John Warren, 1821. 117-18.
The Star. (Part of Sixth Series of "Fragments by L. E. L.").
　　1st line: "Oh, there are sorrows like blighted leaves,"
　　Prefixed lines to series begin: "Gleamings of poetry, — if I may give"
　　in *The Literary Gazette* 368 (Feb. 7, 1824): 91.
The Stars.
　　1st line: "Last night I by my casement leant,"
　　in *The Literary Gazette* 406 (Oct. 30, 1824): 701.
Stern Truth. (One of the "Fragments" from *Ethel Churchill* selected by Blanchard; poem
　　appears elsewhere as "[The Masked Ball]").
　　1st line: "Life is made up of vanities — so small,"
　　in Blanchard, Laman. *Life and Literary Remains of L. E. L.* Vol. 2. London: Henry
　　　Colburn, 1841. 295.
The Storm.
　　1st line: "There was a vessel combating the waves,"
　　in Landon, Letitia E. *The Fate of Adelaide, A Swiss Romantic Tale; and Other Poems.*
　　　London: John Warren, 1821. 141-45.
Storrs, Windermere Lake.
　　1st line: "I would I had a charmed bark,"
　　in Landon, Letitia E. *Fisher's Drawing Room Scrap-Book [for 1832].* London: Fisher,
　　　Son, and Jackson, 1832 [1831]. 14.
Stothard's Erato. (Part of series, "Poetical Catalogue of Pictures").
　　1st line: "Gentlest one, I bow to thee,"
　　in *The Literary Gazette* 342 (Aug. 9, 1823): 507.
Strada Reale — Corfu.
　　1st line: "I am weary of the green wood"
　　in Landon, Letitia E. *Fisher's Drawing Room Scrap Book, 1837.* London, Paris, and
　　　New York: Fisher, Son; Germany: Black and Armstrong, and Asher, 1836. 36.
Strada St. Ursola, — Malta.
　　1st line: "Young knight, that broidered cloak undo,"
　　in Landon, Letitia E. *Fisher's Drawing Room Scrap-Book, 1837.* London, Paris, and
　　　New York: Fisher, Son; Germany: Black and Armstrong, and Asher, 1836. 44.

The Student. (Poem appears elsewhere as "The Gentle Student").

　　1st line: "Bend, gentle student, o'er the page,"
　　in *The Christian Keepsake, and Missionary Annual, for 1849*. Philadelphia: Brower, Hayes, 1849. 247.

[Success]. (Suggested poem title, as poem is motto for Chapter 10 titled "Success"; poem appears elsewhere as "What is Success?").

　　1st line: "All things are symbols; and we find"
　　in Landon, Letitia E. *Ethel Churchill: or, The Two Brides*.Vol. 2. London: Henry Colburn, 1837. 73-74.

Success Alone Seen. (One of the "Fragments" from *Ethel Churchill* selected by Blanchard; poem appears elsewhere as an "[untitled poem]").

　　1st line: "Few know of life's beginnings — men behold"
　　in Blanchard, Laman. *Life and Literary Remains of L. E. L.*Vol. 2. London: Henry Colburn, 1841. 260.

The Suicide's Grave.

　　1st line: "Look on this mound; the newly-turn'd-up earth"
　　in *Friendship's Offering, or, the Annual Remembrancer: A Christmas Present, or New Year's Gift, for 1825*. London: Lupton Relfe, [1824]. 197-200.

The Sultana's Remonstrance. (One of the "Sketches from History").

　　1st line: "It suits thee well to weep,"
　　in Landon, Letitia E. *The Troubadour; Catalogue of Pictures, and Historical Sketches*. London: Hurst, Robinson; Edinburgh: A. Constable, 1825. 305-08.

A Summer Day.

　　1st line: "Sweet valley, whose streams flow as sparkling and bright"
　　in Landon, Letitia E. *The Venetian Bracelet, The Lost Pleiad, A History of the Lyre, and Other Poems*. London: Longman, Rees, Orme, Brown, and Green, 1829. 236-38.

A Summer Evening's Tale.

　　1st line: "Come, let thy careless sail float on the wind;"
　　in Landon, Letitia E. *The Venetian Bracelet, The Lost Pleiad, A History of the Lyre, and Other Poems*. London: Longman, Rees, Orme, Brown, and Green, 1829. 249-64.

A Supper of Madame de Brinvilliers. (No. II in second series of "Subjects for Pictures" in *The New Monthly*; no.V in "Subjects for Pictures" in *Life and Literary Remains*).

　　1st line: "Small but gorgeous was the chamber"
　　Prefixed lines to "Subjects for Pictures" begin: "What seek I here to gather into words?"
　　in *The New Monthly Magazine* 48 (1836): 22-24;
　　in Blanchard, Laman. *Life and Literary Remains of L. E. L.* Vol. 2. London: Henry Colburn, 1841. 207-10.

A Suttee. (Poem appears elsewhere as "Immolation of a Hindoo Widow").

　　1st line: "Gather her raven hair in one rich cluster,"
　　in *The Zenana and Minor Poems of L.E.L.* London: Fisher, Son; Paris: Quai de L'Ecole, [1839]. 175-77.

The Swan. (Part of Fifth Series of "Fragments by L. E. L.").

　　1st line: "I pass'd by a lake in its darkness:"
　　Prefixed lines to series begin: "Gleamings of poetry, — if I may give"
　　in *The Literary Gazette* 367 (Jan. 31, 1824): 74.

The Sword.

　　1st line: "'Twas the battle-field, and the cold pale moon"
　　in *Forget Me Not, A Christmas and New Year's Present for 1828*. Ed. Frederic Shoberl.

London: Ackermann, [1827]. 29-30;
in *The Lady's Magazine* 8 (1828): 30-31.
The Taj-Mahal, at Agra. The Tomb of Muntaza Zemani.
    1st line: "'Aye, build it on these banks,' the monarch said,"
    in Landon, Letitia E. *Fisher's Drawing Room Scrap Book [for 1832]*. London: Fisher,
    Son, and Jackson, 1832 [1831]. 20.
A Tale Founded on Fact.
    1st line: "There is a little Vale, made beautiful"
    in *The Literary Gazette* 337 (July 5, 1823): 427-28.
The Temple Garden. (One of the "Fragments" from *Ethel Churchill* selected by Blan-
    chard; poem appears elsewhere as "The Middle Temple Gardens" and as an "[unti-
    tled poem]").
    1st line: "The fountain's low singing is heard in the wind,"
    in Blanchard, Laman. *Life and Literary Remains of L. E. L.* Vol. 2. London: Henry
    Colburn, 1841. 285.
Temple and Fountain at Zagwhan.
    1st line: "Of the vacant temple"
    in Howitt, Mary. *Fisher's Drawing Room Scrap-Book. 1841*. London: Fisher, Son;
    Paris: Quai de L'Ecole, [1840]. 43-45.
The Temple of the Juggernaut.
    1st line: "The winds are stirred with tumult — on the air"
    in Howitt, Mary and Letitia E. Landon. *Fisher's Drawing Room Scrap-Book. 1840*.
    London: Fisher, Son; Paris: Quai de L'Ecole, [1839]. 22.
Ten Years Ago.
    1st line: "'Ten years ago,' the world was then"
    in *The Literary Gazette* 260 (Jan. 12, 1822): 28.
The Thessalian Fountain. (Part of "Classical Sketches"; poem appears elsewhere as an
    untitled poem within the Fourth Series of "Fragments by L. E. L.").
    1st line: "A small clear fountain, with green willow trees"
    Prefixed lines begin: "Gleamings of poetry, — if I may give"
    in Landon, Letitia E. *The Vow of the Peacock, and Other Poems*. London: Saunders
    and Otley, 1835. 149-51.
Think of Me. (Poem appears elsewhere as part of "On a Star," called "Song," and as
    "Farewell! and Never Think of Me")
    1st line: "Farewell! — and never think of me"
    in *The Passion Flower.* The Mirror Library. 5. New York: n.p., 1844. 31.
Thomas Clarkson, Esq. (Poem is "Inscribed to the Right Honourable Lord Brougham
    and Vaux").
    1st line: "Not to the many doth the earth"
    in Howitt, Mary and Letitia E. Landon. *Fisher's Drawing Room Scrap Book. 1840*.
    London: Fisher, Son; Paris: Quai de L'Ecole, [1839]. 20-22.
Thomas Moore, Esq.
    1st line: "If Titania, just wakened from dreams which the rose,"
    in Landon, Letitia E. *Fisher's Drawing Room Scrap-Book, 1839*. London: Fisher, Son;
    Paris: Quai de L'Ecole, [1838]. 14;
    in *The Zenana and Minor Poems of L. E. L.* London: Fisher, Son; Paris: Quai de
    L'Ecole, [1839]. 289-91.
Thoughts.
    1st line: "'Tis not the lover that is lost — the love — for which we grieve"

in *The Album Wreath of Music and Literature [for 1835]*. London: R. Willoughby, [1834?]. 10.

Thoughts on Christmas-day in India. (Poem appears elsewhere as "Sassoor, in the Deccan").

1st line: "It is Christmas, and the sunshine"
in *The Zenana and Minor Poems of L. E. L*. London: Fisher, Son; Paris: Quai de L'Ecole, [1839]. 119-23.

The Three Brothers. (Poem appears elsewhere as "Fame: An Apologue. The Three Brothers").

1st line: "They dwelt in a valley of sunshine, those Brothers;"
in Landon, Letitia E. *The Vow of the Peacock, and Other Poems*. London: Saunders and Otley. 1835. 299-305.

The Three Wells — A Fairy Tale. (No. 1 in series of "Metrical Tales").

1st line: "There's an island which the sea"
Prefixed line from Marmontel: "J'ai grand regret à la fairée."
in *The Literary Gazette* 371 (Feb. 28, 1824): 139.

Thubare, a Port on the Arabian Coast.

1st line: "Thou lovely port of Araby,"
in Landon, Letitia E. *Fisher's Drawing Room Scrap-Book. 1833*. London: H. Fisher, R. Fisher, and P. Jackson, 1833 [1832]. 19-21.

The Thunder-Storm.

1st line: "It comes! — the rushing wind has burst"
Prefixed line: "Fear not, thy God is with thee."
in *Forget Me Not, A Christmas and New Year's Present for 1832*. Ed. Frederic Shoberl. London: Ackermann, [1831]. 151-53.

Time arresting the Career of Pleasure. (Sketch the First in series, "Sketches from Drawings by Mr. Dagley").

1st line: "Stay thee on thy mad career,"
Prefixed lines begin: "His iron hand grasped a Bacchante's arm,"
in *The Literary Gazette* 288 (July 27, 1822): 473.

Tivoli.

1st line: "When last I gazed, fair Tivoli,"
Prefixed lines begin: "Rushing, like uncurbed passion, thro' the rocks"
in *The Bijou; or Annual of Literature and the Arts [for 1829]*. London: William Pickering, 1829 [1828]. 7-9.

To —.

1st line: "Oh! say not, that I love not nature's face,"
in Landon, Letitia E. *The Fate of Adelaide, A Swiss Romantic Tale; and Other Poems*. London: John Warren, 1821. 95-96.

To Alaric A. Watts, Esq. On receiving from him a copy of his "Poetic Sketches." (Poem appears elsewhere as "Lines Addressed to Alaric A. Watts, Esq." and as "To the Author of 'Poetical Sketches'").

1st line: "There is a dear and lovely power"
in *The Literary Magnet* 4 (1826): 215.

To Amelia Read, on her Thirteenth Birthday.

1st line: "Oh, yet in the happiest season!"
in *Ackermann's Juvenile Forget Me Not. 1830*. London: R. Ackermann, [1829]. 177.

To the Author of "Poetical Sketches." (Poem appears elsewhere as "Lines Addressed to
Alaric A. Watts, Esq." and as "To Alaric A. Watts, Esq.").
1st line: "There is a dear and lovely power"
in *The Lyre. Fugitive Poetry of the Nineteenth Century*. London: Tilt and Bogue, 1841.
56.

To the Author of the Sorrows of Rosalie. (Poem appears elsewhere as "Lines to the Author
after Reading the Sorrows of Rosalie").
1st line: "They tell me, lady, that thy face"
in *The Lyre. Fugitive Poetry of the Nineteenth Century*. London: Tilt and Bogue, 1841.
73-76.

To Marguerite, Countess of Blessington
1st line: "I pray thee, ladye, turn these leaves,"
in Landon, Letitia E. *Fisher's Drawing Room Scrap-Book, 1839*. London: Fisher, Son;
Paris: Quai de L'Ecole, [1838]. 52-53.

To the Memory of a Favorite Child, the Daughter of a Friend. (Poem appears elsewhere as
"Matlock. To the Memory of a Favourite Child (the Daughter of a Friend) who
Died There").
1st line: "Her voice is on the haunted air,"
in *The Zenana and Minor Poems of L. E. L.* London: Fisher, Son; Paris: Quai de
L'Ecole, [1839]. 292-97.

To Mrs. —.
1st line: "My own kind friend, long years may pass"
in Blanchard, Laman. *Life and Literary Remains of L. E. L.* Vol. 1. London: Henry
Colburn, 1841. 182-84.

To my Brother. (Poem appears elsewhere as "Captain Cook").
1st line: "Do you recall the fancies of many years ago,"
in *The Zenana and Minor Poems of L. E. L.* London: Fisher, Son; Paris: Quai de
L'Ecole, [1839]. 258-60.

*To Olinthus Gregory, On Hearing of the Death of his Eldest Son, Who Was Drowned as He
Was Returning by Water to his Father's House at Woolwich.* (Appears elsewhere as
"Olinthus Gregory, LL.D., F.R.A.S., &c.").
1st line: "Is there a spot where Pity's foot,"
in *The Zenana and Minor Poems of L. E. L.* London: Fisher, Son; Paris: Quai de
L'Ecole, 1839. 124-26.

To the Queen.
1st line: "Within the page, oh, Royal Ladye! — seeking,"
in Landon, Letitia E. *Fisher's Drawing Room Scrap-Book, 1838*. London, Paris, and
New York: Fisher, Son; Germany: Black and Armstrong, and Asher, 1837. 3.

To Sir John Doyle, Bart.
1st line: "My heart has beat high at the heroes of old,"
in Landon, Letitia E. *The Fate of Adelaide, A Swiss Romantic Tale; and Other Poems*.
London: John Warren, 1821. 146-48.

To Victoria.
1st line: "Violet, grace of the vernal year,"
in Landon, Letitia E. *Flowers of Loveliness; Twelve Groups of Female Figures, Emblematic of Flowers*. London: Ackermann, 1838. N. pag. [1 page].

[The Toilets]. (Suggested poem title, as poem is motto for Chapter 21 titled "The Toilets"; poem appears elsewhere as "Ornaments").
1st line: "Bring from the east, bring from the west,"

in Landon, Letitia E. *Ethel Churchill: or, The Two Brides.* Vol. 1. London: Henry Colburn, 1837. 206.

The Tomb of Aurungzebe.
1st line: "'A mighty tomb, fit for a mighty king,'"
Prefixed lines begin: "Oh, fleeting honours of the dead,"
in Landon, Letitia E. *Fisher's Drawing Room Scrap-Book. 1833.* London: H. Fisher, R. Fisher, and P. Jackson, 1833 [1832]. 54.

The Tomb of Humaioon, Delhi.
1st line: "He stood alone upon a hill,"
in Landon, Letitia E. *Fisher's Drawing Room Scrap-Book. 1833.* London: H. Fisher, R. Fisher, and P. Jackson, 1833 [1832]. 36-38.

Tomb of Mahomed Shah.
1st line: "What do they call a happy end,"
in Landon, Letitia E. *Fisher's Drawing Room Scrap-Book. 1833.* London: H. Fisher, R. Fisher, and P. Jackson, 1833 [1832]. 10.

The Tomb of Romeo and Juliet.
1st line: "Ay, moralize on Love, and deem"
in *The Literary Souvenir; or, Cabinet of Poetry and Romance [for 1826].* Ed. Alaric A. Watts. London: Hurst, Robinson; Edinburgh: A. Constable, 1826 [1825]. 50-51;
in *The Lyre. Fugitive Poetry of the Nineteeth Century.* London: Tilt and Bogue, 1841. 339.

The Tombs of the Kings of Golconda. (Poem appears elsewhere as "The Kings of Golconda").
1st line: "Morning is round the shining palace,"
in Landon, Letitia E. *Fisher's Drawing Room Scrap-Book, 1838.* London, Paris, and New York: Fisher, Son; Germany: Black and Armstrong, and Asher, 1837. 12-14.

Too well I know my Heart. (One of the series of "Songs").
1st line: "Too well I know my heart"
in *The Literary Gazette* 429 (Apr. 9, 1825): 235.

The Tournament.
1st line: "His spur on his heel, his spear in its rest,"
in Landon, Letitia E. *Fisher's Drawing Room Scrap-Book, 1838.* London, Paris, and New York: Fisher, Son; Germany: Black and Armstrong, and Asher, 1837. 9.

Town and Harbour of Ithaca. (Poem appears elsewhere as "Ithaca").
1st line: "By another light surrounded"
in Landon, Letitia E. *Fisher's Drawing Room Scrap-Book, 1837.* London, Paris, and New York: Fisher, Son; Germany: Black and Armstrong, and Asher, 1836. 47-48.

Treryn Castle.
1st line: "A monarch, who had lost his crown,"
in Landon, Letitia E. *Fisher's Drawing Room Scrap-Book. 1833.* London: H. Fisher, R. Fisher, and P. Jackson, 1833 [1832]. 18.

The Troubadour.
1st line: "Call to mind your loveliest dream, —"
in Landon, Letitia E. *The Troubadour; Catalogue of Pictures, and Historical Sketches.* London: Hurst, Robinson; Edinburgh: A. Constable, 1825. 1-254.

The Troubadour. (Tale IV in series of "Metrical Tales").
1st line: "Oh, sleep in silence, or but wake"
in *The Literary Gazette* 374 (Mar. 20, 1824): 186-87.

Truth. (First, a suggested poem title, as poem is the fifth in a group of six poems described as "Six Songs of Love, Constancy, Romance, Inconstancy, Truth, and Marriage"; then poem is given that title in *The Lyre*).

　　1st line: "Oh! would that love had power to raise"

　　in *The Literary Gazette* 251 (Nov. 10, 1821): 716;

　　in *The Lyre. Fugitive Poetry of the Nineteenth Century.* London: Tilt and Bogue, 1841. 324-25.

[The Truth of Presentiments]. (Suggested poem title, as poem is motto for Chapter 37 titled "The Truth of Presentiments"; poem appears elsewhere as "The Heart's Omens").

　　1st line: "I felt my sorrow ere it came,"

　　in Landon, Letitia E. *Ethel Churchill: or, The Two Brides.* Vol. 2. London: Henry Colburn, 1837. 301.

The Tumuli.

　　1st line: "The Dead! the Dead! and sleep they here,"

　　in *The Literary Gazette* 507 (Oct. 7, 1826): 637.

Tunis.

　　1st line: "No more that city's pirate barks"

　　in Landon, Letitia E. *Fisher's Drawing Room Scrap-Book, 1838.* London, Paris, and New York: Fisher, Son; Germany: Black and Armstrong, and Asher, 1837. 15.

Two Doves in a Grove. Mr. Glover's Exhibition.

　　1st line: "June bloom and foliage were upon the trees,"

　　in *The Literary Gazette* 329 (May 10, 1823): 299-300.

Unavailing Regret. (First, a suggested poem title, as poem is motto for Chapter 14 titled "Unavailing Regret"; then, poem is given this title when included in Blanchard's selection of "Fragments" from *Ethel Churchill*; poem is an altered version of "Leonora").

　　1st line: "Farewell! and when the charm of change"

　　in Landon, Letitia E. *Ethel Churchill: or, The Two Brides.* Vol. 2. London: Henry Colburn, 1837. 105;

　　in Blanchard, Laman. *Life and Literary Remains of L. E. L.* Vol. 2. London: Henry Colburn, 1841. 276-77.

Unguided Will. (One of the "Fragments" from *Ethel Churchill* selected by Blanchard; poem appears elsewhere as "[The Assignation]").

　　1st line: "God, in thy mercy, keep us with thy hand!"

　　in Blanchard, Laman. *Life and Literary Remains of L. E. L.* Vol. 2. London: Henry Colburn, 1841. 296.

Unknown Female Head. (Part of series, "Medallion Wafers" in *The Literary Gazette*; one of the "Classical Sketches" in *The Vow of the Peacock, and Other Poems*).

　　1st line: "I know not of thy history, thou sad"

　　in *The Literary Gazette* 316 (Feb. 8, 1823): 91;

　　in Landon, Letitia E. *The Vow of the Peacock, and Other Poems.* London: Saunders and Otley, 1835. 131-32.

The Unknown Grave.

　　1st line: "There is a little lonely grave"

　　in Landon, Letitia E. *Fisher's Drawing Room Scrap-Book, 1837.* London, Paris, and New York: Fisher, Son; Germany: Black and Armstrong, and Asher, 1836. 24;

　　in *The Zenana and Minor Poems of L. E. L.* London: Fisher, Son; Paris: Quai de L'Ecole, [1839]. 225-27.

The Unknown Poet. (Poem appears elsewhere as "The Unknown Poet's Grave").
1st line: "There is no memory of his fate,"
in *The Album Wreath of Music and Literature [for 1835]*. London: R. Willoughby, [1834?]. 10.

The Unknown Poet's Grave. (Poem appears elsewhere as "The Unknown Poet").
1st line: "There is no memory of his fate,"
in *The Amulet; A Christian and Literary Remembrancer [for 1830]*. Ed. S. C. Hall. London: Frederick Westley and A. H. Davis, 1830 [1829]. 59–62.

[untitled poem]. (Poem serves as motto for Chapter 10, an untitled chapter; poem appears elsewhere as "The Visionary and the True").
1st line: "Ah! waking dreams, that mock the day,"
in Landon, Letitia E. *Ethel Churchill: or, The Two Brides*. Vol. 1. London: Henry Colburn, 1837. 102.

[untitled poem]. (Poem serves as motto for untitled chapter, Chapter 19; poem appears elsewhere as "The Wrongs of Love").
1st line: "Alas, how bitter are the wrongs of love!"
in Landon, Letitia E. *Ethel Churchill: or, The Two Brides*. Vol. 1. London: Henry Colburn, 1837. 194.

[untitled poem].
1st line: "And then he kiss'd"
in *The Album Wreath of Music and Literature [for 1835]*. London: R. Willoughby, [1834?]. 81.

[untitled poem]. (Motto for the section, "Miscellaneous Poems").
1st line: "Chance notes struck from the lute — fancies and thoughts —"
in Landon, Letitia E. *The Venetian Bracelet, The Lost Pleiad, A History of the Lyre, and Other Poems*. London: Longman, Rees, Orme, Brown, and Green, 1829. 199.

[untitled poem]. (Printed in the middle of Chapter 3 as written by the poet character, Walter Maynard).
1st line: "Dream no more of that sweet time"
in Landon, Letitia E. *Ethel Churchill: or, The Two Brides*. Vol. 1. London: Henry Colburn, 1837. 32–33.

[untitled poem]. (Poem occurs in middle of Chapter 21 as composed by poet character, Walter Maynard; it appears elsewhere as "A Poet's Love").
1st line: "Faint and more faint amid the world of dreams,"
in Landon, Letitia E. *Ethel Churchill: or, The Two Brides*. Vol. 2. London: Henry Colburn, 1837. 159–60.

[untitled poem].
1st line: "Farewell! for I have schooled my heart"
in *The Literary Gazette* 380 (May 1, 1824): 284.

[untitled poem]. (Poem serves as motto for Chapter 7, an untitled chapter; poem appears elsewhere as "Success Alone Seen").
1st line: "Few know of life's beginnings — men behold"
in Landon, Letitia E. *Ethel Churchill: or, The Two Brides*. Vol. 1. London: Henry Colburn, 1837. 79.

[untitled poem]. (Poem serves as motto for Chapter 20, an untitled chapter; poem appears elsewhere as "The Middle Temple Gardens" and as "The Temple Garden").
1st line: "The fountain's low singing is heard on the wind,"
in Landon, Letitia E. *Ethel Churchill: or, The Two Brides*. Vol. 2. London: Henry Colburn, 1837. 145.

[untitled poem].
　　1st line: "— give me some green laurel leaves"
　　in *The Album Wreath of Music and Literature [for 1835].* London: R. Willoughby,
　　[1834?]. 5.
[untitled poem].
　　1st line: "I did love once, — "
　　in *The New York Literary Gazette* 1 (Mar. 4, 1826): 410.
[untitled poem]. (Poem appears elsewhere as "Violets").
　　1st line: "I do love violets!"
　　in *The Album of Love.* The Mirror Library. 3. New York: n.p., 1844. 11.
[untitled poem].
　　1st line: "It is a lovely lake, with waves as blue"
　　in *The Literary Gazette* 375 (Mar. 27, 1824): 203.
[untitled poem].
　　1st line: "It is the spirits bitterest pain"
　　in *The Album of Love.* The Mirror Library. 3. New York: n.p., 1844. 17.
[untitled poem]. (Poem serves as motto for Chapter 7, an untitled chapter; it appears
　　elsewhere as "Love a Mystery").
　　1st line: "It matters not its history — Love has wings,"
　　in Landon, Letitia E. *Ethel Churchill: or, The Two Brides.* Vol. 3. London: Henry Col-
　　burn, 1837. 45.
[untitled poem]. (Listed as "Verses" in Table of Contents).
　　1st line: "Lady, thy face is very beautiful,"
　　in *The Keepsake for 1829.* Ed. Frederic Mansel Reynolds. London: Hurst, Chance;
　　Robert Jennings, 1828. 121.
[untitled poem]. (Poem serves as motto for Chapter 28, an untitled chapter, and appears
　　beneath heading of letter from "Lady Marchmont to Sir Jasper Meredith"; poem
　　appears elsewhere as "Dear Gifts").
　　1st line: "Life's best gifts are bought dearly. Wealth is won"
　　in Landon, Letitia E. *Ethel Churchill: or, The Two Brides.* Vol. 1. London: Henry Col-
　　burn, 1837. 249.
[untitled poem].
　　1st line: "Love is like the glass"
　　in *The Album of Love.* The Mirror Library. 3. New York: n.p., 1844. 2.
[untitled poem].
　　1st line: "Love, passionate young love, how sweet it is"
　　in *The Album of Love.* The Mirror Library. 3. New York: n.p., 1844. 3.
[untitled poem]. (Poem serves as motto for Chapter 27, an untitled chapter, and appears
　　beneath heading for letter from "Lady Marchmont to Sir Jasper Meredith"; poem
　　appears elsewhere as "The Mind's Unrest").
　　1st line: "Mind, dangerous and glorious gift!"
　　in Landon, Letitia E. *Ethel Churchill: or, The Two Brides.* Vol. 1. London: Henry Col-
　　burn, 1837. 242.
[untitled poem].
　　1st line: "The moon is on the silent lake"
　　in *The Literary Gazette* 484 (Apr. 29, 1826): 266–67.
[untitled poem].
　　1st line: "Oh! if thou lovest,"
　　in *The Album of Love.* The Mirror Library. 3. New York: n.p., 1844. 12.

[untitled poem].
　　1st line: "Oh it is long since we have met!"
　　in *The Literary Gazette* 487 (May 20, 1826): 315.

[untitled poem]. (Poem serves as motto for untitled chapter, Chapter 4; it appears else-
where as "Song" and, in an altered version, as "[Return to Courtenaye Hall]" and
"The Early Dream").
　　1st line: "Oh! never another dream can be"
　　in Landon, Letitia E. *Ethel Churchill: or, The Two Brides.* Vol. 1. London: Henry Col-
burn, 1837. 43.

[untitled poem]. (Poem serves as motto for Chapter 21, an untitled chapter; it appears
elsewhere as "Gifts Misused").
　　1st line: "Oh, what a waste of feeling and of thought"
　　in Landon, Letitia E. *Ethel Churchill: or, The Two Brides.* Vol. 2. London: Henry Col-
burn, 1837. 157.

[untitled poem].
　　1st line: "Oh! Where is there the heart but knows"
　　in *The Album of Love.* The Mirror Library. 3. New York: n.p., 1844. 22.

[untitled poem].
　　1st line: "Our sky has lost another star,"
　　in *The Literary Gazette* 819 (Sept. 29, 1832): 619-20.

[untitled poem].
　　1st line: "Still there clings"
　　in *The Album of Love.* The Mirror Library. 3. New York: n.p., 1844. 3.

[untitled poem]. (Poem serves as motto for Chapter 26, an untitled chapter, beneath
heading for letter "Lady Marchmont to Sir Jasper Meredith"; poem appears else-
where as "Affection").
　　1st line: "There is in life no blessing like affection:"
　　in Landon, Letitia E. *Ethel Churchill: or, The Two Brides.* Vol. 1. London: Henry Col-
burn, 1837. 236.

[untitled poem].
　　1st line: "'Tis something if in absence we can trace"
　　in *The Album of Love.* The Mirror Library. 3. New York: n.p., 1844. 5.

[untitled poem]. (Printed in middle of Chapter 6 beneath "First Letter of Lady March-
mont to Sir Jasper Meredith"; poem appears elsewhere as "Vanity").
　　1st line: "Vanity! guiding power, 'tis thine to rule"
　　in Landon, Letitia E. *Ethel Churchill: or, The Two Brides.* Vol. 1. London: Henry Col-
burn, 1837. 62.

[untitled poem].
　　1st line: "When in the languid noon"
　　in *The Album Wreath of Music and Literature [for 1835].* London: R. Willoughby,
[1834?]. 93.

[untitled poem]. (Printed in middle of Chapter 6 at top of letter from "Lady March-
mont to Sir Jasper Meredith"; poem appears elsewhere as "Life's Mask").
　　1st line: "Which was the true philosopher? — the sage"
　　in Landon, Letitia E. *Ethel Churchill: or, The Two Brides.* Vol. 1. London: Henry Col-
burn, 1837. 71.

[untitled poem]. (Poem serves as motto for Chapter 15, an untitled chapter; poem
appears elsewhere as "The Rose").
　　1st line: "Why, what a history is on the rose!"

in Landon, Letitia E. *Ethel Churchill: or, The Two Brides.* Vol. 2. London: Henry Colburn, 1837. 110.

The Upper Lake of Killarney. (Poem appears elsewhere as "Kate Kearney").
   1st line: "Why doth the maiden turn away"
   in Landon, Letitia E. *Fisher's Drawing Room Scrap-Book [for 1832].* London: Fisher, Son, and Jackson, 1832 [1831]. 17.

[The Usual Destiny of the Imagination]. (Suggested poem title, as poem is motto for Chapter 35 titled "The Usual Destiny of the Imagination"; poem appears elsewhere as "The Poet's Past").
   1st line: "Remembrance makes the poet: 'tis the past"
   in Landon, Letitia E. *Ethel Churchill: or, The Two Brides.* Vol. 3. London: Henry Colburn, 1837. 284.

The Vale of Lonsdale. Lancashire.
   1st line: "I could not dwell here, it is all too fair,"
   in Landon, Letitia E. *Fisher's Drawing Room Scrap-Book [for 1832].* London: Fisher, Son, and Jackson, 1832 [1831]. 30.

Valedictory Lines To a Cadet on embarking for India.
   1st line: "Young Soldier! are not thy hopes"
   in *The Literary Gazette* 336 (June 28, 1823): 411.

Valedictory Stanzas.
   1st line: "Oh not that look to me, my love,"
   in *The Literary Gazette* 329 (May 10, 1823): 299.

Valedictory Stanzas.
   1st line: "Thy voice is yet upon mine ear,"
   in *The Literary Gazette* 418 (Jan. 22, 1825): 59.

Valetta, Capital of Malta.
   1st line: "The vessel swept in with the light of the morn,"
   in Landon, Letitia E. *Fisher's Drawing Room Scrap-Book, 1837.* London, Paris, and New York: Fisher, Son; Germany: Black and Armstrong, and Asher, 1836. 31.

Valley of Linmouth, North Devon.
   1st line: "Tis a gloomy place, but I like it well;"
   in Landon, Letitia E. *Fisher's Drawing Room Scrap-Book, 1836.* London and Paris: Fisher, Son; Berlin: Asher; New York: Jackson, [1835]. 55.

The Valley of Rocks, Near Linton, Devonshire.
   1st line: "Summer, thou hast lost thy power;"
   in Landon, Letitia E. *Fisher's Drawing Room Scrap-Book [for 1832].* London: Fisher, Son, and Jackson, 1832 [1831]. 47-48.

Vandyke consulting his Mistress on a Picture in Cooke's Exhibition. (Part of series, "Poetical Catalogue of Pictures").
   1st line: "Yes, he is seeking in those eyes"
   Prefixed lines begin: "Beautiful Art! my worship is for thee —"
   in *The Literary Gazette* 321 (Mar. 15, 1823): 171.

Vanity. (One of the "Fragments" from *Ethel Churchill* selected by Blanchard; poem appears elsewhere as an "[untitled poem]").
   1st line: "Vanity! guiding power, 'tis thine to rule"
   in Blanchard, Laman. *Life and Literary Remains of L.E.L.* Vol. 2. London: Henry Colburn, 1841. 260.

Vaucluse.
   1st line: "Tall rocks begirt the lovely valley round,"

in *The Literary Gazette* 196 (Oct. 21, 1820): 685.

The Venetian Bracelet.
> 1st line: "Another tale of thine! fair Italie —"
> Prefixed lines begin: "Those subtle poisons which made science crime,"
> in Landon, Letitia E. *The Venetian Bracelet, The Lost Pleiad, A History of the Lyre, and Other Poems.* London: Longman, Rees, Orme, Brown, and Green, 1829. 1-50.

Venice.
> 1st line: "Aye, the Ocean has bright daughters,"
> in *The Literary Souvenir, and Cabinet of Modern Art [for 1835].* Ed. Alaric A. Watts. London: Whittaker, 1835 [1834]. 207-10.

Venice.
> 1st line: "Morn on the Adriatic, every wave"
> in *The Amulet. A Christian and Literary Remembrancer [for 1832].* Ed. S. C. Hall. London: Frederick Westley and A. H. Davis, 1832 [1831]. 147-150;
> in *The Modern Poets and Artists of Great Britain.* Ed. S. C. Hall. London: Whittaker, 1838. Vol. 3 of *The Book of Gems.* 3 vols. 1836-38. 183-85.

Venus Taking the Bow from a Sleeping Cupid.
> 1st line: "Queen of smiles! fling down the bow:"
> in *The Friendship's Offering. A Literary Album [for 1828].* Ed. Thomas K. Hervey. London: Lupton Relfe, 1828 [1827]. 188-89.

The Village Bells.
> 1st line: "There is a lovely English sound"
> Prefixed lines begin: "How soft the music of those village bells,"
> in Landon, Letitia E. *Fishers Drawing Room Scrap Book, 1839.* London: Fisher, Son; Paris: Quai de L'Ecole, [1838]. 59-60.

Village of Koghera, Near the Choor Mountain.
> 1st line: "She raised her palace of the snows"
> in Landon, Letitia E. *Fisher's Drawing Room Scrap-Book, 1839.* London: Fisher, Son; Paris: Quai de L'Ecole, [1838]. 26-28.

The Village of Kursalee.
> 1st line: "High in the azure heavens, ye ancient mountains,"
> in Landon, Letitia E. *Fisher's Drawing Room Scrap Book, 1838.* London, Paris, and New York: Fisher, Son; Germany: Black and Armstrong, and Asher, 1837. 8.

The Village of the Lepers. (Described as "Taken from the account in the Literary Gazette").
> 1st line: "There was a curse on the unhappy race —"
> in Landon, Letitia E. *The Fate of Adelaide, A Swiss Romantic Tale; and Other Poems.* London: John Warren, 1821. 86-87.

A Village Tale. (Sketch IV in Fourth Series of "Poetic Sketches" in *The Literary Gazette*; one of "A Series of Tales" in *The Vow of the Peacock, and Other Poems*).
> 1st line: "It was a low white church: the elm which grew"
> Prefixed lines: "How the spirit clings"
> in *The Literary Gazette* 359 (Dec. 6, 1823): 778-79;
> in Landon, Letitia E. *The Vow of the Peacock, and Other Poems.* London: Saunders and Otley, 1835. 194-207.

The Violet. (One of the "Fragments"; poem appears elsewhere as "Violets").
> 1st line: "Violets! — deep-blue Violets!"
> in Landon, Letitia E. *The Improvisatrice; and Other Poems.* London: Hurst, Robinson; Edinburgh: A. Constable, 1824. 284-85.

The Violet.
> 1st line: "Why better than the lady rose"
> in *The Literary Souvenir [for 1831].* Ed. Alaric A. Watts. London: Longman, Rees, Orme, Brown, and Green, 1831 [1830]. 267-268;
> in Landon, Letitia E. *The Vow of the Peacock, and Other Poems.* London: Saunders and Otley, 1835. 283-86.

Violets. (Poem appears elsewhere as an "[untitled poem]").
> 1st line: "I do love violets!"
> in *Affection's Gift for 1844.* London: H. G. Clarke, [1843?]. 86.

Violets. (Poem appears elsewhere as "The Violet").
> 1st line: "Violets! — deep-blue violets!"
> in *The Bouquet, for 1847.* Ed. Alfred A. Phillips. New York: Nafis and Cornish, 1847. 104.

The Visionary. (Poem appears elsewhere as "Stanzas").
> 1st line: "I pray thee do not speak to me"
> in Landon, Letitia E. *Fisher's Drawing Room Scrap-Book, 1834.* London: H. Fisher, R. Fisher, and P. Jackson; Paris: Rittner and Goupil; Berlin and St. Petersburg: Asher; New York: Jackson, 1833. 54-56.

The Visionary and the True. (One of the "Fragments" from *Ethel Churchill* selected by Blanchard; poem appears elsewhere as an "[untitled poem]").
> 1st line: "Ah! waking dreams that mock the day,"
> in Blanchard, Laman. *Life and Literary Remains of L. E. L.* Vol. 2. London: Henry Colburn, 1841. 264.

The Volcano of Ki-Rau-E-A. Extract from Stewart's Journal of a Residence in the Sandwich Islands.
> 1st line: "An ebbing tide of fire, the evil powers"
> in Landon, Letitia E. *Fisher's Drawing Room Scrap-Book [for 1832].* London: Fisher, Son, and Jackson, 1832 [1831]. 24.

Von Raumer.
> 1st line: "He has recalled the past as still"
> in *The English Bijou Almanac for 1837.* London: Albert Schloss, [1836]. N. pag. [3 pages].

The Vow of the Peacock.
> 1st line: "The present! it is but a drop from the sea"
> in Landon, Letitia E. *The Vow of the Peacock, and Other Poems.* London: Saunders and Otley, 1835. 1-114.

The Wanderer.
> 1st line: "Float on, float on, thou lonely bark,"
> in *The Literary Gazette* 571 (Dec. 29, 1827): 846;
> in *The Beauties of the Magazines* 18 (Jan. 5, 1828): 283.

Want of Sympathy. (One of the "Fragments" from *Ethel Churchill* selected by Blanchard; poem appears elsewhere as "[A Matrimonial Tête-à-tête]").
> 1st line: "These are the things that fret away the heart —"
> in Blanchard, Laman. *Life and Literary Remains of L. E. L.* Vol. 2. London: Henry Colburn, 1841. 279.

Warkworth Castle, Northumberland. (Poem appears elsewhere as "Farewell! Oh My Brother!").
> 1st line: "Come, up with the banner, and on with the sword,"
> in Landon, Letitia E. *Fisher's Drawing Room Scrap-Book, 1838.* London, Paris, and

New York: Fisher, Son; Germany: Black and Armstrong, and Asher, 1837. 35.

Warkworth Hermitage.
   1st line: "The lonely cavern, like a chapel carved,"
   in Landon, Letitia E. *Fisher's Drawing Room Scrap-Book, 1836.* London and Paris: Fisher, Son; Berlin: Asher; New York: Jackson, [1835]. 13.

Warning.
   1st line: "Pray thee, maiden, hear him not!"
   in Landon, Letitia E. *The Venetian Bracelet, The Lost Pleiad, A History of the Lyre, and Other Poems.* London: Longman, Rees, Orme, Brown, and Green, 1829. 218-24.

The Warrior.
   1st line: "It came upon the morning wind"
   in *Death's Doings; Consisting of Numerous Original Compositions, in Prose and Verse.* 2nd ed. London: J. Andrews; W. Cole, 1827. 248-52.

The Warrior. A Sketch. (One of the "Fragments"; poem appears elsewhere as "Sketch").
   1st line: "The warrior went forth in the morning light, —"
   in Landon, Letitia E. *The Improvisatrice; and Other Poems.* London: Hurst, Robinson; Edinburgh: Archibald Constable, 1824. 310-14.

The Watchful Friend.
   1st line: "In a hidden thicket's shade"
   in *The Juvenile Forget-Me-Not: A Christmas and New-Year's Gift, or Birth-day Present. 1837.* Ed. Mrs. S. C. [Anna Maria] Hall. London: R. Ackermann; Westley and Davis, 1837 [1836]. 186-87.

The Water Palace, Mandoo.
   1st line: "He built it, for he was a king,"
   in Landon, Letitia E. *Fisher's Drawing Room Scrap-Book [for 1832].* London: Fisher, Son, and Jackson, 1832 [1831]. 27.

The Water-Lily.
   1st line: "Not 'mid the soil and the shadow of earth,"
   in Landon, Letitia E. *Flowers of Loveliness; Twelve Groups of Female Figures, Emblematic of Flowers.* London: Ackermann, 1838. N. pag. [2 pages].

We Might Have Been! (Part of series, "Three Extracts from the Diary of a Week," in *The New Monthly* and *Life and Literary Remains,* no. I. in the latter; a few stanzas from poem appear elsewhere as "[Lady Marchmont's Journal]").
   1st line: "We might have been! — these are but common words,"
   Prefixed lines begin: "A record of the inward world, whose facts"
   in *The New Monthly Magazine* 49 (1837): 478-79;
   in *The Casket of Literature, Science and Entertainment* 17 (Apr. 29, 1837): 265-66;
   in Blanchard, Laman. *Life and Literary Remains of L. E. L.* Vol. 2. London: Henry Colburn, 1841. 248-50.

Weakness Ends With Love. (One of the "Fragments" from *Ethel Churchill* selected by Blanchard; poem appears elsewhere as "[Pope's Villa]").
   1st line: "I say not, regret me; you will not regret;"
   in Blanchard, Laman. *Life and Literary Remains of L. E. L.* Vol. 2. London: Henry Colburn, 1841. 265.

Wellington.
   1st line: "The Conqueror of a thousand fields!"
   in Landon, Letitia E. *Schloss's English Bijou Almanac for 1839.* London: Albert Schloss, [1838]. N. pag. [3 pages].

What is Success? (One of the "Fragments" from *Ethel Churchill* selected by Blanchard; poem appears elsewhere as "[Success]").

　　1st line: "All things are symbols; and we find"

　　in Blanchard, Laman. *Life and Literary Remains of L. E. L.* Vol. 2. London: Henry Colburn, 1841. 275.

What was Our Parting? (Poem appears elsewhere as the 6th untitled poem within a series of "Songs").

　　1st line: "What was our parting? — one wild kiss,"

　　in *The Literary Sketch-Book* 1 (Nov. 22, 1823): 233.

When Should Lovers Breathe Their Vows? (One of the "Ballads"; poem appears elsewhere as "Stanzas").

　　1st line: "When should lovers breathe their vows?"

　　in Landon, Letitia E. *The Improvisatrice; and Other Poems.* London: Hurst, Robinson; Edinburgh: A. Constable, 1824. 326-27.

The White Ship.

　　1st line: "'Strike the sails again, and drop'"

　　in *The Literary Gazette* 545 (June 30, 1827): 429.

Why Looked I on that Fatal Line.

　　1st line: "Why looked I on that fatal line,"

　　in *Ladies' Penny Gazette* 2 (Sept. 6, 1834): 351.

The Widow's Mite.

　　1st line: "It is the fruit of waking hours"

　　in Landon, Letitia E. *Fisher's Drawing Room Scrap-Book, 1836.* London and Paris: Fisher, Son; Berlin: Asher; New York: Jackson, [1835]. 34.

William IV.

　　1st line: "A Thousand torches light the air,"

　　in Landon, Letitia E. *The English Bijou Almanac for 1838.* London: Albert Schloss, [1837]. N. pag. [3 pages].

Wm. Wilberforce, Esq. Born August 24th, 1759. — Died July 19th, 1823.

　　1st line: "He sleeps — yet little of him sleeps below,"

　　in Landon, Letitia E. *Fisher's Drawing Room Scrap Book, 1837.* London, Paris, and New York: Fisher, Son; Gemany: Black and Armstrong, and Asher, 1836. 40.

Willow Leaves. (Described as a "Translation of Les Feuilles de Saule. Par Mde. Aimable Tastu").

　　1st line: "The hour was fair, but Autumn's dying"

　　in *The Literary Gazette* 523 (Jan. 27, 1827): 59.

Windleshaw Abbey. (Poem appears elsewhere as "The Funeral").

　　1st line: "Mark you not yon sad procession,"

　　in Landon, Letitia E. *Fisher's Drawing Room Scrap-Book. 1835.* London: H. Fisher, R. Fisher, and P. Jackson. 1835 [1834]. 53.

The Wish.

　　1st line: "Oh, it is not on lip or brow"

　　in *The New Monthly Magazine* 17 (1826): 232-33.

Wishes.

　　1st line: "It was a summer night,"

　　in *The Amulet; or, Christian and Literary Remembrancer [for 1827].* London: W. Baynes and Son, and Wightman and Cramp, 1827. 349-50.

The Wishing Gate.

　　1st line: "Wishes, no! I have not one,"

in Landon, Letitia E. *Fisher's Drawing Room Scrap Book, 1834.* London: H.Fisher, R. Fisher, and P. Jackson; Paris: Rittner and Goupil; Berlin and St. Petersburg: Asher; New York: Jackson, 1833. 44.

The Withered Flowers.
1st line: "There is a white Vase in my hall,"
in *The Literary Gazette* 388 (June 26, 1824): 411.

Woman's Destiny.
1st line "'I am a woman: — tell me not of fame!'"
in *The Ladies' Wreath; A Selection from the Female Poetic Writers of England and America.* Ed. Mrs. Sarah J. Hale. Boston: Marsh, Capen, and Lyon; New York: D. Appleton, 1837. 132.

The Woodland Brook.
1st line: "Thou art flowing, thou art flowing,"
in Landon, Letitia E. *Fisher's Drawing Room Scrap-Book, 1837.* London, Paris, and New York: Fisher, Son; Germany: Black and Armstrong, and Asher, 1836. 26;
in *The Zenana and Minor Poems of L. E. L.* London: Fisher, Son; Paris: Quai de L'Ecole, [1839]. 228-29.

The World.
1st line: "Alas! alas! to pass in peace,"
in *The Album Wreath of Music and Literature [for 1835].* London: R. Willoughby, [1834?]. 54.

The World As It Is.
1st line: "Farewell, farewell, and light farewell"
in *The Literary Gazette* 500 (Aug. 19, 1826): 524.

The World Within. (One of the "Fragments" from *Ethel Churchill* selected by Blanchard; poem appears elsewhere as "[Different Views of Youth and Age]").
1st line: "There was a shadow on his face, that spake"
in Blanchard, Laman. *Life and Literary Remains of L. E. L.* Vol. 2. London: Henry Colburn, 1841. 262.

The Worshipper.
1st line: "It is a shrine, a sunny shrine,"
in *The Literary Gazette* 470 (Jan. 21, 1826): 43.

The Wreath.
1st line: "Nay, fling not down those faded flowers,"
in Landon, Letitia E. *The Venetian Bracelet, The Lost Pleiad, A History of the Lyre, and Other Poems.* London: Longman, Rees, Orme, Brown, and Green, 1829. 239-41.

The Wreck.
1st line: "The moonlight fell on the stately ship;"
in Landon, Letitia E. *The Vow of the Peacock, and Other Poems..* London: Saunders and Otley, 1835. 249-53.

Written after seeing Maid Marian performed. (Printed as No. XIII in series, "Fragments in Rhyme": should be read correctly as No. XII).
1st line: "Oh, for the days of the bow and the spear,"
in *The Literary Gazette* 311 (Jan. 4, 1823): 12.

The Wrongs of Love. (One of the "Fragments" from *Ethel Churchill* selected by Blanchard; poem appears elsewhere as an "[untitled poem]").
1st line: "Alas, how bitter are the wrongs of love!"
in Blanchard, Laman. *Life and Literary Remains of L. E. L.* Vol. 2. London: Henry Colburn, 1841. 270.

The Young Destructive.
    1st line: "In truth, I do not wonder"
    in Landon, Letitia E. *Fisher's Drawing Room Scrap-Book, 1836.* London and Paris:
    Fisher, Son; Berlin: Asher; New York: Jackson, [1835]. 24.
The Young Poet's Fate. (One of the "Fragments" from *Ethel Churchill* selected by Blan-
    chard; poem appears elsewhere as "[A Request]").
    1st line: "Trace the young poet's fate"
    in Blanchard, Laman. *Life and Literary Remains of L. E. L.* Vol. 2. London: Henry
    Colburn, 1841. 297.
Youth.
    1st line: "Oh! the hours! the happy hours"
    in *The Literary Gazette* 812 (Aug. 11, 1832): 508.
Youth and Love. (One of the "Fragments" from *Ethel Churchill* selected by Blanchard;
    poem appears elsewhere as "[The Disclosure]").
    1st line: "Young, loving, and beloved — these are brief words;"
    in Blanchard, Laman. *Life and Literary Remains of L. E. L.* Vol. 2. London: Henry
    Colburn, 1841. 299.
*A Youth, with a Lyre in his hand, kneeling to a Female half turning to him, as in the act of rec-
    onciliation.* (Part of the series, "Medallion Wafers").
    1st line: "Yes! I have sinned 'gainst love and thee!"
    in *The Literary Gazette* 316 (Feb. 8, 1823): 91.
The Youthful Mariners.
    1st line: "How now, my youthful mariners!"
    in *The Amulet. A Christian and Literary Remembrancer [for 1833].* Ed. S.C. Hall. Lon-
    don: Frederick Westley and A. H. Davis, 1833 [1832]. 127-29.
The Zegri Lady's Vigil. (Printed as No. I in fourth series of "Subjects for Pictures" in
    The New Monthly: series should be numbered the fifth; no. XII in "Subjects for
    Pictures" in *Life and Literary Remains*).
    1st line: "Ever sits the Lady weeping —"
    Prefixed lines to "Subjects for Pictures" begin: "What seek I here to gather into
    words?"
    in *The New Monthly Magazine* 53 (1838): 77-79;
    in Blanchard, Laman. *Life and Literary Remains of L. E. L.* Vol. 2. London: Henry
    Colburn, 1841. 225-28.
The Zenana.
    1st line: "What is there that the world hath not"
    in Landon, Letitia E. *Fisher's Drawing Room Scrap-Book, 1834.* London: H. Fisher, R.
    Fisher, and P. Jackson; Paris: Rittner and Goupil; Berlin and St. Petersburg: Asher;
    New York: Jackson, 1833. 3-33;
    as "The Zenana. An Eastern Tale" in *The Zenana and Minor Poems of L. E. L.* Lon-
    don: Fisher, Son; Paris: Quai de L'Ecole, [1839]. 1-71.
Zenobia.
    1st line: "On wild wind, bring me back a sound;"
    in [Collier, J. and Letitia E. Landon]. *The Pictorial Album; or, Cabinet of Paintings. For
    the Year 1837.* Illus. George Baxter. London: Chapman and Hall, 1837.

Bibliography

Armstrong, Isobel. *Victorian Poetry: Poetry, Poetics, and Politics*. London: Routledge, 1992.

Bates, William, ed. *The Maclise Portrait Gallery*. London: Chatto, 1883.

Berkeley, Grantley. *My Life and Recollections*. London: Hurst, 1865. 4 vols.

Blain, Virginia. "Letitia Elizabeth Landon, Eliza Mary Hamilton, and the Genealogy of the Victorian Poetess." *Victorian Poetry* 33.1 (1995): 31-51.

Blanchard, [Samuel] Laman. "Memoir of L.E.L., with a Portrait." *New Monthly Magazine* 50 (May 1837): 78-82.

——. *Life and Literary Remains of L.E.L.* London: Colburn, 1841. 2 vols.

Boyle, Andrew. *An Index to the Annuals*. Worcester: Andrew Boyle, 1967.

Chorley, Henry. "Mrs. Maclean." *The Athenaeum* (5 January 1839): 14.

——. *Recent Art and Society*. New York: Holt, 1874.

Cruikshank, Brodie. *Eighteen Years on the Gold Coast of Africa*. London: Hurst, 1853.

Devey, Louisa. *The Life of Rosina, Lady Lytton*. London: Sonnenschein, 1887.

Ellis, S[tewart] M[arsh], ed. *Unpublished Letters of Lady Bulwer Lytton to A. E. Chalon, R. A.* London: Eveleigh Nash, 1914.

Elwood, Anne Katharine. *Memoirs of the Literary Ladies of England*. 1843. New York: AMS, 1973. 2 vols.

Faxon, Frederick W. *Literary Annuals and Gift Books—A Bibliography 1823-1903*. Middlesex: Private Libraries Association, 1973.

Greer, Germaine, "The Tulsa Center for the Study of Women's Literature: What We Are Doing and Why We Are Doing It." *Tulsa Studies in Women's Literature* 1.1 (1982): 5-26.

Hall, S[amuel] C[arter]. *A Book of Memories of Great Men and Women of the Age*. London: Virtue, 1871.

——. *Retrospect of a Long Life*. New York: Appleton, 1883.

Hall, S[amuel] C[arter] and Anna Maria Hall, "Memories of Authors: Miss Landon." *Atlantic Monthly* 15 (1865): 333.

Howitt, William. *Homes and Haunts of the Most Eminent British Poets*. London: Bentley, 1847. 2 vols.

Jerdan, William. *The Autobiography of William Jerdan*. London: Hall, 1852-54. 4 vols.

Lawford, Cynthia. "Bijous Beyond Possession: The Prima Donnas of L.E.L.'s Album Poems." *Gender and Genre: Essays on Women's Poetry, Late Romantics to Late Victorians, 1830-1900.* Eds. Virginia Blain and Isobel Armstrong. London: Macmillan, 1997.

Leighton, Angela. *Victorian Women Poets: Writing Against the Heart.* London: Harvester, 1992.

L'Estrange, Rev. A.G. *The Life of Mary Russell Mitford.* New York: Harper, 1870.

———. *The Friendships of Mary Russell Mitford.* London: Hurst, 1882. 2 vols.

Madden, Richard Robert. *The Literary Life and Correspondence of the Countess of Blessington.* 1855. New York: AMS, 1973. 3 vols.

McGann, Jerome. *Poetics of Sensibility. A Revolution in Literary Style.* Oxford: Oxford UP, 1996.

Mellor, Anne. *Romanticism & Gender.* New York: Routledge, 1993.

Metcalfe, George Edgar. *Maclean of the Gold Coast: The Life and Times of George Maclean, 1801-1847.* London: Oxford UP, 1962.

Moulton, Charles Wells, ed. *The Library of Literary Criticism of English and American Authors.* New York: Malkan, 1910. 8 vols.

Raymond, Meredeth B., and Mary Rose Sullivan, eds. *Letters of Elizabeth Barrett Browning to Mary Russell Mitford.* Kansas City: Wedgestone P, 1983. 3 vols.

Renton, Richard. *John Forster and His Friendships.* London: Chapman, 1912.

Riess, Daniel. "Laetitia Landon and the Dawn of English Post-Romanticism." *Studies in English Literature* 36.4 (Autumn 1996): 807-27.

Roberts, Emma. "Memoir of L.E.L." *The Zenana and Minor Poems of L.E.L.* London: Fisher, 1839.

Rowton, Frederic. *The Female Poets of Great Britain.* Philadelphia: Baird, 1849.

Sadleir, Michael. *Bulwer: A Panorama, Edward and Rosina, 1803-1836.* London: Constable, 1931.

Sheppard, S[arah]. *Characteristics of the Genius and Writings of L.E.L.* London: Longman, 1841.

Stephenson, Glennis. "Letitia Landon and the Victorian Improvisatrice: The Construction of L.E.L." *Victorian Poetry* 30.1 (1992): 1-17.

———. *Letitia Landon: The Woman Behind L.E.L.* New York: Manchester UP, 1995.

Stevenson, Lionel. "Miss Landon, 'The Milk-and-Watery Moon of Our Darkness,' 1824-30." *Modern Language Quarterly* 8.3 (1947): 355-63.

Sypher, F. J. "The Magical Letters of L.E.L." *Columbia Library Columns* 39.3 (1990): 3-9.

Thomson, Katherine. *Recollections of Literary Characters and Celebrated Places.* London: Bentley, 1854. 2 vols.

Thomson, Katherine, and Antony Todd Thomson. ["Grace and Philip Wharton."] *The Queens of Society.* London: Hogg, 1860.

Thrall, Miriam. *Rebellious Fraser's.* New York: Columbia UP, 1934.

Toynbee, William, ed. *The Diaries of William Charles Macready, 1833-1851.* London: Chapman, 1912. 2 vols.

Watts, Alaric. *Alaric Watts: A Narrative of His Life.* 1884. New York: AMS, 1974. 2 vols.

Wyly, Anne Ethel. *Letitia Elizabeth Landon: Her Career, Her "Mysterious" Death, and Her Poetry.* Unpublished thesis, Duke U, 1942.

Rossetti
responding
to
Browning
on
Landon
on
Hemans